Glencoe

Accounting

Chapter Study Guides and Working Papers

Chapters
1-29

MHEonline.com

Send all inquiries to:
McGraw-Hill Education
8787 Orion Place
Columbus, OH 43240

ISBN: 978-0-07-671856-6 (Student Edition)
MHID: 0-07-671856-5 (Student Edition)

Printed in the United States of America.

7 8 9 10 LOV 23 22 21

CONTENTS

Name Date Class

CHAPTER 1 You and the World of Accounting

Study Guide

Section Assessment

Section 1 *Read Section 1 on pages 7–12 and complete the following exercises on page 13.*
- ☐ Reinforce the Main Idea
- ☐ Math for Accounting
- ☐ Problem 1-1 *Studying Yourself*
- ☐ Problem 1-2 *Gathering Career Resources*

Section 2 *Read Section 2 on pages 14–18 and complete the following exercises on page 19.*
- ☐ Reinforce the Main Idea
- ☐ Math for Accounting
- ☐ Problem 1-3 *Checking Out Accounting Careers*
- ☐ Problem 1-4 *Matching Interests and Careers*
- ☐ Problem 1-5 *Researching Public Accounting Firms*
- ☐ Problem 1-6 *Interviewing Accountants*

Chapter Assessment

Summary *Review the Chapter 1 Visual Summary on page 20 in your textbook.*
- ☐ Key Concepts

Review and Activities *Complete the following questions and exercises on page 21 in your textbook.*
- ☐ After You Read: Answering the Essential Question
- ☐ Vocabulary Check
- ☐ Concept Check

Standardized Test Practice *Complete the exercises on page 22 in your textbook.*

Problems *Complete the following End-of-Chapter Problems for Chapter 1 in your textbook.*
- ☐ Problem 1-7 *Researching Careers in Your Library*
- ☐ Problem 1-8 *Researching Careers in Your Local Newspaper*
- ☐ Problem 1-9 *Assessing Your Skills and Interests*
- ☐ Problem 1-10 *Working with Others*
- ☐ Problem 1-11 *Summarizing Personal Traits*
- ☐ Problem 1-12 *Gathering Career Information*
- ☐ Problem 1-13 *Exploring Careers in Accounting*

Challenge Problem
- ☐ Problem 1-14 *Exploring Global Careers*

Real-World Applications and Connections *Complete the following applications on pages 26–27 in your textbook.*
- ☐ Case Study
- ☐ 21st Century Skills
- ☐ Career Wise
- ☐ Spotlight on Personal Finance
- ☐ A Matter of Ethics

Working Papers *for Section Problems*

Problem 1-1 Studying Yourself *(textbook p. 13)*

List at least five personal interests or skills.

Identify one or more careers that match the interests and skills you listed above.

Choose one of the above careers and write a description of how your skills and interests fit into this career.

Name Date Class

Problem 1-2 Gathering Career Resources *(textbook p. 13)*

Personal Career Profile Form	
Name: **Date:**	**Career:**
Your Values	Career Values
Your Interests	Career Duties and Responsibilities
Your Personality	Personality Type Needed
Skills and Aptitudes	Skills and Aptitudes Required
Education/Training Acceptable	Education/Training Required

Name Date Class

Problem 1-2 (continued)

Personal Career Profile Form	
Name: **Date:**	**Career:**
Your Values	Career Values
Your Interests	Career Duties and Responsibilities
Your Personality	Personality Type Needed
Skills and Aptitudes	Skills and Aptitudes Required
Education/Training Acceptable	Education/Training Required

Name Date Class

Problem 1-2 (concluded)

Personal Career Profile Form	
Name: **Date:**	**Career:**
Your Values	Career Values
Your Interests	Career Duties and Responsibilities
Your Personality	Personality Type Needed
Skills and Aptitudes	Skills and Aptitudes Required
Education/Training Acceptable	Education/Training Required

Name Date Class

Problem 1-3 Checking Out Accounting Careers *(textbook p. 19)*

Career	Formal Training Needed	Work Experience Needed

Which of the careers listed above do you prefer? ____________________

Why does this career appeal to you?

____

____

____

____

____

Name Date Class

Problem 1-4 Matching Interests and Careers *(textbook p. 19)*

List the personal interests and skills of the accountants described in the text.

List three types of businesses (or actual companies) for which you might like to work.

How would you learn about accounting career opportunities in the above companies?

Aside from pursuing needed training and education, what else would you do to prepare to work in that career?

Name Date Class

Problem 1-5 Researching Public Accounting Firms *(textbook p. 19)*

Company's name: Web site:	Services provided:
Company's name: Web site:	Services provided:
Company's name: Web site:	Services provided:
Company's name: Web site:	Services provided:

Problem 1-6 Interviewing Accountants *(textbook p. 19)*

Name Date Class

Working Papers *for End-of-Chapter Problems*

Problem 1-7 Researching Careers in Your Library *(textbook p. 23)*

Problem 1-8 Researching Careers in Your Local Newspaper *(textbook p. 23)*

Job Title	Skills Required	Education Required

Name Date Class

Problem 1-9 Assessing Your Skills and Interests *(textbook p. 23)*

What are your aptitudes and abilities?

What are your interests?

What are your values?

Do you like working with people?

Do you like working with data?

Do you like working with numbers?

Using your answers above, list three careers that might match your skills and interests.

Name Date Class

Problem 1-10 Working with Others *(textbook p. 23)*

Situation	Skills Needed	How can you get those skills?
Training new hires in the accounting department		
Discuss project cost overruns with a department manager		
Present operating results to senior managers		

Problem 1-11 Summarizing Personal Traits *(textbook p. 24)*

1. __________ __________ __________
2. __________ __________ __________
3. __________ __________ __________
4. __________ __________ __________
5. __________ __________ __________
6. __________ __________ __________
7. __________ __________ __________
8. __________ __________ __________
9. __________ __________ __________
10. __________ __________ __________

Which five characteristics were mentioned most often?

Do these descriptions match your self-perception? Why or why not?

Name Date Class

Problem 1-12 Gathering Career Information *(textbook p. 24)*

Name Date Class

Problem 1-13 Exploring Careers in Accounting *(textbook p. 24)*

Problem 1-14 Exploring Global Careers *(textbook p. 24)*

Name Date Class

Notes

Name Date Class

CHAPTER 2 The World of Business and Accounting

Study Guide

Section Assessment

Section 1 *Read Section 1 on pages 31–34 and complete the following exercises on page 35.*

- ☐ Reinforce the Main Idea
- ☐ Math for Accounting
- ☐ Problem 2-1 *Assess Your Entrepreneurship Potential*

Section 2 *Read Section 2 on pages 36–38 and complete the following exercises on page 39.*

- ☐ Reinforce the Main Idea
- ☐ Math for Accounting
- ☐ Problem 2-2 *Using Financial Information*
- ☐ Problem 2-3 *Identifying Accounting Assumptions*

Chapter Assessment

Summary *Review the Chapter 2 Visual Summary on page 40 in your textbook.*

- ☐ Key Concepts

Review and Activities *Complete the following questions and exercises on page 41 in your textbook.*

- ☐ After You Read: Answering the Essential Question
- ☐ Vocabulary Check
- ☐ Concept Check

Standardized Test Practice *Complete the exercises on page 42 in your textbook.*

Problems *Complete the following End-of-Chapter Problems for Chapter 2 in your textbook.*

- ☐ Problem 2-4 *Identifying Types of Businesses*
- ☐ Problem 2-5 *Understanding Accounting Assumptions*
- ☐ Problem 2-6 *Understanding Business Operations*
- ☐ Problem 2-7 *Categorizing Forms of Business Organizations*

Challenge Problem

- ☐ Problem 2-8 *Working as an Entrepreneur*

Real-World Applications and Connections *Complete the following applications on pages 46–47 in your textbook.*

- ☐ Case Study
- ☐ 21st Century Skills
- ☐ Career Wise
- ☐ Spotlight on Personal Finance
- ☐ Global Accounting

Name Date Class

Working Papers *for Section Problems*

Problem 2-1 Assess Your Entrepreneurship Potential *(textbook p. 35)*

	Most Like Me				Least Like Me
Persistent	5	4	3	2	1
Creative	5	4	3	2	1
Responsible	5	4	3	2	1
Inquisitive	5	4	3	2	1
Goal-oriented	5	4	3	2	1
Independent	5	4	3	2	1
Demanding	5	4	3	2	1
Self-confident	5	4	3	2	1
Risk-taking	5	4	3	2	1
Restless	5	4	3	2	1

Problem 2-2 Using Financial Information *(textbook p. 39)*

Name Date Class

Problem 2-3 Identifying Accounting Assumptions *(textbook p. 39)*

Working Papers *for End-of-Chapter Problems*

Problem 2-4 Identifying Types of Businesses *(textbook p. 43)*

1. ____ **5.** ____ **9.** ____
2. ____ **6.** ____ **10.** ____
3. ____ **7.** ____ **11.** ____
4. ____ **8.** ____ **12.** ____

Problem 2-5 Understanding Accounting Assumptions *(textbook p. 43)*

1. ____ **3.** ____ **5.** ____
2. ____ **4.** ____ **6.** ____

Problem 2-6 Understanding Business Operations *(textbook p. 44)*

1. ____

2. profit on bread sales: ____

calculations:

3. ____

Name Date Class

Problem 2-7 Categorizing Forms of Business Organizations *(textbook p. 44)*

1. ______
2. ______
3. ______
4. ______
5. ______
6. ______
7. ______
8. ______
9. ______
10. ______

Problem 2-8 Working as an Entrepreneur *(textbook p. 44)*

	Advantage	Disadvantage
1. Risking the loss of your savings		
2. Deciding what you and everyone else needs to do each day		
3. Lacking steady wages and employee benefits		
4. Choosing when and where to work		
5. Keeping the financial benefits of your hard work		
6. Choosing the people you want to work with		
7. Paying all the expenses of a new business		

Name Date Class

CHAPTER 3 Business Transactions and the Accounting Equation

Study Guide

Section Assessment

Section 1 *Read Section 1 on pages 53–55 and complete the following exercises on page 56.*

- ☐ Reinforce the Main Idea
- ☐ Math for Accounting
- ☐ Problem 3-1 *Balancing the Accounting Equation*

Section 2 *Read Section 2 on pages 57–61 and complete the following exercises on page 62.*

- ☐ Reinforce the Main Idea
- ☐ Math for Accounting
- ☐ Problem 3-2 *Determining the Effects of Transactions on the Accounting Equation*

Section 3 *Read Section 3 on pages 63–65 and complete the following exercises on page 66.*

- ☐ Reinforce the Main Idea
- ☐ Math for Accounting
- ☐ Problem 3-3 *Determining the Effect of Transactions on the Accounting Equation*

Chapter Assessment

Summary *Review the Chapter 3 Visual Summary on page 67 in your textbook.*

- ☐ Key Concepts

Review and Activities *Complete the following questions and exercises on page 68 in your textbook.*

- ☐ After You Read: Answering the Essential Question
- ☐ Vocabulary Check
- ☐ Concept Check

Standardized Test Practice *Complete the exercises on page 69 in your textbook.*

Computerized Accounting *Read the Computerized Accounting information on page 70 in your textbook.*

- ☐ Exploring Electronic Spreadsheets

Problems *Complete the following End-of-Chapter Problems for Chapter 3 in your textbook.*

- ☐ Problem 3-4 *Classifying Accounts*
- ☐ Problem 3-5 *Completing the Accounting Equation*
- ☐ Problem 3-6 *Classifying Accounts Within the Accounting Equation*
- ☐ Problem 3-7 *Determining Increases and Decreases in Accounts*
- ☐ Problem 3-8 *Determining the Effects of Transactions on the Accounting Equation*
- ☐ Problem 3-9 *Determining the Effects of Transactions on the Accounting Equation*
- ☐ Problem 3-10 *Describing Business Transactions*

Challenge Problem

- ☐ Problem 3-11 *Completing the Accounting Equation*

Real-World Applications and Connections *Complete the following applications on pages 76–77 in your textbook.*

- ☐ Career Wise
- ☐ 21st Century Skills
- ☐ A Matter of Ethics
- ☐ Spotlight on Personal Finance
- ☐ H.O.T. Audit

Working Papers *for Section Problems*

Problem 3-1 Balancing the Accounting Equation *(textbook p. 56)*

	Assets	=	Liabilities	+	Owner's Equity
1	$17,000	=	$ 7,000	+	10,000
2	26K	=	$ 6,000	+	$20,000
3	$10,000	=	3,000	+	$ 7,000
4	26,000	=	$ 9,000	+	$17,000
5	$ 8,000	=	$ 2,000	+	6,000
6	$20,000	=	$ 7,000	+	13,000
7	16,000	=	$12,000	+	$ 4,000
8	$30,000	=	8,000	+	$22,000
9	$22,000	=	$ 1,000	+	21,000
10	$25,000	=	$ 5,000	+	20,000
11	35,000	=	$10,000	+	$25,000
12	$ 7,500	=	4,500	+	$ 3,000

Problem 3-2 Determining the Effects of Transactions on the Accounting Equation *(textbook p. 62)*

Trans	Assets							=	Liabilities	+	Owner's Equity
	Cash in Bank	+	Accounts Receivable	+	Computer Equipment	+	Office Furniture	=	Accounts Payable	+	Jan Swift, Capital
1	+30K										+30K
2							+700				+700
3	− 4K				+4K						
4							+5000		+5000		
5			+700				−700				
6	−2000								−2000		
Bal.	24K	+	700	+	4K	+	5K	=	3000	+	30700

Name Date Class

Problem 3-3 Determining the Effect of Transactions on the Accounting Equation *(textbook p. 66)*

	Assets							=	Liabilities	+	Owner's Equity
Trans.	Cash in Bank	+	Accounts Receivable	+	Computer Equipment	+	Office Equipment	=	Accounts Payable	+	Jan Swift, Capital
Bal.	24,000		700		4,000		5,000		3,000		30,700
1	-50										-50
2	+1K										+1K
3	-600										-600
4	-800										-800
5	+200		[illegible]				[illegible]				
Bal.	23,550	+	900	+	4000	+	4,800	=	3,000	+	30,250

33,250 = 33,250

Working Papers *for End-of-Chapter Problems*

Problem 3-4 Classifying Accounts *(textbook p. 71)*

1. owners equity
2. asset
3. asset
4. liability
5. asset
6. asset
7. asset
8. asset
9. asset
10. asset

Analyze:

Problem 3-5 Completing the Accounting Equation *(textbook p. 71)*

Assets		=	Liabilities		+	Owner's Equity	
Cash in Bank	$ 4,500		Accts. Pay.	1,550		Mike Murray, Capital	$9,250
Accts. Rec.	1,350						
Office Equipment	5,000						
	10,800						

Analyze:

Problem 3-6 Classifying Accounts Within the Accounting Equation *(textbook p. 71)*

	Account Name	Balance
(1)	Cash	5000
	office equipment	3000
	camping equipment	12000
	Accounts Receivable	2000
	Total	22000
(2)	Accounts payable	2000
(3)	Capital	15000

Name Date Class

Problem 3-6 (concluded)

Analyze:

Assets				= Liabilities	+ Owner's Equity
Accounts Receivable +	Camping Equipment +	Cash in Bank +	Office Equipment =	Accounts Payable +	Ronald Hicks, Capital
2000, +	12000, +	5000, +	3000	2000	15000

Problem 3-7 Determining Increases and Decreases in Accounts *(textbook p. 72)*

Transaction	Accounts Affected	Classification	Amount of Increase (+) or Decrease (-)
1	*Cash in Bank* *Regina Delgado, Capital*	*Asset* *Owner's Equity*	+ *$25,000* + *$25,000*
2	cash in bank ~~capital~~ car wash ~~equipment~~	asset asset ~~owners equity~~	− ~~[illegible]~~ 12000 +12000 ~~[illegible]~~
3	office equipment ~~[illegible]~~ accounts payable	asset liability	+2500 +2500
4	cash in bank capital	~~asset~~ revenue owners equity	+1000 +1000
5	cash capital	asset owners equity	-600 -600
6	office furniture ~~cash~~ capital accounts payable	asset asset owners equity liability	+1000 -200 -200 +800
7	cash capital	asset owners equity	-800 -800
8	accounts receivable capital	asset owners equity	+600 +600

Analyze: transaction 6

Problem 3-8 Determining the Effects of Transactions on the Accounting Equation *(textbook p. 73)*

Trans.	Assets				=	Liabilities	+	Owner's Equity
	Cash in Bank	Accounts Receivable	Office Equipment	Grooming Equipment	=	Accounts Payable	+	Abe Schultz, Capital
1	+ $10,000							+ $10,000
Balance	10,000	—	—	—		—		10000
2	−1,000	—	—	+1,000		—		—
Balance	9,000	—	—	1,000		—		10000
3	−900	—	—	—		—		−900
Balance	8,100	—	—	1,000		—		9100
4	—	—	+6000	—		+6000		—
Balance	8100	—	6,000	1000		6000		[illegible]
5	+700	—	—	—		—		+700
Balance	8800	—	6000	1000		6000		9800
6	−2000	—	—	—		−2000		—
Balance	6800	—	6000	1000		4000		9800
7	—	+500	—	—		—		+500
Balance	6800	500	6000	1000		4000		10300

Analyze: 14,300 = 14300

Name Date Class

Problem 3-9 Determining the Effects of Transactions on the Accounting Equation *(textbook p. 73)*

	Assets					=	Liabilities	+	Owner's Equity
Trans.	Cash in Bank	Accounts Receivable	Hiking Equipment	Rafting Equipment	Office Equipment	=	Accounts Payable	+	Juanita Ortega, Capital
1	60,000								60000
Balance									
2	-3000								-3000
Balance									
3	-24,000			+24000					
Balance									
4	-3000		+3000						
Balance									
5	+2500								+2500
Balance									
6	[illegible]				+4000		+4000		
Balance									
7					+450				+450
Balance									
8	-3000								-3000
Balance									
9	-1500						-1500		
Balance									
10		+1200							+1200
Balance	28,000	1200	3000	24000	4,450		2500		58,150

Analyze: ______________________________

Name Date Class

Problem 3-10 Describing Business Transactions *(textbook p. 74)*

1. *The owner invested $30,000 in the business.*
2. Bought office equipment with cash worth 2000
3. Bought 8000 dollars of video equipment on account
4. Owner invested 200 into business
5. business received 500 on account from a transaction
6. owner contributed $200 worth of office equipment
7. paid off previous purchase 3000 on account
8. Sold office equipment on account
9. creditor paid 500 of debt
10. owner took 1,000 for personal use

Analyze:

Problem 3-11 Completing the Accounting Equation *(textbook p. 75)*

	Assets					=	Liabilities	+	Owner's Equity
	Cash in Bank	+	Accounts Receivable	+	Business Equipment	=	Accounts Payable	+	Richard Tang, Capital
1		+	$ 2,000	+	$ 1,000	=	$ 500	+	$ 7,500
2	$ 3,000	+	$ 9,000	+		=	$ 2,000	+	$ 16,000
3	$ 8,000	+	$ 1,000	+	$ 10,000	=		+	$ 15,000
4	$ 4,000	+		+	$ 4,000	=	$ 1,000	+	$ 17,000
5	$ 9,000	+	$ 7,000	+	$ 6,000	=	$ 5,000	+	
6	$ 10,000	+	$ 14,000	+		=	$ 6,000	+	$ 32,000
7	$ 6,000	+	$ 4,000	+	$ 10,000	=		+	$ 15,000
8		+	$ 5,000	+	$ 9,000	=	$ 1,000	+	

Analyze:

Name Date Class

CHAPTER 7 Posting Journal Entries to General Ledger Accounts

Study Guide

Section Assessment

Section 1 *Read Section 1 on pages 167–169 and complete the following exercises on page 170.*
- ☐ Reinforce the Main Idea
- ☐ Math for Accounting
- ☐ Problem 7-1 *Opening Ledger Accounts*

Section 2 *Read Section 2 on pages 171–177 and complete the following exercises on page 178.*
- ☐ Reinforce the Main Idea
- ☐ Math for Accounting
- ☐ Problem 7-2 *Posting from the General Journal to the Ledger*

Section 3 *Read Section 3 on pages 179–182 and complete the following exercises on page 183.*
- ☐ Reinforce the Main Idea
- ☐ Math for Accounting
- ☐ Problem 7-3 *Analyzing a Source Document*
- ☐ Problem 7-4 *Recording and Posting a Correcting Entry*

Chapter Assessment

Summary *Review the Chapter 7 Visual Summary on page 184 in your textbook.*
- ☐ Key Concepts

Review and Activities *Complete the following questions and exercises on page 185 in your textbook.*
- ☐ After You Read: Answering the Essential Question
- ☐ Vocabulary Check
- ☐ Concept Check

Standardized Test Practice *Complete the exercises on page 186 in your textbook.*

Computerized Accounting *Read the Computerized Accounting information on page 187 in your textbook.*
- ☐ Making the Transition from a Manual to a Computerized System

Problems *Complete the following End-of-Chapter Problems for Chapter 7 in your textbook.*
- ☐ Problem 7-5 *Posting General Journal Transactions*
- ☐ Problem 7-6 *Preparing a Trial Balance*
- ☐ Problem 7-7 *Journalizing and Posting Business Transactions*
- ☐ Problem 7-8 *Journalizing and Posting Business Transactions*

Challenge Problem
- ☐ Problem 7-9 *Recording and Posting Correcting Entries*

Real-World Applications and Connections *Complete the following applications on pages 192–193 in your textbook.*
- ☐ Career Wise
- ☐ Global Accounting
- ☐ A Matter of Ethics
- ☐ Spotlight on Personal Finance
- ☐ H.O.T Audit

Name Date Class

Working Papers *for Section Problems*

Problem 7-1 Opening Ledger Accounts *(textbook p. 170)*

GENERAL LEDGER

ACCOUNT ______ ACCOUNT NO. ______

DATE		DESCRIPTION	POST. REF.	DEBIT	CREDIT	BALANCE	
						DEBIT	CREDIT

ACCOUNT ______ ACCOUNT NO. ______

DATE		DESCRIPTION	POST. REF.	DEBIT	CREDIT	BALANCE	
						DEBIT	CREDIT

ACCOUNT ______ ACCOUNT NO. ______

DATE		DESCRIPTION	POST. REF.	DEBIT	CREDIT	BALANCE	
						DEBIT	CREDIT

ACCOUNT ______ ACCOUNT NO. ______

DATE		DESCRIPTION	POST. REF.	DEBIT	CREDIT	BALANCE	
						DEBIT	CREDIT

ACCOUNT ______ ACCOUNT NO. ______

DATE		DESCRIPTION	POST. REF.	DEBIT	CREDIT	BALANCE	
						DEBIT	CREDIT

Name Date Class

Problem 7-2 Posting from the General Journal to the Ledger *(textbook p. 178)*

GENERAL JOURNAL PAGE *1*

	DATE		DESCRIPTION	POST. REF.	DEBIT	CREDIT	
1	*20--*						1
2	*May*	*1*	*Cash in Bank*		*10 000 00*		2
3			*David Serlo, Capital*			*10 000 00*	3
4			*Memorandum 101*				4
5							5
6							6
7							7

GENERAL LEDGER (PARTIAL)

ACCOUNT *Cash in Bank* ACCOUNT NO. *101*

DATE		DESCRIPTION	POST. REF.	DEBIT	CREDIT	BALANCE DEBIT	BALANCE CREDIT

ACCOUNT *David Serlo, Capital* ACCOUNT NO. *301*

DATE		DESCRIPTION	POST. REF.	DEBIT	CREDIT	BALANCE DEBIT	BALANCE CREDIT

Problem 7-3 Analyzing a Source Document *(textbook p. 183)*

FUNTIME
AMUSEMENT ARCADE

MEMORANDUM 47

TO: *Accounting Clerk*
FROM: *Dan Vonderhaar*
DATE: *May 20, 20--*
SUBJECT: *Correction of error*

On May 10, we purchased an office copier for $1,500. I noticed in the general journal that the entry was recorded and posted to the Computer Equipment account. Please record the necessary entry to correct this error.

GENERAL JOURNAL

PAGE *6*

	DATE		DESCRIPTION	POST. REF.	DEBIT	CREDIT	
1	*20--*						1
2	*May*	*10*	*Computer Equipment*	*120*	*1500 00*		2
3			*Cash in Bank*	*101*		*1500 00*	3
4			*Check 8099*				4
5							5
6							6
7							7
8							8
9							9

GENERAL LEDGER (PARTIAL)

ACCOUNT *Office Equipment* ACCOUNT NO. *115*

DATE		DESCRIPTION	POST. REF.	DEBIT	CREDIT	BALANCE DEBIT	BALANCE CREDIT
20--							
May	*1*	*Balance*	*✓*			*700 00*	

ACCOUNT *Computer Equipment* ACCOUNT NO. *120*

DATE		DESCRIPTION	POST. REF.	DEBIT	CREDIT	BALANCE DEBIT	BALANCE CREDIT
20--							
May	*1*	*Balance*	*✓*			*3000 00*	
	10		*G6*	*1500 00*		*4500 00*	

Problem 7-4 Recording and Posting a Correcting Entry *(textbook p. 183)*

GENERAL JOURNAL PAGE 5

	DATE		DESCRIPTION	POST. REF.	DEBIT	CREDIT	
1	20--						1
2	July	3	Rent Expense	530	300 00		2
3			Cash in Bank	101		300 00	3
4			Check 1903				4
5							5
6							6
7							7
8							8
9							9

GENERAL LEDGER (PARTIAL)

ACCOUNT *Advertising Expense* ACCOUNT NO. *502*

DATE		DESCRIPTION	POST. REF.	DEBIT	CREDIT	BALANCE DEBIT	BALANCE CREDIT
20--							
July	1	Balance	✓			2,600 00	

ACCOUNT *Rent Expense* ACCOUNT NO. *530*

DATE		DESCRIPTION	POST. REF.	DEBIT	CREDIT	BALANCE DEBIT	BALANCE CREDIT
20--							
July	1	Balance	✓			15,000 00	
	3		G5	300 00		15,300 00	

Working Papers *for End-of-Chapter Problems*

Problem 7-5 Posting General Journal Transactions *(textbook p. 188)*

GENERAL JOURNAL PAGE ____

	DATE		DESCRIPTION	POST. REF.	DEBIT	CREDIT	
1	20--						1
2	Mar.	1	Cash in Bank		5000 00		2
3			Ronald Hicks, Capital			5000 00	3
4			Memorandum 21				4
5		3	Office Equipment		3000 00		5
6			Accts. Pay.—Digital Tech Computers			3000 00	6
7			Invoice 500				7
8		4	Camping Equipment		2500 00		8
9			Accts. Pay.—Adventure Equip.			2500 00	9
10			Invoice 318				10
11		6	Office Equipment		100 00		11
12			Ronald Hicks, Capital			100 00	12
13			Memorandum 22				13
14		8	Cash in Bank		6000 00		14
15			Equipment Rental Revenue			6000 00	15
16			Receipt 226				16
17		10	Accts. Pay.—Digital Tech Computers		1500 00		17
18			Cash in Bank			1500 00	18
19			Check 461				19
20		12	Accts. Rec.—Helen Katz		1000 00		20
21			Equipment Rental Revenue			1000 00	21
22			Sales Invoice 354				22
23		15	Ronald Hicks, Withdrawals		2000 00		23
24			Cash in Bank			2000 00	24
25			Check 462				25
26		19	Accts. Pay.—Adventure Equip.		1200 00		26
27			Cash in Bank			1200 00	27
28			Check 463				28
29		28	Cash in Bank		1000 00		29
30			Accts. Rec.—Helen Katz			1000 00	30
31			Receipt 227				31
32		29	Accts. Rec.—Polk and Co.		2400 00		32
33			Equipment Rental Revenue			2400 00	33
34			Sales Invoice 355				34
35		30	Advertising Expense		300 00		35
36			Cash in Bank			300 00	36
37			Check 464				37

Problem 7-5 (continued)

GENERAL LEDGER

ACCOUNT *Cash in Bank* ACCOUNT NO. *101*

DATE		DESCRIPTION	POST. REF.	DEBIT	CREDIT	BALANCE DEBIT	BALANCE CREDIT

ACCOUNT *Accounts Receivable—Helen Katz* ACCOUNT NO. *105*

DATE		DESCRIPTION	POST. REF.	DEBIT	CREDIT	BALANCE DEBIT	BALANCE CREDIT

ACCOUNT *Accounts Receivable—Polk and Co.* ACCOUNT NO. *110*

DATE		DESCRIPTION	POST. REF.	DEBIT	CREDIT	BALANCE DEBIT	BALANCE CREDIT

ACCOUNT *Office Equipment* ACCOUNT NO. *120*

DATE		DESCRIPTION	POST. REF.	DEBIT	CREDIT	BALANCE DEBIT	BALANCE CREDIT

ACCOUNT *Camping Equipment* ACCOUNT NO. *125*

DATE		DESCRIPTION	POST. REF.	DEBIT	CREDIT	BALANCE DEBIT	BALANCE CREDIT

Name Date Class

Problem 7-5 (concluded)

ACCOUNT *Accounts Payable—Adventure Equipment Inc.* ACCOUNT NO. *201*

DATE		DESCRIPTION	POST. REF.	DEBIT	CREDIT	BALANCE	
						DEBIT	CREDIT

ACCOUNT *Accounts Payable—Digital Tech Computers* ACCOUNT NO. *203*

DATE		DESCRIPTION	POST. REF.	DEBIT	CREDIT	BALANCE	
						DEBIT	CREDIT

ACCOUNT *Ronald Hicks, Capital* ACCOUNT NO. *301*

DATE		DESCRIPTION	POST. REF.	DEBIT	CREDIT	BALANCE	
						DEBIT	CREDIT

ACCOUNT *Ronald Hicks, Withdrawals* ACCOUNT NO. *305*

DATE		DESCRIPTION	POST. REF.	DEBIT	CREDIT	BALANCE	
						DEBIT	CREDIT

ACCOUNT *Equipment Rental Revenue* ACCOUNT NO. *401*

DATE		DESCRIPTION	POST. REF.	DEBIT	CREDIT	BALANCE	
						DEBIT	CREDIT

ACCOUNT *Advertising Expense* ACCOUNT NO. *501*

DATE		DESCRIPTION	POST. REF.	DEBIT	CREDIT	BALANCE	
						DEBIT	CREDIT

Analyze:

Problem 7-6 Preparing a Trial Balance *(textbook p. 188)*

GENERAL LEDGER

ACCOUNT *Cash in Bank* ACCOUNT NO. *101*

DATE		DESCRIPTION	POST. REF.	DEBIT	CREDIT	BALANCE DEBIT	BALANCE CREDIT
20--							
Mar.	1	Balance	✓			15,000 00	
	15		G1	4,000 00		19,000 00	
	31		G2		2,000 00	17,000 00	

ACCOUNT *Accounts Receivable—Valley Auto* ACCOUNT NO. *110*

DATE		DESCRIPTION	POST. REF.	DEBIT	CREDIT	BALANCE DEBIT	BALANCE CREDIT
20--							
Mar.	1	Balance	✓			2,000 00	
	12		G1		1,000 00	1,000 00	

ACCOUNT *Detergent Supplies* ACCOUNT NO. *120*

DATE		DESCRIPTION	POST. REF.	DEBIT	CREDIT	BALANCE DEBIT	BALANCE CREDIT
20--							
Mar.	1	Balance	✓			1,500 00	
	17		G1	500 00		2,000 00	

ACCOUNT *Car Wash Equipment* ACCOUNT NO. *135*

DATE		DESCRIPTION	POST. REF.	DEBIT	CREDIT	BALANCE DEBIT	BALANCE CREDIT
20--							
Mar.	1	Balance	✓			20,000 00	

ACCOUNT *Accounts Payable—Allen Vacuum Systems* ACCOUNT NO. *201*

DATE		DESCRIPTION	POST. REF.	DEBIT	CREDIT	BALANCE DEBIT	BALANCE CREDIT
20--							
Mar.	1	Balance	✓				1,000 00
	31		G2	500 00			500 00

ACCOUNT *Regina Delgado, Capital* ACCOUNT NO. *301*

DATE		DESCRIPTION	POST. REF.	DEBIT	CREDIT	BALANCE DEBIT	BALANCE CREDIT
20--							
Mar.	1	Balance	✓				40,000 00

Problem 7-6 (continued)

ACCOUNT *Regina Delgado, Withdrawals* ACCOUNT NO. *305*

DATE		DESCRIPTION	POST. REF.	DEBIT	CREDIT	BALANCE DEBIT	BALANCE CREDIT
20--							
Mar.	*1*	*Balance*	✓			*2 000 00*	
	31		*G2*	*2 000 00*		*4 000 00*	

ACCOUNT *Income Summary* ACCOUNT NO. *310*

DATE		DESCRIPTION	POST. REF.	DEBIT	CREDIT	BALANCE DEBIT	BALANCE CREDIT

ACCOUNT *Wash Revenue* ACCOUNT NO. *401*

DATE		DESCRIPTION	POST. REF.	DEBIT	CREDIT	BALANCE DEBIT	BALANCE CREDIT
20--							
Mar.	*1*	*Balance*	✓				*4 000 00*
	31		*G2*		*3 500 00*		*7 500 00*

ACCOUNT *Wax Revenue* ACCOUNT NO. *405*

DATE		DESCRIPTION	POST. REF.	DEBIT	CREDIT	BALANCE DEBIT	BALANCE CREDIT
20--							
Mar.	*1*	*Balance*	✓				*500 00*
	31		*G2*		*800 00*		*1 300 00*

ACCOUNT *Interior Detailing Revenue* ACCOUNT NO. *410*

DATE		DESCRIPTION	POST. REF.	DEBIT	CREDIT	BALANCE DEBIT	BALANCE CREDIT
20--							
Mar.	*1*	*Balance*	✓				*1 000 00*
	31		*G2*		*200 00*		*1 200 00*

ACCOUNT *Utilities Expense* ACCOUNT NO. *530*

DATE		DESCRIPTION	POST. REF.	DEBIT	CREDIT	BALANCE DEBIT	BALANCE CREDIT
20--							
Mar.	*1*	*Balance*	✓			*6 000 00*	
	15		*G1*	*500 00*		*6 500 00*	

Problem 7-6 (concluded)

Analyze:

Name _______________ Date _______________ Class _______________

Problem 7-7 Journalizing and Posting Business Transactions *(textbook p. 188)*

GENERAL LEDGER

ACCOUNT _______________ ACCOUNT NO. _______________

DATE	DESCRIPTION	POST. REF.	DEBIT	CREDIT	BALANCE DEBIT	BALANCE CREDIT

ACCOUNT _______________ ACCOUNT NO. _______________

DATE	DESCRIPTION	POST. REF.	DEBIT	CREDIT	BALANCE DEBIT	BALANCE CREDIT

ACCOUNT _______________ ACCOUNT NO. _______________

DATE	DESCRIPTION	POST. REF.	DEBIT	CREDIT	BALANCE DEBIT	BALANCE CREDIT

ACCOUNT _______________ ACCOUNT NO. _______________

DATE	DESCRIPTION	POST. REF.	DEBIT	CREDIT	BALANCE DEBIT	BALANCE CREDIT

ACCOUNT _______________ ACCOUNT NO. _______________

DATE	DESCRIPTION	POST. REF.	DEBIT	CREDIT	BALANCE DEBIT	BALANCE CREDIT

Problem 7-7 (continued)

ACCOUNT ______ ACCOUNT NO. ______

DATE		DESCRIPTION	POST. REF.	DEBIT	CREDIT	BALANCE DEBIT	BALANCE CREDIT

ACCOUNT ______ ACCOUNT NO. ______

DATE		DESCRIPTION	POST. REF.	DEBIT	CREDIT	BALANCE DEBIT	BALANCE CREDIT

ACCOUNT ______ ACCOUNT NO. ______

DATE		DESCRIPTION	POST. REF.	DEBIT	CREDIT	BALANCE DEBIT	BALANCE CREDIT

ACCOUNT ______ ACCOUNT NO. ______

DATE		DESCRIPTION	POST. REF.	DEBIT	CREDIT	BALANCE DEBIT	BALANCE CREDIT

ACCOUNT ______ ACCOUNT NO. ______

DATE		DESCRIPTION	POST. REF.	DEBIT	CREDIT	BALANCE DEBIT	BALANCE CREDIT

ACCOUNT ______ ACCOUNT NO. ______

DATE		DESCRIPTION	POST. REF.	DEBIT	CREDIT	BALANCE DEBIT	BALANCE CREDIT

Problem 7-7 (continued)

GENERAL JOURNAL

PAGE ____

	DATE		DESCRIPTION	POST. REF.	DEBIT	CREDIT	
1							1
2							2
3							3
4							4
5							5
6							6
7							7
8							8
9							9
10							10
11							11
12							12
13							13
14							14
15							15
16							16
17							17
18							18
19							19
20							20
21							21
22							22
23							23
24							24
25							25
26							26
27							27
28							28
29							29
30							30
31							31
32							32
33							33
34							34
35							35
36							36

Problem 7-7 (concluded)

Analyze:

Name Date Class

Problem 7-8 Journalizing and Posting Business Transactions *(textbook p. 189)*

Instructions: *Use the following source documents to record the transactions for this problem.*

MEMORANDUM 35

Outback Guide Service
705 Fernhill Road
Encinitas, CA 92024

TO: *Accounting Clerk*
FROM: *Juanita Ortega*
DATE: *March 1, 20--*
SUBJECT: *Investment in business*

I have invested $20,000 in cash and rafting equipment valued at $5,000 in the business. Please record the journal entry.

PEAK EQUIPMENT INC.
402 Industry Blvd.
San Diego, CA 92122

INVOICE NO. 101
DATE: *March 3, 20--*
ORDER NO.:
SHIPPED BY: *Speedy Delivery*
TERMS: *Payable in 30 days*

TO *Outback Guide Service*
705 Fernhill Road
Encinitas, CA 92024

QTY.	ITEM	UNIT PRICE	TOTAL
3	Daypacks -- DP41714-0	$100.00	$300.00
2	Backpacks -- BP43714-1	150.00	300.00
			$600.00

Premier Processors
5775 Lemon Grove Drive
San Diego, CA 92107

INVOICE NO. 616
DATE: *March 5, 20--*
ORDER NO.:
SHIPPED BY: *Pick up*
TERMS: *Payable in 60 days*

TO *Outback Guide Service*
705 Fernhill Road
Encinitas, CA 92024

QTY.	ITEM	UNIT PRICE	TOTAL
1	Computer system -- IEF407	$2,800.00	$2,800.00

RECEIPT No. 310

Outback Guide Service
705 Fernhill Road
Encinitas, CA 92024

March 2 20--

RECEIVED FROM *Cathy & Jonathon Smith* $ *135.00*

One hundred thirty-five and 00/100 DOLLARS

FOR *Guide Service*

RECEIVED BY *Juanita Ortega*

RECEIPT No. 311

Outback Guide Service
705 Fernhill Road
Encinitas, CA 92024

March 2 20--

RECEIVED FROM *Chad Schmidt* $ *80.00*

Eighty and 00/100 DOLLARS

FOR *Guide Service*

RECEIVED BY *Juanita Ortega*

RECEIPT No. 312

Outback Guide Service
705 Fernhill Road
Encinitas, CA 92024

March 3 20--

RECEIVED FROM *Jason & Brittany Kelley* $ *135.00*

One hundred thirty-five and 00/100 DOLLARS

FOR *Guide Service*

RECEIVED BY *Juanita Ortega*

RECEIPT No. 313

Outback Guide Service
705 Fernhill Road
Encinitas, CA 92024

March 5 20--

RECEIVED FROM *Clancey McMichael* $ *80.00*

Eighty and 00/100 DOLLARS

FOR *Guide Service*

RECEIVED BY *Juanita Ortega*

RECEIPT No. 314

Outback Guide Service
705 Fernhill Road
Encinitas, CA 92024

March 5 20--

RECEIVED FROM *Louise Wicker & Dudley Hartel* $ *135.00*

One hundred thirty-five and 00/100 DOLLARS

FOR *Guide Service*

RECEIVED BY *Juanita Ortega*

Problem 7-8 (continued)

Outback Guide Service
705 Fernhill Road
Encinitas, CA 92024

RECEIPT
No. 315

March 7 20--

RECEIVED FROM *Greg & Ann Ingram* $ *135.00*

One hundred thirty-five and 00/100 DOLLARS

FOR *Guide Service*

RECEIVED BY *Juanita Ortega*

$ *1,400.00* **No. 654**
Date *March 18* 20--
To *Premier Processors*
For *On account*

	Dollars	Cents
Balance brought forward	19,500	00
Add deposits		
Total	19,500	00
Less this check	1,400	00
Balance carried forward	18,100	00

$ *400.00* **No. 652**
Date *March 9* 20--
To *Daily Courier*
For *Ad*

	Dollars	Cents
Balance brought forward	0	00
Add deposits 2/1	20,000	00
2/7	700	00
Total	20,700	00
Less this check	400	00
Balance carried forward	20,300	00

Outback Guide Service
705 Fernhill Road
Encinitas, CA 92024

RECEIPT
No. 316

March 22 20--

RECEIVED FROM *Podaski Systems Inc.* $ *900.00*

Nine hundred and 00/100 DOLLARS

FOR *Payment on account*

RECEIVED BY *Juanita Ortega*

Outback Guide Service
705 Fernhill Road, Encinitas, CA 92024

INVOICE NO. 352

DATE: *March 12, 20--*
ORDER NO.:
SHIPPED BY:
TERMS: *Payment due upon receipt*

TO *Podaski Systems Inc.*
115 Beach Blvd.
San Diego, CA 92103

DATE	SERVICE	AMOUNT
3/10/--	Group rafting trip	$900.00

$ *500.00* **No. 655**
Date *March 27* 20--
To *Live TV*
For *Ad*

	Dollars	Cents
Balance brought forward	18,100	00
Add deposits 2/22	900	00
Total	19,000	00
Less this check	500	00
Balance carried forward	18,500	00

$ *800.00* **No. 653**
Date *March 15* 20--
To *Cash*
For *Personal use*

	Dollars	Cents
Balance brought forward	20,300	00
Add deposits		
Total		
Less this check	800	00
Balance carried forward	19,500	00

$ *600.00* **No. 656**
Date *March 28* 20--
To *Peak Equipment Inc.*
For *On account*

	Dollars	Cents
Balance brought forward	18,500	00
Add deposits		
Total	18,500	00
Less this check	600	00
Balance carried forward	17,900	00

Problem 7-8 (continued)

GENERAL LEDGER

ACCOUNT ______ ACCOUNT NO. ______

DATE		DESCRIPTION	POST. REF.	DEBIT	CREDIT	BALANCE	
						DEBIT	CREDIT

ACCOUNT ______ ACCOUNT NO. ______

DATE		DESCRIPTION	POST. REF.	DEBIT	CREDIT	BALANCE	
						DEBIT	CREDIT

ACCOUNT ______ ACCOUNT NO. ______

DATE		DESCRIPTION	POST. REF.	DEBIT	CREDIT	BALANCE	
						DEBIT	CREDIT

ACCOUNT ______ ACCOUNT NO. ______

DATE		DESCRIPTION	POST. REF.	DEBIT	CREDIT	BALANCE	
						DEBIT	CREDIT

ACCOUNT ______ ACCOUNT NO. ______

DATE		DESCRIPTION	POST. REF.	DEBIT	CREDIT	BALANCE	
						DEBIT	CREDIT

Name Date Class

Problem 7-8 (continued)

ACCOUNT ______________________ ACCOUNT NO. ________

DATE		DESCRIPTION	POST. REF.	DEBIT	CREDIT	BALANCE	
						DEBIT	CREDIT

ACCOUNT ______________________ ACCOUNT NO. ________

DATE		DESCRIPTION	POST. REF.	DEBIT	CREDIT	BALANCE	
						DEBIT	CREDIT

ACCOUNT ______________________ ACCOUNT NO. ________

DATE		DESCRIPTION	POST. REF.	DEBIT	CREDIT	BALANCE	
						DEBIT	CREDIT

ACCOUNT ______________________ ACCOUNT NO. ________

DATE		DESCRIPTION	POST. REF.	DEBIT	CREDIT	BALANCE	
						DEBIT	CREDIT

ACCOUNT ______________________ ACCOUNT NO. ________

DATE		DESCRIPTION	POST. REF.	DEBIT	CREDIT	BALANCE	
						DEBIT	CREDIT

ACCOUNT ______________________ ACCOUNT NO. ________

DATE		DESCRIPTION	POST. REF.	DEBIT	CREDIT	BALANCE	
						DEBIT	CREDIT

Name Date Class

Problem 7-8 (continued)

GENERAL JOURNAL PAGE ______

	DATE	DESCRIPTION	POST. REF.	DEBIT	CREDIT	
1						1
2						2
3						3
4						4
5						5
6						6
7						7
8						8
9						9
10						10
11						11
12						12
13						13
14						14
15						15
16						16
17						17
18						18
19						19
20						20
21						21
22						22
23						23
24						24
25						25
26						26
27						27
28						28
29						29
30						30
31						31
32						32
33						33
34						34
35						35
36						36

Name Date Class

Problem 7-8 (concluded)

Analyze:

Name Date Class

Problem 7-9 Recording and Posting Correcting Entries *(textbook p. 190)*

GENERAL JOURNAL PAGE *21*

	DATE		DESCRIPTION	POST. REF.	DEBIT	CREDIT	
1	*20--*						1
2	*Mar.*	*3*	*Office Furniture*	*135*	*125 00*		2
3			*Cash in Bank*	*101*		*125 00*	3
4			*Check 1401*				4
5		*5*	*Cash in Bank*	*101*	*400 00*		5
6			*Accts. Rec.—James Coletti*	*110*		*400 00*	6
7			*Receipt 602*				7
8		*7*	*Accts. Pay.—Broad Street Office Supply*	*201*	*200 00*		8
9			*Cash in Bank*	*101*		*200 00*	9
10			*Check 1402*				10
11		*9*	*Office Furniture*	*135*	*500 00*		11
12			*Cash in Bank*	*101*		*500 00*	12
13			*Check 1403*				13
14		*13*	*Greg Failla, Capital*	*301*	*1 200 00*		14
15			*Cash in Bank*	*101*		*1 200 00*	15
16			*Check 1404*				16
17		*17*	*Cash in Bank*	*101*	*2 000 00*		17
18			*Greg Failla, Capital*	*301*		*2 000 00*	18
19			*Receipt 603*				19
20		*19*	*Cash in Bank*	*101*	*75 00*		20
21			*Accts. Rec.—Shannon Flannery*	*113*		*75 00*	21
22			*Receipt 604*				22
23		*20*	*Cash in Bank*	*101*	*100 00*		23
24			*Accts. Rec.—James Coletti*	*110*		*100 00*	24
25			*Receipt 605*				25
26		*24*	*Utilities Expense*	*530*	*75 00*		26
27			*Cash in Bank*	*101*		*75 00*	27
28			*Check 1405*				28
29		*27*	*Cash in Bank*	*101*	*3 000 00*		29
30			*Greg Failla, Withdrawals*	*305*		*3 000 00*	30
31			*Memorandum 40*				31
32		*29*	*Cash in Bank*	*101*	*1 000 00*		32
33			*HD projector Rental Revenue*	*405*		*1 000 00*	33
34			*Receipt 606*				34
35							35
36							36

Name Date Class

Problem 7-9 (continued)

GENERAL LEDGER

ACCOUNT *Cash in Bank* ACCOUNT NO. *101*

DATE		DESCRIPTION	POST. REF.	DEBIT	CREDIT	BALANCE DEBIT	BALANCE CREDIT
20--							
Mar.	1	Balance	✓			9,855 00	
	3		G21		125 00	9,730 00	
	5		G21	400 00		10,130 00	
	7		G21		200 00	9,930 00	
	9		G21		500 00	9,430 00	
	13		G21		1,200 00	8,230 00	
	17		G21	2,000 00		10,230 00	
	19		G21	75 00		10,305 00	
	20		G21	100 00		10,405 00	
	24		G21		75 00	10,330 00	
	27		G21	3,000 00		13,330 00	
	29		G21	1,000 00		14,330 00	

ACCOUNT *Accounts Receivable—Shannon Flannery* ACCOUNT NO. *113*

DATE		DESCRIPTION	POST. REF.	DEBIT	CREDIT	BALANCE DEBIT	BALANCE CREDIT
20--							
Mar.	1	Balance	✓			300 00	
	19		G21		57 00	243 00	

ACCOUNT *Office Supplies* ACCOUNT NO. *120*

DATE		DESCRIPTION	POST. REF.	DEBIT	CREDIT	BALANCE DEBIT	BALANCE CREDIT
20--							
Mar.	1	Balance	✓			120 00	

ACCOUNT *Office Furniture* ACCOUNT NO. *135*

DATE		DESCRIPTION	POST. REF.	DEBIT	CREDIT	BALANCE DEBIT	BALANCE CREDIT
20--							
Mar.	1	Balance	✓			1,500 00	
	3		G21	125 00		1,625 00	
	9		G21	500 00		2,125 00	

Problem 7-9 (continued)

ACCOUNT *Accounts Payable—Broad Street Office Supply* ACCOUNT NO. *201*

DATE		DESCRIPTION	POST. REF.	DEBIT	CREDIT	BALANCE DEBIT	BALANCE CREDIT
20--							
Mar.	1	Balance	✓				220000

ACCOUNT *Greg Failla, Capital* ACCOUNT NO. *301*

DATE		DESCRIPTION	POST. REF.	DEBIT	CREDIT	BALANCE DEBIT	BALANCE CREDIT
20--							
Mar.	1	Balance	✓				1300000
	13		G21	120000			1180000
	17		G21		200000		1380000

ACCOUNT *Greg Failla, Withdrawals* ACCOUNT NO. *305*

DATE		DESCRIPTION	POST. REF.	DEBIT	CREDIT	BALANCE DEBIT	BALANCE CREDIT
20--							
Mar.	27		G21		300000		300000

ACCOUNT *DVD Rental Revenue* ACCOUNT NO. *401*

DATE		DESCRIPTION	POST. REF.	DEBIT	CREDIT	BALANCE DEBIT	BALANCE CREDIT

ACCOUNT *HD projector Rental Revenue* ACCOUNT NO. *405*

DATE		DESCRIPTION	POST. REF.	DEBIT	CREDIT	BALANCE DEBIT	BALANCE CREDIT
20--							
Mar.	29		G21		100000		100000

Name Date Class

Problem 7-9 (concluded)

GENERAL JOURNAL PAGE ______

	DATE		DESCRIPTION	POST. REF.	DEBIT	CREDIT	
1							1
2							2
3							3
4							4
5							5
6							6
7							7
8							8
9							9
10							10
11							11
12							12
13							13
14							14
15							15
16							16
17							17
18							18
19							19
20							20
21							21
22							22
23							23
24							24
25							25
26							26
27							27
28							28
29							29
30							30
31							31
32							32
33							33
34							34

Analyze: ____________________

Name Date Class

Notes

Name Date Class

MINI PRACTICE SET 1

TechVision Web Design

Audit Test

Directions: *Use your completed solutions to answer the following questions. Write the answer in the space to the left of each question.*

______________________ **1.** In the entry to record the May 1 transaction, which account was debited?

______________________ **2.** Were assets increased, decreased, or unaffected by the May 3 transaction?

______________________ **3.** What type of account is Web Server?

______________________ **4.** Which account was credited in the May 9, 17, and 26 transactions?

______________________ **5.** What account was credited for the purchase of the Web server on May 7?

______________________ **6.** What was the source document for the May 17 transaction?

______________________ **7.** How does the May 20 transaction affect the owner's capital account?

______________________ **8.** Was Accounts Receivable—Sunshine Products increased or decreased by the transaction on May 21?

______________________ **9.** What was the balance of Cash in Bank on May 27?

______________________ **10.** What were the account numbers entered in the posting Reference column of the general journal for the May 25 transaction?

______________________ **11.** Which account was debited to record the issue of Check 110?

______________________ **12.** What is the ending balance of the Utilities Expense account?

______________________ **13.** Has the amount owed to Office Systems been paid off?

______________________ **14.** How many transactions recorded during May affected the Cash in Bank account?

15. What was the total cost of the office equipment purchased during the month?

16. How many checks were written by the business during May?

17. What was the total amount credited to Web Services Fees during May?

18. What was the total amount debited to Cash in Bank for May?

19. At the end of the month, did the Jack Hines, Withdrawals account have a debit or credit balance?

20. On May 30, what was the total amount owed to TechVision Web Design for services performed for clients?

21. What was the date of the trial balance?

22. What was the amount of the debit and credit totals on the trial balance?

23. How many accounts are listed in the trial balance for TechVision Web Design?

24. How many accounts on the trial balance have debit balances?

25. Which account on the trial balance has the largest balance?

Name Date Class

CHAPTER 9 Financial Statements for a Sole Proprietorship

Study Guide

Section Assessment

Section 1 *Read Section 1 on pages 223–226 and complete the following exercises page 227.*
- ☐ Reinforce the Main Idea
- ☐ Math for Accounting
- ☐ Problem 9-1 *Analyzing a Source Document*

Section 2 *Read Section 2 on pages 228–231 and complete the following exercises on ,e 232.*
- ☐ Reinforce the Main Idea
- ☐ Math for Accounting
- ☐ Problem 9-2 *Determining Ending Capital Balances*

Section 3 *Read Section 3 on pages 233–238 and complete the following exercises on pa 39.*
- ☐ Reinforce the Main Idea
- ☐ Math for Accounting
- ☐ Problem 9-3 *Calculating Return on Sales*

apter Assessment

Summary *Review the Chapter 9 Visual Summary on page 240 in your textbook.*
- ☐ Key Concepts

Review and Activities *Complete the following questions and exercises on page 241 in your textbook.*
- ☐ After You Read: Answering the Essential Question
- ☐ Vocabulary Check
- ☐ Concept Check

Standardized Test Practice *Complete the exercises on page 242 in your textbook.*

omputerized Accounting *Read the Computerized Accounting information on page 243 in your textbook.*
- ☐ Making the Transition from a Manual to a Computerized System

Problems *Complete the following end-of-chapter Problems for Chapter 9 in your textbook.*
- ☐ Problem 9-4 *Preparing an Income Statement*
- ☐ Problem 9-5 *Preparing a Statement of Changes in Owner's Equity*
- ☐ Problem 9-6 *Preparing Financial Statements*
- ☐ Problem 9-7 *Preparing Financial Statements*

Chall e Problem
- ☐ Problem 9-8 *Preparing a Statement of Changes in Owner's Equity*

eal-World App tions and nnections *Complete the following applications on pages 248–249 in your textbook.*
- ☐ Career Wise
- ☐ Global Accounting
- ☐ Analyzing Financial Reports
- ☐ H.O.T. Audit

Name Date Class

Working Papers *for Section Problems*

Problem 9-1 Analyzing a Source Document *(textbook p. 227)*

1. ______
2. ______
3. ______
4. ______
5. ______
6. ______
7. ______

Problem 9-2 Determining Ending Capital Balances *(textbook p. 232)*

	Beginning Capital	Investments	Revenue	Expenses	Withdrawals	Ending Capital
1	$60,000	$ 500	$ 5,100	$ 2,400	$ 700	
2	$24,075	$ 0	$13,880	$ 7,240	$ 800	
3	$28,800	$ 1,000	$ 6,450	$ 6,780	$ 0	
4	$ 0	$10,500	$ 5,320	$ 4,990	$ 200	
5	$ 6,415	$ 0	$ 4,520	$ 3,175	$ 700	
6	$20,870	$ 1,300	$13,980	$ 9,440	$ 1,700	

Problem 9-3 Calculating Return on Sales *(textbook p. 239)*

Return on sales ______ %

Space for calculations:

Name Date Class

Working Papers *for End-of-Chapter Problems*

Problem 9-4 Preparing an Income Statement *(textbook p. 244)*

Wilderness Rentals
Work Sheet
For the Month Ended September 30, 20--

	ACCT. NO.	ACCOUNT NAME	TRIAL BALANCE DEBIT	TRIAL BALANCE CREDIT	INCOME STATEMENT DEBIT	INCOME STATEMENT CREDIT	BALANCE SHEET DEBIT	BALANCE SHEET CREDIT	
1	101	Cash in Bank	5510 00				5510 00		1
2	105	Accts. Rec.—Helen Katz	929 00				929 00		2
3	110	Accts. Rec.—Polk and Co.	467 00				467 00		3
4	115	Office Supplies	974 00				974 00		4
5	120	Office Equipment	4519 00				4519 00		5
6	125	Camping Equipment	6300 00				6300 00		6
7	201	Accts. Pay.—Adventure Equip.		2316 00				2316 00	7
8	203	Accts. Pay.—Digital Tech		1109 00				1109 00	8
9	205	Accts. Pay.—Greg Mollaro		902 00				902 00	9
10	301	Ronald Hicks, Capital		13260 00				13260 00	10
11	305	Ronald Hicks, Withdrawals	700 00				700 00		11
12	310	Income Summary	—	—	—	—			12
13	401	Equipment Rental Revenue		10629 00		10629 00			13
14	501	Advertising Expense	2113 00		2113 00				14
15	505	Maintenance Expense	1200 00		1200 00				15
16	515	Rent Expense	3500 00		3500 00				16
17	525	Utilities Expense	2004 00		2004 00				17
18			28216 00	28216 00	8817 00	10629 00	19399 00	17587 00	18
19		Net Income			1812 00			1812 00	19
20					10629 00	10629 00	19399 00	19399 00	20
21									21
22									22
23									23
24									24
25									25

Problem 9-4 (concluded)

Analyze:

Problem 9-5 Preparing a Statement of Changes in Owner's Equity *(textbook p. 244)*

Name Date Class

Problem 9-5 (concluded)

Analyze:

Name Date Class

Problem 9-6 Preparing Financial Statements *(textbook p. 244)*

(1)

Hot Suds Car Wash

Work Sheet

For the Quarter Ended September 30, 20--

	ACCT. NO.	ACCOUNT NAME	TRIAL BALANCE DEBIT	TRIAL BALANCE CREDIT	INCOME STATEMENT DEBIT	INCOME STATEMENT CREDIT	BALANCE SHEET DEBIT	BALANCE SHEET CREDIT	
1	101	Cash in Bank	8457 00						1
2	105	Accts. Rec.—Linda Brown	584 00						2
3	110	Accts. Rec.—Valley Auto	619 00						3
4	115	Detailing Supplies	810 00						4
5	120	Detergent Supplies	460 00						5
6	125	Office Equipment	15240 00						6
7	130	Office Furniture	2160 00						7
8	135	Car Wash Equipment	7522 00						8
9	201	Accts. Pay.—Allen Vacuum		3528 00					9
10	204	Accts. Pay.—O'Brian's Office		1215 00					10
11	301	Regina Delgado, Capital		23845 00					11
12	305	Regina Delgado, Withdrawals	1500 00						12
13	310	Income Summary	—	—					13
14	401	Wash Revenue		9623 00					14
15	405	Wax Revenue		8019 00					15
16	410	Interior Detailing Revenue		2628 00					16
17	501	Advertising Expense	1963 00						17
18	505	Equipment Rental Expense	4137 00						18
19	510	Maintenance Expense	1186 00						19
20	520	Rent Expense	3500 00						20
21	530	Utilities Expense	720 00						21
22			48858 00	48858 00					22
23									23
24									24
25									25

Problem 9-6 (continued)

(2)

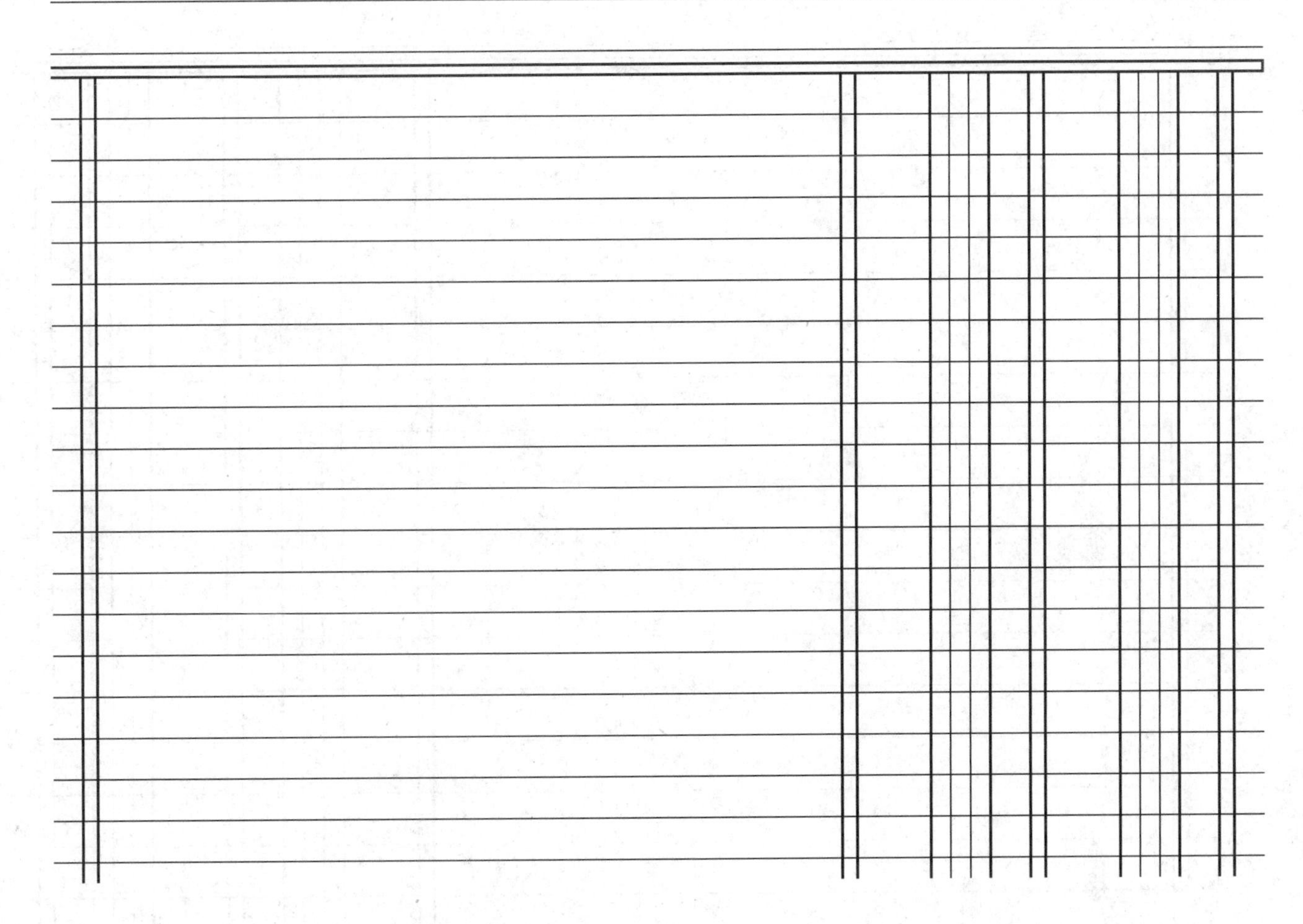

(3)

Name Date Class

Problem 9-6 (concluded)

(4)

Analyze:

Name Date Class

Problem 9-7 Preparing Financial Statements *(textbook p. 245)*

(1)

	ACCT. NO.	ACCOUNT NAME	TRIAL BALANCE DEBIT	TRIAL BALANCE CREDIT	INCOME STATEMENT DEBIT	INCOME STATEMENT CREDIT	BALANCE SHEET DEBIT	BALANCE SHEET CREDIT	
1									1
2									2
3									3
4									4
5									5
6									6
7									7
8									8
9									9
10									10
11									11
12									12
13									13
14									14
15									15
16									16
17									17
18									18
19									19
20									20
21									21
22									22
23									23
24									24
25									25
26									26

Name Date Class

Problem 9-7 (continued)

(2)

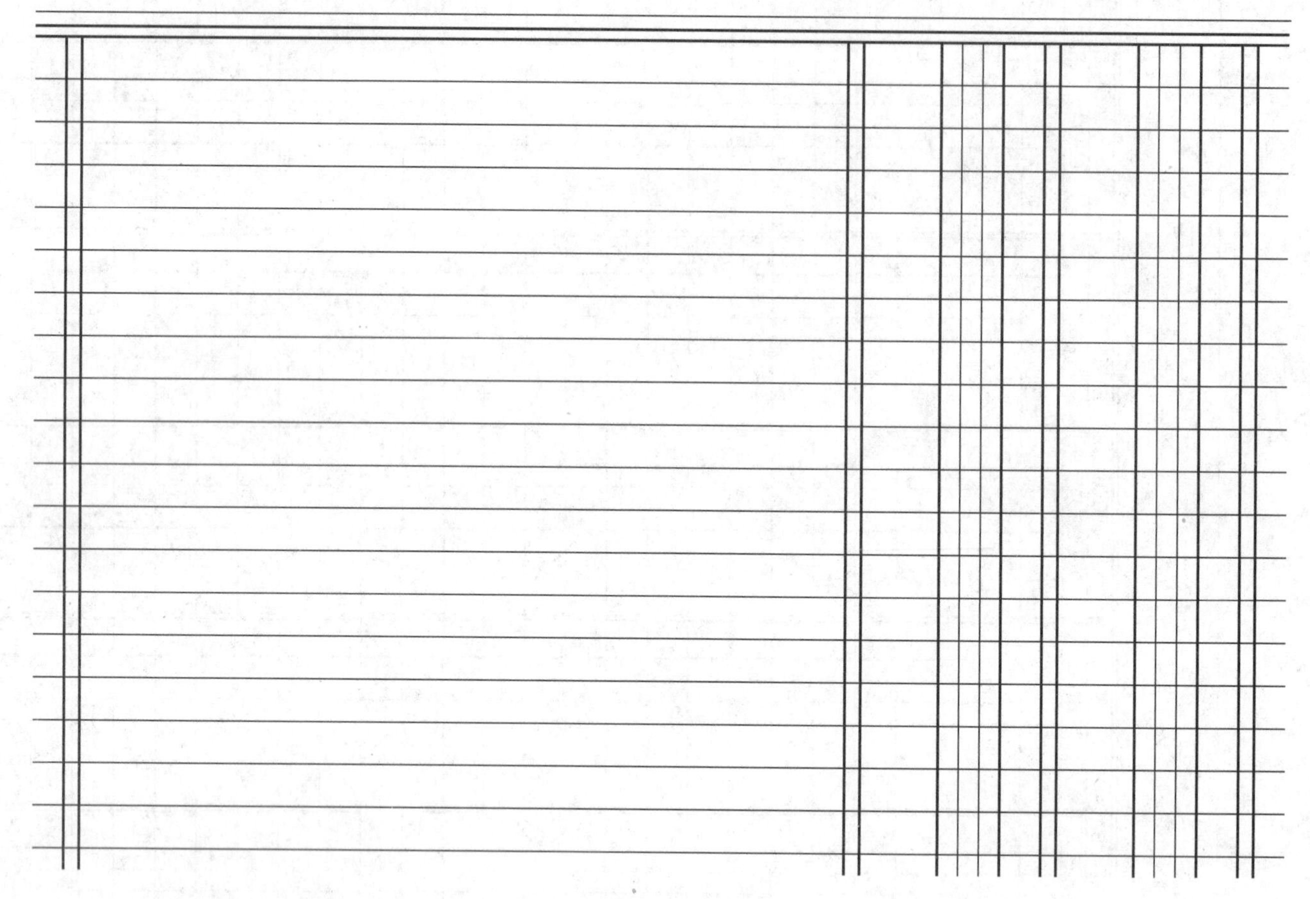

(3)

Name Date Class

Problem 9-7 (concluded)

(4)

Analyze:

Name Date Class

Problem 9-8 Preparing a Statement of Changes in Owner's Equity *(textbook p. 245)*

Analyze:

Problem 10-9 (continued)

ACCOUNT *Advertising Expense* ACCOUNT NO. *501*

DATE		DESCRIPTION	POST. REF.	DEBIT	CREDIT	BALANCE DEBIT	BALANCE CREDIT
20--							
Dec.	*31*	*Balance*	✓			*3 000 00*	

ACCOUNT *Maintenance Expense* ACCOUNT NO. *505*

DATE		DESCRIPTION	POST. REF.	DEBIT	CREDIT	BALANCE DEBIT	BALANCE CREDIT
20--							
Dec.	*31*	*Balance*	✓			*800 00*	

ACCOUNT *Miscellaneous Expense* ACCOUNT NO. *510*

DATE		DESCRIPTION	POST. REF.	DEBIT	CREDIT	BALANCE DEBIT	BALANCE CREDIT
20--							
Dec.	*31*	*Balance*	✓			*800 00*	

ACCOUNT *Rent Expense* ACCOUNT NO. *520*

DATE		DESCRIPTION	POST. REF.	DEBIT	CREDIT	BALANCE DEBIT	BALANCE CREDIT
20--							
Dec.	*31*	*Balance*	✓			*2 000 00*	

ACCOUNT *Utilities Expense* ACCOUNT NO. *530*

DATE		DESCRIPTION	POST. REF.	DEBIT	CREDIT	BALANCE DEBIT	BALANCE CREDIT
20--							
Dec.	*31*	*Balance*	✓			*900 00*	

Name Date Class

Problem 10-9 (concluded)

(5)

Analyze:

Scholastic Success Tutoring Service

CHART OF ACCOUNTS

ASSETS

101	Cash in Bank
110	Accounts Receivable—Carla DiSario
120	Accounts Receivable—George McGarty
140	Office Supplies
150	Office Equipment
155	Instructional Equipment

LIABILITIES

210	Accounts Payable—Educational Software
215	Accounts Payable—T & N School Equip.

OWNER'S EQUITY

301	Lisa Adams, Capital
305	Lisa Adams, Withdrawals
310	Income Summary

REVENUE

401	Group Lessons Fees
405	Private Lessons Fees

EXPENSES

505	Maintenance Expense
510	Miscellaneous Expense
515	Rent Expense
525	Utilities Expense

Mini Practice Set 2 *(textbook p. 304)*

Instructions: *Use the following source documents to record the transactions for this practice set.*

Scholastic Success Tutoring Service
75 Knoll Ridge Drive
Austin, TX 78708

MEMORANDUM 1

TO: *Accounting Clerk*
FROM: *Owner*
DATE: *December 1, 20--*
SUBJECT: *Investment*

Prepare entry to record $25,000 cash investment by Jennifer Rachael.

Scholastic Success Tutoring Service
75 Knoll Ridge Drive
Austin, TX 78708

RECEIPT
No. 1

December 5 20 --

RECEIVED FROM *Shirley Stevenson* $ *950.00*

Nine hundred fifty and 00/100 DOLLARS

FOR *Private instruction*

RECEIVED BY *Lisa Adams*

Scholastic Success Tutoring Service
75 Knoll Ridge Drive
Austin, TX 78708

101
71-627/3222

DATE *December 2* 20 --

PAY TO THE ORDER OF *Office Max* $ *525.00*

Five hundred twenty-five and 00/100 DOLLARS

Citibank

MEMO *cash register* *Lisa Adams*

⑆3222 7⑆627⑆ 1123 4533⑈ 0101

EDUCATIONAL SOFTWARE
913 Walnut St., #2
Coxville, TX 78701

INVOICE NO. 395

DATE: *Dec. 6, 20--*
ORDER NO.:
SHIPPED BY:
TERMS:

TO *Scholastic Success Tutoring Service*
75 Knoll Ridge Drive
Austin, TX 78708

QTY.	ITEM	UNIT PRICE	TOTAL
	Software (Windows NT, MS Office, Goldmine)		*$8494.00*
			$8494.00

Scholastic Success Tutoring Service
75 Knoll Ridge Drive
Austin, TX 78708

102
71-627/3222

DATE *December 2* 20 --

PAY TO THE ORDER OF *Office Depot* $ *73.00*

Seventy-three and 00/100 DOLLARS

Citibank

MEMO *office supplies* *Lisa Adams*

⑆3222 7⑆627⑆ 1123 4533⑈ 0102

Scholastic Success Tutoring Service
75 Knoll Ridge Drive
Austin, TX 78708

INVOICE NO. 101

DATE: *Dec. 8, 20--*
ORDER NO.:
SHIPPED BY:
TERMS:

TO *Carla DiSario*
99 Louise St.
Austin, TX 78708

QTY.	ITEM	UNIT PRICE	TOTAL
2	*Group Classes*	*$18.00*	*$36.00*

Scholastic Success Tutoring Service
75 Knoll Ridge Drive
Austin, TX 78708

103
71-627/3222

DATE *December 5* 20 --

PAY TO THE ORDER OF *Best Buy* $ *13,924.00*

Thirteen thousand nine hundred twenty-four and 00/100 DOLLARS

Citibank

MEMO *computers* *Lisa Adams*

⑆3222 7⑆627⑆ 1123 4533⑈ 0103

Scholastic Success Tutoring Service
75 Knoll Ridge Drive
Austin, TX 78708

104
71-627/3222

DATE *December 9* 20 --

PAY TO THE ORDER OF *Carlo Property Realty* $ *850.00*

Eight hundred fifty and 00/100 DOLLARS

Citibank

MEMO *rent* *Lisa Adams*

⑆3222 7⑆627⑆ 1123 4533⑈ 0104

Name Date Class

Mini Practice Set 2 (continued)

Scholastic Success Tutoring Service
75 Knoll Ridge Drive
Austin, TX 78708

INVOICE NO. 102

DATE: *Dec. 10, 20--*
ORDER NO.:
SHIPPED BY:
TERMS:

TO *George McGarty*
31 Vale Street
Austin, TX 78705

QTY.	ITEM	UNIT PRICE	TOTAL
5	*Special Group Classes*	*$55.00*	*$275.00*

T&N School Equipment
111 Stratford Drive, #2A
Rollingwood, TX 77081

INVOICE NO. 5495

DATE: *Dec. 10, 20--*
ORDER NO.:
SHIPPED BY:
TERMS:

TO *Scholastic Success Tutoring Service*
75 Knoll Ridge Drive
Austin, TX 78708

QTY.	ITEM	UNIT PRICE	TOTAL
	Microcomputer System		*$2,375.00*

Scholastic Success Tutoring Service
75 Knoll Ridge Drive
Austin, TX 78708

RECEIPT
No. 2

December 11 20 --

RECEIVED FROM *Cash customers* $ *695.00*

Six hundred ninety-five and 00/100 DOLLARS

FOR *20 private lessons between 12/1 and 12/10*

RECEIVED BY *Lisa Adams*

Scholastic Success Tutoring Service
75 Knoll Ridge Drive
Austin, TX 78708

RECEIPT
No. 3

December 13 20 --

RECEIVED FROM *Carla DiSario* $ *36.00*

Thirty-six and 00/100 DOLLARS

FOR *Payment for lessons*

RECEIVED BY *Lisa Adams*

Scholastic Success Tutoring Service
75 Knoll Ridge Drive
Austin, TX 78708

105
71-627/3222

DATE *December 14* 20--

PAY TO THE ORDER OF *Educational Software* $ *200.00*

Two hundred and 00/100 DOLLARS

Citibank

MEMO *software* *Lisa Adams*

⑆3222 71627⑆ 1123 4533⑈ 0105

Scholastic Success Tutoring Service
75 Knoll Ridge Drive
Austin, TX 78708

106
71-627/3222

DATE *December 15* 20--

PAY TO THE ORDER OF *Union Painting Service* $ *750.00*

Seven hundred fifty and 00/100 DOLLARS

Citibank

MEMO *painting* *Lisa Adams*

⑆3222 71627⑆ 1123 4533⑈ 0106

Scholastic Success Tutoring Service
75 Knoll Ridge Drive
Austin, TX 78708

107
71-627/3222

DATE *December 18* 20--

PAY TO THE ORDER OF *Lisa Adams* $ *500.00*

Five hundred and 00/100 DOLLARS

Citibank

MEMO *personal withdrawal* *Lisa Adams*

⑆3222 71627⑆ 1123 4533⑈ 0107

Scholastic Success Tutoring Service
75 Knoll Ridge Drive
Austin, TX 78708

108
71-627/3222

DATE *December 20* 20--

PAY TO THE ORDER OF *Edison Electric* $ *183.00*

One hundred eighty-three and 00/100 DOLLARS

Citibank

MEMO *electricity bill* *Lisa Adams*

⑆3222 71627⑆ 1123 4533⑈ 0108

Scholastic Success Tutoring Service
75 Knoll Ridge Drive
Austin, TX 78708

109
71-627/3222

DATE *December 24* 20--

PAY TO THE ORDER OF *U.S. Postal Service* $ *45.00*

Forty-five and 00/100 DOLLARS

Citibank

MEMO *stamps* *Lisa Adams*

⑆3222 71627⑆ 1123 4533⑈ 0109

Name Date Class

Mini Practice Set 2 (continued)

(3)

GENERAL JOURNAL PAGE ______

	DATE		DESCRIPTION	POST. REF.	DEBIT	CREDIT	
1							1
2							2
3							3
4							4
5							5
6							6
7							7
8							8
9							9
10							10
11							11
12							12
13							13
14							14
15							15
16							16
17							17
18							18
19							19
20							20
21							21
22							22
23							23
24							24
25							25
26							26
27							27
28							28
29							29
30							30
31							31
32							32
33							33
34							34
35							35
36							36
37							37

Mini Practice Set 2 (continued)

GENERAL JOURNAL PAGE ______

	DATE		DESCRIPTION	POST. REF.	DEBIT	CREDIT	
1							1
2							2
3							3
4							4
5							5
6							6
7							7
8							8
9							9
10							10
11							11
12							12
13							13
14							14
15							15
16							16
17							17
18							18
19							19
20							20
21							21
22							22
23							23
24							24
25							25
26							26
27							27
28							28
29							29
30							30
31							31
32							32
33							33
34							34
35							35
36							36
37							37

Mini Practice Set 2 (continued)

(4)

GENERAL LEDGER

ACCOUNT ______________________ ACCOUNT NO. ______

DATE		DESCRIPTION	POST. REF.	DEBIT	CREDIT	BALANCE	
						DEBIT	CREDIT

ACCOUNT ______________________ ACCOUNT NO. ______

DATE		DESCRIPTION	POST. REF.	DEBIT	CREDIT	BALANCE	
						DEBIT	CREDIT

Name Date Class

Mini Practice Set 2 (continued)

ACCOUNT ACCOUNT NO.

DATE		DESCRIPTION	POST. REF.	DEBIT	CREDIT	BALANCE	
						DEBIT	CREDIT

ACCOUNT ACCOUNT NO.

DATE		DESCRIPTION	POST. REF.	DEBIT	CREDIT	BALANCE	
						DEBIT	CREDIT

ACCOUNT ACCOUNT NO.

DATE		DESCRIPTION	POST. REF.	DEBIT	CREDIT	BALANCE	
						DEBIT	CREDIT

ACCOUNT ACCOUNT NO.

DATE		DESCRIPTION	POST. REF.	DEBIT	CREDIT	BALANCE	
						DEBIT	CREDIT

ACCOUNT ACCOUNT NO.

DATE		DESCRIPTION	POST. REF.	DEBIT	CREDIT	BALANCE	
						DEBIT	CREDIT

ACCOUNT ACCOUNT NO.

DATE		DESCRIPTION	POST. REF.	DEBIT	CREDIT	BALANCE	
						DEBIT	CREDIT

Name Date Class

Mini Practice Set 2 (continued)

ACCOUNT ______ ACCOUNT NO. ______

DATE		DESCRIPTION	POST. REF.	DEBIT	CREDIT	BALANCE	
						DEBIT	CREDIT

ACCOUNT ______ ACCOUNT NO. ______

DATE		DESCRIPTION	POST. REF.	DEBIT	CREDIT	BALANCE	
						DEBIT	CREDIT

ACCOUNT ______ ACCOUNT NO. ______

DATE		DESCRIPTION	POST. REF.	DEBIT	CREDIT	BALANCE	
						DEBIT	CREDIT

ACCOUNT ______ ACCOUNT NO. ______

DATE		DESCRIPTION	POST. REF.	DEBIT	CREDIT	BALANCE	
						DEBIT	CREDIT

ACCOUNT ______ ACCOUNT NO. ______

DATE		DESCRIPTION	POST. REF.	DEBIT	CREDIT	BALANCE	
						DEBIT	CREDIT

Name Date Class

Mini Practice Set 2 (continued)

ACCOUNT ______ ACCOUNT NO. ______

DATE		DESCRIPTION	POST. REF.	DEBIT	CREDIT	BALANCE DEBIT	BALANCE CREDIT

ACCOUNT ______ ACCOUNT NO. ______

DATE		DESCRIPTION	POST. REF.	DEBIT	CREDIT	BALANCE DEBIT	BALANCE CREDIT

ACCOUNT ______ ACCOUNT NO. ______

DATE		DESCRIPTION	POST. REF.	DEBIT	CREDIT	BALANCE DEBIT	BALANCE CREDIT

ACCOUNT ______ ACCOUNT NO. ______

DATE		DESCRIPTION	POST. REF.	DEBIT	CREDIT	BALANCE DEBIT	BALANCE CREDIT

Mini Practice Set 2 (continued)

(5)

BANK RECONCILIATION FORM

PLEASE EXAMINE YOUR STATEMENT AT ONCE. ANY DISCREPANCY SHOULD BE REPORTED TO THE BANK IMMEDIATELY.

1. Record any transactions appearing on this statement but not listed in your checkbook.
2. List any checks still outstanding in the space provided to the right.
3. Enter the balance shown on this statement here.
4. Enter deposits recorded in your checkbook but not shown on this statement.
5. Total Lines 3 and 4 and enter here.
6. Enter total checks outstanding here.
7. Subtract Line 6 from Line 5. This adjusted bank balance should agree with your checkbook balance.

CHECKS OUTSTANDING		
Number	Amount	
TOTAL		

(7)

$ ______ No. 114
Date ______ 20___
To ______
For ______

	Dollars	Cents
Balance brought forward		
Add deposits		
Total		
Less this check		
Balance carried forward		

Scholastic Success Tutoring Service
75 Knoll Ridge Drive
Austin, TX 78708

114

71-627
3222

DATE ______ 20___

PAY TO THE ORDER OF ______ $ ______

______ DOLLARS

Citibank

MEMO ______

⑆3222 71627⑆ 1123 4533⑈ 0114

Name Date Class

Mini Practice Set 2 (continued)

(8)

	ACCT. NO.	ACCOUNT NAME	TRIAL BALANCE DEBIT	TRIAL BALANCE CREDIT	INCOME STATEMENT DEBIT	INCOME STATEMENT CREDIT	BALANCE SHEET DEBIT	BALANCE SHEET CREDIT	
1									1
2									2
3									3
4									4
5									5
6									6
7									7
8									8
9									9
10									10
11									11
12									12
13									13
14									14
15									15
16									16
17									17
18									18
19									19
20									20
21									21
22									22

Mini Practice Set 2 (continued)

(9)

(9)

Name Date Class

Mini Practice Set 2 (concluded)

(9)

(11)

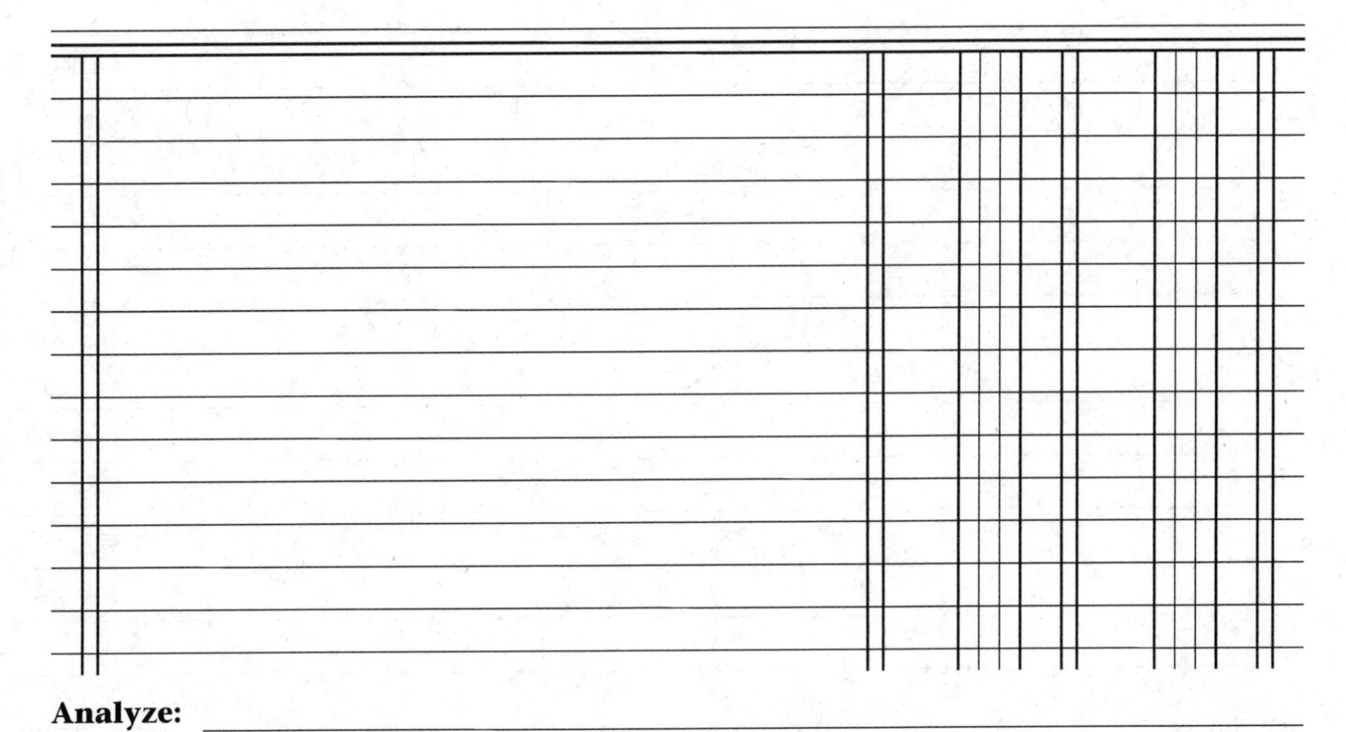

Analyze:

Name Date Class

Notes

Name ______________________ Date __________ Class __________

MINI PRACTICE SET 2

Scholastic Success Tutoring Service

Audit Test

Directions: *Use your completed solutions to answer the following questions. Write the answer in the space to the left of each question.*

________________ **1.** Did the transaction on December 18 increase or decrease owner's capital?

________________ **2.** What was the balance in the Private Lessons Fees account on December 23?

________________ **3.** Did the transaction on December 8 increase or decrease accounts receivable?

________________ **4.** What was the amount of office supplies purchased during the month?

________________ **5.** What was the checkbook balance after the bank service charge was recorded on the check stub?

________________ **6.** What account was debited to record the bank service charge amount?

________________ **7.** What was the total amount of outstanding checks listed on the bank reconciliation statement?

________________ **8.** To which creditor did Scholastic Success Tutoring Service owe the most money on December 31?

________________ **9.** What was the balance of the owner's capital account reported on the trial balance?

________________ **10.** To what section of the work sheet was the balance of the Lisa Adams, Withdrawals account extended?

________ 11. What was the total of the Income Statement Debit column of the work sheet before the net income or net loss was determined?

________ 12. What was the amount of net income or net loss for December?

________ 13. What was the amount of total revenue for the period?

________ 14. From what source did Scholastic Success Tutoring Service earn most of its revenue?

________ 15. What were the total expenses for the month?

________ 16. Did all the temporary capital accounts appear on the income statement?

________ 17. How many asset accounts were listed on the balance sheet?

________ 18. What were Scholastic Success Tutoring Service's total liabilities at the end of the month?

________ 19. How many closing entries were needed to close the temporary accounts?

________ 20. To close Rent Expense, was the account debited or credited?

________ 21. How many accounts in the general ledger were closed?

________ 22. The final closing entry closed which account?

________ 23. How many accounts were listed on the post-closing trial balance?

________ 24. What was the balance in the Lisa Adams, Capital account reported on the post-closing trial balance?

________ 25. What were the debit and credit totals of the post-closing trial balance?

Name Date Class

CHAPTER 12 Payroll Accounting

Study Guide

Section Assessment

Section 1 *Read Section 1 on pages 313–316 and complete the following exercises on page 317.*

- ☐ Reinforce the Main Idea
- ☐ Math for Accounting
- ☐ Problem 12-1 *Calculating Gross Earnings*

Section 2 *Read Section 2 on pages 318–321 and complete the following exercises on page 322.*

- ☐ Reinforce the Main Idea
- ☐ Math for Accounting
- ☐ Problem 12-2 *Determining Taxes on Gross Earnings*
- ☐ Problem 12-3 *Analyzing a Source Document*

Section 3 *Read Section 3 on pages 323–327 and complete the following exercises on page 328.*

- ☐ Reinforce the Main Idea
- ☐ Math for Accounting
- ☐ Problem 12-4 *Preparing a Payroll Check*

Chapter Assessment

Summary *Review the Chapter 12 Visual Summary on page 329 in your textbook.*

- ☐ Key Concepts

Review and Activities *Complete the following questions and exercises on page 330 in your textbook.*

- ☐ After You Read: Answering the Essential Question
- ☐ Vocabulary Check
- ☐ Concept Check

Standardized Test Practice *Complete the exercises on page 331 in your textbook.*

Computerized Accounting *Read the Computerized Accounting information on page 332 in your textbook.*

- ☐ Enter and Maintain Employee Information; Process Payroll

Problems *Complete the following End-of-Chapter Problems for Chapter 12 in your textbook.*

- ☐ Problem 12-5 *Calculating Gross Pay*
- ☐ Problem 12-6 *Preparing a Payroll Register*
- ☐ Problem 12-7 *Preparing Payroll Checks and Employee's Earnings Records*
- ☐ Problem 12-8 *Preparing the Payroll*
- ☐ Problem 12-9 *Preparing the Payroll Register*

Challenge Problem

- ☐ Problem 12-10 *Calculating Gross Earnings*

Real-World Applications and Connections *Complete the following applications on pages 338–339 in your textbook.*

- ☐ Case Study
- ☐ 21st Century Skills
- ☐ Career Wise
- ☐ H.O.T Audit

Working Papers *for Section Problems*

Problem 12-1 Calculating Gross Earnings *(textbook p. 317)*

Employee	Total Hours	Pay Rate	Regular Earnings	Overtime Earnings	Gross Earnings
Clune, David	*33½*	*$7.75*	*$259.63*	*–0–*	*$259.63*
Lang, Richard					
Longas, Jane					
Quinn, Betty					
Sullivan, John					
Talbert, Kelly					
Trimbell, Gene					
Varney, Heidi					
Wallace, Kevin					

Problem 12-2 Determining Taxes on Gross Earnings *(textbook p. 322)*

				Deductions					
Employee	Marital Status	Allowances	Gross Earnings	Social Security Tax	Medicare Tax	Federal Inc. Tax	State Inc. Tax	Total	Net
Cleary, Kevin	S	0	155.60						
Halley, James	S	1	184.10						
Hong, Kim	S	0	204.65						
Jackson, Marvin	M	1	216.40						
Sell, Richard	M	2	196.81						
Totals									

Problem 12-3 Analyzing a Source Document *(textbook p. 322)*

Employee Pay Statement
Detach and retain this statement. **260**

Period Ending	Earnings			Deductions							Net Pay
	Regular	Overtime	Total	Social Security Tax	Med. Tax	Federal Income Tax	State Income Tax	Hosp. Ins.	Other	Total	
1/15/20--	*315.00*	*-0-*	*315.00*	*2)*	*1)*	*3)*					

Problem 12-4 Preparing a Payroll Check *(textbook p. 328)*

PAYROLL REGISTER

PAY PERIOD ENDING *March 23* 20 *--* DATE OF PAYMENT *March 23, 20--*

EMPLOYEE NUMBER	NAME	MAR. STATUS	ALLOW.	TOTAL HOURS	RATE	EARNINGS			DEDUCTIONS							NET PAY	CK. NO.
						REGULAR	OVERTIME	TOTAL	SOC. SEC. TAX	MED. TAX	FED. INC. TAX	STATE INC. TAX	HOSP. INS.	OTHER	TOTAL		
18	*Burns, Janice*	*S*	*1*	*42*	*7.80*	*312 00*	*23 40*	*335 40*	*20 79*	*4 86*	*35 00*	*6 71*	*4 10*	—	*71 46*	*263 94*	*79*

Heather's Dance School
23 Kingdom Street
Danbury, TX 75430

79

63-947
670

Date ______________ 20 ____

Pay to the Order of ______________________ $ __________

______________________________________ Dollars

Worster Bank
PATTON, TEXAS

⑆067009471⑆ 3939 043 417⑈

Employee Pay Statement
Detach and retain this statement.

79

Period Ending	Earnings			Deductions							Net Pay
	Regular	Overtime	Total	Social Security Tax	Med. Tax	Federal Income Tax	State Income Tax	Hosp. Ins.	Other	Total	

Name Date Class

Working Papers *for End-of-Chapter Problems*

Problem 12-5 Calculating Gross Pay *(textbook p. 333)*

Name	Regular Hours	Overtime Hours	Total Hours	Hourly Rate	Salary	Commission	Gross Pay
Driscoll, Tom							
Gilmartin, John							
Ryan, Ann							
Stone, Arlene							

Analyze: ________________________________

Name ______________________ Date ______________ Class ______________

Problem 12-6 Preparing a Payroll Register *(textbook p. 333)*

PAYROLL REGISTER

PAY PERIOD ENDING ______________________ 20 ______ DATE OF PAYMENT ______________________

	EMPLOYEE NUMBER	NAME	MAR. STATUS	ALLOW.	TOTAL HOURS	RATE	EARNINGS			DEDUCTIONS							NET PAY	CK. NO.	
							REGULAR	OVERTIME	TOTAL	SOC. SEC. TAX	MED. TAX	FED. INC. TAX	STATE INC. TAX	HOSP. INS.	OTHER	TOTAL			
1																			1
2																			2
3																			3
4																			4
25																			25
						TOTALS													

Other Deductions: Write the appropriate code letter to the left of the amount: B—U.S. Savings Bonds; C—Credit Union; UD—Union Dues; UW—United Way.

Analyze: ____

____

Name Date Class

Problem 12-7 Preparing Payroll Checks and Employees' Earnings Records *(textbook p. 334)*

PAYROLL REGISTER

PAY PERIOD ENDING *October 17* 20 *—* DATE OF PAYMENT *October 17, 20—*

EMPLOYEE NUMBER	NAME	MAR. STATUS	ALLOW.	TOTAL HOURS	RATE	EARNINGS: REGULAR	EARNINGS: OVERTIME	EARNINGS: TOTAL	DEDUCTIONS: SOC. SEC. TAX	DEDUCTIONS: MED. TAX	DEDUCTIONS: FED. INC. TAX	DEDUCTIONS: STATE INC. TAX	DEDUCTIONS: HOSP. INS.	DEDUCTIONS: OTHER	DEDUCTIONS: TOTAL	NET PAY	CK. NO.
162	Hurd, Mildred	S	0	38	7.60	288 80		288 80	17 91	4 19	35 00	7 22		B 5 00	69 32	219 48	
157	Montego, José	S	1	39	7.90	308 10		308 10	19 10	4 47	30 00	7 70	5 10		66 37	241 73	
151	Pilly, Amanda	M	2	36	8.10	291 60		291 60	18 08	4 23	10 00	7 29	7 60	B 5 00	52 20	239 40	
163	Steams, Margaret	S	0	41	7.60	304 00	11 40	315 40	19 55	4 57	40 00	7 89			72 01	243 39	
					TOTALS	1,192 50	11 40	1,203 90	74 64	17 46	115 00	30 10	12 70	10 00	259 90	944 00	

Other Deductions: Write the appropriate code letter to the left of the amount: B—U.S. Savings Bonds; C—Credit Union; UD—Union Dues; UW—United Way.

Name Date Class

Problem 12-7 (continued)

92

KITS & PUPS GROOMING

63-947
670

Date ______ 20 ___

Pay to the Order of ______ $ ______

______ Dollars

Shoreline National Bank
PENSACOLA, FLORIDA

⑆0670094 7⑆ 0092 043 417⑈

Employee Pay Statement
Detach and retain this statement.

92

Period Ending	Earnings			Deductions							Net Pay
	Regular	Overtime	Total	Social Security Tax	Med. Tax	Federal Income Tax	State Income Tax	Hosp. Ins.	Other	Total	

93

KITS & PUPS GROOMING

63-947
670

Date ______ 20 ___

Pay to the Order of ______ $ ______

______ Dollars

Shoreline National Bank
PENSACOLA, FLORIDA

⑆0670094 7⑆ 0093 043 417⑈

Employee Pay Statement
Detach and retain this statement.

93

Period Ending	Earnings			Deductions							Net Pay
	Regular	Overtime	Total	Social Security Tax	Med. Tax	Federal Income Tax	State Income Tax	Hosp. Ins.	Other	Total	

Problem 12-7 (continued)

KITS & PUPS GROOMING

94

63-947
670

Date ______________ 20 ___

Pay to the Order of ______________ $ ______

______________ Dollars

Shoreline National Bank
PENSACOLA, FLORIDA

⑆067009471⑆ 0094 043 417⑈

Employee Pay Statement
Detach and retain this statement.

94

Period Ending	Earnings			Deductions							Net Pay
	Regular	Overtime	Total	Social Security Tax	Med. Tax	Federal Income Tax	State Income Tax	Hosp. Ins.	Other	Total	

KITS & PUPS GROOMING

95

63-947
670

Date ______________ 20 ___

Pay to the Order of ______________ $ ______

______________ Dollars

Shoreline National Bank
PENSACOLA, FLORIDA

⑆067009471⑆ 0095 043 417⑈

Employee Pay Statement
Detach and retain this statement.

95

Period Ending	Earnings			Deductions							Net Pay
	Regular	Overtime	Total	Social Security Tax	Med. Tax	Federal Income Tax	State Income Tax	Hosp. Ins.	Other	Total	

Problem 12-7 (continued)

EMPLOYEE'S EARNINGS RECORD FOR QUARTER ENDING *October 31, 20--*

Montego (Last Name) *José* (First) *M.* (Initial)

EMPLOYEE NO. *157* MARTIAL STATUS *S* ALLOWANCES *1*

28 Cambell Avenue (Address)

POSITION *Sales Associate*

Pensacola, FL 32526

RATE OF PAY *$7.90* SOC. SEC. NO. *021-54-7641*

PAY PERIOD		EARNINGS			DEDUCTIONS							NET PAY	ACCUMULATED EARNINGS
NO.	ENDED	REGULAR	OVERTIME	TOTAL	SOC. SEC. TAX	MED. TAX	FED. INC. TAX	STATE INC. TAX	HOSP. INS.	OTHER	TOTAL		*9414 32*
1	*10/3*	*260 70*		*260 70*	*16 16*	*3 78*	*24 00*	*6 52*	*5 10*	—	*55 56*	*205 14*	*9675 02*
2	*10/10*	*300 20*		*300 20*	*18 61*	*4 35*	*30 00*	*7 51*	*5 10*	—	*65 57*	*234 63*	*9975 22*
3													
4													
5													
6													
7													
8													
9													
10													
11													
12													
13													
QUARTERLY TOTALS													

Other Deductions: B—U.S. Savings Bonds; C—Credit Union; UD—Union Dues; UW—United Way.

Name Date Class

Problem 12-7 (concluded)

EMPLOYEE'S EARNINGS RECORD FOR QUARTER ENDING *October 31, 20--*

Pilly (Last Name) *Amanda* (First) *G.* (Initial)
EMPLOYEE NO. *151* MARTIAL STATUS *M* ALLOWANCES *2*

162 Clinton Avenue (Address)
POSITION *Assistant Manager*

Pensacola, FL 32502
RATE OF PAY *$8.10* SOC. SEC. NO. *021-56-7302*

PAY PERIOD		EARNINGS			DEDUCTIONS							NET PAY	ACCUMULATED EARNINGS
NO.	ENDED	REGULAR	OVERTIME	TOTAL	SOC. SEC. TAX	MED. TAX	FED. INC. TAX	STATE INC. TAX	HOSP. INS.	OTHER	TOTAL		9655 30
1	10/3	275 40		275 40	17 07	3 99	7 00	6 89	7 60	B 5 00	47 55	227 85	9930 70
2	10/10	315 90		315 90	19 59	4 58	13 00	7 90	7 60	B 5 00	57 67	258 23	10,246 60
3													
4													
5													
6													
7													
8													
9													
10													
11													
12													
13													
QUARTERLY TOTALS													

Other Deductions: B—U.S. Savings Bonds; C—Credit Union; UD—Union Dues; UW—United Way.

Analyze:

Problem 12-8 Preparing the Payroll *(textbook p. 335)*

NO. 73
NAME Ted Dame
SOC. SEC. NO. 093-48-7423
WEEK ENDING 10/17/20--

DAY	IN	OUT	IN	OUT	IN	OUT	TOTAL
M	8:58	12:03	12:55	5:09			
T	8:55	11:55	1:00	4:00			
W	9:30	12:10	1:04	3:30			
Th	8:57	12:03	12:59	6:00			
F	8:58	12:00	1:00	6:05			
S	9:00	12:00					
S							
					TOTAL HOURS		

	HOURS	RATE	AMOUNT
REGULAR			
OVERTIME			
TOTAL EARNINGS			

SIGNATURE ____________ DATE ____________

NO. 92
NAME James Usdavin
SOC. SEC. NO. 087-46-3875
WEEK ENDING 10/17/20--

DAY	IN	OUT	IN	OUT	IN	OUT	TOTAL
M	8:55	12:06	1:01	5:40			
T	7:58	11:01	12:03	6:38			
W	9:03	1:10	2:00	6:00			
Th	7:59	11:55	1:10	4:51			
F	9:01	12:06	1:05	3:47			
S	9:00	12:03					
S							
					TOTAL HOURS		

	HOURS	RATE	AMOUNT
REGULAR			
OVERTIME			
TOTAL EARNINGS			

SIGNATURE ____________ DATE ____________

PAYROLL REGISTER

PAY PERIOD ENDING ____________ 20 ____ DATE OF PAYMENT ____________

	EMPLOYEE NUMBER	NAME	MAR. STATUS	ALLOW.	TOTAL HOURS	RATE	EARNINGS			DEDUCTIONS							NET PAY	CK. NO.	
							REGULAR	OVERTIME	TOTAL	SOC. SEC. TAX	MED. TAX	FED. INC. TAX	STATE INC. TAX	HOSP. INS.	OTHER	TOTAL			
1																			1
2																			2
3																			3
4																			4
5																			5
6																			6
25																			25
		TOTALS																	

Other Deductions: Write the appropriate code letter to the left of the amount: B—U.S. Savings Bonds; C—Credit Union; UD—Union Dues; UW—United Way.

Problem 12-8 (continued)

(3)

Outback Guide Service

82

91-182
1721

Date____________ 20 ___

Pay to the Order of____________________ $ ________

______________________________ Dollars

CNB Canyon National Bank
MARIPOSA, CALIFORNIA

⑆1721091182⑆ 082 015 1189064⑈

Employee Pay Statement
Detach and retain this statement.

82

Period Ending	Earnings			Deductions							Net Pay
	Regular	Overtime	Total	Social Security Tax	Med. Tax	Federal Income Tax	State Income Tax	Hosp. Ins.	Other	Total	

Outback Guide Service

83

91-182
1721

Date____________ 20 ___

Pay to the Order of____________________ $ ________

______________________________ Dollars

CNB Canyon National Bank
MARIPOSA, CALIFORNIA

⑆1721091182⑆ 083 015 1189064⑈

Employee Pay Statement
Detach and retain this statement.

83

Period Ending	Earnings			Deductions							Net Pay
	Regular	Overtime	Total	Social Security Tax	Med. Tax	Federal Income Tax	State Income Tax	Hosp. Ins.	Other	Total	

Name Date Class

Problem 12-8 (continued)

Outback Guide Service

84

91-182
1721

Date ______________ 20 ____

Pay to the Order of ______________________ $ ________

______________________________________ Dollars

CNB Canyon National Bank
MARIPOSA, CALIFORNIA

⑆172109118 2⑆ 084 015 1189064⑈

Employee Pay Statement
Detach and retain this statement.

84

Period Ending	Earnings			Deductions							Net Pay
	Regular	Overtime	Total	Social Security Tax	Med. Tax	Federal Income Tax	State Income Tax	Hosp. Ins.	Other	Total	

Outback Guide Service

85

91-182
1721

Date ______________ 20 ____

Pay to the Order of ______________________ $ ________

______________________________________ Dollars

CNB Canyon National Bank
MARIPOSA, CALIFORNIA

⑆172109118 2⑆ 085 015 1189064⑈

Employee Pay Statement
Detach and retain this statement.

85

Period Ending	Earnings			Deductions							Net Pay
	Regular	Overtime	Total	Social Security Tax	Med. Tax	Federal Income Tax	State Income Tax	Hosp. Ins.	Other	Total	

Name Date Class

Problem 12-8 (continued)

Outback Guide Service

86

91-182
1721

Date ______________ 20 ___

Pay to the
Order of ______________________________ $ ________

______________________________ Dollars

CNB Canyon National Bank
MARIPOSA, CALIFORNIA

____

⑆172109118 2⑆ 086 015 1189064⑈

Employee Pay Statement
Detach and retain this statement.

86

Period Ending	Earnings			Deductions							Net Pay
	Regular	Overtime	Total	Social Security Tax	Med. Tax	Federal Income Tax	State Income Tax	Hosp. Ins.	Other	Total	

Outback Guide Service

87

91-182
1721

Date ______________ 20 ___

Pay to the
Order of ______________________________ $ ________

______________________________ Dollars

CNB Canyon National Bank
MARIPOSA, CALIFORNIA

____

⑆172109118 2⑆ 087 015 1189064⑈

Employee Pay Statement
Detach and retain this statement.

87

Period Ending	Earnings			Deductions							Net Pay
	Regular	Overtime	Total	Social Security Tax	Med. Tax	Federal Income Tax	State Income Tax	Hosp. Ins.	Other	Total	

Problem 12-8 (continued)

(4)

EMPLOYEE'S EARNINGS RECORD FOR QUARTER ENDING *December 31, 20--*

Cummings (Last Name) *Carol* (First) *T.* (Initial) EMPLOYEE NO. *83* MARTIAL STATUS *M* ALLOWANCES *1*

289 Eaton Avenue (Address) POSITION *Director*

Mariposa, CA 95338 RATE OF PAY *$270.00 Salary* SOC. SEC. NO. *091-56-7024*

PAY PERIOD		EARNINGS			DEDUCTIONS							NET PAY	ACCUMULATED EARNINGS
NO.	ENDED	REGULAR	OVERTIME	TOTAL	SOC. SEC. TAX	MED. TAX	FED. INC. TAX	STATE INC. TAX	HOSP. INS.	OTHER	TOTAL		*12,150 00*
1	*10/10*	*270 00*		*270 00*	*16 74*	*3 92*	*15 00*	*4 05*	*9 37*	——	*49 08*	*220 92*	*12,420 00*
2													
3													
4													
5													
6													
7													
8													
9													
10													
11													
12													
13													
QUARTERLY TOTALS													

Other Deductions: B—U.S. Savings Bonds; C—Credit Union; UD—Union Dues; UW—United Way.

Problem 12-8 (continued)

EMPLOYEE'S EARNINGS RECORD FOR QUARTER ENDING *December 31, 20--*

Dame (Last Name) *Ted* (First) *K.* (Initial)
EMPLOYEE NO. *73* MARTIAL STATUS *S* ALLOWANCES *0*

14 Merton Avenue (Address)
POSITION *Equipment Clerk*

Mariposa, CA 95338
RATE OF PAY *$7.60* SOC. SEC. NO. *093-48-7423*

PAY PERIOD		EARNINGS			DEDUCTIONS							NET PAY	ACCUMULATED EARNINGS
NO.	ENDED	REGULAR	OVERTIME	TOTAL	SOC. SEC. TAX	MED. TAX	FED. INC. TAX	STATE INC. TAX	HOSP. INS.	OTHER	TOTAL		*4,016 22*
1	*10/10*	*264 10*		*264 10*	*16 37*	*3 83*	*32 00*	*3 96*	*5 43*		*61 59*	*202 51*	*4,280 32*
2													
3													
4													
5													
6													
7													
8													
9													
10													
11													
12													
13													
QUARTERLY TOTALS													

Other Deductions: B—U.S. Savings Bonds; C—Credit Union; UD—Union Dues; UW—United Way.

Name Date Class

Problem 12-8 (continued)

EMPLOYEE'S EARNINGS RECORD FOR QUARTER ENDING *December 31, 20--*

Lengyel (Last Name) *Tom* (First) *B.* (Initial)
EMPLOYEE NO. *79* MARTIAL STATUS *M* ALLOWANCES *1*

926 Amsterdam Avenue (Address)
POSITION *Guide*

Mariposa, CA 95338
RATE OF PAY *$160.00 + 5%* SOC. SEC. NO. *210-50-7261*

PAY PERIOD NO.	PAY PERIOD ENDED	EARNINGS REGULAR	EARNINGS OVERTIME	EARNINGS TOTAL	DEDUCTIONS SOC. SEC. TAX	MED. TAX	FED. INC. TAX	STATE INC. TAX	HOSP. INS.	OTHER	TOTAL	NET PAY	ACCUMULATED EARNINGS
													4,818 00
1	10/10	219 40		219 40	13 60	3 18	6 00	3 29	9 37	B 10 00	45 44	173 96	5,037 40
2													
3													
4													
5													
6													
7													
8													
9													
10													
11													
12													
13													
QUARTERLY TOTALS													

Other Deductions: B—U.S. Savings Bonds; C—Credit Union; UD—Union Dues; UW—United Way.

Problem 12-8 (continued)

EMPLOYEE'S EARNINGS RECORD FOR QUARTER ENDING *December 31, 20--*

Robinson (Last Name) *Jean* (First) *A.* (Initial) EMPLOYEE NO. *46* MARTIAL STATUS *S* ALLOWANCES *1*

12 Meadow Avenue (Address) POSITION *Guide*

Mariposa, CA 95338 RATE OF PAY *$140.00 + 5%* SOC. SEC. NO. *036-59-7206*

PAY PERIOD		EARNINGS			DEDUCTIONS							NET PAY	ACCUMULATED EARNINGS
NO.	ENDED	REGULAR	OVERTIME	TOTAL	SOC. SEC. TAX	MED. TAX	FED. INC. TAX	STATE INC. TAX	HOSP. INS.	OTHER	TOTAL		*2,786.35*
1	*10/10*	*209.30*		*209.30*	*12.98*	*3.03*	*15.00*	*3.14*	*5.43*		*39.58*	*169.72*	*2,995.65*
2													
3													
4													
5													
6													
7													
8													
9													
10													
11													
12													
13													
QUARTERLY TOTALS													

Other Deductions: B—U.S. Savings Bonds; C—Credit Union; UD—Union Dues; UW—United Way.

Problem 12-8 (continued)

EMPLOYEE'S EARNINGS RECORD FOR QUARTER ENDING *December 31, 20--*

Usdavin (Last Name) *James* (First) *P.* (Initial)	EMPLOYEE NO. *92* MARTIAL STATUS *S* ALLOWANCES *0*
19 Paterson Avenue (Address)	POSITION *Stock Clerk*
Mariposa, CA 95338	RATE OF PAY *$7.40* SOC. SEC. NO. *087-46-3875*

PAY PERIOD		EARNINGS			DEDUCTIONS							NET PAY	ACCUMULATED EARNINGS
NO.	ENDED	REGULAR	OVERTIME	TOTAL	SOC. SEC. TAX	MED. TAX	FED. INC. TAX	STATE INC. TAX	HOSP. INS.	OTHER	TOTAL		*3,172 15*
1	*10/10*	*206 15*		*206 15*	*12 78*	*2 99*	*23 00*	*3 09*	*5 43*		*47 29*	*158 86*	*3,378 30*
2													
3													
4													
5													
6													
7													
8													
9													
10													
11													
12													
13													
QUARTERLY TOTALS													

Other Deductions: B—U.S. Savings Bonds; C—Credit Union; UD—Union Dues; UW—United Way.

Problem 12-8 (concluded)

EMPLOYEE'S EARNINGS RECORD FOR QUARTER ENDING *December 31, 20--*

Wong (Last Name)	*Kim* (First)	*P.* (Initial)
28 Millrose Avenue (Address)		
Mariposa, CA 95338		

EMPLOYEE NO. *66* MARTIAL STATUS *S* ALLOWANCES *0*

POSITION *Guide*

RATE OF PAY *$140.00 + 5%* SOC. SEC. NO. *019-53-7302*

PAY PERIOD		EARNINGS			DEDUCTIONS							NET PAY	ACCUMULATED EARNINGS
NO.	ENDED	REGULAR	OVERTIME	TOTAL	SOC. SEC. TAX	MED. TAX	FED. INC. TAX	STATE INC. TAX	HOSP. INS.	OTHER	TOTAL		*3,672 45*
1	*10/10*	*211 20*		*211 20*	*13 09*	*3 06*	*23 00*	*3 17*	*5 43*	*B 10 00*	*57 75*	*153 45*	*3,883 65*
2													
3													
4													
5													
6													
7													
8													
9													
10													
11													
12													
13													
QUARTERLY TOTALS													

Other Deductions: B—U.S. Savings Bonds; C—Credit Union; UD—Union Dues; UW—United Way.

Analyze:

Name Date Class

Problem 12-9 Preparing the Payroll Register *(textbook p. 336)*

PAYROLL REGISTER

PAY PERIOD ENDING ____________ 20___ DATE OF PAYMENT ____________

	EMPLOYEE NUMBER	NAME	MAR. STATUS	ALLOW.	TOTAL HOURS	RATE	EARNINGS			DEDUCTIONS							NET PAY	CK. NO.	
							REGULAR	OVERTIME	TOTAL	SOC. SEC. TAX	MED. TAX	FED. INC. TAX	STATE INC. TAX	HOSP. INS.	OTHER	TOTAL			
1																			1
2																			2
3																			3
4																			4
5																			5
6																			6
7																			7
8																			8
9																			9
10																			10
11																			11
12																			12
13																			13
14																			14
15																			15
16																			16
17																			17
18																			18
25		TOTALS																	25

Other Deductions: Write the appropriate code letter to the left of the amount: B—U.S. Savings Bonds; C—Credit Union; UD—Union Dues; UW—United Way.

Analyze: ____

Problem 12-10 Calculating Gross Earnings *(textbook p. 337)*

Instructions: *Use the following source documents to record the transactions for this problem.*

Job Connect
4457 Market Street
Kingston, NC 28150

INTEROFFICE MEMORANDUM

TO: *Payroll Clerk*
FROM: *Richard Tang*
DATE: *10/24/20--*
SUBJECT: *Payroll*

Please note the following information necessary for preparing payroll for the week ending October 24. Total office sales were $8,420.00, and phone sales were $1,375.00. Pam Darrah made seven (7) job placements.

NO. 14
NAME Susan Dilloway
SOC. SEC. NO.
WEEK ENDING 10/24/20--

DAY	IN	OUT	IN	OUT	IN	OUT	TOTAL
M	9:03	12:01	12:32	5:28			*8*
T	8:30	12:29	1:00	3:29			*6½*
W	9:01	12:03	12:29	5:31			*8*
Th	9:02	11:59	12:31	5:30			*8*
F	9:01	12:00	12:31	5:29			*8*
S							
S							
						TOTAL HOURS	*38½*

	HOURS	RATE	AMOUNT
REGULAR			
OVERTIME			
TOTAL EARNINGS			

SIGNATURE________ DATE________

NO. 15
NAME Doris Franco
SOC. SEC. NO.
WEEK ENDING 10/24/20--

DAY	IN	OUT	IN	OUT	IN	OUT	TOTAL
M	9:00	12:01	12:35	5:35			*8*
T	9:01	12:02	12:37	5:36			*8*
W	8:00	11:59	12:28	5:31			*9*
Th	8:58	12:01	12:29	5:46			*8¼*
F	9:02	11:58	12:31	5:29			*8*
S							
S							
						TOTAL HOURS	*41¼*

	HOURS	RATE	AMOUNT
REGULAR			
OVERTIME			
TOTAL EARNINGS			

SIGNATURE________ DATE________

NO. 17
NAME David Facini
SOC. SEC. NO.
WEEK ENDING 10/24/20--

DAY	IN	OUT	IN	OUT	IN	OUT	TOTAL
M	3:00	8:01					*5*
T	2:59	8:02					*5*
W	3:01	8:02					*5*
Th	3:00	8:00					*5*
F	3:00	6:01					*3*
S							
S							
						TOTAL HOURS	*23*

	HOURS	RATE	AMOUNT
REGULAR			
OVERTIME			
TOTAL EARNINGS			

SIGNATURE________ DATE________

Name Date Class

Problem 12-10 (concluded)

Name	Gross Earnings
Austin, Lynn	
Darrah, Pam	
Dilloway, Susan	
Facini, David	
Franco, Doris	
Miller, Barbara	
Womack, Charlene	
Total Gross Earnings	

Analyze: ______________________________

Notes

Name Date Class

CHAPTER 13 Payroll Liabilities and Tax Records

Study Guide

Section Assessment

Section 1 *Read Section 1 on pages 343–347 and complete the following exercises on page 348.*
- ☐ Reinforce the Main Idea
- ☐ Math for Accounting
- ☐ Problem 13-1 *Determining Payroll Amounts*

Section 2 *Read Section 2 on pages 349–352 and complete the following exercises on page 353.*
- ☐ Reinforce the Main Idea
- ☐ Math for Accounting
- ☐ Problem 13-2 *Calculating Employer's Payroll Taxes*
- ☐ Problem 13-3 *Identifying Entries for Payroll Liabilities*

Section 3 *Read Section 3 on pages 354–362 and complete the following exercises on page 363.*
- ☐ Reinforce the Main Idea
- ☐ Math for Accounting
- ☐ Problem 13-4 *Payment of Payroll Liabilities*
- ☐ Problem 13-5 *Analyzing a Source Document*

Chapter Assessment

Summary *Review the Chapter 13 Visual Summary on page 364 in your textbook.*
- ☐ Key Concepts

Review and Activities *Complete the following questions and exercises on page 365 in your textbook.*
- ☐ After You Read: Answering the Essential Question
- ☐ Vocabulary Check
- ☐ Concept Check

Standardized Test Practice *Complete the exercises on page 366 in your textbook.*

Computerized Accounting *Read the Computerized Accounting information on page 367 in your textbook.*
- ☐ Record and Post Payroll Entries; Pay Payroll Tax Liabilities

Problems *Complete the following End-of-Chapter Problems for Chapter 13 in your textbook.*
- ☐ Problem 13-6 *Calculating Employer's Payroll Taxes*
- ☐ Problem 13-7 *Recording the Payment of the Payroll*
- ☐ Problem 13-8 *Journalizing Payroll Transactions*
- ☐ Problem 13-9 *Recording and Posting Payroll Transactions*

Challenge Problem
- ☐ Problem 13-10 *Recording and Posting Payroll Transactions*

Real-World Applications and Connections *Complete the following applications on pages 372–373 in your textbook.*
- ☐ Career Wise
- ☐ Global Accounting
- ☐ 21st Century Skills
- ☐ A Matter of Ethics
- ☐ Analyzing Financial Reports

Name Date Class

Working Papers *for Section Problems*

Problem 13-1 Determining Payroll Amounts *(textbook p. 348)*

1. ______
2. ______
3. ______
4. ______
5. ______

Problem 13-2 Calculating Employer's Payroll Taxes *(textbook p. 353)*

Social Security Tax Payable $ ______

Medicare Tax Payable $ ______

Federal Unemployment Tax Payable $ ______

State Unemployment Tax Payable $ ______

Problem 13-3 Identifying Entries for Payroll Liabilities *(textbook p. 353)*

Payroll Item	Entry to Record Payroll	Entry to Record Employer's Payroll Taxes
Employees' federal income tax		
Employer's social security tax		
U.S. savings bonds		
Employer's Medicare tax		
Federal unemployment tax		
Employees' state income tax		
Union dues		
Employees' social security tax		
State unemployment tax		
Employees' Medicare tax		

Name Date Class

Problem 13-4 Payment of Payroll Liabilities *(textbook p. 363)*

GENERAL JOURNAL PAGE ____

	DATE		DESCRIPTION	POST. REF.	DEBIT	CREDIT	
1							1
2							2
3							3
4							4
5							5
6							6
7							7
8							8
9							9
10							10

Problem 13-5 Analyzing a Source Document *(textbook p. 363)*

GENERAL JOURNAL PAGE *14*

	DATE		DESCRIPTION	POST. REF.	DEBIT	CREDIT	
1							1
2							2
3							3
4							4
5							5
6							6
7							7
8							8
9							9
10							10

Working Papers *for End-of-Chapter Problems*

Problem 13-6 Calculating Employer's Payroll Taxes *(textbook p. 368)*

Total Gross Earnings	Social Security Tax	Medicare Tax	Federal Unemployment Tax	State Unemployment Tax
$ 914.80				
1,113.73				
2,201.38				
791.02				
1,245.75				

Analyze:

Problem 13-7 Recording the Payment of the Payroll *(textbook p. 368)*

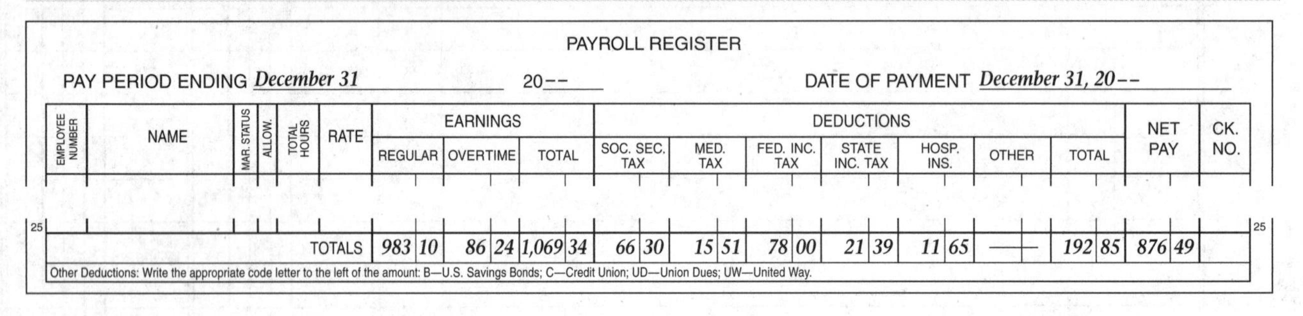

PAYROLL REGISTER

PAY PERIOD ENDING *December 31* 20*--* DATE OF PAYMENT *December 31, 20--*

EMPLOYEE NUMBER	NAME	MAR. STATUS	ALLOW.	TOTAL HOURS	RATE	EARNINGS			DEDUCTIONS							NET PAY	CK. NO.
						REGULAR	OVERTIME	TOTAL	SOC. SEC. TAX	MED. TAX	FED. INC. TAX	STATE INC. TAX	HOSP. INS.	OTHER	TOTAL		
					TOTALS	*983 10*	*86 24*	*1,069 34*	*66 30*	*15 51*	*78 00*	*21 39*	*11 65*	—	*192 85*	*876 49*	

Other Deductions: Write the appropriate code letter to the left of the amount: B—U.S. Savings Bonds; C—Credit Union; UD—Union Dues; UW—United Way.

Name Date Class

Problem 13-7 (continued)

(1)

GENERAL JOURNAL PAGE 46

	DATE		DESCRIPTION	POST. REF.	DEBIT	CREDIT	
1							1
2							2
3							3
4							4
5							5
6							6
7							7
8							8
9							9
10							10

(2)

GENERAL LEDGER (PARTIAL)

ACCOUNT *Cash in Bank* ACCOUNT NO. *101*

DATE		DESCRIPTION	POST. REF.	DEBIT	CREDIT	BALANCE DEBIT	BALANCE CREDIT
20--							
Dec.	*24*	*Balance*	✓			*17352 10*	

ACCOUNT *Employees' Federal Income Tax Payable* ACCOUNT NO. *210*

DATE		DESCRIPTION	POST. REF.	DEBIT	CREDIT	BALANCE DEBIT	BALANCE CREDIT
20--							
Dec.	*24*	*Balance*	✓				*240 00*

ACCOUNT *Employees' State Income Tax Payable* ACCOUNT NO. *215*

DATE		DESCRIPTION	POST. REF.	DEBIT	CREDIT	BALANCE DEBIT	BALANCE CREDIT
20--							
Dec.	*24*	*Balance*	✓				*180 79*

Name Date Class

Problem 13-7 (concluded)

ACCOUNT *Social Security Tax Payable* ACCOUNT NO. *235*

DATE		DESCRIPTION	POST. REF.	DEBIT	CREDIT	BALANCE DEBIT	BALANCE CREDIT
20--							
Dec.	*24*	*Balance*	✓				*191 25*

ACCOUNT *Medicare Tax Payable* ACCOUNT NO. *230*

DATE		DESCRIPTION	POST. REF.	DEBIT	CREDIT	BALANCE DEBIT	BALANCE CREDIT
20--							
Dec.	*24*	*Balance*	✓				*45 31*

ACCOUNT *Hospital Insurance Premiums Payable* ACCOUNT NO. *225*

DATE		DESCRIPTION	POST. REF.	DEBIT	CREDIT	BALANCE DEBIT	BALANCE CREDIT
20--							
Dec.	*24*	*Balance*	✓				*52 26*

ACCOUNT *Salaries Expense* ACCOUNT NO. *525*

DATE		DESCRIPTION	POST. REF.	DEBIT	CREDIT	BALANCE DEBIT	BALANCE CREDIT
20--							
Dec.	*24*	*Balance*	✓			*48,417 86*	

Analyze:

Name Date Class

Problem 13-8 Journalizing Payroll Transactions *(textbook p. 368)*

GENERAL JOURNAL PAGE *15*

	DATE		DESCRIPTION	POST. REF.	DEBIT	CREDIT	
1							1
2							2
3							3
4							4
5							5
6							6
7							7
8							8
9							9
10							10
11							11
12							12
13							13
14							14
15							15
16							16
17							17
18							18
19							19
20							20

Analyze:

Problem 13-9 Recording and Posting Payroll Transactions *(textbook p. 369)*

Instructions: *Use the following source documents to record the transactions for this problem.*

PAYROLL REGISTER

PAY PERIOD ENDING *December 13* 20-- DATE OF PAYMENT *December 13, 20--*

	EMPLOYEE NUMBER	NAME	MAR. STATUS	ALLOW.	TOTAL HOURS	RATE	EARNINGS REGULAR	EARNINGS OVERTIME	EARNINGS TOTAL	DEDUCTIONS SOC. SEC. TAX	MED. TAX	FED. INC. TAX	STATE INC. TAX	HOSP. INS.	OTHER	TOTAL	NET PAY	CK. NO.	
1	105	Arcompora, M.	M	2					627 00	38 87	9 09	106 59	15 68	3 00	B 5 00	178 23	448 77		1
2	137	Fox, B.	M	1					430 00	26 66	6 24	73 10	10 75	3 00	—	119 75	310 25		2
25																			25
		TOTALS							3,840 58	238 12	55 69	639 00	96 02	21 00	B 20 00	1,069 83	2,770 75	2206	

Other Deductions: Write the appropriate code letter to the left of the amount: B—U.S. Savings Bonds; C—Credit Union; UD—Union Dues; UW—United Way.

$ *2,770.75* No. 2206
Date *December 13* 20--
To *Payroll Account*
For *Salaries Expense*

	Dollars	Cents
Balance brought forward	21,932	14
Add deposits		
Total	21,932	14
Less this check	2,770	75
Balance carried forward	19,161	39

$ *100.00* No. 2216
Date *December 16* 20--
To *Northwest Bank*
For *U.S. Savings Bonds*

	Dollars	Cents
Balance brought forward	17,934	77
Add deposits		
Total	17,934	77
Less this check	100	00
Balance carried forward	17,834	77

SHOWBIZ VIDEO
7575 Ingram Blvd.
Spokane, WA 99204

INTEROFFICE MEMORANDUM

TO: *Payroll Clerk*
FROM: *Greg Failla*
DATE: *December 13, 20--*
SUBJECT: *Payroll tax rates*

Social security—6.2%
Medicare—1.45%
Fed. unemployment—0.8%
State unemployment—5.4%

$ *148.00* No. 2217
Date *December 16* 20--
To *American Insurance Co.*
For *Hospital Insurance*

	Dollars	Cents
Balance brought forward	17,834	77
Add deposits		
Total	17,834	77
Less this check	148	00
Balance carried forward	17,686	77

$ *1,226.62* No. 2215
Date *December 16* 20--
To *Internal Revenue Service*
For *Fed. income and FICA taxes*

	Dollars	Cents
Balance brought forward	19,161	39
Add deposits		
Total	19,161	39
Less this check	1,226	62
Balance carried forward	17,934	77

Name _______________ Date _______________ Class _______________

Problem 13-9 (continued)

(1), (3)

GENERAL JOURNAL PAGE _______

	DATE		DESCRIPTION	POST. REF.	DEBIT	CREDIT	
1							1
2							2
3							3
4							4
5							5
6							6
7							7
8							8
9							9
10							10
11							11
12							12
13							13
14							14
15							15
16							16
17							17
18							18
19							19
20							20
21							21
22							22
23							23
24							24
25							25
26							26
27							27
28							28
29							29

Name Date Class

Problem 13-9 (continued)

(2), (3)

GENERAL LEDGER (PARTIAL)

ACCOUNT *Cash in Bank* ACCOUNT NO. *101*

DATE		DESCRIPTION	POST. REF.	DEBIT	CREDIT	BALANCE DEBIT	BALANCE CREDIT
20--							
Dec.	*6*	*Balance*	✓			*21932 14*	

ACCOUNT *Employees' Federal Income Tax Payable* ACCOUNT NO. *210*

DATE		DESCRIPTION	POST. REF.	DEBIT	CREDIT	BALANCE DEBIT	BALANCE CREDIT

ACCOUNT *Employees' State Income Tax Payable* ACCOUNT NO. *215*

DATE		DESCRIPTION	POST. REF.	DEBIT	CREDIT	BALANCE DEBIT	BALANCE CREDIT
20--							
Dec.	*6*	*Balance*	✓				*286 08*

ACCOUNT *Social Security Tax Payable* ACCOUNT NO. *235*

DATE		DESCRIPTION	POST. REF.	DEBIT	CREDIT	BALANCE DEBIT	BALANCE CREDIT

ACCOUNT *Medicare Tax Payable* ACCOUNT NO. *230*

DATE		DESCRIPTION	POST. REF.	DEBIT	CREDIT	BALANCE DEBIT	BALANCE CREDIT

Problem 13-9 (continued)

ACCOUNT *Hospital Insurance Premiums Payable* ACCOUNT NO. *225*

DATE		DESCRIPTION	POST. REF.	DEBIT	CREDIT	BALANCE DEBIT	BALANCE CREDIT
20--							
Dec.	6	Balance	✓				127 00

ACCOUNT *U.S. Savings Bonds Payable* ACCOUNT NO. *245*

DATE		DESCRIPTION	POST. REF.	DEBIT	CREDIT	BALANCE DEBIT	BALANCE CREDIT
20--							
Dec.	6	Balance	✓				80 00

ACCOUNT *Federal Unemployment Tax Payable* ACCOUNT NO. *220*

DATE		DESCRIPTION	POST. REF.	DEBIT	CREDIT	BALANCE DEBIT	BALANCE CREDIT

ACCOUNT *State Unemployment Tax Payable* ACCOUNT NO. *240*

DATE		DESCRIPTION	POST. REF.	DEBIT	CREDIT	BALANCE DEBIT	BALANCE CREDIT

ACCOUNT *Payroll Tax Expense* ACCOUNT NO. *515*

DATE		DESCRIPTION	POST. REF.	DEBIT	CREDIT	BALANCE DEBIT	BALANCE CREDIT
20--							
Dec.	6	Balance	✓			4,614 13	

ACCOUNT *Salaries Expense* ACCOUNT NO. *525*

DATE		DESCRIPTION	POST. REF.	DEBIT	CREDIT	BALANCE DEBIT	BALANCE CREDIT
20--							
Dec.	6	Balance	✓			33,655 22	

Name Date Class

Problem 13-9 (concluded)

Analyze:

Problem 13-10 Recording and Posting Payroll Transactions *(textbook p. 370)*

GENERAL JOURNAL PAGE

	DATE		DESCRIPTION	POST. REF.	DEBIT	CREDIT	
1							1
2							2
3							3
4							4
5							5
6							6
7							7
8							8
9							9
10							10
11							11
12							12
13							13
14							14
15							15
16							16
17							17
18							18
19							19
20							20
21							21
22							22
23							23
24							24
25							25
26							26
27							27
28							28
29							29

Name Date Class

Problem 13-10 (continued)

GENERAL LEDGER (PARTIAL)

ACCOUNT *Cash in Bank* ACCOUNT NO. *101*

DATE		DESCRIPTION	POST. REF.	DEBIT	CREDIT	BALANCE DEBIT	BALANCE CREDIT
20--							
Dec.	*31*	*Balance*	✓			*29,441.61*	

ACCOUNT *Employees' Federal Income Tax Payable* ACCOUNT NO. *210*

DATE		DESCRIPTION	POST. REF.	DEBIT	CREDIT	BALANCE DEBIT	BALANCE CREDIT

ACCOUNT *Employees' State Income Tax Payable* ACCOUNT NO. *215*

DATE		DESCRIPTION	POST. REF.	DEBIT	CREDIT	BALANCE DEBIT	BALANCE CREDIT

ACCOUNT *Federal Unemployment Tax Payable* ACCOUNT NO. *220*

DATE		DESCRIPTION	POST. REF.	DEBIT	CREDIT	BALANCE DEBIT	BALANCE CREDIT
20--							
Dec.	*15*	*Balance*	✓				*464.11*

ACCOUNT *Medicare Tax Payable* ACCOUNT NO. *230*

DATE		DESCRIPTION	POST. REF.	DEBIT	CREDIT	BALANCE DEBIT	BALANCE CREDIT

Name Date Class

Problem 13-10 (continued)

ACCOUNT *Social Security Tax Payable* ACCOUNT NO. *235*

DATE		DESCRIPTION	POST. REF.	DEBIT	CREDIT	BALANCE DEBIT	BALANCE CREDIT

ACCOUNT *State Unemployment Tax Payable* ACCOUNT NO. *240*

DATE		DESCRIPTION	POST. REF.	DEBIT	CREDIT	BALANCE DEBIT	BALANCE CREDIT
20--							
Dec.	*15*	*Balance*	✓				*3132 73*

ACCOUNT *Payroll Tax Expense* ACCOUNT NO. *515*

DATE		DESCRIPTION	POST. REF.	DEBIT	CREDIT	BALANCE DEBIT	BALANCE CREDIT
20--							
Dec.	*15*	*Balance*	✓			*7953 65*	

ACCOUNT *Salaries Expense* ACCOUNT NO. *525*

DATE		DESCRIPTION	POST. REF.	DEBIT	CREDIT	BALANCE DEBIT	BALANCE CREDIT
20--							
Dec.	*15*	*Balance*	✓			*58013 45*	

Analyze:

Problem 13-10 (continued)

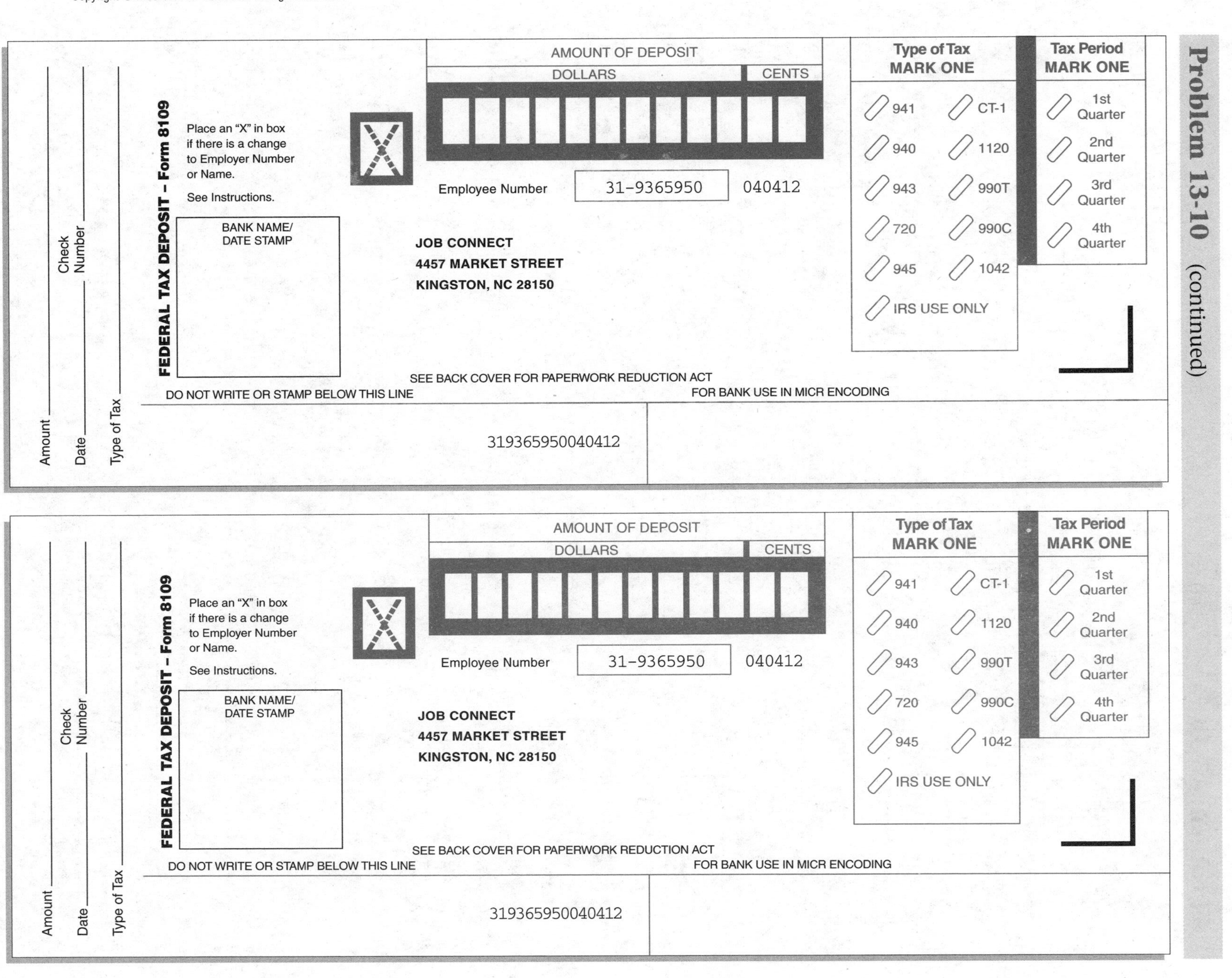
AMOUNT OF DEPOSIT
DOLLARS | CENTS

Type of Tax
MARK ONE
941 | CT-1
940 | 1120
943 | 990T
720 | 990C
945 | 1042
IRS USE ONLY

Tax Period
MARK ONE
1st Quarter
2nd Quarter
3rd Quarter
4th Quarter

Place an "X" in box if there is a change to Employer Number or Name.
See Instructions.

Employee Number 31-9365950 040412

BANK NAME/
DATE STAMP

JOB CONNECT
4457 MARKET STREET
KINGSTON, NC 28150

FEDERAL TAX DEPOSIT – Form 8109

SEE BACK COVER FOR PAPERWORK REDUCTION ACT

DO NOT WRITE OR STAMP BELOW THIS LINE

FOR BANK USE IN MICR ENCODING

319365950040412

Amount
Date
Check Number
Type of Tax

AMOUNT OF DEPOSIT
DOLLARS | CENTS

Type of Tax
MARK ONE
941 | CT-1
940 | 1120
943 | 990T
720 | 990C
945 | 1042
IRS USE ONLY

Tax Period
MARK ONE
1st Quarter
2nd Quarter
3rd Quarter
4th Quarter

Place an "X" in box if there is a change to Employer Number or Name.
See Instructions.

Employee Number 31-9365950 040412

BANK NAME/
DATE STAMP

JOB CONNECT
4457 MARKET STREET
KINGSTON, NC 28150

FEDERAL TAX DEPOSIT – Form 8109

SEE BACK COVER FOR PAPERWORK REDUCTION ACT

DO NOT WRITE OR STAMP BELOW THIS LINE

FOR BANK USE IN MICR ENCODING

319365950040412

Amount
Date
Check Number
Type of Tax

Problem 13-10 (concluded)

$ ________ No. 1602
Date ________ 20___
To ________
For ________

	Dollars	Cents
Balance brought forward	29,441	61
Add deposits		
Total		
Less this check		
Balance carried forward		

Job Connect
4457 Market Street
Kingstown, NC 28150

1602
4-58/810

DATE ________ 20___

PAY TO THE ORDER OF ________ $ ________

________ DOLLARS

SNB Security National Bank
KINGSTOWN, NC

MEMO ________ ________

⑆0810 0058⑆ 4163 697⑈ 1602

$ ________ No. 1603
Date ________ 20___
To ________
For ________

	Dollars	Cents
Balance brought forward		
Add deposits		
Total		
Less this check		
Balance carried forward		

Job Connect
4457 Market Street
Kingstown, NC 28150

1603
4-58/810

DATE ________ 20___

PAY TO THE ORDER OF ________ $ ________

________ DOLLARS

SNB Security National Bank
KINGSTOWN, NC

MEMO ________ ________

⑆0810 0058⑆ 4163 697⑈ 1603

$ ________ No. 1604
Date ________ 20___
To ________
For ________

	Dollars	Cents
Balance brought forward		
Add deposits		
Total		
Less this check		
Balance carried forward		

Job Connect
4457 Market Street
Kingstown, NC 28150

1604
4-58/810

DATE ________ 20___

PAY TO THE ORDER OF ________ $ ________

________ DOLLARS

SNB Security National Bank
KINGSTOWN, NC

MEMO ________ ________

⑆0810 0058⑆ 4163 697⑈ 1604

$ ________ No. 1605
Date ________ 20___
To ________
For ________

	Dollars	Cents
Balance brought forward		
Add deposits		
Total		
Less this check		
Balance carried forward		

Job Connect
4457 Market Street
Kingstown, NC 28150

1605
4-58/810

DATE ________ 20___

PAY TO THE ORDER OF ________ $ ________

________ DOLLARS

SNB Security National Bank
KINGSTOWN, NC

MEMO ________ ________

⑆0810 0058⑆ 4163 697⑈ 1605

Name Date Class

MINI PRACTICE SET 3

Happy Trees Landscaping Service

Instructions: *Complete the following time cards and use the record payroll information in the payroll register.*

(1)

NO. 019
NAME Michael Alter
SOC. SEC. NO. 049-71-8436
WEEK ENDING 7/25/20--

DAY	IN	OUT	IN	OUT	IN	OUT	TOTAL
M			2:00	5:00			
T			2:00	6:00			
W							
Th			2:00	6:00			
F			2:00	6:00			
S			9:00	2:00			
S							
						TOTAL HOURS	

	HOURS	RATE	AMOUNT
REGULAR			
OVERTIME			
TOTAL EARNINGS			

SIGNATURE ______ DATE ______

NO. 018
NAME Christine Cuddy
SOC. SEC. NO. 223-56-0992
WEEK ENDING 7/25/20--

DAY	IN	OUT	IN	OUT	IN	OUT	TOTAL
M	9:00	12:00	12:30	5:00			
T	9:00	11:30	12:00	5:00			
W	9:00	1:00					
Th	9:00	12:00	12:30	4:00			
F	8:30	1:00	1:30	3:00			
S	9:00	1:30					
S							
						TOTAL HOURS	

	HOURS	RATE	AMOUNT
REGULAR			
OVERTIME			
TOTAL EARNINGS			

SIGNATURE ______ DATE ______

NO. 013
NAME Joclyn Filley
SOC. SEC. NO. 042-97-3814
WEEK ENDING 7/25/20--

DAY	IN	OUT	IN	OUT	IN	OUT	TOTAL
M	9:00	12:00	1:00	3:00			
T	9:00	12:00	1:00	5:00			
W	8:00	12:00	1:00	5:00			
Th	9:00	12:00	1:00	3:30			
F	9:00	12:00	1:00	4:00			
S	9:00	12:00					
S							
						TOTAL HOURS	

	HOURS	RATE	AMOUNT
REGULAR			
OVERTIME			
TOTAL EARNINGS			

SIGNATURE ______ DATE ______

NO. 016
NAME Daniel Ripp
SOC. SEC. NO. 011-79-2118
WEEK ENDING 7/25/20--

DAY	IN	OUT	IN	OUT	IN	OUT	TOTAL
M	9:00	12:00	12:30	5:00			
T	9:00	12:30	1:00	6:00			
W	9:00	12:00	1:00	4:30			
Th	8:30	12:30	1:00	5:00			
F	9:00	11:30	12:00	5:00			
S	9:00	1:00					
S							
						TOTAL HOURS	

	HOURS	RATE	AMOUNT
REGULAR			
OVERTIME			
TOTAL EARNINGS			

SIGNATURE ______ DATE ______

Name Date Class

Mini Practice Set 3 *(textbook p. 374)*

Federal Income Tax Table

SINGLE Persons—**WEEKLY** Payroll Period

(For Wages Paid in 20--)

If the wages are—		And the number of withholding allowances claimed is—										
At least	But less than	0	1	2	3	4	5	6	7	8	9	10
		The amount of income tax to be withheld is—										
125	130	11	4	0	0	0	0	0	0	0	0	0
130	135	12	5	0	0	0	0	0	0	0	0	0
135	140	13	5	0	0	0	0	0	0	0	0	0
140	145	14	6	0	0	0	0	0	0	0	0	0
145	150	14	7	0	0	0	0	0	0	0	0	0
150	155	15	8	0	0	0	0	0	0	0	0	0
155	160	16	8	1	0	0	0	0	0	0	0	0
160	165	17	9	1	0	0	0	0	0	0	0	0
165	170	17	10	2	0	0	0	0	0	0	0	0
170	175	18	11	3	0	0	0	0	0	0	0	0
175	180	19	11	4	0	0	0	0	0	0	0	0
180	185	20	12	4	0	0	0	0	0	0	0	0
185	190	20	13	5	0	0	0	0	0	0	0	0
190	195	21	14	6	0	0	0	0	0	0	0	0
195	200	22	14	7	0	0	0	0	0	0	0	0
200	210	23	15	8	0	0	0	0	0	0	0	0
210	220	25	17	9	2	0	0	0	0	0	0	0
220	230	26	18	11	3	0	0	0	0	0	0	0
230	240	28	20	12	5	0	0	0	0	0	0	0
240	250	29	21	14	6	0	0	0	0	0	0	0
250	260	31	23	15	8	0	0	0	0	0	0	0
260	270	32	24	17	9	2	0	0	0	0	0	0
270	280	34	26	18	11	3	0	0	0	0	0	0
280	290	35	27	20	12	5	0	0	0	0	0	0
290	300	37	29	21	14	6	0	0	0	0	0	0
300	310	38	30	23	15	8	0	0	0	0	0	0
310	320	40	32	24	17	9	1	0	0	0	0	0
320	330	41	33	26	18	11	3	0	0	0	0	0
330	340	43	35	27	20	12	4	0	0	0	0	0
340	350	44	36	29	21	14	6	0	0	0	0	0

Mini Practice Set 3 (continued)

Federal Income Tax Table (continued)

MARRIED Persons—WEEKLY Payroll Period
(For Wages Paid in 20--)

If the wages are—		And the number of withholding allowances claimed is—										
At least	But less than	0	1	2	3	4	5	6	7	8	9	10
		The amount of income tax to be withheld is—										
340	350	33	26	18	10	3	0	0	0	0	0	0
350	360	35	27	19	12	4	0	0	0	0	0	0
360	370	36	29	21	13	6	0	0	0	0	0	0
370	380	38	30	22	15	7	0	0	0	0	0	0
380	390	39	32	24	16	9	1	0	0	0	0	0
390	400	41	33	25	18	10	2	0	0	0	0	0
400	410	42	35	27	19	12	4	0	0	0	0	0
410	420	44	36	28	21	13	5	0	0	0	0	0
420	430	45	38	30	22	15	7	0	0	0	0	0
430	440	47	39	31	24	16	8	1	0	0	0	0
440	450	48	41	33	25	18	10	2	0	0	0	0
450	460	50	42	34	27	19	11	4	0	0	0	0
460	470	51	44	36	28	21	13	5	0	0	0	0
470	480	53	45	37	30	22	14	7	0	0	0	0
480	490	54	47	39	31	24	16	8	1	0	0	0
490	500	56	48	40	33	25	17	10	2	0	0	0
500	510	57	50	42	34	27	19	11	4	0	0	0
510	520	59	51	43	36	28	20	13	5	0	0	0
520	530	60	53	45	37	30	22	14	7	0	0	0
530	540	62	54	46	39	31	23	16	8	0	0	0
540	550	63	56	48	40	33	25	17	10	2	0	0
550	560	65	57	49	42	34	26	19	11	3	0	0
560	570	66	59	51	43	36	28	20	13	5	0	0
570	580	68	60	52	45	37	29	22	14	6	0	0
580	590	69	62	54	46	39	31	23	16	8	0	0
590	600	71	63	55	48	40	32	25	17	9	2	0
600	610	72	65	57	49	42	34	26	19	11	3	0
610	620	74	66	58	51	43	35	28	20	12	5	0
620	630	75	68	60	52	45	37	29	22	14	6	0
630	640	77	69	61	54	46	38	31	23	15	8	0
640	650	78	71	63	55	48	40	32	25	17	9	2
650	660	80	72	64	57	49	41	34	26	18	11	3
660	670	81	74	66	58	51	43	35	28	20	12	5
670	680	83	75	67	60	52	44	37	29	21	14	6
680	690	84	77	69	61	54	46	38	31	23	15	8
690	700	86	78	70	63	55	47	40	32	24	17	9
700	710	87	80	72	64	57	49	41	34	26	18	11
710	720	89	81	73	66	58	50	43	35	27	20	12
720	730	90	83	75	67	60	52	44	37	29	21	14
730	740	92	84	76	69	61	53	46	38	30	23	15

Name Date Class

Mini Practice Set 3 (continued) (2), (3), (4), (5), (6)

PAYROLL REGISTER

PAY PERIOD ENDING ____________ 20____ DATE OF PAYMENT ____________

	EMPLOYEE NUMBER	NAME	MAR. STATUS	ALLOW.	TOTAL HOURS	RATE	EARNINGS			DEDUCTIONS							NET PAY	CK. NO.	
							REGULAR	OVERTIME	TOTAL	SOC. SEC. TAX	MED. TAX	FED. INC. TAX	STATE INC. TAX	HOSP. INS.	OTHER	TOTAL			
1																			1
2																			2
3																			3
4																			4
5																			5
6																			6
7																			7
8																			8
9																			9
10																			10
11																			11
12																			12
13																			13
14																			14
15																			15
16																			16
17																			17
18																			18
19																			19
20																			20
21																			21
22																			22
23																			23
24																			24
25																			25
	TOTALS																		

Other Deductions: Write the appropriate code letter to the left of the amount: B—U.S. Savings Bonds; C—Credit Union; UD—Union Dues; UW—United Way.

Name Date Class

Mini Practice Set 3 (continued)

(7)

$	No. 972
Date	20
To	
For	

	Dollars	Cents
Balance brought forward	*8,371*	*42*
Add deposits		
Total		
Less this check		
Balance carried forward		

Happy Trees
Landscaping service
456 Lindenhurst Street
Kingsbury, Michigan 03855

972

53-215
113

DATE ______ 20___

PAY TO THE ORDER OF ______ $______

______ DOLLARS

Lexington Bank
KINGSBURY, MICHIGAN

MEMO ______

⑆011302153⑆ 331 234 9⑈ 0972

(12)

$	No. 973
Date	20
To	
For	

	Dollars	Cents
Balance brought forward		
Add deposits		
Total		
Less this check		
Balance carried forward		

Happy Trees
Landscaping service
456 Lindenhurst Street
Kingsbury, Michigan 03855

973

53-215
113

DATE ______ 20___

PAY TO THE ORDER OF ______ $______

______ DOLLARS

Lexington Bank
KINGSBURY, MICHIGAN

MEMO ______

⑆011302153⑆ 331 234 9⑈ 0973

(14)

$	No. 974
Date	20
To	
For	

	Dollars	Cents
Balance brought forward		
Add deposits		
Total		
Less this check		
Balance carried forward		

Happy Trees
Landscaping service
456 Lindenhurst Street
Kingsbury, Michigan 03855

974

53-215
113

DATE ______ 20___

PAY TO THE ORDER OF ______ $______

______ DOLLARS

Lexington Bank
KINGSBURY, MICHIGAN

MEMO ______

⑆011302153⑆ 331 234 9⑈ 0974

(7)

Patriot Bank
CONCORD, MASSACHUSETTS

Date ______ **20** ___

Checks and other items are received for deposit subject to the terms and conditions of this bank's collection agreement.

Happy Trees
Landscaping service
PAYROLL ACCOUNT
456 Lindenhurst Street
Kingsbury, Michigan 03855

⑆011302153⑆ 0001 290 3⑈

BE SURE EACH ITEM IS ENDORSED

	DOLLARS	CENTS
CASH		
CHECKS (List Singly)		
1		
2		
3		
4		
5		
6		
7		
8.		
TOTAL		

Name Date Class

Mini Practice Set 3 (continued)

(8), (11), (13), (14)

GENERAL JOURNAL PAGE ______

	DATE		DESCRIPTION	POST. REF.	DEBIT	CREDIT	
1							1
2							2
3							3
4							4
5							5
6							6
7							7
8							8
9							9
10							10
11							11
12							12
13							13
14							14
15							15
16							16
17							17
18							18
19							19
20							20
21							21
22							22
23							23
24							24
25							25
26							26
27							27
28							28
29							29
30							30
31							31
32							32
33							33
34							34
35							35
36							36

Name Date Class

Mini Practice Set 3 (continued)

GENERAL LEDGER (PARTIAL)

ACCOUNT *Cash in Bank* ACCOUNT NO. *101*

DATE		DESCRIPTION	POST. REF.	DEBIT	CREDIT	BALANCE DEBIT	BALANCE CREDIT
20--							
July	*18*	*Balance*	✓			*8,371 42*	

ACCOUNT *Employees' Federal Income Tax Payable* ACCOUNT NO. *205*

DATE		DESCRIPTION	POST. REF.	DEBIT	CREDIT	BALANCE DEBIT	BALANCE CREDIT
20--							
July	*18*	*Balance*	✓				*183 00*

ACCOUNT *Employees' State Income Tax Payable* ACCOUNT NO. *210*

DATE		DESCRIPTION	POST. REF.	DEBIT	CREDIT	BALANCE DEBIT	BALANCE CREDIT
20--							
July	*18*	*Balance*	✓				*245 74*

ACCOUNT *Social Security Tax Payable* ACCOUNT NO. *215*

DATE		DESCRIPTION	POST. REF.	DEBIT	CREDIT	BALANCE DEBIT	BALANCE CREDIT
20--							
July	*18*	*Balance*	✓				*217 96*

Name Date Class

Mini Practice Set 3 (continued)

ACCOUNT *Medicare Tax Payable* ACCOUNT NO. *220*

DATE		DESCRIPTION	POST. REF.	DEBIT	CREDIT	BALANCE DEBIT	BALANCE CREDIT
20--							
July	18	Balance	✓				54 44

ACCOUNT *Insurance Premiums Payable* ACCOUNT NO. *225*

DATE		DESCRIPTION	POST. REF.	DEBIT	CREDIT	BALANCE DEBIT	BALANCE CREDIT
20--							
July	18	Balance	✓				171 00

ACCOUNT *Federal Unemployment Tax Payable* ACCOUNT NO. *235*

DATE		DESCRIPTION	POST. REF.	DEBIT	CREDIT	BALANCE DEBIT	BALANCE CREDIT
20--							
July	4	Balance	✓				30 71
	11		G18		16 43		47 14
	18		G18		14 36		61 50

ACCOUNT *State Unemployment Tax Payable* ACCOUNT NO. *240*

DATE		DESCRIPTION	POST. REF.	DEBIT	CREDIT	BALANCE DEBIT	BALANCE CREDIT
20--							
July	4	Balance	✓				206 20
	11		G18		104 16		310 36
	18		G18		96 79		407 15

Mini Practice Set 3 (continued)

ACCOUNT *U.S. Savings Bonds Payable* ACCOUNT NO. *245*

DATE		DESCRIPTION	POST. REF.	DEBIT	CREDIT	BALANCE DEBIT	BALANCE CREDIT
20--							
July	4	Balance	✓				40 00
	11		G18		20 00		60 00
	18		G18		20 00		80 00

ACCOUNT *United Way Payable* ACCOUNT NO. *250*

DATE		DESCRIPTION	POST. REF.	DEBIT	CREDIT	BALANCE DEBIT	BALANCE CREDIT
20--							
July	4	Balance	✓				12 00
	11		G18		12 00		24 00
	18		G18		12 00		36 00

ACCOUNT *Payroll Tax Expense* ACCOUNT NO. *620*

DATE		DESCRIPTION	POST. REF.	DEBIT	CREDIT	BALANCE DEBIT	BALANCE CREDIT
20--							
July	4	Balance	✓			5 689 20	
	11		G18	369 41		6 058 61	
	18		G18	366 17		6 424 78	

ACCOUNT *Salaries Expense* ACCOUNT NO. *630*

DATE		DESCRIPTION	POST. REF.	DEBIT	CREDIT	BALANCE DEBIT	BALANCE CREDIT
20--							
July	11	Balance	✓			43 947 39	
	18		G18	2 963 14		46 910 53	

Mini Practice Set 3 (continued)

(9)

Happy Trees
Landscaping service
PAYROLL ACCOUNT
456 Lindenhurst Street
Kingsbury, Michigan 03855

310

53-215
113

Date ________ 20 ____

Pay to the Order of ________ $ ________

________ Dollars

Patriot Bank
CONCORD, MASSACHUSETTS

⑆011302153⑆ 0001 290 3⑈ 0310

Employee Pay Statement
Detach and retain this statement.

310

Period Ending	Earnings			Deductions							Net Pay
	Regular	Overtime	Total	Social Security Tax	Med. Tax	Federal Income Tax	State Income Tax	Hosp. Ins.	Other	Total	

Happy Trees
Landscaping service
PAYROLL ACCOUNT
456 Lindenhurst Street
Kingsbury, Michigan 03855

311

53-215
113

Date ________ 20 ____

Pay to the Order of ________ $ ________

________ Dollars

Patriot Bank
CONCORD, MASSACHUSETTS

⑆011302153⑆ 0001 290 3⑈ 0311

Employee Pay Statement
Detach and retain this statement.

311

Period Ending	Earnings			Deductions							Net Pay
	Regular	Overtime	Total	Social Security Tax	Med. Tax	Federal Income Tax	State Income Tax	Hosp. Ins.	Other	Total	

Mini Practice Set 3 (continued)

Happy Trees
Landscaping service
PAYROLL ACCOUNT
456 Lindenhurst Street
Kingsbury, Michigan 03855

312

53-215
113

Date ____________ 20 ____

Pay to the Order of ____________________ $ ________

____________________ Dollars

Patriot Bank
CONCORD, MASSACHUSETTS

⑆0113021531⑆ 0001 290 3⑈ 0312

Employee Pay Statement
Detach and retain this statement.

312

Period Ending	Earnings			Deductions							Net Pay
	Regular	Overtime	Total	Social Security Tax	Med. Tax	Federal Income Tax	State Income Tax	Hosp. Ins.	Other	Total	

Happy Trees
Landscaping service
PAYROLL ACCOUNT
456 Lindenhurst Street
Kingsbury, Michigan 03855

313

53-215
113

Date ____________ 20 ____

Pay to the Order of ____________________ $ ________

____________________ Dollars

Patriot Bank
CONCORD, MASSACHUSETTS

⑆0113021531⑆ 0001 290 3⑈ 0313

Employee Pay Statement
Detach and retain this statement.

313

Period Ending	Earnings			Deductions							Net Pay
	Regular	Overtime	Total	Social Security Tax	Med. Tax	Federal Income Tax	State Income Tax	Hosp. Ins.	Other	Total	

Mini Practice Set 3 (continued)

Happy Trees
Landscaping service
PAYROLL ACCOUNT
456 Lindenhurst Street
Kingsbury, Michigan 03855

314

53-215
113

Date ____________ 20 ___

Pay to the Order of ________________________ $ ________

____ *Dollars*

Patriot Bank
CONCORD, MASSACHUSETTS

⑆011302153⑆ 0001 290 3⑈ 0314

Employee Pay Statement
Detach and retain this statement.

314

Period Ending	Earnings			Deductions							Net Pay
	Regular	Overtime	Total	Social Security Tax	Med. Tax	Federal Income Tax	State Income Tax	Hosp. Ins.	Other	Total	

Happy Trees
Landscaping service
PAYROLL ACCOUNT
456 Lindenhurst Street
Kingsbury, Michigan 03855

315

53-215
113

Date ____________ 20 ___

Pay to the Order of ________________________ $ ________

____ *Dollars*

Patriot Bank
CONCORD, MASSACHUSETTS

⑆011302153⑆ 0001 290 3⑈ 0315

Employee Pay Statement
Detach and retain this statement.

315

Period Ending	Earnings			Deductions							Net Pay
	Regular	Overtime	Total	Social Security Tax	Med. Tax	Federal Income Tax	State Income Tax	Hosp. Ins.	Other	Total	

Mini Practice Set 3 (continued)

Happy Trees
Landscaping service
PAYROLL ACCOUNT
456 Lindenhurst Street
Kingsbury, Michigan 03855

316

53-215
113

Date __________ 20 ___

Pay to the
Order of __________ $ ______

__________ Dollars

Patriot Bank
CONCORD, MASSACHUSETTS

⑆011302153⑆ 0001 290 3⑈ 0316

Employee Pay Statement
Detach and retain this statement.

316

Period Ending	Earnings			Deductions							Net Pay
	Regular	Overtime	Total	Social Security Tax	Med. Tax	Federal Income Tax	State Income Tax	Hosp. Ins.	Other	Total	

Happy Trees
Landscaping service
PAYROLL ACCOUNT
456 Lindenhurst Street
Kingsbury, Michigan 03855

317

53-215
113

Date __________ 20 ___

Pay to the
Order of __________ $ ______

__________ Dollars

Patriot Bank
CONCORD, MASSACHUSETTS

⑆011302153⑆ 0001 290 3⑈ 0317

Employee Pay Statement
Detach and retain this statement.

317

Period Ending	Earnings			Deductions							Net Pay
	Regular	Overtime	Total	Social Security Tax	Med. Tax	Federal Income Tax	State Income Tax	Hosp. Ins.	Other	Total	

Mini Practice Set 3 (continued)

(10)

EMPLOYEE'S EARNINGS RECORD FOR QUARTER ENDING *September 30, 20--*

Alter (Last Name) *Michael* (First) (Initial)

479 Lindon Street (Address)

Kingsbury, Michigan

EMPLOYEE NO. *019* MARTIAL STATUS *S* ALLOWANCES *1*

POSITION *Supply Clerk*

RATE OF PAY *7.10* SOC. SEC. NO. *049-71-8436*

PAY PERIOD		EARNINGS			DEDUCTIONS							NET PAY	ACCUMULATED EARNINGS
NO.	ENDED	REGULAR	OVERTIME	TOTAL	SOC. SEC. TAX	MED. TAX	FED. INC. TAX	STATE INC. TAX	HOSP. INS.	OTHER	TOTAL		2,572 10
1	7/4	158 60		158 60	9 83	2 30	8 00	3 17	6 00	5 00	34 30	124 30	2,730 70
2	7/11	154 10		154 10	9 55	2 23	8 00	3 08	6 00	5 00	33 86	120 24	2,884 80
3	7/18	147 30		147 30	9 13	2 13	6 00	2 94	6 00	5 00	31 20	116 10	3,032 10
4													
5													
6													
7													
8													
9													
10													
11													
12													
13													
QUARTERLY TOTALS													

Other Deductions: B—U.S. Savings Bonds; C—Credit Union; UD—Union Dues; UW—United Way.

Mini Practice Set 3 (continued)

EMPLOYEE'S EARNINGS RECORD FOR QUARTER ENDING *September 30, 20--*

Millette *Greg*
Last Name First Initial

EMPLOYEE NO. *011* MARTIAL STATUS *M* ALLOWANCES *2*

86 Meadow Road
Address

POSITION *Salesperson*

Kingsbury, Michigan

RATE OF PAY *$450/week + 10%* SOC. SEC. NO. *046-29-8403*

PAY PERIOD		EARNINGS			DEDUCTIONS							NET PAY	ACCUMULATED EARNINGS
NO.	ENDED	REGULAR	OVERTIME	TOTAL	SOC. SEC. TAX	MED. TAX	FED. INC. TAX	STATE INC. TAX	HOSP. INS.	OTHER	TOTAL		*9,349 20*
1	*7/4*	*526 10*		*526 10*	*32 62*	*7 63*	*44 00*	*10 52*	*9 00*	*5 00*	*108 77*	*417 33*	*9,875 30*
2	*7/11*	*519 60*		*519 60*	*32 22*	*7 53*	*42 00*	*10 39*	*9 00*	*5 00*	*106 14*	*413 46*	*10,394 90*
3	*7/18*	*584 20*		*584 20*	*36 22*	*8 47*	*51 00*	*11 68*	*9 00*	*5 00*	*121 37*	*462 83*	*10,979 10*
4													
5													
6													
7													
8													
9													
10													
11													
12													
13													
QUARTERLY TOTALS													

Other Deductions: B—U.S. Savings Bonds; C—Credit Union; UD—Union Dues; UW—United Way.

Name Date Class

Mini Practice Set 3 (concluded)

(12)

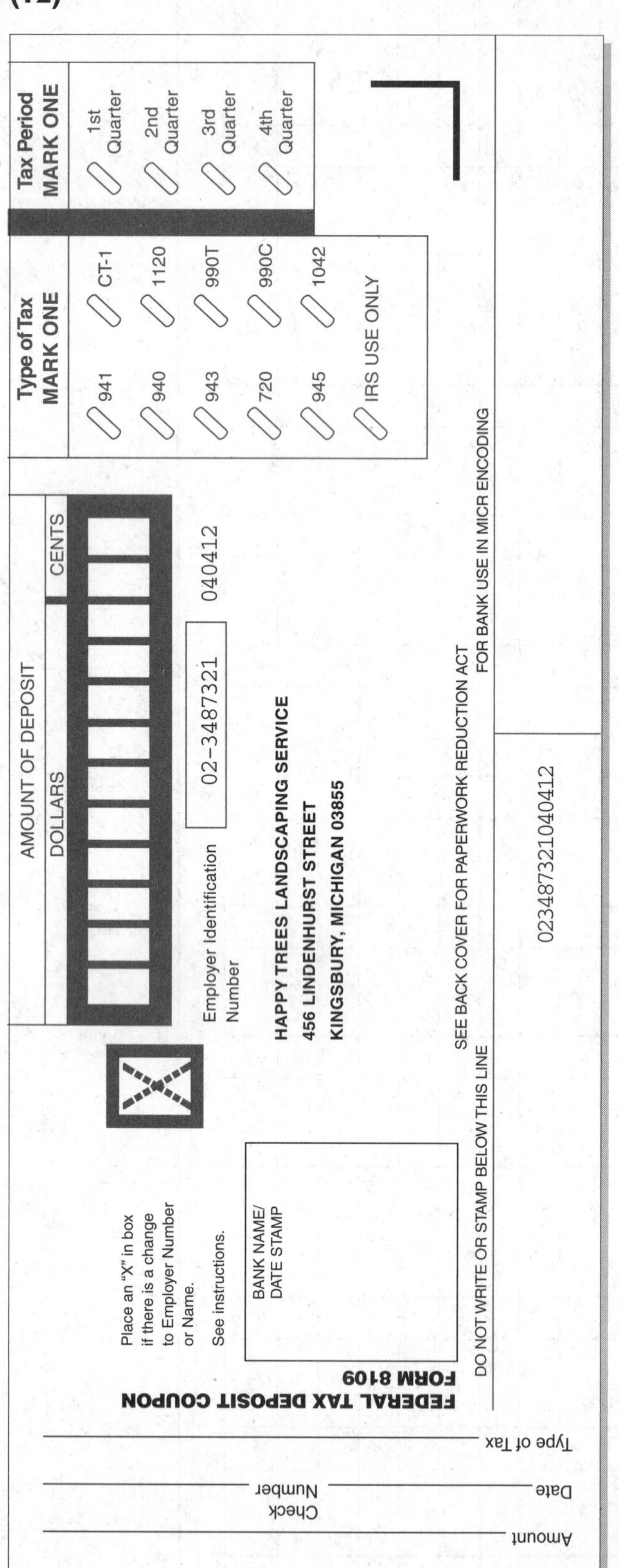

Amount

Check Number

Date

Type of Tax

FEDERAL TAX DEPOSIT COUPON
FORM 8109

Place an "X" in box if there is a change to Employer Number or Name.

See instructions.

BANK NAME/ DATE STAMP

AMOUNT OF DEPOSIT

DOLLARS	CENTS

Employer Identification Number: 02-3487321

040412

HAPPY TREES LANDSCAPING SERVICE
456 LINDENHURST STREET
KINGSBURY, MICHIGAN 03855

Type of Tax MARK ONE

941	CT-1
940	1120
943	990T
720	990C
945	1042
IRS USE ONLY	

Tax Period MARK ONE

1st Quarter
2nd Quarter
3rd Quarter
4th Quarter

SEE BACK COVER FOR PAPERWORK REDUCTION ACT

FOR BANK USE IN MICR ENCODING

DO NOT WRITE OR STAMP BELOW THIS LINE

023487321040412

Analyze:

Name Date Class

MINI PRACTICE SET 3

Happy Trees Landscaping Service

Audit Test

Instructions: *Use your completed solutions to answer the following questions. Write the answer in the space to the left of each question.*

Answer

_______________ **1.** What rate is used to compute employee state income tax?

_______________ **2.** What rate is used to compute the employer's Federal unemployment tax?

_______________ **3.** What commission amount did Greg Millette earn?

_______________ **4.** How many employees reached the maximum taxable amount for the social security tax this period?

_______________ **5.** What was the total net pay for the pay period ending July 25?

_______________ **6.** How many payroll checks were issued for this period?

_______________ **7.** What was the amount of check 972?

_______________ **8.** What was the amount paid to American Insurance Company for employee hospital insurance?

_______________ **9.** What accounts were debited when check 973 was recorded in the general ledger?

_______________ **10.** What is the ending balance of the Employees' Federal Income Tax Payable account at July 31?

11. What is the ending balance of the Cash in Bank account at month end?

12. What is the amount of payroll check 312?

13. What is the amount of accumulated earnings for Michael Alter after the July 25 paycheck?

14. What amount was remitted with the Federal Tax Deposit Coupon Form 8109 on July 25?

15. What total amount of federal income tax was withheld from the paycheck of Greg Millette at the July 25 pay period?

16. What is the total of payroll liabilities at July 25?

17. What amount was debited to Salaries Expense on July 25?

18. What is the balance in the Happy Trees Landscaping Service regular bank account after check 974 is recorded?

19. What is the next pay period date for this business?

Name Date Class

CHAPTER 15 Accounting for Purchases and Cash Payments

Study Guide

Section Assessment

Section 1 *Read Section 1 on pages 419–422 and complete the following exercises on page 423.*
- ☐ Reinforce the Main Idea
- ☐ Math for Accounting
- ☐ Problem 15-1 *Analyzing a Purchase Order*

Section 2 *Read Section 2 on pages 424–429 and complete the following exercises on page 430.*
- ☐ Reinforce the Main Idea
- ☐ Math for Accounting
- ☐ Problem 15-2 *Recording Purchases Transactions*
- ☐ Problem 15-3 *Analyzing a Source Document*

Section 3 *Read Section 3 on pages 431–436 and complete the following exercises on page 437.*
- ☐ Reinforce the Main Idea
- ☐ Math for Accounting
- ☐ Problem 15-4 *Recording Cash Payment Transactions*

Chapter Assessment

Summary *Review the Chapter 15 Visual Summary on page 438 in your textbook.*
- ☐ Key Concepts

Review and Activities *Complete the following questions and exercises on page 439 in your textbook.*
- ☐ After You Read: Answering the Essential Question
- ☐ Vocabulary Check
- ☐ Concept Check

Standardized Test Practice *Complete the exercises on page 440 in your textbook.*

Computerized Accounting *Read the Computerized Accounting information on page 441 in your textbook.*
- ☐ Recording Purchase and Cash Payment Transactions

Problems *Complete the following End-of-Chapter Problems for Chapter 15 in your textbook.*
- ☐ Problem 15-5 *Determining Due Dates and Discount Amounts*
- ☐ Problem 15-6 *Analyzing Purchases and Cash Payments*
- ☐ Problem 15-7 *Recording Purchases Transactions*
- ☐ Problem 15-8 *Recording Cash Payment Transactions*
- ☐ Problem 15-9 *Recording Purchases and Cash Payment Transactions*

Challenge Problem
- ☐ Problem 15-10 *Recording and Posting Purchases and Cash Payment Transactions*

Real-World Applications and Connections *Complete the following applications on pages 448–449 in your textbook.*
- ☐ Career Wise
- ☐ Global Accounting
- ☐ A Matter of Ethics
- ☐ Analyzing Financial Reports
- ☐ H.O.T. Audit

Name ____________________ Date __________ Class __________

Working Papers *for Section Problems*

Problem 15-1 Analyzing a Purchase Order *(textbook p. 423)*

1. ______________________________
2. ______________________________
3. ______________________________
4. ______________________________
5. ______________________________
6. ______________________________
7. ______________________________
8. ______________________________
9. ______________________________
10. ______________________________

Problem 15-2 Recording Purchases Transactions *(textbook p. 430)*

GENERAL JOURNAL PAGE ______

	DATE		DESCRIPTION	POST. REF.	DEBIT	CREDIT	
1							1
2							2
3							3
4							4
5							5
6							6
7							7
8							8
9							9
10							10
11							11
12							12

Problem 15-3 Analyzing a Source Document *(textbook p. 430)*

GENERAL JOURNAL PAGE ______

	DATE		DESCRIPTION	POST. REF.	DEBIT	CREDIT	
1							1
2							2
3							3
4							4
5							5
6							6
7							7
8							8
9							9
10							10
11							11
12							12

Name Date Class

Problem 15-4 Recording Cash Payment Transactions *(textbook p. 437)*

GENERAL JOURNAL PAGE ______

	DATE		DESCRIPTION	POST. REF.	DEBIT	CREDIT	
1							1
2							2
3							3
4							4
5							5
6							6
7							7
8							8
9							9
10							10
11							11
12							12

Working Papers *for End-of-Chapter Problems*

Problem 15-5 Determining Due Dates and Discount Amounts *(textbook p. 442)*

Invoice Number	Invoice Date	Credit Terms	Invoice Amount	Due Date	Discount Amount	Amount to be Paid
24574	Mar. 5	2/10, n/30	$3,000.00	Mar. 15	$ 60.00	$2,940.00
530992	Mar. 7	3/10, n/30	***$5,550.00***			
211145	Mar. 12	2/15, n/60	***$ 729.95***			
45679	Mar. 16	n/45	***$ 345.67***			
34120	Mar. 23	2/10, n/30	***$1,526.50***			
00985	Mar. 27	n/30	***$ 700.00***			

Analyze: ____________________

Name Date Class

Problem 15-6 Analyzing Purchases and Cash Payments *(textbook p. 443)*

Cash in Bank

Supplies

Prepaid Insurance

Accounts Payable

Purchases

Transportation In

Purchases Discounts

Purchases Returns and Allowances

ACCOUNTS PAYABLE SUBSIDIARY LEDGER

NightVision & Company

Temple Store Supply

Analyze:

Name Date Class

Problem 15-7 Recording Purchases Transactions *(textbook p. 443)*

GENERAL JOURNAL PAGE ______

	DATE	DESCRIPTION	POST. REF.	DEBIT	CREDIT	
1						1
2						2
3						3
4						4
5						5
6						6
7						7
8						8
9						9
10						10
11						11
12						12
13						13
14						14
15						15
16						16
17						17
18						18
19						19
20						20
21						21
22						22
23						23
24						24
25						25
26						26
27						27
28						28
29						29
30						30
31						31
32						32
33						33
34						34
35						35

Analyze: ______

Name Date Class

Problem 15-8 Recording Cash Payment Transactions *(textbook p. 444)*

GENERAL JOURNAL PAGE ______

	DATE		DESCRIPTION	POST. REF.	DEBIT	CREDIT	
1							1
2							2
3							3
4							4
5							5
6							6
7							7
8							8
9							9
10							10
11							11
12							12
13							13
14							14
15							15
16							16
17							17
18							18
19							19
20							20
21							21
22							22
23							23
24							24
25							25
26							26
27							27
28							28
29							29
30							30
31							31
32							32
33							33
34							34
35							35

Analyze:

Name Date Class

Problem 15-9 Recording Purchases and Cash Payment Transactions *(textbook p. 445)*

GENERAL JOURNAL PAGE ______

	DATE		DESCRIPTION	POST. REF.	DEBIT	CREDIT	
1							1
2							2
3							3
4							4
5							5
6							6
7							7
8							8
9							9
10							10
11							11
12							12
13							13
14							14
15							15
16							16
17							17
18							18
19							19
20							20
21							21
22							22
23							23
24							24
25							25
26							26
27							27
28							28
29							29
30							30
31							31
32							32
33							33
34							34
35							35

Analyze: ______________________________

Problem 15-10 Recording and Posting Purchases and Cash Payment Transactions *(textbook p. 446)*

Instructions: *Use the following source documents to record the transactions for this problem.*

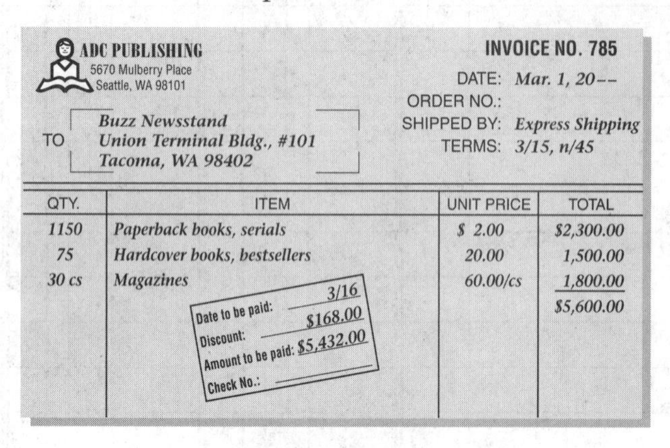

ADC PUBLISHING
5670 Mulberry Place
Seattle, WA 98101

INVOICE NO. 785

DATE: *Mar. 1, 20--*
ORDER NO.:
SHIPPED BY: *Express Shipping*
TERMS: *3/15, n/45*

TO *Buzz Newsstand*
Union Terminal Bldg., #101
Tacoma, WA 98402

QTY.	ITEM	UNIT PRICE	TOTAL
1150	*Paperback books, serials*	*$ 2.00*	*$2,300.00*
75	*Hardcover books, bestsellers*	*20.00*	*1,500.00*
30 cs	*Magazines*	*60.00/cs*	*1,800.00*
			$5,600.00

Date to be paid: *3/16*
Discount: *$168.00*
Amount to be paid: *$5,432.00*
Check No.:

$ *588.00* No. 1402
Date *March 7* 20--
To *Delta Press*
For *on account*

	Dollars	Cents
Balance brought forward	*10,990*	*00*
Add deposits		
Total	*10,990*	*00*
Less this check	*588*	*00*
Balance carried forward	*10,402*	*00*

Delta Press
One Triangle Park
Vancouver, WA 98661

INVOICE NO. DP166

DATE: *Feb. 25, 20--*
ORDER NO.:
SHIPPED BY: *Rizzo's Trucking Co.*
TERMS: *2/10, n/30*

TO *Buzz Newsstand*
Union Terminal Bldg., #101
Tacoma, WA 98402

QTY.	ITEM	UNIT PRICE	TOTAL
30	*Hardcover books*	*$20.00*	*$ 600.00*

Date to be paid: *3/7*
Discount: *$12.00*
Amount to be paid: *$588.00*
Check No.: *1402*

REC'D FEB 27

$ *735.00* No. 1400
Date *March 3* 20--
To *Pine Forest Publications*
For *on account*

	Dollars	Cents
Balance brought forward	*12,000*	*00*
Add deposits		
Total	*12,000*	*00*
Less this check	*735*	*00*
Balance carried forward	*11,265*	*00*

Pine Forest Publications
103 Mt. Thor Road
Spokane, WA 99210

...CE NO. PFP98

DATE: *Feb. 25, 20--*
ORDER NO.:
SHIPPED BY: *Rizzo's Trucking Co.*
TERMS: *2/10, n/30*

TO *Buzz Newsstand*
Union Terminal Bldg., #101
Tacoma, WA 98402

QTY.	ITEM	UNIT PRICE	TOTAL
50	*Trade paperback books*	*$15.00*	*$ 750.00*

Date to be paid: *3/3*
Discount: *$15.00*
Amount to be paid: *$735.00*
Check No.: *1400*

REC'D FEB 27

DEBIT MEMORANDUM No. 33
Date: *Mar. 9, 20--*
Invoice No.: *ATP77*

BUZZ NEWSSTAND
Union Terminal Building, #101
Tacoma, WA 98402

To: *American Trend Publishers*
1313 Maple Drive
Seattle, WA 98148

This day we have debited your account as follows:

Quantity	Item	Unit Price	Total
50	*Paperback books*	*$2.00*	*$100.00*

$ *275.00* No. 1401
Date *March 5* 20--
To *Rizzo's Trucking Company*
For *transportation charges*

	Dollars	Cents
Balance brought forward	*11,265*	*00*
Add deposits		
Total	*11,265*	*00*
Less this check	*275*	*00*
Balance carried forward	*10,990*	*00*

$ *3,200.00* No. 1403
Date *March 11* 20--
To *Keystone Insurance Company*
For *business insurance*

	Dollars	Cents
Balance brought forward	*10,402*	*00*
Add deposits		
Total	*10,402*	*00*
Less this check	*3,200*	*00*
Balance carried forward	*7,202*	*00*

Problem 15-10 (continued)

$ 5,432.00 No. 1404
Date March 15 20--
To ADC Publishing
For on account—Invoice 785

	Dollars	Cents
Balance brought forward	7,202	00
Add deposits		
Total	7,202	00
Less this check	5,432	00
Balance carried forward	1,770	00

$ 120.00 No. 1406
Date March 30 20--
To ADC Publishing
For merchandise

	Dollars	Cents
Balance brought forward	970	00
Add deposits		
Total	970	00
Less this check	120	00
Balance carried forward	850	00

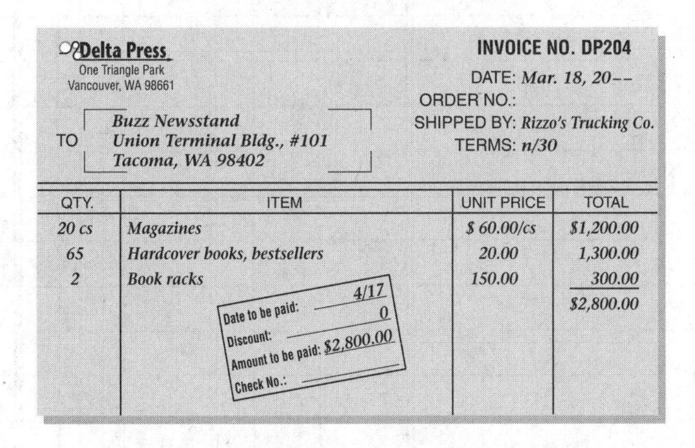
Delta Press
One Triangle Park
Vancouver, WA 98661

INVOICE NO. DP204
DATE: Mar. 18, 20--
ORDER NO.:
SHIPPED BY: Rizzo's Trucking Co.
TERMS: n/30

TO Buzz Newsstand
Union Terminal Bldg., #101
Tacoma, WA 98402

QTY.	ITEM	UNIT PRICE	TOTAL
20 cs	Magazines	$ 60.00/cs	$1,200.00
65	Hardcover books, bestsellers	20.00	1,300.00
2	Book racks	150.00	300.00
			$2,800.00

Date to be paid: 4/17
Discount: 0
Amount to be paid: $2,800.00
Check No.:

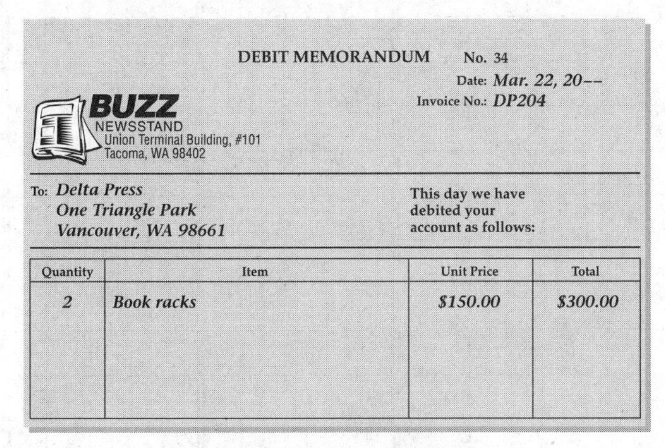
DEBIT MEMORANDUM No. 34
Date: Mar. 22, 20--
Invoice No.: DP204

BUZZ NEWSSTAND
Union Terminal Building, #101
Tacoma, WA 98402

To: Delta Press
One Triangle Park
Vancouver, WA 98661

This day we have debited your account as follows:

Quantity	Item	Unit Price	Total
2	Book racks	$150.00	$300.00

$ 800.00 No. 1405
Date March 28 20--
To American Trend Publishers
For on account

	Dollars	Cents
Balance brought forward	1,770	00
Add deposits		
Total	1,770	00
Less this check	800	00
Balance carried forward	970	00

Name Date Class

Problem 15-10 (continued)

GENERAL JOURNAL PAGE ________

	DATE		DESCRIPTION	POST. REF.	DEBIT	CREDIT	
1							1
2							2
3							3
4							4
5							5
6							6
7							7
8							8
9							9
10							10
11							11
12							12
13							13
14							14
15							15
16							16
17							17
18							18
19							19
20							20
21							21
22							22
23							23
24							24
25							25
26							26
27							27
28							28
29							29
30							30
31							31
32							32
33							33
34							34
35							35
36							36
37							37
38							38

Problem 15-10 (continued)

ACCOUNT *Cash in Bank* ACCOUNT NO. *101*

DATE		DESCRIPTION	POST. REF.	DEBIT	CREDIT	BALANCE DEBIT	BALANCE CREDIT
20--							
Mar.	*1*	*Balance*	✓			*12,000.00*	

ACCOUNT *Prepaid Insurance* ACCOUNT NO. *140*

DATE		DESCRIPTION	POST. REF.	DEBIT	CREDIT	BALANCE DEBIT	BALANCE CREDIT

ACCOUNT *Accounts Payable* ACCOUNT NO. *201*

DATE		DESCRIPTION	POST. REF.	DEBIT	CREDIT	BALANCE DEBIT	BALANCE CREDIT
20--							
Mar.	*1*	*Balance*	✓				*2,250.00*

Name Date Class

Problem 15-10 (continued)

ACCOUNT *Purchases* ACCOUNT NO. *501*

DATE		DESCRIPTION	POST. REF.	DEBIT	CREDIT	BALANCE DEBIT	BALANCE CREDIT
20--							
Mar.	*1*	*Balance*	✓			*8000 00*	

ACCOUNT *Transportation In* ACCOUNT NO. *505*

DATE		DESCRIPTION	POST. REF.	DEBIT	CREDIT	BALANCE DEBIT	BALANCE CREDIT
20--							
Mar.	*1*	*Balance*	✓			*1500 00*	

ACCOUNT *Purchases Discounts* ACCOUNT NO. *510*

DATE		DESCRIPTION	POST. REF.	DEBIT	CREDIT	BALANCE DEBIT	BALANCE CREDIT

ACCOUNT *Purchases Returns and Allowances* ACCOUNT NO. *515*

DATE		DESCRIPTION	POST. REF.	DEBIT	CREDIT	BALANCE DEBIT	BALANCE CREDIT

Problem 15-10 (concluded)

ACCOUNTS PAYABLE SUBSIDIARY LEDGER

Name *ADC Publishing*

Address *5670 Mulberry Place, Seattle, WA 98101*

DATE		DESCRIPTION	POST. REF.	DEBIT	CREDIT	BALANCE

Name *American Trend Publishers*

Address *1313 Maple Drive, Seattle, WA 98148*

DATE		DESCRIPTION	POST. REF.	DEBIT	CREDIT	BALANCE
20--						
Mar.	*1*	*Balance*	✓			*900 00*

Name *Delta Press*

Address *One Triangle Park, Vancouver, WA 98661*

DATE		DESCRIPTION	POST. REF.	DEBIT	CREDIT	BALANCE
20--						
Mar.	*1*	*Balance*	✓			*600 00*

Name *Pine Forest Publications*

Address *103 Mt. Thor Road, Spokane, WA 99210*

DATE		DESCRIPTION	POST. REF.	DEBIT	CREDIT	BALANCE
20--						
Mar.	*1*	*Balance*	✓			*750 00*

Analyze:

Notes

Name Date Class

CHAPTER 16 Special Journals: Sales and Cash Receipts

Study Guide

Section Assessment

Section 1 *Read Section 1 on pages 453–460 and complete the following exercises on page 461.*

- ☐ Reinforce the Main Idea
- ☐ Math for Accounting
- ☐ Problem 16-1 *Posting Column Totals from the Sales Journal*
- ☐ Problem 16-2 *Analyzing a Source Document*

Section 2 *Read Section 2 on pages 462–471 and complete the following exercises on page 472.*

- ☐ Reinforce the Main Idea
- ☐ Math for Accounting
- ☐ Problem 16-3 *Completing the Cash Receipts Journal*

Chapter Assessment

Summary *Review the Chapter 16 Visual Summary on page 473 in your textbook.*

- ☐ Key Concepts

Review and Activities *Complete the following questions and exercises on page 474 in your textbook.*

- ☐ After You Read: Answering the Essential Question
- ☐ Vocabulary Check
- ☐ Concept Check

Standardized Test Practice *Complete the exercises on page 475 in your textbook.*

Computerized Accounting *Read the Computerized Accounting information on page 476 in your textbook.*

- ☐ Making the Transition from a Manual to a Computerized System

Problems *Complete the following End-of-Chapter Problems for Chapter 16 in your textbook.*

- ☐ Problem 16-4 *Recording and Posting Sales Transactions*
- ☐ Problem 16-5 *Recording and Posting Cash Receipts*

Challenge Problem

- ☐ Problem 16-6 *Recording and Posting Sales and Cash Receipts*

Real-World Applications and Connections *Complete the following applications on pages 480–481 in your textbook.*

- ☐ Case Study
- ☐ 21st Century Skills
- ☐ Career Wise
- ☐ Spotlight on Personal Finance
- ☐ H.O.T. Audit

Name Date Class

Working Papers *for Section Problems*

Problem 16-1 Posting Column Totals from the Sales Journal
(textbook p. 461)

SALES JOURNAL

PAGE 4

	DATE		SALES SLIP NO.	CUSTOMER'S ACCOUNT DEBITED	POST. REF.	SALES CREDIT	SALES TAX PAYABLE CREDIT	ACCOUNTS RECEIVABLE DEBIT	
1	20--								1
2	Apr.	1	47	Amy Anderson	✓	800 00	48 00	848 00	2
31		30		Totals		12,000 00	720 00	12,720 00	31
32									32
33									33

GENERAL LEDGER

ACCOUNT *Accounts Receivable* ACCOUNT NO. *115*

DATE		DESCRIPTION	POST. REF.	DEBIT	CREDIT	BALANCE DEBIT	BALANCE CREDIT
20--							
Apr.	1	Balance	✓			15,000 00	

ACCOUNT *Sales Tax Payable* ACCOUNT NO. *220*

DATE		DESCRIPTION	POST. REF.	DEBIT	CREDIT	BALANCE DEBIT	BALANCE CREDIT
20--							
Apr.	1	Balance	✓				1,300 00

ACCOUNT *Sales* ACCOUNT NO. *401*

DATE		DESCRIPTION	POST. REF.	DEBIT	CREDIT	BALANCE DEBIT	BALANCE CREDIT
20--							
Apr.	1	Balance	✓				25,000 00

Name Date Class

Problem 16-2 Analyzing a Source Document *(textbook p. 461)*

SALES JOURNAL

PAGE ______

	DATE		SALES SLIP NO.	CUSTOMER'S ACCOUNT DEBITED	POST. REF.	SALES CREDIT	SALES TAX PAYABLE CREDIT	ACCOUNTS RECEIVABLE DEBIT	
1									1
2									2
3									3
4									4
5									5
6									6
7									7

Name *M&M Consultants*

Address *2816 Mt. Odin Drive, Williamsburg, VA 23185*

DATE		DESCRIPTION	POST. REF.	DEBIT	CREDIT	BALANCE
20--						
June	*1*	*Balance*	✓			*300 00*

Problem 16-3 Completing the Cash Receipts Journal *(textbook p. 472)*

CASH RECEIPTS JOURNAL

PAGE *10*

	DATE		DOC. NO.	ACCOUNT NAME	POST. REF.	GENERAL CREDIT	SALES CREDIT	SALES TAX PAYABLE CREDIT	ACCOUNTS RECEIVABLE CREDIT	SALES DISCOUNTS DEBIT	CASH IN BANK DEBIT	
1	*20—*											1
2	*Jan.*	*3*	*R502*	*Jennifer Smith*	✓				*80 00*		*80 00*	2
3		*5*	*R503*	*Wilton High School*	✓				*3100 00*	*62 00*	*3038 00*	3
4		*8*	*R504*	*Store Equipment*	*155*	*75 00*					*75 00*	4
5		*15*	*T42*	*Cash Sales*	—		*5000 00*	*300 00*			*5300 00*	5
6		*15*	*T42*	*Bankcard Sales*	—		*1200 00*	*72 00*			*1272 00*	6
7		*20*	*R505*	*Norwin High School*	✓				*2400 00*	*48 00*	*2352 00*	7
8		*30*	*R506*	*Supplies*	*115*	*30 00*					*30 00*	8
9												9
10												10
11												11
12												12
13												13
14												14
15												15
16												16
17												17
18												18
19												19
20												20
21												21
22												22
23												23
24												24
25												25
26												26

Name Date Class

Working Papers *for End-of-Chapter Problems*

Problem 16-4 Recording and Posting Sales Transactions

(textbook p. 477)

(1), (3)

SALES JOURNAL

PAGE ______

	DATE		SALES SLIP NO.	CUSTOMER'S ACCOUNT DEBITED	POST. REF.	SALES CREDIT	SALES TAX PAYABLE CREDIT	ACCOUNTS RECEIVABLE DEBIT	
1									1
2									2
3									3
4									4
5									5
6									6
7									7
8									8
9									9
10									10
11									11
12									12
13									13
14									14
15									15
16									16
17									17
18									18
19									19
20									20
21									21
22									22
23									23
24									24
25									25
26									26
27									27
28									28
29									29
30									30
31									31
32									32
33									33

Problem 16-4 (continued)

(1)

CASH RECEIPTS JOURNAL

PAGE ____

	DATE	DOC. NO.	ACCOUNT NAME	POST. REF.	GENERAL CREDIT	SALES CREDIT	SALES TAX PAYABLE CREDIT	ACCOUNTS RECEIVABLE CREDIT	SALES DISCOUNTS DEBIT	CASH IN BANK DEBIT	
1											1
2											2
3											3
4											4
5											5
6											6
7											7
8											8
9											9
10											10
11											11
12											12
13											13
14											14
15											15
16											16
17											17
18											18
19											19
20											20
21											21
22											22
23											23
24											24
25											25

Problem 16-4 (continued)

(2)

ACCOUNTS RECEIVABLE SUBSIDIARY LEDGER

Name *FastForward Productions*

Address *3 Oakhill Mall, Decatur, AL 35601*

DATE		DESCRIPTION	POST. REF.	DEBIT	CREDIT	BALANCE

Name *Yoko Nakata*

Address *19 Hawthorne Street, Tuscaloosa, AL 35401*

DATE		DESCRIPTION	POST. REF.	DEBIT	CREDIT	BALANCE
20--						
May	*1*	*Balance*	✓			*600 00*

Name *Heather Sullivan*

Address *835 Aspen Lane, Huntsville, AL 35801*

DATE		DESCRIPTION	POST. REF.	DEBIT	CREDIT	BALANCE
20--						
May	*1*	*Balance*	✓			*50 00*

Name Date Class

Problem 16-4 (concluded)

(4)

GENERAL LEDGER

ACCOUNT *Cash in Bank* ACCOUNT NO. *101*

DATE		DESCRIPTION	POST. REF.	DEBIT	CREDIT	BALANCE DEBIT	BALANCE CREDIT
20--							
May	*1*	*Balance*	✓			*5,000.00*	

ACCOUNT *Accounts Receivable* ACCOUNT NO. *115*

DATE		DESCRIPTION	POST. REF.	DEBIT	CREDIT	BALANCE DEBIT	BALANCE CREDIT
20--							
May	*1*	*Balance*	✓			*650.00*	

ACCOUNT *Sales Tax Payable* ACCOUNT NO. *215*

DATE		DESCRIPTION	POST. REF.	DEBIT	CREDIT	BALANCE DEBIT	BALANCE CREDIT
20--							
May	*1*	*Balance*	✓				*1,200.00*

ACCOUNT *Sales* ACCOUNT NO. *401*

DATE		DESCRIPTION	POST. REF.	DEBIT	CREDIT	BALANCE DEBIT	BALANCE CREDIT
20--							
May	*1*	*Balance*	✓				*30,000.00*

(5)

Analyze:

Name ______________________ Date ______________ Class ______________

Problem 16-5 Recording and Posting Cash Receipts *(textbook p. 477)*

CASH RECEIPTS JOURNAL

PAGE ______

	DATE	DOC. NO.	ACCOUNT NAME	POST. REF.	GENERAL CREDIT	SALES CREDIT	SALES TAX PAYABLE CREDIT	ACCOUNTS RECEIVABLE CREDIT	SALES DISCOUNTS DEBIT	CASH IN BANK DEBIT	
1											1
2											2
3											3
4											4
5											5
6											6
7											7
8											8
9											9
10											10
11											11
12											12
13											13
14											14
15											15
16											16
17											17
18											18
19											19
20											20
21											21
22											22
23											23
24											24
25											25
26											26

Name Date Class

Problem 16-5 (continued)

GENERAL LEDGER

ACCOUNT *Cash in Bank* ACCOUNT NO. *101*

DATE		DESCRIPTION	POST. REF.	DEBIT	CREDIT	BALANCE DEBIT	BALANCE CREDIT
20--							
May	*1*	*Balance*	✓			*7500 00*	

ACCOUNT *Accounts Receivable* ACCOUNT NO. *115*

DATE		DESCRIPTION	POST. REF.	DEBIT	CREDIT	BALANCE DEBIT	BALANCE CREDIT
20--							
May	*1*	*Balance*	✓			*6900 00*	

ACCOUNT *Store Equipment* ACCOUNT NO. *150*

DATE		DESCRIPTION	POST. REF.	DEBIT	CREDIT	BALANCE DEBIT	BALANCE CREDIT
20--							
May	*1*	*Balance*	✓			*3000 00*	

ACCOUNT *Sales Tax Payable* ACCOUNT NO. *215*

DATE		DESCRIPTION	POST. REF.	DEBIT	CREDIT	BALANCE DEBIT	BALANCE CREDIT
20--							
May	*1*	*Balance*	✓				*250 00*

ACCOUNT *Sales* ACCOUNT NO. *401*

DATE		DESCRIPTION	POST. REF.	DEBIT	CREDIT	BALANCE DEBIT	BALANCE CREDIT
20--							
May	*1*	*Balance*	✓				*40000 00*

ACCOUNT *Sales Discounts* ACCOUNT NO. *405*

DATE		DESCRIPTION	POST. REF.	DEBIT	CREDIT	BALANCE DEBIT	BALANCE CREDIT
20--							
May	*1*	*Balance*	✓			*1200 00*	

Problem 16-5 (continued)

ACCOUNTS RECEIVABLE SUBSIDIARY LEDGER

Name *Adventure River Tours*

Address *Box 101, Jackson, WY 83001*

DATE		DESCRIPTION	POST. REF.	DEBIT	CREDIT	BALANCE
20--						
May	1	Balance	✓			3 000 00

Name *Paul Drake*

Address *125 Rodeo Road, Cody, WY 82414*

DATE		DESCRIPTION	POST. REF.	DEBIT	CREDIT	BALANCE
20--						
May	1	Balance	✓			800 00

Name *Celeste Everett*

Address *1824 Grays Gable, Laramie, WY 82070*

DATE		DESCRIPTION	POST. REF.	DEBIT	CREDIT	BALANCE
20--						
May	1	Balance	✓			400 00

Name *Isabel Rodriguez*

Address *626 Buffalo Road, Cheyenne, WY 82001*

DATE		DESCRIPTION	POST. REF.	DEBIT	CREDIT	BALANCE
20--						
May	1	Balance	✓			200 00

Name Date Class

Problem 16-5 (concluded)

ACCOUNTS RECEIVABLE SUBSIDIARY LEDGER

Name *Wildwood Resorts*

Address *601 Ponderosa Trail, Moose, WY 83012*

DATE		DESCRIPTION	POST. REF.	DEBIT	CREDIT	BALANCE
20--						
May	*1*	*Balance*	✓			*2500 00*

Analyze:

Name Date Class

Problem 16-6 Recording and Posting Sales and Cash Receipts *(textbook p. 478)*

Instructions: *Use the following source documents to record the transactions for this problem.*

BUZZ NEWSSTAND
Union Terminal Building, #101
Tacoma, WA 98402

DATE: *May 1, 20--* NO. *170*

SOLD TO: *Ilya Bodonski*
20 Maplewood Terrace
Lakewood, WA 98259

CLERK	CASH	CHARGE	TERMS
BA		*✓*	*n/30*

QTY.	DESCRIPTION	UNIT PRICE	AMOUNT
2 cs	*Magazines*	*100/cs*	*200 00*
10	*Entertainment software*	*10.00*	*100 00*
		SUBTOTAL	*300 00*
		SALES TAX	*18 00*
		TOTAL	*318 00*

Thank You!

BUZZ NEWSSTAND
Union Terminal Building, #101
Tacoma, WA 98402

RECEIPT
No. 147

May 7 20 *--*

RECEIVED FROM *Rothwell Management Inc.* $ *294.00*

Two hundred ninety-four and 00/100 DOLLARS

FOR *on account (300 less 2% discount)*

RECEIVED BY *Kathy Harper*

BUZZ NEWSSTAND
Union Terminal Building, #101
Tacoma, WA 98402

DATE: *April 30, 20--* NO. *162*

SOLD TO: *Rothwell Management Inc.*
16 University Place
Vancouver, WA 98661

CLERK	CASH	CHARGE	TERMS
BA		*✓*	*2/10, n/30*

QTY.	DESCRIPTION	UNIT PRICE	AMOUNT
2 cs	*Magazines*	*100/cs*	*200 00*
75	*Daily newspapers*	*1.00*	*75 00*
1 bx	*Pocket combs*	*8.02*	*8 02*
		SUBTOTAL	*283 02*
		SALES TAX	*16 98*
		TOTAL	*300 00*

COPY

Thank You!

BUZZ NEWSSTAND
Union Terminal Building, #101
Tacoma, WA 98402

RECEIPT
No. 145

May 3 20 *--*

RECEIVED FROM *Katz Properties* $ *490.00*

Four hundred ninety and 00/100 DOLLARS

FOR *on account (500.00 less 2% discount)*

RECEIVED BY *Kathy Harper*

BUZZ NEWSSTAND
Union Terminal Building, #101
Tacoma, WA 98402

DATE: *April 26, 20--* NO. *159*

SOLD TO: *Katz Properties*
103 Prospect Point
Bellevue, WA 98009

CLERK	CASH	CHARGE	TERMS
BA		*✓*	*2/10, n/30*

QTY.	DESCRIPTION	UNIT PRICE	AMOUNT
4 cs	*Magazines*	*100/cs*	*400 00*
2	*Desk lamps*	*35.85*	*71 70*
		SUBTOTAL	*471 70*
		SALES TAX	*28 30*
		TOTAL	*500 00*

COPY

Thank You!

BUZZ NEWSSTAND
Union Terminal Building, #101
Tacoma, WA 98402

DATE: *May 9, 20--* NO. *171*

SOLD TO: *Saba Nadal*
943 Peachtree Drive
Spokane, WA 99210

CLERK	CASH	CHARGE	TERMS
BA		*✓*	*n/30*

QTY.	DESCRIPTION	UNIT PRICE	AMOUNT
25	*Paperback books*	*4.00*	*100 00*
		SUBTOTAL	*100 00*
		SALES TAX	*6 00*
		TOTAL	*106 00*

Thank You!

BUZZ NEWSSTAND
Union Terminal Building, #101
Tacoma, WA 98402

DATE: *May 10, 20--* NO. *172*

SOLD TO: *Java Shops, Inc.*
449 Country Place
Auburn, WA 98002

CLERK	CASH	CHARGE	TERMS
BA		*✓*	*2/10, n/30*

QTY.	DESCRIPTION	UNIT PRICE	AMOUNT
3 cs	*Magazines*	*100/cs*	*300 00*
12	*Hardcover books*	*25.00*	*300 00*
		SUBTOTAL	*600 00*
		SALES TAX	*36 00*
		TOTAL	*636 00*

Thank You!

BUZZ NEWSSTAND
Union Terminal Building, #101
Tacoma, WA 98402

RECEIPT
No. 146

May 5 20 *--*

RECEIVED FROM *Straka Stores* $ *60.00*

Sixty and 00/100 DOLLARS

FOR *supplies*

RECEIVED BY *Kathy Harper*

Name Date Class

Problem 16-6 (continued)

BUZZ NEWSSTAND
Union Terminal Building, #101
Tacoma, WA 98402

DATE: *May 12, 20--* NO. *173*

SOLD TO: *Lee Adkins, 720 Dogwood Lane, Seattle, WA 98101*

CLERK	CASH	CHARGE	TERMS
BA		✓	*n/30*

QTY.	DESCRIPTION	UNIT PRICE	AMOUNT
½ cs	*Magazines*	*100/cs*	*50 00*
		SUBTOTAL	*50 00*
		SALES TAX	*3 00*
		TOTAL	*53 00*

Thank You!

BUZZ NEWSSTAND
Union Terminal Building, #101
Tacoma, WA 98402

DATE: *May 18, 20--* NO. *174*

SOLD TO: *Katz Properties, 103 Prospect Point, Bellevue, WA 98009*

CLERK	CASH	CHARGE	TERMS
BA		✓	*2/10, n/30*

QTY.	DESCRIPTION	UNIT PRICE	AMOUNT
32	*Hardcover books*	*25.00*	*800 00*
200	*Daily newspapers*	*1.00*	*200 00*
		SUBTOTAL	*1,000 00*
		SALES TAX	*60 00*
		TOTAL	*1,060 00*

Thank You!

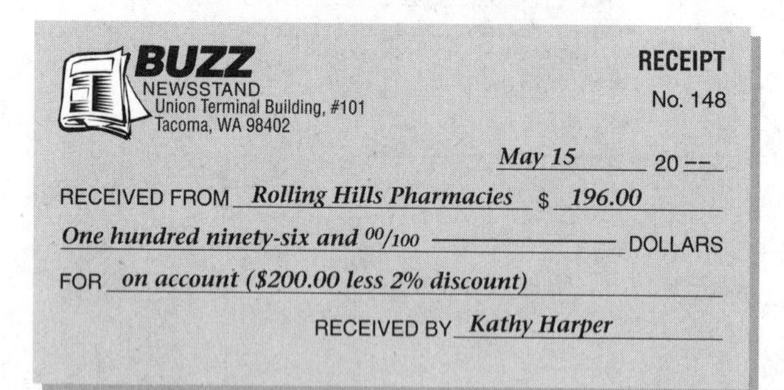

BUZZ NEWSSTAND
Union Terminal Building, #101
Tacoma, WA 98402

RECEIPT No. 148

May 15 20 *--*

RECEIVED FROM *Rolling Hills Pharmacies* $ *196.00*

One hundred ninety-six and 00/100 DOLLARS

FOR *on account ($200.00 less 2% discount)*

RECEIVED BY *Kathy Harper*

BUZZ NEWSSTAND
Union Terminal Building, #101
Tacoma, WA 98402

RECEIPT No. 149

May 20 20 *--*

RECEIVED FROM *Ilya Bodonski* $ *100.00*

One hundred and 00/100 DOLLARS

FOR *on account*

RECEIVED BY *Kathy Harper*

May 15
Tape 33

2,400.00 CA
144.00 ST

May 15
Tape 33

2,000.00 BCS
120.00 ST

BUZZ NEWSSTAND
Union Terminal Building, #101
Tacoma, WA 98402

DATE: *May 22, 20--* NO. *175*

SOLD TO: *Rothwell Management Inc., 16 University Place, Vancouver, WA 98661*

CLERK	CASH	CHARGE	TERMS
BA		✓	*2/10, n/30*

QTY.	DESCRIPTION	UNIT PRICE	AMOUNT
4 cs	*Magazines*	*100/cs*	*400 00*
200	*Daily newspapers*	*1.00*	*200 00*
5	*Travel planning software*	*40.00*	*200 00*
		SUBTOTAL	*800 00*
		SALES TAX	*48 00*
		TOTAL	*848 00*

Thank You!

Problem 16-6 (continued)

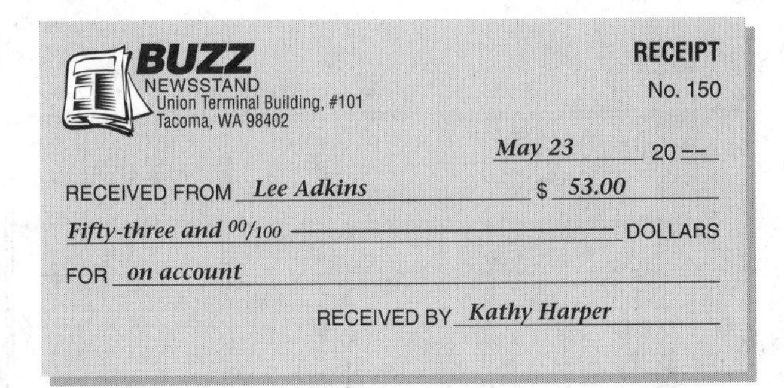

BUZZ NEWSSTAND
Union Terminal Building, #101
Tacoma, WA 98402

RECEIPT
No. 150

May 23 20--

RECEIVED FROM *Lee Adkins* $ *53.00*

Fifty-three and 00/100 DOLLARS

FOR *on account*

RECEIVED BY *Kathy Harper*

BUZZ NEWSSTAND
Union Terminal Building, #101
Tacoma, WA 98402

RECEIPT
No. 153

May 28 20--

RECEIVED FROM *Brown's Books and More* $ *75.00*

Seventy-five and 00/100 DOLLARS

FOR *used store equipment*

RECEIVED BY *Kathy Harper*

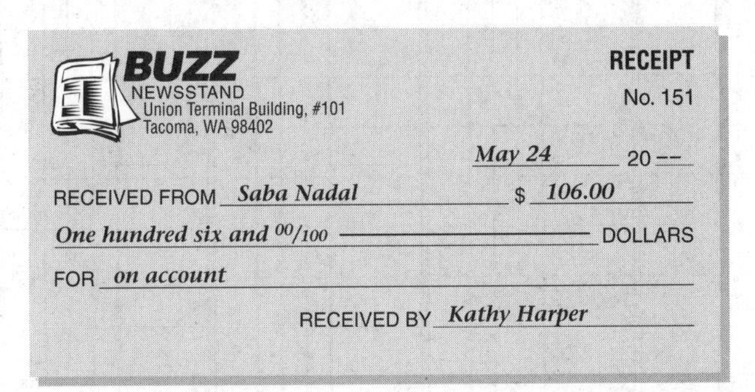

BUZZ NEWSSTAND
Union Terminal Building, #101
Tacoma, WA 98402

RECEIPT
No. 151

May 24 20--

RECEIVED FROM *Saba Nadal* $ *106.00*

One hundred six and 00/100 DOLLARS

FOR *on account*

RECEIVED BY *Kathy Harper*

May 30
Tape 34

2,600.00 CA
156.00 ST

BUZZ NEWSSTAND
Union Terminal Building, #101
Tacoma, WA 98402

RECEIPT
No. 152

May 26 20--

RECEIVED FROM *Java Shops, Inc.* $ *200.00*

Two hundred and 00/100 DOLLARS

FOR *on account*

RECEIVED BY *Kathy Harper*

May 30
Tape 34

2,200.00 BCS
132.00 ST

BUZZ NEWSSTAND
Union Terminal Building, #101
Tacoma, WA 98402

DATE: *May 27, 20--* NO. *176*

SOLD TO: *Lee Adkins*
720 Dogwood Lane
Seattle, WA 98101

CLERK	CASH	CHARGE	TERMS
BA		✓	*n/30*

QTY.	DESCRIPTION	UNIT PRICE	AMOUNT	
2 cs	*Magazines*	*100/cs*	*200*	*00*
		SUBTOTAL	*200*	*00*
		SALES TAX	*12*	*00*
		TOTAL	*212*	*00*

Thank You!

Name Date Class

Problem 16-6 Recording and Posting Sales and Cash Receipts

(1), (4)

SALES JOURNAL

PAGE ______

	DATE	SALES SLIP NO.	CUSTOMER'S ACCOUNT DEBITED	POST. REF.	SALES CREDIT	SALES TAX PAYABLE CREDIT	ACCOUNTS RECEIVABLE DEBIT	
1								1
2								2
3								3
4								4
5								5
6								6
7								7
8								8
9								9
10								10
11								11
12								12
13								13
14								14
15								15
16								16
17								17
18								18
19								19
20								20
21								21
22								22
23								23
24								24
25								25
26								26
27								27
28								28
29								29
30								30
31								31
32								32
33								33

Name Date Class

Problem 16-6 (continued)

CASH RECEIPTS JOURNAL

PAGE ____

	DATE	DOC. NO.	ACCOUNT NAME	POST. REF.	GENERAL CREDIT	SALES CREDIT	SALES TAX PAYABLE CREDIT	ACCOUNTS RECEIVABLE CREDIT	SALES DISCOUNTS DEBIT	CASH IN BANK DEBIT	
1											1
2											2
3											3
4											4
5											5
6											6
7											7
8											8
9											9
10											10
11											11
12											12
13											13
14											14
15											15
16											16
17											17
18											18
19											19
20											20
21											21
22											22
23											23
24											24
25											25
26											26

Name Date Class

Problem 16-6 (continued)

(2) ACCOUNTS RECEIVABLE SUBSIDIARY LEDGER

Name *Lee Adkins*

Address *720 Dogwood Lane, Seattle, WA 98101*

DATE		DESCRIPTION	POST. REF.	DEBIT	CREDIT	BALANCE

Name *Ilya Bodonski*

Address *20 Maplewood Terrace, Lakewood, WA 98259*

DATE		DESCRIPTION	POST. REF.	DEBIT	CREDIT	BALANCE

Name *Java Shops Inc.*

Address *449 Country Place, Auburn, WA 98002*

DATE		DESCRIPTION	POST. REF.	DEBIT	CREDIT	BALANCE

Name *Katz Properties*

Address *103 Prospect Point, Bellevue, WA 98009*

DATE		DESCRIPTION	POST. REF.	DEBIT	CREDIT	BALANCE
20--						
May	*1*	*Balance*	✓			*500 00*

Name Date Class

Problem 16-6 (continued)

Name *Saba Nadal*

Address *943 Peachtree Drive, Spokane, WA 99210*

DATE		DESCRIPTION	POST. REF.	DEBIT	CREDIT	BALANCE

Name *Rolling Hills Pharmacies*

Address *16 Meadow Lane, Tacoma, WA 98402*

DATE		DESCRIPTION	POST. REF.	DEBIT	CREDIT	BALANCE
20--						
May	*5*	*Balance*	✓			*200 00*

Name *Rothwell Management Inc.*

Address *16 University Place, Vancouver, WA 98661*

DATE		DESCRIPTION	POST. REF.	DEBIT	CREDIT	BALANCE
20--						
May	*1*	*Balance*	✓			*300 00*

Name Date Class

Problem 16-6 (continued)

GENERAL LEDGER

ACCOUNT *Cash in Bank* ACCOUNT NO. *101*

DATE		DESCRIPTION	POST. REF.	DEBIT	CREDIT	BALANCE DEBIT	BALANCE CREDIT
20--							
May	1	Balance	✓			500000	

ACCOUNT *Accounts Receivable* ACCOUNT NO. *115*

DATE		DESCRIPTION	POST. REF.	DEBIT	CREDIT	BALANCE DEBIT	BALANCE CREDIT
20--							
May	1	Balance	✓			100000	

ACCOUNT *Supplies* ACCOUNT NO. *135*

DATE		DESCRIPTION	POST. REF.	DEBIT	CREDIT	BALANCE DEBIT	BALANCE CREDIT
20--							
May	1	Balance	✓			30000	

ACCOUNT *Store Equipment* ACCOUNT NO. *150*

DATE		DESCRIPTION	POST. REF.	DEBIT	CREDIT	BALANCE DEBIT	BALANCE CREDIT
20--							
May	1	Balance	✓			400000	

ACCOUNT *Sales Tax Payable* ACCOUNT NO. *215*

DATE		DESCRIPTION	POST. REF.	DEBIT	CREDIT	BALANCE DEBIT	BALANCE CREDIT
20--							
May	1	Balance	✓				40000

Problem 16-6 (concluded)

ACCOUNT *Sales* ACCOUNT NO. *401*

DATE		DESCRIPTION	POST. REF.	DEBIT	CREDIT	BALANCE DEBIT	BALANCE CREDIT
20--							
May	*1*	*Balance*	✓				*2000000*

ACCOUNT *Sales Discounts* ACCOUNT NO. *405*

DATE		DESCRIPTION	POST. REF.	DEBIT	CREDIT	BALANCE DEBIT	BALANCE CREDIT
20--							
May	*1*	*Balance*	✓			*50000*	

(7)

--

Analyze:

Name Date Class

Notes

Name Date Class

CHAPTER 17 Special Journals: Purchases and Cash Payments

Study Guide

Section Assessment

Section 1 *Read Section 1 on pages 485–490 and complete the following exercises on page 491.*

- ☐ Reinforce the Main Idea
- ☐ Math for Accounting
- ☐ Problem 17-1 *Recording Transactions in the Purchases Journal*

Section 2 *Read Section 2 on pages 492–504 and complete the following exercises on page 505.*

- ☐ Reinforce the Main Idea
- ☐ Math for Accounting
- ☐ Problem 17-2 *Preparing a Cash Proof*
- ☐ Problem 17-3 *Analyzing a Source Document*

Chapter Assessment

Summary *Review the Chapter 17 Visual Summary on page 506 in your textbook.*

- ☐ Key Concepts

Review and Activities *Complete the following questions and exercises on page 507 in your textbook.*

- ☐ After You Read: Answering the Essential Question
- ☐ Vocabulary Check
- ☐ Concept Check

Standardized Test Practice *Complete the exercises on page 508 in your textbook.*

Computerized Accounting *Read the Computerized Accounting information on page 509 in your textbook.*

- ☐ Making the Transition from a Manual to a Computerized System

Problems *Complete the following End-of-Chapter Problems for Chapter 17 in your textbook.*

- ☐ Problem 17-4 *Recording Payment of the Payroll*
- ☐ Problem 17-5 *Recording Transactions in the Purchases Journal*
- ☐ Problem 17-6 *Recording and Posting Purchases*
- ☐ Problem 17-7 *Recording and Posting Cash Payments*

Challenge Problem

- ☐ Problem 17-8 *Recording and Posting Purchases and Cash Payments*

Real-World Applications and Connections *Complete the following applications on pages 516–517 in your textbook.*

- ☐ Career Wise
- ☐ Global Accounting
- ☐ A Matter of Ethics
- ☐ Analyzing Financial Reports
- ☐ H.O.T. Audit

Name Date Class

Working Papers *for Section Problems*

Problem 17-1 Recording Transactions in the Purchases Journal *(textbook p. 491)*

PURCHASES JOURNAL PAGE ____

	DATE	INVOICE NO.	CREDITOR'S ACCOUNT CREDITED	POST. REF.	ACCOUNTS PAYABLE CREDIT	PURCHASES DEBIT	GENERAL			
							ACCOUNT DEBITED	POST. REF.	DEBIT	
1										1
2										2
3										3
4										4
5										5
6										6
7										7
8										8
9										9
10										10
11										11
12										12
13										13
14										14
15										15
16										16
17										17
18										18
19										19
20										20
21										21
22										22
23										23
24										24
25										25
26										26

Problem 17-2 Preparing a Cash Proof *(textbook p. 505)*

Name Date Class

Problem 17-3 Analyzing a Source Document *(textbook p. 505)*

$ 873.00		No. 104
Date November 2		20 --
To Colonial Products Inc.		
For Inv. 323—$900 less 3% disc., $27.00		
	Dollars	Cents
Balance brought forward	3,468	29
Add deposits		
Total	3,468	29
Less this check	873	00
Balance carried forward	2,595	29

CASH PAYMENTS JOURNAL

PAGE ______

	DATE		DOC. NO.	ACCOUNT NAME	POST. REF.	GENERAL DEBIT	GENERAL CREDIT	ACCOUNTS PAYABLE DEBIT	PURCHASES DISCOUNTS CREDIT	CASH IN BANK CREDIT	
1											1
2											2
3											3
4											4

Working Papers *for End-of-Chapter Problems*

Problem 17-4 Recording Payment of the Payroll *(textbook p. 510)*

CASH PAYMENTS JOURNAL

PAGE ____

	DATE	DOC. NO.	ACCOUNT NAME	POST. REF.	GENERAL DEBIT	GENERAL CREDIT	ACCOUNTS PAYABLE DEBIT	PURCHASES DISCOUNTS CREDIT	CASH IN BANK CREDIT	
1										1
2										2
3										3
4										4
5										5
6										6
7										7

Analyze:

Name Date Class

Problem 17-5 Recording Transactions in the Purchases Journal *(textbook p. 510)*

PURCHASES JOURNAL

PAGE ____

	DATE	INVOICE NO.	CREDITOR'S ACCOUNT CREDITED	POST. REF.	ACCOUNTS PAYABLE CREDIT	PURCHASES DEBIT	GENERAL			
							ACCOUNT DEBITED	POST. REF.	DEBIT	
1										1
2										2
3										3
4										4
5										5
6										6
7										7
8										8
9										9
10										10
11										11
12										12
13										13
14										14
15										15
16										16
17										17
18										18
19										19
20										20
21										21

Analyze:

Name Date Class

Problem 17-6 Recording and Posting Purchases *(textbook p. 511)*

PURCHASES JOURNAL

PAGE ____

	DATE	INVOICE NO.	CREDITOR'S ACCOUNT CREDITED	POST. REF.	ACCOUNTS PAYABLE CREDIT	PURCHASES DEBIT	GENERAL ACCOUNT DEBITED	GENERAL POST. REF.	GENERAL DEBIT	
1										1
2										2
3										3
4										4
5										5
6										6
7										7
8										8
9										9
10										10
11										11
12										12
13										13
14										14
15										15
16										16
17										17
18										18
19										19
20										20
21										21
22										22
23										23
24										24
25										25

Problem 17-6 (continued)

(2), (3), (4), (5)

ACCOUNTS PAYABLE SUBSIDIARY LEDGER

Name *Allen's Repair*

Address *Two Deauville Place, Birmingham, AL 35203*

DATE		DESCRIPTION	POST. REF.	DEBIT	CREDIT	BALANCE

Name *Digital Precision Equipment*

Address *16 Military Complex, Huntsville, AL 35801*

DATE		DESCRIPTION	POST. REF.	DEBIT	CREDIT	BALANCE
20--						
July	*1*	*Balance*	✓			*1 000 00*

Name *Photo Emporium*

Address *Center Mall, Mobile, AL 36601*

DATE		DESCRIPTION	POST. REF.	DEBIT	CREDIT	BALANCE

Name *ProStudio Supply*

Address *Penn Center Blvd., Montgomery, AL 36104*

DATE		DESCRIPTION	POST. REF.	DEBIT	CREDIT	BALANCE
20--						
July	*1*	*Balance*	✓			*2 000 00*

Problem 17-6 (continued)

Name *State Street Office Supply*

Address *16 Garden Drive, Tuscaloosa, AL 35401*

DATE		DESCRIPTION	POST. REF.	DEBIT	CREDIT	BALANCE

Name *U-Tech Products*

Address *42 Ridgeway Drive, Decatur, AL 35601*

DATE		DESCRIPTION	POST. REF.	DEBIT	CREDIT	BALANCE
20--						
July	*1*	*Balance*	✓			*1500 00*

Name *Video Optics Inc.*

Address *Three Oxford Place, Auburn, AL 36830*

DATE		DESCRIPTION	POST. REF.	DEBIT	CREDIT	BALANCE

Problem 17-6 (continued)

GENERAL LEDGER (PARTIAL)

ACCOUNT *Supplies* ACCOUNT NO. *130*

DATE		DESCRIPTION	POST. REF.	DEBIT	CREDIT	BALANCE DEBIT	BALANCE CREDIT
20--							
July	*1*	*Balance*	✓			*300 00*	

ACCOUNT *Store Equipment* ACCOUNT NO. *140*

DATE		DESCRIPTION	POST. REF.	DEBIT	CREDIT	BALANCE DEBIT	BALANCE CREDIT
20--							
July	*1*	*Balance*	✓			*2,500 00*	

ACCOUNT *Accounts Payable* ACCOUNT NO. *201*

DATE		DESCRIPTION	POST. REF.	DEBIT	CREDIT	BALANCE DEBIT	BALANCE CREDIT
20--							
July	*1*	*Balance*	✓				*4,500 00*

ACCOUNT *Purchases* ACCOUNT NO. *501*

DATE		DESCRIPTION	POST. REF.	DEBIT	CREDIT	BALANCE DEBIT	BALANCE CREDIT
20--							
July	*1*	*Balance*	✓			*15,000 00*	

ACCOUNT *Maintenance Expense* ACCOUNT NO. *640*

DATE		DESCRIPTION	POST. REF.	DEBIT	CREDIT	BALANCE DEBIT	BALANCE CREDIT
20--							
July	*1*	*Balance*	✓			*200 00*	

Problem 17-6 (concluded)

(6)

Analyze:

Problem 17-7 Recording and Posting Cash Payments *(textbook p. 512)*

(1), (4), (5)

CASH PAYMENTS JOURNAL

PAGE ______

	DATE	DOC. NO.	ACCOUNT NAME	POST. REF.	GENERAL DEBIT	GENERAL CREDIT	ACCOUNTS PAYABLE DEBIT	PURCHASES DISCOUNTS CREDIT	CASH IN BANK CREDIT	
1										1
2										2
3										3
4										4
5										5
6										6
7										7
8										8
9										9
10										10
11										11
12										12
13										13
14										14
15										15
16										16
17										17
18										18
19										19
20										20
21										21
22										22

Problem 17-7 (continued)

(2)

ACCOUNTS PAYABLE SUBSIDIARY LEDGER

Name *Mohican Falls Kayak Wholesalers*

Address *Box 17, Buffalo Road, Jackson, WY 83001*

DATE		DESCRIPTION	POST. REF.	DEBIT	CREDIT	BALANCE
20--						
July	*1*	*Balance*	✓			*500 00*

Name *North American Waterways Suppliers*

Address *Horse Creek Road, Casper, WY 82601*

DATE		DESCRIPTION	POST. REF.	DEBIT	CREDIT	BALANCE
20--						
July	*1*	*Balance*	✓			*1 400 00*

Name *Office Max*

Address *142 Park Plaza, Cody, WY 82414*

DATE		DESCRIPTION	POST. REF.	DEBIT	CREDIT	BALANCE
20--						
July	*1*	*Balance*	✓			*150 00*

Name *Pacific Wholesalers*

Address *497 State Street, Laramie, WY 82070*

DATE		DESCRIPTION	POST. REF.	DEBIT	CREDIT	BALANCE
20--						
July	*1*	*Balance*	✓			*1 300 00*

Problem 17-7 (continued)

Name *Rollins Plumbing Service*

Address *14 Ponderosa Road, Gillette, WY 82716*

DATE		DESCRIPTION	POST. REF.	DEBIT	CREDIT	BALANCE
20--						
July	1	Balance	✓			200 00

Name *StoreMart Supply*

Address *Box 182 Yellowstone Creek, Sheridan, WY 82801*

DATE		DESCRIPTION	POST. REF.	DEBIT	CREDIT	BALANCE
20--						
July	1	Balance	✓			900 00

Name *Trailhead Canoes*

Address *800 Trail Road, Cheyenne, WY 82001*

DATE		DESCRIPTION	POST. REF.	DEBIT	CREDIT	BALANCE
20--						
July	1	Balance	✓			700 00

Problem 17-7 (continued)

(3)

GENERAL LEDGER (PARTIAL)

ACCOUNT *Cash in Bank* ACCOUNT NO. *101*

DATE		DESCRIPTION	POST. REF.	DEBIT	CREDIT	BALANCE DEBIT	BALANCE CREDIT
20--							
July	*1*	*Balance*	✓			*800000*	
	31		*CP18*	*700000*		*1500000*	

ACCOUNT *Supplies* ACCOUNT NO. *135*

DATE		DESCRIPTION	POST. REF.	DEBIT	CREDIT	BALANCE DEBIT	BALANCE CREDIT
20--							
July	*1*	*Balance*	✓			*15000*	

ACCOUNT *Prepaid Insurance* ACCOUNT NO. *140*

DATE		DESCRIPTION	POST. REF.	DEBIT	CREDIT	BALANCE DEBIT	BALANCE CREDIT

ACCOUNT *Store Equipment* ACCOUNT NO. *150*

DATE		DESCRIPTION	POST. REF.	DEBIT	CREDIT	BALANCE DEBIT	BALANCE CREDIT
20--							
July	*1*	*Balance*	✓			*300000*	

ACCOUNT *Accounts Payable* ACCOUNT NO. *201*

DATE		DESCRIPTION	POST. REF.	DEBIT	CREDIT	BALANCE DEBIT	BALANCE CREDIT
20--							
July	*1*	*Balance*	✓				*515000*

Problem 17-7 (continued)

ACCOUNT *Transportation In* ACCOUNT NO. *505*

DATE		DESCRIPTION	POST. REF.	DEBIT	CREDIT	BALANCE DEBIT	BALANCE CREDIT
20--							
July	1	Balance	✓			650 00	

ACCOUNT *Purchases Discounts* ACCOUNT NO. *510*

DATE		DESCRIPTION	POST. REF.	DEBIT	CREDIT	BALANCE DEBIT	BALANCE CREDIT
20--							
July	1	Balance	✓				1500 00

ACCOUNT *Advertising Expense* ACCOUNT NO. *601*

DATE		DESCRIPTION	POST. REF.	DEBIT	CREDIT	BALANCE DEBIT	BALANCE CREDIT
20--							
July	1	Balance	✓			1800 00	

ACCOUNT *Miscellaneous Expense* ACCOUNT NO. *655*

DATE		DESCRIPTION	POST. REF.	DEBIT	CREDIT	BALANCE DEBIT	BALANCE CREDIT

Problem 17-7 (concluded)

(6), (7)

Analyze:

Problem 17-8 Recording and Posting Purchases and Cash Payments *(textbook p. 513)*

Instructions: *Use the following source documents to record the transactions for this problem.*

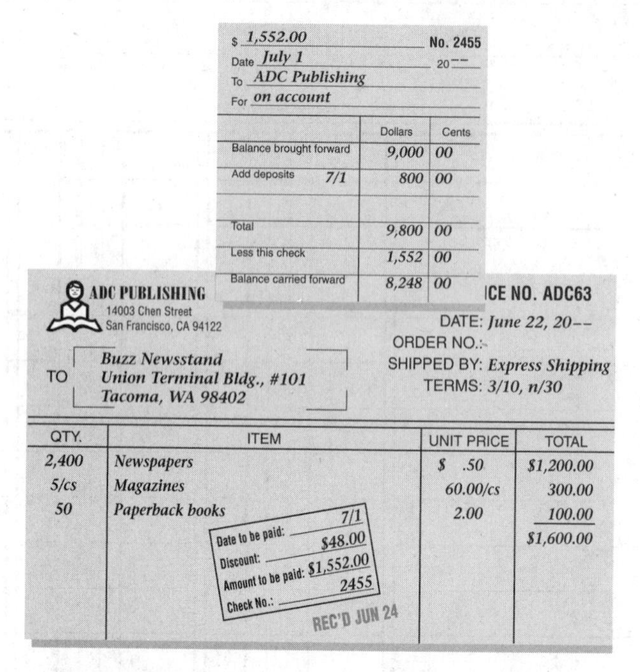

$ 1,552.00 No. 2455
Date July 1 20--
To ADC Publishing
For on account

	Dollars	Cents
Balance brought forward	9,000	00
Add deposits 7/1	800	00
Total	9,800	00
Less this check	1,552	00
Balance carried forward	8,248	00

ADC PUBLISHING
14003 Chen Street
San Francisco, CA 94122

INVOICE NO. ADC63
DATE: June 22, 20--
ORDER NO.:
SHIPPED BY: Express Shipping
TERMS: 3/10, n/30

TO Buzz Newsstand
Union Terminal Bldg., #101
Tacoma, WA 98402

QTY.	ITEM	UNIT PRICE	TOTAL
2,400	Newspapers	$ .50	$1,200.00
5/cs	Magazines	60.00/cs	300.00
50	Paperback books	2.00	100.00
			$1,600.00

Date to be paid: 7/1
Discount: $48.00
Amount to be paid: $1,552.00
Check No.: 2455

REC'D JUN 24

$ 1,358.00 No. 2456
Date July 2 20--
To Candlelight Software
For on account

	Dollars	Cents
Balance brought forward	8,248	00
Add deposits		
Total	8,248	00
Less this check	1,358	00
Balance carried forward	6,890	00

Candlelight Software
1466 San Diego Avenue
Tacoma, WA 98407

INVOICE NO. CS92
DATE: June 18, 20--
ORDER NO.:
SHIPPED BY: Picked up
TERMS: 3/15, n/30

TO Buzz Newsstand
Union Terminal Bldg., #101
Tacoma, WA 98402

QTY.	ITEM	UNIT PRICE	TOTAL
40	Travel planning software	$25.00	$1,000.00
80	Entertainment software	5.00	400.00
			$1,400.00

Date to be paid: 7/2
Discount: $42.00
Amount to be paid: $1,358.00
Check No.: 2456

REC'D JUN 20

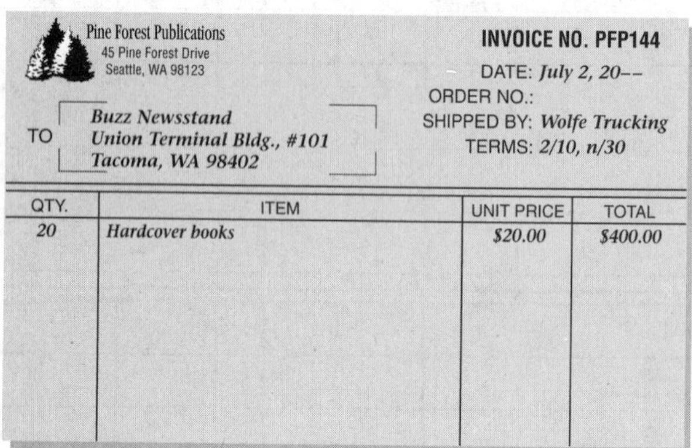

Pine Forest Publications
45 Pine Forest Drive
Seattle, WA 98123

INVOICE NO. PFP144
DATE: July 2, 20--
ORDER NO.:
SHIPPED BY: Wolfe Trucking
TERMS: 2/10, n/30

TO Buzz Newsstand
Union Terminal Bldg., #101
Tacoma, WA 98402

QTY.	ITEM	UNIT PRICE	TOTAL
20	Hardcover books	$20.00	$400.00

$ 350.00 No. 2457
Date July 4 20--
To Nomad Computer Sales
For on account

	Dollars	Cents
Balance brought forward	6,890	00
Add deposits		
Total	6,890	00
Less this check	350	00
Balance carried forward	6,540	00

CorpTech Office Supply
818 McCain Street
Tacoma, WA 98402

INVOICE NO. CT67
DATE: July 5, 20--
ORDER NO.:
SHIPPED BY: Picked up
TERMS: n/30

TO Buzz Newsstand
Union Terminal Bldg., #101
Tacoma, WA 98402

QTY.	ITEM	UNIT PRICE	TOTAL
5	Bookshelves	$300.00	$1,500.00
2	Book racks	193.00	386.00
			$1,886.00
		TX	114.00
			$2,000.00

$ 125.00 No. 2458
Date July 7 20--
To Wolfe Trucking
For transportation charges

	Dollars	Cents
Balance brought forward	6,540	00
Add deposits 7/5	1,000	00
Total	7,540	00
Less this check	125	00
Balance carried forward	7,415	00

Problem 17-8 (continued)

American Trend Publishers
766 Goldrush Way
Denver, CO 80207

INVOICE NO. ATP98
DATE: *July 9, 20--*
ORDER NO.:
SHIPPED BY: *Wolfe Trucking*
TERMS: *2/10, n/30*

TO *Buzz Newsstand*
Union Terminal Bldg., #101
Tacoma, WA 98402

QTY.	ITEM	UNIT PRICE	TOTAL
250	Paperback books	$2.00	$500.00
800	Newspapers	.50	400.00
			$900.00

	Dollars	Cents
$ 882.00		No. 2461
Date July 16 20--		
To American Trend Publishers		
For on account (900 less 2% disc.)		
Balance brought forward	7,265	00
Add deposits		
Total	7,265	00
Less this check	882	00
Balance carried forward	6,383	00

CorpTech Office Supply
818 McCain Street
Tacoma, WA 98402

INVOICE NO. CT72
DATE: *July 12, 20--*
ORDER NO.:
SHIPPED BY: *Picked up*
TERMS: *n/30*

TO *Buzz Newsstand*
Union Terminal Bldg., #101
Tacoma, WA 98402

QTY.	ITEM	UNIT PRICE	TOTAL
2 cs	Office paper	$66.50/cs	$133.00
3	Inkjet ink cartridges	50.00/ea	150.00
			$283.00
			TX 17.00
			$300.00

Candlelight Software
1466 San Diego Avenue
Tacoma, WA 98407

INVOICE NO. CS101
DATE: *July 18, 20--*
ORDER NO.:
SHIPPED BY: *Picked up*
TERMS: *n/30*

TO *Buzz Newsstand*
Union Terminal Bldg., #101
Tacoma, WA 98402

QTY.	ITEM	UNIT PRICE	TOTAL
100	Entertainment software	$5.00	$500.00

	Dollars	Cents
$ 750.00		No. 2459
Date July 14 20--		
To Delta Press		
For on account		
Balance brought forward	7,415	00
Add deposits		
Total	7,415	00
Less this check	750	00
Balance carried forward	6,665	00

Nomad COMPUTER SALES
1601 San Diego Avenue
Tacoma, WA 98407

INVOICE NO. NC56
DATE: *July 20, 20--*
ORDER NO.:
SHIPPED BY: *Picked up*
TERMS: *2/10, n/30*

TO *Buzz Newsstand*
Union Terminal Bldg., #101
Tacoma, WA 98402

QTY.	ITEM	UNIT PRICE	TOTAL
20	Pocket electronic organizers	$10.00	$200.00

	Dollars	Cents
$ 1,600.00		No. 2460
Date July 15 20--		
To SeaTac Insurance Co.		
For prepaid insurance		
Balance brought forward	6,665	00
Add deposits 7/15	2,200	00
Total	8,865	00
Less this check	1,600	00
Balance carried forward	7,265	00

	Dollars	Cents
$ 100.00		No. 2462
Date July 22 20--		
To Pine Forest Publications		
For on account		
Balance brought forward	6,383	00
Add deposits 7/18	1,500	00
7/20	2,000	00
Total	9,883	00
Less this check	100	00
Balance carried forward	9,783	00

Problem 17-8 (continued)

$ 2,000.00		No. 2463
Date July 23		20--
To CorpTech Office Supply		
For on account		
	Dollars	Cents
Balance brought forward	9,783	00
Add deposits		
Total	9,783	00
Less this check	2,000	00
Balance carried forward	7,783	00

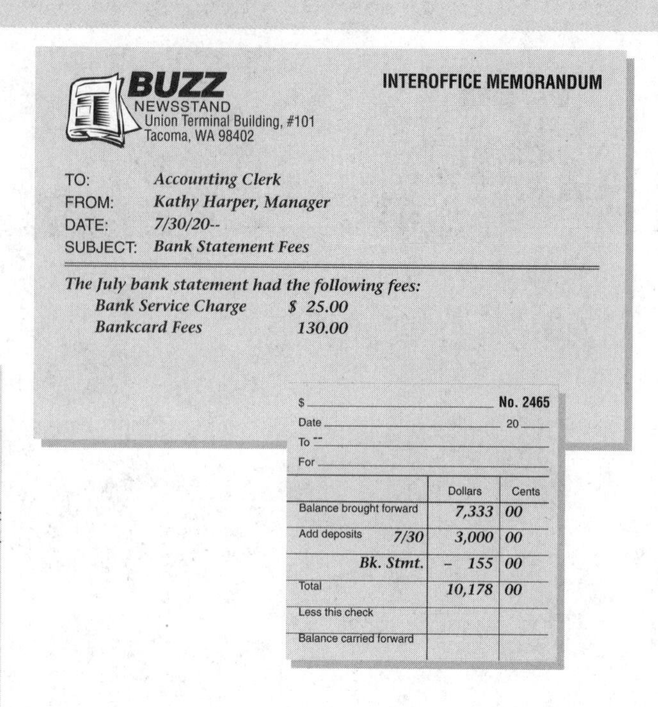
BUZZ NEWSSTAND
Union Terminal Building, #101
Tacoma, WA 98402

INTEROFFICE MEMORANDUM

TO: *Accounting Clerk*
FROM: *Kathy Harper, Manager*
DATE: *7/30/20--*
SUBJECT: *Bank Statement Fees*

The July bank statement had the following fees:

Bank Service Charge	*$ 25.00*
Bankcard Fees	*130.00*

$		No. 2465
Date		20
To --		
For		
	Dollars	Cents
Balance brought forward	7,333	00
Add deposits 7/30	3,000	00
Bk. Stmt.	– 155	00
Total	10,178	00
Less this check		
Balance carried forward		

ADC PUBLISHING
14003 Chen Street
San Francisco, CA 94122

INVOICE NO. ADC70
DATE: *July 25, 20--*
ORDER NO.:
SHIPPED BY: *Express Shipping*
TERMS: *2/10, n/30*

TO *Buzz Newsstand*
Union Terminal Bldg., #101
Tacoma, WA 98402

QTY.	ITEM	UNIT PRICE	TOTAL
800	Newspapers	$ .50	$400.00
100	Paperback books	2.00	200.00
			$600.00

$ 450.00		No. 2464
Date July 28		20--
To Nomad Computer Sales		
For on account		
	Dollars	Cents
Balance brought forward	7,783	00
Add deposits		
Total	7,783	00
Less this check	450	00
Balance carried forward	7,333	00

Name Date Class

Problem 17-8 (continued)

(1), (3), (4)

CASH PAYMENTS JOURNAL

PAGE ____

	DATE	DOC. NO.	ACCOUNT NAME	POST. REF.	GENERAL DEBIT	GENERAL CREDIT	ACCOUNTS PAYABLE DEBIT	PURCHASES DISCOUNTS CREDIT	CASH IN BANK CREDIT	
1										1
2										2
3										3
4										4
5										5
6										6
7										7
8										8
9										9
10										10
11										11
12										12
13										13
14										14
15										15
16										16
17										17
18										18
19										19
20										20
21										21
22										22

Name Date Class

Problem 17-8 (continued)

(1), (3), (4)

PURCHASES JOURNAL PAGE ______

	DATE	INVOICE NO.	CREDITOR'S ACCOUNT CREDITED	POST. REF.	ACCOUNTS PAYABLE CREDIT	PURCHASES DEBIT	GENERAL ACCOUNT DEBITED	GENERAL POST. REF.	GENERAL DEBIT	
1										1
2										2
3										3
4										4
5										5
6										6
7										7
8										8
9										9
10										10
11										11
12										12
13										13
14										14
15										15
16										16
17										17
18										18
19										19
20										20
21										21
22										22

Name Date Class

Problem 17-8 (continued)

(5), (6)

GENERAL LEDGER (PARTIAL)

ACCOUNT *Cash in Bank* ACCOUNT NO. *101*

DATE		DESCRIPTION	POST. REF.	DEBIT	CREDIT	BALANCE DEBIT	BALANCE CREDIT
20--							
July	1	Balance	✓			900000	
	30		CR12	1050000		1950000	

ACCOUNT *Supplies* ACCOUNT NO. *135*

DATE		DESCRIPTION	POST. REF.	DEBIT	CREDIT	BALANCE DEBIT	BALANCE CREDIT
20--							
July	1	Balance	✓			15000	

ACCOUNT *Prepaid Insurance* ACCOUNT NO. *140*

DATE		DESCRIPTION	POST. REF.	DEBIT	CREDIT	BALANCE DEBIT	BALANCE CREDIT

ACCOUNT *Store Equipment* ACCOUNT NO. *150*

DATE		DESCRIPTION	POST. REF.	DEBIT	CREDIT	BALANCE DEBIT	BALANCE CREDIT
20--							
July	1	Balance	✓			600000	

ACCOUNT *Accounts Payable* ACCOUNT NO. *201*

DATE		DESCRIPTION	POST. REF.	DEBIT	CREDIT	BALANCE DEBIT	BALANCE CREDIT
20--							
July	1	Balance	✓				570000

Problem 17-8 (continued)

ACCOUNT *Purchases* ACCOUNT NO. *501*

DATE		DESCRIPTION	POST. REF.	DEBIT	CREDIT	BALANCE DEBIT	BALANCE CREDIT
20--							
July	1	Balance	✓			2500000	

ACCOUNT *Transportation In* ACCOUNT NO. *505*

DATE		DESCRIPTION	POST. REF.	DEBIT	CREDIT	BALANCE DEBIT	BALANCE CREDIT
20--							
July	1	Balance	✓			80000	

ACCOUNT *Purchases Discounts* ACCOUNT NO. *510*

DATE		DESCRIPTION	POST. REF.	DEBIT	CREDIT	BALANCE DEBIT	BALANCE CREDIT
20--							
July	1	Balance	✓				160000

ACCOUNT *Bankcard Fees Expense* ACCOUNT NO. *605*

DATE		DESCRIPTION	POST. REF.	DEBIT	CREDIT	BALANCE DEBIT	BALANCE CREDIT
20--							
July	1	Balance	✓			110000	

ACCOUNT *Miscellaneous Expense* ACCOUNT NO. *650*

DATE		DESCRIPTION	POST. REF.	DEBIT	CREDIT	BALANCE DEBIT	BALANCE CREDIT
20--							
July	1	Balance	✓			20000	

Problem 17-8 (continued)

(2)

ACCOUNTS PAYABLE SUBSIDIARY LEDGER

Name *ADC Publishing*

Address *5670 Mulberry Place, Seattle, WA 98101*

DATE		DESCRIPTION	POST. REF.	DEBIT	CREDIT	BALANCE
20--						
July	*1*	*Balance*	✓			*1600 00*

Name *American Trend Publishers*

Address *1313 Maple Drive, Seattle, WA 98148*

DATE		DESCRIPTION	POST. REF.	DEBIT	CREDIT	BALANCE

Name *Candlelight Software*

Address *Six Evergreen Park, Tacoma, WA 98402*

DATE		DESCRIPTION	POST. REF.	DEBIT	CREDIT	BALANCE
20--						
July	*1*	*Balance*	✓			*1400 00*

Name *CorpTech Office Supply*

Address *601 Cascade Park, Bellevue, WA 98009*

DATE		DESCRIPTION	POST. REF.	DEBIT	CREDIT	BALANCE

Problem 17-8 (continued)

Name *Delta Press*

Address *One Triangle Park, Vancouver, WA 98661*

DATE		DESCRIPTION	POST. REF.	DEBIT	CREDIT	BALANCE
20--						
July	1	Balance	✓			1500 00

Name *Nomad Computer Sales*

Address *16 Point Drive, Ft. Lewis, WA 98433*

DATE		DESCRIPTION	POST. REF.	DEBIT	CREDIT	BALANCE
20--						
July	1	Balance	✓			1200 00

Name *Pine Forest Publications*

Address *103 Mt. Thor Road, Spokane, WA 99210*

DATE		DESCRIPTION	POST. REF.	DEBIT	CREDIT	BALANCE

Name Date Class

Problem 17-8 (concluded)

(7)

(8)

Analyze:

Name Date Class

Notes

Name Date Class

CHAPTER 18 Adjustments and the Ten-Column Work Sheet

Study Guide

Section Assessment

Section 1 *Read Section 1 on pages 521–525 and complete the following exercises on page 526.*

- ☐ Reinforce the Main Idea
- ☐ Math for Accounting
- ☐ Problem 18-1 *Analyzing the Adjustment for Merchandise Inventory*

Section 2 *Read Section 2 on pages 527–530 and complete the following exercises on page 531.*

- ☐ Reinforce the Main Idea
- ☐ Math for Accounting
- ☐ Problem 18-2 *Analyzing Adjustments*

Section 3 *Read Section 3 on pages 532–539 and complete the following exercises on page 540.*

- ☐ Reinforce the Main Idea
- ☐ Math for Accounting
- ☐ Problem 18-3 *Analyzing the Work Sheet*
- ☐ Problem 18-4 *Analyzing a Source Document*

Chapter Assessment

Summary *Review the Chapter 18 Visual Summary on page 541 in your textbook.*

- ☐ Key Concepts

Review and Activities *Complete the following questions and exercises on page 542 in your textbook.*

- ☐ After You Read: Answering the Essential Question
- ☐ Vocabulary Check
- ☐ Concept Check

Standardized Test Practice *Complete the exercises on page 543 in your textbook.*

Computerized Accounting *Read the Computerized Accounting information on page 544 in your textbook.*

- ☐ Making the Transition from a Manual to a Computerized System

Problems *Complete the following End-of-Chapter Problems for Chapter 18 in your textbook.*

- ☐ Problem 18-5 *Completing a Ten-Column Work Sheet*
- ☐ Problem 18-6 *Completing a Ten-Column Work Sheet*
- ☐ Problem 18-7 *Completing a Ten-Column Work Sheet*
- ☐ Problem 18-8 *Completing a Ten-Column Work Sheet*

Challenge Problem

- ☐ Problem 18-9 *Locating Errors on the Work Sheet*

Real-World Applications and Connections *Complete the following applications on pages 550–551 in your textbook.*

- ☐ Case Study
- ☐ 21st Century Skills
- ☐ Spotlight on Personal Finance
- ☐ Analyzing Financial Reports
- ☐ H.O.T. Audit

Name _______________ Date _______ Class _______

Working Papers *for Section Problems*

Problem 18-1 Analyzing the Adjustment for Merchandise Inventory *(textbook p. 526)*

1. ______________________________
2. ______________________________
3. ______________________________
4. ______________________________

Problem 18-2 Analyzing Adjustments *(textbook p. 531)*

1. Amount of Adjustment ______________
   Account Debited ______________
   Account Credited ______________
2. Amount of Adjustment ______________
   Account Debited ______________
   Account Credited ______________
3. Amount of Adjustment ______________
   Account Debited ______________
   Account Credited ______________

Problem 18-3 Analyzing the Work Sheet *(textbook p. 540)*

1. Amount? ______________
2. Section? ______________
3. Amount? ______________
4. Amount? ______________

Problem 18-4 Analyzing a Source Document *(textbook p. 540)*

1. ______________________________
2. ______________________________
3. ______________________________
4. ______________________________
5. ______________________________

Name Date Class

Notes

Name Date Class

Working Papers *for End-of-Chapter Problems*

Problem 18-5 Completing a Ten-Column Work Sheet *(textbook p. 545)*

InBeat

Work

For the Month Ended

	ACCT. NO.	ACCOUNT NAME	TRIAL BALANCE		ADJUSTMENTS	
			DEBIT	CREDIT	DEBIT	CREDIT
1	101	Cash in Bank	14974 00			
2	115	Accounts Receivable	3774 00			
3	130	Merchandise Inventory	86897 00			
4	135	Supplies	2940 00			
5	140	Prepaid Insurance	1975 00			
6	150	Office Equipment	10819 00			
7	201	Accounts Payable		7740 00		
8	207	Fed. Corporate Income Tax Pay.				
9	210	Employees' Fed. Inc. Tax Pay.		291 00		
10	211	Employees' State Inc. Tax Pay.		86 00		
11	212	Social Security Tax Payable		106 00		
12	213	Medicare Tax Payable		21 00		
13	215	Fed. Unemployment Tax Pay.		32 00		
14	216	State Unemployment Tax Pay.		106 00		
15	217	Sales Tax Payable		1370 00		
16	301	Capital Stock		55000 00		
17	305	Retained Earnings		30928 00		
18	310	Income Summary				
19	401	Sales		149136 00		
20	501	Purchases	93874 00			
21	625	Fed. Corporate Income Tax Exp.	2200 00			
22	630	Insurance Expense				
23	647	Payroll Tax Expense	2170 00			
24	650	Miscellaneous Expense	3662 00			
25	655	Rent Expense	9225 00			
26	660	Salaries Expense	12306 00			
27	665	Supplies Expense				
28						
29			244816 00	244816 00		
30						
31						
32						
33						

CD Shop

Sheet

August 31, 20--

ADJUSTED TRIAL BALANCE		INCOME STATEMENT		BALANCE SHEET		
DEBIT	CREDIT	DEBIT	CREDIT	DEBIT	CREDIT	
						1
						2
						3
						4
						5
						6
						7
						8
						9
						10
						11
						12
						13
						14
						15
						16
						17
						18
						19
						20
						21
						22
						23
						24
						25
						26
						27
						28
						29
						30
						31
						32
						33

Analyze:

Name Date Class

Problem 18-6 Completing a Ten-Column Work Sheet *(textbook p. 545)*

Shutterbug
Work
For the Month Ended

	ACCT. NO.	ACCOUNT NAME	TRIAL BALANCE DEBIT	TRIAL BALANCE CREDIT	ADJUSTMENTS DEBIT	ADJUSTMENTS CREDIT
1	101	Cash in Bank				
2	115	Accounts Receivable				
3	125	Merchandise Inventory				
4	130	Supplies				
5	135	Prepaid Insurance				
6	140	Store Equipment				
7	201	Accounts Payable				
8	207	Fed. Corporate Income Tax Pay.				
9	210	Employees' Fed. Inc. Tax Pay.				
10	211	Employees' State Inc. Tax Pay.				
11	212	Social Security Tax Payable				
12	213	Medicare Tax Payable				
13	215	Sales Tax Payable				
14	216	Fed. Unemployment Tax Pay.				
15	217	State Unemployment Tax Pay.				
16	301	Capital Stock				
17	305	Retained Earnings				
18	310	Income Summary				
19	401	Sales				
20	405	Sales Discounts				
21	410	Sales Returns and Allowances				
22	501	Purchases				
23	505	Transportation In				
24	510	Purchases Discounts				
25	515	Purchases Returns and Allow.				
26	601	Advertising Expense				
27	605	Bankcard Fees Expense				
28	620	Fed. Corporate Income Tax Exp.				
29		Carried Forward				
30						
31						
32						

Cameras

Sheet

August 31, 20--

ADJUSTED TRIAL BALANCE		INCOME STATEMENT		BALANCE SHEET		
DEBIT	CREDIT	DEBIT	CREDIT	DEBIT	CREDIT	
						1
						2
						3
						4
						5
						6
						7
						8
						9
						10
						11
						12
						13
						14
						15
						16
						17
						18
						19
						20
						21
						22
						23
						24
						25
						26
						27
						28
						29
						30
						31
						32

Name Date Class

Problem 18-6 (concluded)

Shutterbug
Work Sheet
For the Month Ended

	ACCT. NO.	ACCOUNT NAME	TRIAL BALANCE DEBIT	TRIAL BALANCE CREDIT	ADJUSTMENTS DEBIT	ADJUSTMENTS CREDIT
1		*Brought Forward*				
2						
3	*630*	*Insurance Expense*				
4	*640*	*Maintenance Expense*				
5	*645*	*Miscellaneous Expense*				
6	*647*	*Payroll Tax Expense*				
7	*650*	*Rent Expense*				
8	*655*	*Salaries Expense*				
9	*660*	*Supplies Expense*				
10	*670*	*Utilities Expense*				
11						
12						
13						
14						
15						
16						
17						
18						
19						
20						
21						
22						
23						
24						
25						
26						
27						
28						
29						
30						
31						
32						

Cameras

(continued)

August 31, 20--

ADJUSTED TRIAL BALANCE		INCOME STATEMENT		BALANCE SHEET		
DEBIT	CREDIT	DEBIT	CREDIT	DEBIT	CREDIT	
						1
						2
						3
						4
						5
						6
						7
						8
						9
						10
						11
						12
						13
						14
						15
						16
						17
						18
						19
						20
						21
						22
						23
						24
						25
						26
						27
						28
						29
						30
						31
						32

Analyze:

Name Date Class

Problem 18-7 Completing a Ten-Column Work Sheet *(textbook p. 547)*

Cycle Tech

Work

For the Month Ended

	ACCT. NO.	ACCOUNT NAME	TRIAL BALANCE DEBIT	TRIAL BALANCE CREDIT	ADJUSTMENTS DEBIT	ADJUSTMENTS CREDIT
1	101	Cash in Bank				
2	115	Accounts Receivable				
3	125	Merchandise Inventory				
4	130	Supplies				
5	135	Prepaid Insurance				
6	140	Store Equipment				
7	145	Office Equipment				
8	201	Accounts Payable				
9	210	Fed. Corporate Income Tax Pay.				
10	211	Employees' Fed. Inc. Tax Pay.				
11	212	Employees' State Inc. Tax Pay.				
12	213	Social Security Tax Payable				
13	214	Medicare Tax Payable				
14	215	Sales Tax Payable				
15	216	Fed. Unemployment Tax Pay.				
16	217	State Unemployment Tax Pay.				
17	301	Capital Stock				
18	305	Retained Earnings				
19	310	Income Summary				
20	401	Sales				
21	405	Sales Discounts				
22	410	Sales Returns and Allowances				
23	501	Purchases				
24	505	Transportation In				
25	510	Purchases Discounts				
26	515	Purchases Returns and Allow.				
27	601	Advertising Expense				
28	605	Bankcard Fees Expense				
29		Carried Forward				
30						
31						
32						

Name Date Class

Bicycles

Sheet

August 31, 20--

ADJUSTED TRIAL BALANCE		INCOME STATEMENT		BALANCE SHEET		
DEBIT	CREDIT	DEBIT	CREDIT	DEBIT	CREDIT	
						1
						2
						3
						4
						5
						6
						7
						8
						9
						10
						11
						12
						13
						14
						15
						16
						17
						18
						19
						20
						21
						22
						23
						24
						25
						26
						27
						28
						29
						30
						31
						32

Name Date Class

Problem 18-7 (concluded)

Cycle Tech
Work Sheet
For the Month Ended

	ACCT. NO.	ACCOUNT NAME	TRIAL BALANCE DEBIT	TRIAL BALANCE CREDIT	ADJUSTMENTS DEBIT	ADJUSTMENTS CREDIT
1		*Brought Forward*				
2						
3	625	*Fed. Corporate Income Tax Exp.*				
4	630	*Insurance Expense*				
5	645	*Maintenance Expense*				
6	650	*Miscellaneous Expense*				
7	655	*Payroll Tax Expense*				
8	657	*Rent Expense*				
9	660	*Salaries Expense*				
10	665	*Supplies Expense*				
11	675	*Utilities Expense*				
12						
13						
14						
15						
16						
17						
18						
19						
20						
21						
22						
23						
24						
25						
26						
27						
28						
29						
30						
31						
32						

Name Date Class

Bicycles

(continued)

August 31, 20--

ADJUSTED TRIAL BALANCE		INCOME STATEMENT		BALANCE SHEET		
DEBIT	CREDIT	DEBIT	CREDIT	DEBIT	CREDIT	
						1
						2
						3
						4
						5
						6
						7
						8
						9
						10
						11
						12
						13
						14
						15
						16
						17
						18
						19
						20
						21
						22
						23
						24
						25
						26
						27
						28
						29
						30
						31
						32

Analyze:

Name Date Class

Problem 18-8 Completing a Ten-Column Work Sheet *(textbook p. 548)*

(1)

River's Edge

Work

For the Year Ended

	ACCT. NO.	ACCOUNT NAME	TRIAL BALANCE DEBIT	TRIAL BALANCE CREDIT	ADJUSTMENTS DEBIT	ADJUSTMENTS CREDIT
1	*101*	*Cash in Bank*				
2	*115*	*Accounts Receivable*				
3	*130*	*Merchandise Inventory*				
4	*135*	*Supplies*				
5	*140*	*Prepaid Insurance*				
6	*145*	*Delivery Equipment*				
7	*150*	*Store Equipment*				
8	*201*	*Accounts Payable*				
9	*204*	*Fed. Corporate Income Tax Pay.*				
10	*210*	*Employees' Fed. Inc. Tax Pay.*				
11	*211*	*Employees' State Inc. Tax Pay.*				
12	*212*	*Social Security Tax Payable*				
13	*213*	*Medicare Tax Payable*				
14	*215*	*Sales Tax Payable*				
15	*216*	*Fed. Unemployment Tax Pay.*				
16	*217*	*State Unemployment Tax Pay.*				
17	*219*	*U.S. Savings Bonds Pay.*				
18	*301*	*Capital Stock*				
19	*305*	*Retained Earnings*				
20	*310*	*Income Summary*				
21	*401*	*Sales*				
22	*405*	*Sales Discounts*				
23	*410*	*Sales Returns and Allowances*				
24	*501*	*Purchases*				
25	*505*	*Transportation In*				
26	*510*	*Purchases Discounts*				
27	*515*	*Purchases Returns and Allow.*				
28	*601*	*Advertising Expense*				
29		*Carried Forward*				
30						
31						
32						

Name Date Class

Canoe & Kayak

Sheet

August 31, 20--

ADJUSTED TRIAL BALANCE		INCOME STATEMENT		BALANCE SHEET		
DEBIT	CREDIT	DEBIT	CREDIT	DEBIT	CREDIT	
						1
						2
						3
						4
						5
						6
						7
						8
						9
						10
						11
						12
						13
						14
						15
						16
						17
						18
						19
						20
						21
						22
						23
						24
						25
						26
						27
						28
						29
						30
						31
						32

Name Date Class

Problem 18-8 (continued)

River's Edge
Work Sheet
For the Year Ended

	ACCT. NO.	ACCOUNT NAME	TRIAL BALANCE DEBIT	TRIAL BALANCE CREDIT	ADJUSTMENTS DEBIT	ADJUSTMENTS CREDIT
1		*Brought Forward*				
2						
3	*605*	*Bankcard Fees Expense*				
4	*625*	*Fed. Corporate Income Tax Exp.*				
5	*635*	*Insurance Expense*				
6	*650*	*Maintenance Expense*				
7	*655*	*Miscellaneous Expense*				
8	*658*	*Payroll Tax Expense*				
9	*660*	*Rent Expense*				
10	*665*	*Salaries Expense*				
11	*670*	*Supplies Expense*				
12	*680*	*Utilities Expense*				
13						
14						
15						
16						
17						
18						
19						
20						
21						
22						
23						
24						
25						
26						
27						
28						
29						
30						
31						
32						

Name Date Class

Canoe & Kayak

(continued)

August 31, 20--

ADJUSTED TRIAL BALANCE		INCOME STATEMENT		BALANCE SHEET		
DEBIT	CREDIT	DEBIT	CREDIT	DEBIT	CREDIT	
						1
						2
						3
						4
						5
						6
						7
						8
						9
						10
						11
						12
						13
						14
						15
						16
						17
						18
						19
						20
						21
						22
						23
						24
						25
						26
						27
						28
						29
						30
						31
						32

Name Date Class

Problem 18-8 (continued)

(2)

GENERAL JOURNAL PAGE ____

	DATE		DESCRIPTION	POST. REF.	DEBIT	CREDIT	
1							1
2							2
3							3
4							4
5							5
6							6
7							7
8							8
9							9
10							10
11							11
12							12

(3)

GENERAL LEDGER

ACCOUNT *Merchandise Inventory* ACCOUNT NO. *130*

DATE		DESCRIPTION	POST. REF.	DEBIT	CREDIT	BALANCE DEBIT	BALANCE CREDIT
20--							
Aug.	*1*	*Balance*	✓			*49,205 00*	

ACCOUNT *Supplies* ACCOUNT NO. *135*

DATE		DESCRIPTION	POST. REF.	DEBIT	CREDIT	BALANCE DEBIT	BALANCE CREDIT
20--							
Aug.	*1*	*Balance*	✓			*3,027 00*	

ACCOUNT *Prepaid Insurance* ACCOUNT NO. *140*

DATE		DESCRIPTION	POST. REF.	DEBIT	CREDIT	BALANCE DEBIT	BALANCE CREDIT
20--							
Aug.	*1*	*Balance*	✓			*1,680 00*	

Problem 18-8 (concluded)

ACCOUNT *Federal Corporate Income Tax Payable* ACCOUNT NO. *204*

DATE		DESCRIPTION	POST. REF.	DEBIT	CREDIT	BALANCE DEBIT	BALANCE CREDIT

ACCOUNT *Income Summary* ACCOUNT NO. *310*

DATE		DESCRIPTION	POST. REF.	DEBIT	CREDIT	BALANCE DEBIT	BALANCE CREDIT

ACCOUNT *Federal Corporate Income Tax Expense* ACCOUNT NO. *625*

DATE		DESCRIPTION	POST. REF.	DEBIT	CREDIT	BALANCE DEBIT	BALANCE CREDIT
20--							
Aug.	*1*	*Balance*	✓			*2480 00*	

ACCOUNT *Insurance Expense* ACCOUNT NO. *635*

DATE		DESCRIPTION	POST. REF.	DEBIT	CREDIT	BALANCE DEBIT	BALANCE CREDIT

ACCOUNT *Supplies Expense* ACCOUNT NO. *670*

DATE		DESCRIPTION	POST. REF.	DEBIT	CREDIT	BALANCE DEBIT	BALANCE CREDIT

Analyze:

Name Date Class

Problem 18-9 Locating Errors on the Work Sheet *(textbook p. 549)*

Buzz Newsstand

Work Sheet

For the Month Ended August 31, 20--

	ACCT. NO.	ACCOUNT NAME	TRIAL BALANCE DEBIT	TRIAL BALANCE CREDIT	ADJUSTMENTS DEBIT	ADJUSTMENTS CREDIT
1	101	Cash in Bank	8131 00			
2	115	Accounts Receivable	363 00			
3	130	Merchandise Inventory	5120 00			(a) 12950 00
4	135	Supplies	974 00			(b) 454 00
5	140	Prepaid Insurance	980 00			(c) 245 00
6	145	Delivery Equipment	7600 00			
7	150	Store Equipment	2854 00			
8	201	Accounts Payable		4515 00		
9	204	Fed. Corporate Income Tax Pay.		—		(d) 249 00
10	210	Employees' Fed. Inc. Tax Pay.		149 00		
11	211	Employees' State Inc. Tax Pay.	26 00			
12	215	Sales Tax Payable		421 00		
13	216	Social Security Tax Payable		79 00		
14	217	Medicare Tax Payable		10 00		
15	301	Capital Stock		25000 00		
16	305	Retained Earnings		5120 00		
17	310	Income Summary	—	—	(a) 12950 00	
18	401	Sales		11034 00		
19	410	Sales Returns and Allowances		126 00		
20	501	Purchases	16819 00			
21	510	Purchases Discounts		—		
22	515	Purchases Returns and Allow.		246 00		
23	601	Advertising Expense	125 00			
24	625	Fed. Corporate Income Tax Exp.	—		(d) 249 00	
25	635	Insurance Expense	—		(c) 245 00	
26	650	Miscellaneous Expense	45 00			
27	655	Rent Expense	1700 00			
28	657	Payroll Tax Expense	156 00			
29	660	Salaries Expense	1265 00			
30	665	Supplies Expense	—			
31	675	Utilities Expense	342 00			
32			41380 00	41580 00		
33		Corrected TOTALS				

Analyze:

Name Date Class

CHAPTER 19 Financial Statements for a Corporation

Study Guide

Section Assessment

Section 1 *Read Section 1 on pages 555–558 and complete the following exercises on page 559.*

- ☐ Reinforce the Main Idea
- ☐ Math for Accounting
- ☐ Problem 19-1 *Analyzing Stockholders' Equity Accounts*
- ☐ Problem 19-2 *Analyzing a Source Document*

Section 2 *Read Section 2 on pages 560–566 and complete the following exercises on page 567.*

- ☐ Reinforce the Main Idea
- ☐ Math for Accounting
- ☐ Problem 19-3 *Calculating Amounts on the Income Statement*

Section 3 *Read Section 3 on pages 568–573 and complete the following exercises on page 574.*

- ☐ Reinforce the Main Idea
- ☐ Math for Accounting
- ☐ Problem 19-4 *Analyzing a Balance Sheet*

Chapter Assessment

Summary *Review the Chapter 19 Visual Summary on page 575 in your textbook.*

- ☐ Key Concepts

Review and Activities *Complete the following questions and exercises on page 576 in your textbook.*

- ☐ After You Read: Answering the Essential Question
- ☐ Vocabulary Check
- ☐ Concept Check

Standardized Test Practice *Complete the exercises on page 577 in your textbook.*

Computerized Accounting *Read the Computerized Accounting information on page 578 in your textbook.*

- ☐ Making the Transition from a Manual to a Computerized System

Problems *Complete the following End-of-Chapter Problems for Chapter 19 in your textbook.*

- ☐ Problem 19-5 *Preparing an Income Statement*
- ☐ Problem 19-6 *Preparing a Statement of Retained Earnings and a Balance Sheet*
- ☐ Problem 19-7 *Preparing Financial Statements*
- ☐ Problem 19-8 *Completing a Work Sheet and Financial Statements*

Challenge Problem

- ☐ Problem 19-9 *Evaluating the Effect of an Error on the Income Statement*

Real-World Applications and Connections *Complete the following applications on pages 582–583 in your textbook.*

- ☐ Career Wise
- ☐ Global Accounting
- ☐ A Matter of Ethics
- ☐ Analyzing Financial Reports
- ☐ H.O.T. Audit

Name Date Class

Working Papers *for Section Problems*

Problem 19-1 Analyzing Stockholders' Equity Accounts *(textbook p. 559)*

1. ______________________
2. ______________________
3. ______________________

Problem 19-2 Analyzing a Source Document *(textbook p. 559)*

Cindy's Curtains
432 Meadowbrook Street
Wilcoxson, GA 30345-8417
404-555-2488

DATE: June 26, 20-- NO. 1441

SOLD TO	Rachel C. Washington 59 Priscilla Drive Park Ridge, IL 60068		
CLERK K.C.	CASH ✓	CHARGE	TERMS

QTY.	DESCRIPTION	UNIT PRICE	AMOUNT	
2	Curtain Rods #21847	$ 14.95	$ 29	09
4	Anchor Pieces #23104	6.75	27	00
15	Feet of ribbon/per ft.	.89	13	00
		SUBTOTAL	$ 69	09
		SALES TAX	2	76
		TOTAL	$ 71	85

Thank You!

Name ____________________ Date __________ Class __________

Problem 19-3 Calculating Amounts on the Income Statement *(textbook p. 567)*

1. Cost of merchandise available for sale ____________

2. Gross profit on sales ____________

3. Cost of delivered merchandise ____________

4. Cost of merchandise sold ____________

Problem 19-4 Analyzing a Balance Sheet *(textbook p. 574)*

1. ____________

2. ____________

3. ____________

4. ____________

5. ____________

6. ____________

Name Date Class

Working Papers *for End-of-Chapter Problems*

Problem 19-5 Preparing an Income Statement *(textbook p. 579)*

Sunset

Work

For the Year Ended

	ACCT. NO.	ACCOUNT NAME	TRIAL BALANCE DEBIT	TRIAL BALANCE CREDIT	ADJUSTMENTS DEBIT	ADJUSTMENTS CREDIT
1	101	Cash in Bank	15274 00			
2	115	Accounts Receivable	4124 00			
3	130	Merchandise Inventory	84097 00			(a) 9025 00
4	135	Supplies	3740 00			(b) 2722 00
5	140	Prepaid Insurance	1584 00			(c) 528 00
6	145	Store Equipment	7231 00			
7	150	Office Equipment	4619 00			
8	201	Accounts Payable		9340 00		
9	204	Fed. Corporate Income Tax Pay.				(d) 122 00
10	205	Employees' Fed. Inc. Tax Pay.		311 00		
11	208	Employees' State Inc. Tax Pay.		89 00		
12	210	Social Security Tax Payable		132 00		
13	211	Medicare Tax Payable		21 00		
14	212	Fed. Unemployment Tax Pay.		37 00		
15	213	State Unemployment Tax Pay.		134 00		
16	215	Sales Tax Payable		2670 00		
17	301	Capital Stock		60000 00		
18	305	Retained Earnings		14920 00		
19	310	Income Summary			(a) 9025 00	
20	401	Sales		137711 00		
21	405	Sales Discounts	2336 00			
22	410	Sales Returns and Allowances	4188 00			
23	501	Purchases	71097 00			
24	505	Transportation In	928 00			
25	510	Purchases Discounts		1823 00		
26	515	Purchases Returns and Allow.		2108 00		
27	601	Advertising Expense	840 00			
28	605	Bankcard Fees Expense	374 00			
29	630	Fed. Corporate Income Tax Exp.	2600 00		(d) 122 00	
30		Carried Forward	203032 00	229296 00	9147 00	12397 00
31						
32						
33						

Name Date Class

Surfwear

Sheet

December 31, 20--

ADJUSTED TRIAL BALANCE		INCOME STATEMENT		BALANCE SHEET		
DEBIT	CREDIT	DEBIT	CREDIT	DEBIT	CREDIT	
15274 00				15274 00		1
4124 00				4124 00		2
75072 00				75072 00		3
1018 00				1018 00		4
1056 00				1056 00		5
7231 00				7231 00		6
4619 00				4619 00		7
	9340 00				9340 00	8
	122 00				122 00	9
	311 00				311 00	10
	89 00				89 00	11
	132 00				132 00	12
	21 00				21 00	13
	37 00				37 00	14
	134 00				134 00	15
	2670 00				2670 00	16
	60000 00				60000 00	17
	14920 00				14920 00	18
9025 00		9025 00				19
	137711 00		137711 00			20
2336 00		2336 00				21
4188 00		4188 00				22
71097 00		71097 00				23
928 00		928 00				24
	1823 00		1823 00			25
	2108 00		2108 00			26
840 00		840 00				27
374 00		374 00				28
2722 00		2722 00				29
199904 00	229418 00	91510 00	141642 00	108394 00	87776 00	30
						31
						32
						33

Name Date Class

Problem 19-5 (continued)

Sunset

Work Sheet

For the Year Ended

	ACCT. NO.	ACCOUNT NAME	TRIAL BALANCE DEBIT	TRIAL BALANCE CREDIT	ADJUSTMENTS DEBIT	ADJUSTMENTS CREDIT
1		*Brought Forward*	203032 00	229296 00	9147 00	12397 00
2						
3	635	*Insurance Expense*			(c) 528 00	
4	645	*Maintenance Expense*	1231 00			
5	650	*Miscellaneous Expense*	2860 00			
6	652	*Payroll Tax Expense*	2170 00			
7	655	*Rent Expense*	9270 00			
8	660	*Salaries Expense*	10733 00			
9	685	*Supplies Expense*			(b) 2722 00	
10			229296 00	229296 00	12397 00	12397 00
11		*Net Income*				
12						
13						
14						
15						
16						
17						
18						
19						
20						
21						
22						
23						
24						
25						
26						
27						
28						
29						
30						
31						
32						
33						

Surfwear

(continued)

December 31, 20--

ADJUSTED TRIAL BALANCE		INCOME STATEMENT		BALANCE SHEET		
DEBIT	CREDIT	DEBIT	CREDIT	DEBIT	CREDIT	
199904 00	229418 00	91510 00	141642 00	108394 00	87776 00	1
						2
528 00		528 00				3
1231 00		1231 00				4
2860 00		2860 00				5
2170 00		2170 00				6
9270 00		9270 00				7
10733 00		10733 00				8
2722 00		2722 00				9
229418 00	229418 00	121024 00	141642 00	108394 00	87776 00	10
		20618 00			20618 00	11
		141642 00	141642 00	108394 00	108394 00	12
						13
						14
						15
						16
						17
						18
						19
						20
						21
						22
						23
						24
						25
						26
						27
						28
						29
						30
						31
						32
						33

Name Date Class

Problem 19-5 (concluded)

Analyze:

Name Date Class

Problem 19-6 Preparing a Statement of Retained Earnings and a Balance Sheet *(textbook p. 579)*

Name Date Class

Problem 19-6 (concluded)

Analyze:

Name Date Class

Notes

Name ____________________ Date ____________________ Class ____________________

Problem 19-7 Preparing Financial Statements *(textbook p. 579)*

(1)

Shutterbug

Work

For the Year Ended

	ACCT. NO.	ACCOUNT NAME	TRIAL BALANCE DEBIT	TRIAL BALANCE CREDIT	ADJUSTMENTS DEBIT	ADJUSTMENTS CREDIT
1	101	Cash in Bank	13603 00			
2	115	Accounts Receivable	5418 00			
3	125	Merchandise Inventory	82763 00			(a) 4451 00
4	130	Supplies	2522 00			(b) 2039 00
5	135	Prepaid Insurance	1350 00			(c) 475 00
6	140	Store Equipment	26769 00			
7	201	Accounts Payable		14481 00		
8	207	Fed. Corporate Income Tax Pay.				(d) 261 00
9	210	Employees' Fed. Inc. Tax Pay.		189 00		
10	211	Employees' State Inc. Tax Pay.		52 00		
11	212	Social Security Tax Payable		138 00		
12	213	Medicare Tax Payable		28 00		
13	215	Sales Tax Payable		891 00		
14	216	Fed. Unemployment Tax Pay.		19 00		
15	217	State Unemployment Tax Pay.		96 00		
16	301	Capital Stock		80000 00		
17	305	Retained Earnings		19192 00		
18	310	Income Summary			(a) 4451 00	
19	401	Sales		92867 00		
20	405	Sales Discounts	105 00			
21	410	Sales Returns and Allowances	885 00			
22	501	Purchases	37491 00			
23	505	Transportation In	1805 00			
24	510	Purchases Discounts		644 00		
25	515	Purchases Returns and Allow.		231 00		
26	601	Advertising Expense	650 00			
27	605	Bankcard Fees Expense	213 00			
28	620	Fed. Corporate Income Tax Exp.	1720 00		(d) 261 00	
29		Carried Forward	175294 00	208828 00	4712 00	7226 00
30						
31						
32						
33						

Name Date Class

Cameras

Sheet

December 31, 20--

Adjusted Trial Balance		Income Statement		Balance Sheet		
Debit	Credit	Debit	Credit	Debit	Credit	
13,603.00						1
5,418.00						2
78,312.00						3
483.00						4
875.00						5
26,769.00						6
	14,481.00					7
	261.00					8
	189.00					9
	52.00					10
	138.00					11
	28.00					12
	891.00					13
	19.00					14
	96.00					15
	80,000.00					16
	19,192.00					17
4,451.00						18
	92,867.00					19
105.00						20
885.00						21
37,491.00						22
1,805.00						23
	644.00					24
	231.00					25
650.00						26
213.00						27
1,981.00						28
173,041.00	209,089.00					29
						30
						31
						32
						33

Problem 19-7 (continued)

Shutterbug
Work Sheet
For the Year Ended

	ACCT. NO.	ACCOUNT NAME	TRIAL BALANCE DEBIT	TRIAL BALANCE CREDIT	ADJUSTMENTS DEBIT	ADJUSTMENTS CREDIT
1		*Brought Forward*	175 294 00	208 828 00	4 712 00	7 226 00
2						
3	630	*Insurance Expense*			(c) 475 00	
4	640	*Maintenance Expense*	2 552 00			
5	645	*Miscellaneous Expense*	285 00			
6	647	*Payroll Tax Expense*	1 920 00			
7	650	*Rent Expense*	9 700 00			
8	655	*Salaries Expense*	18 720 00			
9	660	*Supplies Expense*			(b) 2 039 00	
10	670	*Utilities Expense*	357 00			
11						
12			208 828 00	208 828 00	7 226 00	7 226 00
13						
14						
15						
16						
17						
18						
19						
20						
21						
22						
23						
24						
25						
26						
27						
28						
29						
30						
31						
32						

Cameras

(continued)

December 31, 20--

ADJUSTED TRIAL BALANCE		INCOME STATEMENT		BALANCE SHEET		
DEBIT	CREDIT	DEBIT	CREDIT	DEBIT	CREDIT	
173,041.00	209,089.00					1
						2
475.00						3
2,552.00						4
285.00						5
1,920.00						6
9,700.00						7
18,720.00						8
2,039.00						9
357.00						10
						11
209,089.00	209,089.00					12
						13
						14
						15
						16
						17
						18
						19
						20
						21
						22
						23
						24
						25
						26
						27
						28
						29
						30
						31
						32

Name Date Class

Problem 19-7 (continued)

(2)

Name Date Class

Problem 19-7 (concluded)

(3)

(4)

Analyze:

Name Date Class

Problem 19-8 Completing a Work Sheet and Financial Statements *(textbook p. 580)*

(1)

Cycle Tech
Work
For the Year Ended

	ACCT. NO.	ACCOUNT NAME	TRIAL BALANCE DEBIT	TRIAL BALANCE CREDIT	ADJUSTMENTS DEBIT	ADJUSTMENTS CREDIT
1	101	Cash in Bank	21,931.00			
2	115	Accounts Receivable	1,782.00			
3	125	Merchandise Inventory	24,028.00			
4	130	Supplies	4,159.00			
5	135	Prepaid Insurance	1,800.00			
6	140	Store Equipment	24,895.00			
7	145	Office Equipment	16,113.00			
8	201	Accounts Payable		11,224.00		
9	210	Fed. Corporate Income Tax Pay.				
10	211	Employees' Fed. Inc. Tax Pay.		522.00		
11	212	Employees' State Inc. Tax Pay.		144.00		
12	213	Social Security Tax Payable		413.00		
13	214	Medicare Tax Payable		134.00		
14	215	Sales Tax Payable		1,915.00		
15	216	Fed. Unemployment Tax Pay.		54.00		
16	217	State Unemployment Tax Pay.		271.00		
17	301	Capital Stock		40,000.00		
18	305	Retained Earnings		11,091.00		
19	310	Income Summary				
20	401	Sales		127,151.00		
21	405	Sales Discounts	246.00			
22	410	Sales Returns and Allowances	1,328.00			
23	501	Purchases	66,107.00			
24	505	Transportation In	983.00			
25	510	Purchases Discounts		822.00		
26	515	Purchases Returns and Allow.		376.00		
27	601	Advertising Expense	2,380.00			
28	605	Bankcard Fees Expense	181.00			
29	625	Fed. Corporate Income Tax Exp.	3,340.00			
30		Carried Forward	169,273.00	194,117.00		
31						
32						

Name **Date** **Class**

Bicycles

Sheet

December 31, 20--

ADJUSTED TRIAL BALANCE		INCOME STATEMENT		BALANCE SHEET		
DEBIT	CREDIT	DEBIT	CREDIT	DEBIT	CREDIT	
						1
						2
						3
						4
						5
						6
						7
						8
						9
						10
						11
						12
						13
						14
						15
						16
						17
						18
						19
						20
						21
						22
						23
						24
						25
						26
						27
						28
						29
						30
						31
						32

Name Date Class

Problem 19-8 (continued)

Cycle Tech
Work Sheet
For the Year Ended

	ACCT. NO.	ACCOUNT NAME	TRIAL BALANCE DEBIT	TRIAL BALANCE CREDIT	ADJUSTMENTS DEBIT	ADJUSTMENTS CREDIT
1		*Brought Forward*	169,273.00	194,117.00		
2						
3	630	*Insurance Expense*				
4	645	*Maintenance Expense*	1,950.00			
5	650	*Miscellaneous Expense*	1,831.00			
6	655	*Payroll Tax Expense*	834.00			
7	657	*Rent Expense*	10,800.00			
8	660	*Salaries Expense*	4,734.00			
9	665	*Supplies Expense*				
10	675	*Utilities Expense*	4,695.00			
11						
12			194,117.00	194,117.00		
13						
14						
15						
16						
17						
18						
19						
20						
21						
22						
23						
24						
25						
26						
27						
28						
29						
30						
31						
32						

Name Date Class

Bicycles

(continued)

December 31, 20--

ADJUSTED TRIAL BALANCE		INCOME STATEMENT		BALANCE SHEET		
DEBIT	CREDIT	DEBIT	CREDIT	DEBIT	CREDIT	
						1
						2
						3
						4
						5
						6
						7
						8
						9
						10
						11
						12
						13
						14
						15
						16
						17
						18
						19
						20
						21
						22
						23
						24
						25
						26
						27
						28
						29
						30
						31
						32

Name Date Class

Problem 19-8 (continued)

(2)

Name Date Class

Problem 19-8 (concluded)

(3)

(4)

Analyze:

Problem 19-9 Evaluating the Effect of an Error on the Income Statement *(textbook p. 581)*

River's Edge Canoe & Kayak
Income Statement
For the Year Ended December 31, 20--

Revenue:				
Sales			324784 00	
Less: Sales Discounts		3839 00		
Sales Returns and Allowances		1209 00	5048 00	
Net Sales				319736 00
Cost of Merchandise Sold:				
Merchandise Inventory, Jan. 1, 20--			84921 00	
Purchases	208416 00			
Cost of Delivered Merchandise		208416 00		
Less: Purchases Discounts	9623 00			
Purchases Returns and Allow.	4721 00	14344 00		
Net Purchases			194072 00	
Cost of Merchandise Available			278993 00	
Merchandise Inv., Dec. 31, 20--			81385 00	
Cost of Merchandise Sold				197608 00
Gross Profit on Saless				122128 00
Operating Expenses:				
Advertising Expense			2570 00	
Bankcard Fees Expense			4182 00	
Insurance Expense			275 00	
Maintenance Expense			3552 00	
Miscellaneous Expense			344 00	
Payroll Tax Expense			3824 00	
Rent Expense			15000 00	
Salaries Expense			29381 00	
Supplies Expense			3710 00	
Utilities Expense			2378 00	
Total Operating Expenses				65216 00
Operating Income				56912 00
Less: Fed. Corporate Inc. Tax Exp.				9436 00
Net Income				47476 00

Name Date Class

Problem 19-9 (concluded)

1. ______________________________
2. ______________________________
3. ______________________________
4. ______________________________
5. ______________________________

Analyze: ______________________________

____

Notes

Name Date Class

MINI PRACTICE SET 4

Cordova Electronics

CHART OF ACCOUNTS

ASSETS
101 Cash in Bank
105 Accounts Receivable
110 Merchandise Inventory
115 Supplies
120 Prepaid Insurance
150 Store Equipment
155 Office Equipment

LIABILITIES
201 Accounts Payable
205 Sales Tax Payable
210 Employees' Federal Income Tax Payable
211 Employees' State Income Tax Payable
212 Social Security Tax Payable
213 Medicare Tax Payable
214 Federal Unemployment Tax Payable
215 State Unemployment Tax Payable

STOCKHOLDERS' EQUITY
301 Capital Stock
302 Retained Earnings
303 Income Summary

REVENUE
401 Sales
405 Sales Discounts
410 Sales Returns and Allowances

COST OF MERCHANDISE
501 Purchases
505 Transportation In
510 Purchases Discounts
515 Purchases Returns and Allowances

EXPENSES
605 Advertising Expense
610 Bankcard Fees Expense
615 Miscellaneous Expense
620 Payroll Tax Expense
625 Rent Expense
630 Salaries Expense
635 Utilities Expense

Accounts Receivable Subsidiary Ledger
LOR Sam Lorenzo
MAR Marianne Martino
MCC Mark McCormick
SCO Sue Ellen Scott
TRO Tom Trout

Accounts Payable Subsidiary Ledger
COM Computer Systems Inc.
DES Desktop Wholesalers
HIT Hi-Tech Electronics Outlet
LAS Laser & Ink Jet Products
OFF Office Suppliers Inc.

Name Date Class

Mini Practice Set 4 Source Documents *(textbook p. 584)*

Instructions: *Use the following source documents to record the transactions for this practice set.*

Cardova Electronics
612 Kent Avenue
Brooklyn, NY 11205

DATE: *May 16, 20--* NO. *607*

SOLD TO *Sam Lorenzo*

CLERK	CASH	CHARGE	TERMS

QTY.	DESCRIPTION	UNIT PRICE	AMOUNT
2	*stereo speakers*	*$60.00*	*$120 00*
		SUBTOTAL	*$120 00*
		SALES TAX	*6 00*
		TOTAL	*$126 00*

Thank You!

Cordova Electronics
612 Kent Avenue
Brooklyn, NY 11205

893
74-103/720

DATE *May 19* 20--

PAY TO THE ORDER OF *Computer Systems, Inc.* $ *1,200.00*

One thousand two hundred and 00/100 DOLLARS

UB Union Bank

MEMO *on account* *Pedro Cordova*

⑆0720 0⑆033⑆ 6171 5222 ⑈0893

Cordova Electronics
612 Kent Avenue
Brooklyn, NY 11205

894
74-103/720

DATE *May 19* 20--

PAY TO THE ORDER OF *Hi-Tech Electronics Outlet* $ *1,750.00*

One thousand seven hundred fifty and 00/100 DOLLARS

UB Union Bank

MEMO *on account* *Tina Cordova*

⑆0720 0⑆033⑆ 6171 5222 ⑈0894

Cordova Electronics
612 Kent Avenue
Brooklyn, NY 11205

RECEIPT
No. 356

May 17 20--

RECEIVED FROM *Tom Trout* $ *126.00*

One hundred twenty-six and 00/100 DOLLARS

FOR *Payment on account*

RECEIVED BY *Tina Cordova*

Cordova Electronics
612 Kent Avenue
Brooklyn, NY 11205

895
74-103/720

DATE *May 19* 20--

PAY TO THE ORDER OF *Office Suppliers, Inc.* $ *770.00*

Seven hundred seventy and 00/100 DOLLARS

UB Union Bank

MEMO *on account* *Pedro Cordova*

⑆0720 0⑆033⑆ 6171 5222 ⑈0895

Cordova Electronics
612 Kent Avenue
Brooklyn, NY 11205

892
74-103/720

DATE *May 17* 20--

PAY TO THE ORDER OF *Desktop Wholesalers* $ *800.00*

Eight hundred and 00/100 DOLLARS

UB Union Bank

MEMO *Pedro Cordova*

⑆0720 0⑆033⑆ 6171 5222 ⑈0892

Cordova Electronics
612 Kent Avenue
Brooklyn, NY 11205

RECEIPT
No. 357

May 20 20--

RECEIVED FROM *Bob Bell* $ *90.00*

Ninety and 00/100 DOLLARS

FOR *employee purchase of office equipment*

RECEIVED BY *Pedro Cordova*

DEBIT MEMORANDUM No. 38

Date: *May 18, 20--*
Invoice No.: *N/A*

Cordova Electronics
612 Kent Avenue
Brooklyn, NY 11205

To: *Laser & Ink Jet Products*
1412 Abrams Avenue
Brooklyn, NY 11205

This day we have debited your account as follows:

Quantity	Item	Unit Price	Total
1	*Ink Jet Cartridge*	*$75.00*	*$75.00*

Name Date Class

Mini Practice Set 4 (continued)

Desktop Wholesalers
6190 Grand Street
Bronx, NY 10451

INVOICE NO. DW87
DATE: *May 20, 20--*
ORDER NO.:
SHIPPED BY:
TERMS: *n/30*

TO *Cordova Electronics*
612 Kent Avenue
Brooklyn, NY 11205

QTY.	ITEM	UNIT PRICE	TOTAL
3	Car Stereo System	$ 300.00	$ 900.00
1	Television	300.00	300.00
	Total		$ 1,200.00

Cordova Electronics
612 Kent Avenue
Brooklyn, NY 11205

RECEIPT
No. 360

May 21 20--
RECEIVED FROM *Marianne Martino* $ *94.50*
Ninety-four and 50/100 DOLLARS
FOR *Payment on account*
RECEIVED BY *Pedro Cordova*

Cordova Electronics
612 Kent Avenue
Brooklyn, NY 11205

RECEIPT
No. 358

May 20 20--
RECEIVED FROM *Mark McCormick* $ *210.00*
Two hundred ten and 00/100 DOLLARS
FOR *Payment on account*
RECEIVED BY *Kelly Briggs*

Cordova Electronics
612 Kent Avenue
Brooklyn, NY 11205

DATE: *May 21, 20--* NO. *608*

SOLD TO *Mark McCormick*

CLERK	CASH	CHARGE	TERMS
			2/10, n/30

QTY.	DESCRIPTION	UNIT PRICE	AMOUNT
5	answering machines	$80.00	$400 00
		SUBTOTAL	$400 00
		SALES TAX	20 00
		TOTAL	$420 00

Thank You!

Cordova Electronics
612 Kent Avenue
Brooklyn, NY 11205

RECEIPT
No. 359

May 20 20--
RECEIVED FROM *Sue Ellen Scott* $ *308.70*
Three hundred eight and 70/100 DOLLARS
FOR *Paid $315 less 2% on account*
RECEIVED BY *Tina Cordova*

Cordova Electronics
612 Kent Avenue
Brooklyn, NY 11205

896
74-103/720

DATE *May 22* 20--
PAY TO THE ORDER OF *Desktop Wholesalers* $ *1,200.00*
One thousand two hundred and 00/100 DOLLARS
UB Union Bank
MEMO *Tina Cordova*
⑆0720 01033⑆ 6171 5222 ⑈0896

Hi-Tech Electronics Outlet
265 Pixie Drive
New York, NY 10006

INVOICE NO. HT99
DATE: *May 21, 20--*
ORDER NO.:
SHIPPED BY:
TERMS: *2/10, n/30*

TO *Cordova Electronics*
612 Kent Avenue
Brooklyn, NY 11205

QTY.	ITEM	UNIT PRICE	TOTAL
2	Sony VCR Systems	$ 250.00	$ 500.00
5	Intercom Systems	200.00	1,000.00
			$ 1,500.00

Cordova Electronics
612 Kent Avenue
Brooklyn, NY 11205

DATE: *May 23, 20--* NO. *609*

SOLD TO *Sue Ellen Scott*

CLERK	CASH	CHARGE	TERMS
			2/10, n/30

QTY.	DESCRIPTION	UNIT PRICE	AMOUNT
1	Sony DVD player	$500.00	$500 00
		SUBTOTAL	$500 00
		SALES TAX	25 00
		TOTAL	$525 00

Thank You!

Mini Practice Set 4 (continued)

Cordova Electronics
612 Kent Avenue
Brooklyn, NY 11205

CREDIT MEMORANDUM NO. 55

ORIGINAL SALES DATE	ORIGINAL SALES SLIP	APPROVAL	MDSE RET
May 12, 20--	605	TC	X

DATE: May 24, 20--
NAME: Mark McCormick
ADDRESS: 2724 S. 1st Street
Brooklyn, NY 11205

QTY.	DESCRIPTION	AMOUNT
1	Clarion accessory	$100.00

REASON FOR RETURN: wrong model
SUB TOTAL: $100.00
THE TOTAL SHOWN AT THE RIGHT WILL BE CREDITED TO YOUR ACCOUNT.
SALES TAX: 5.00
TOTAL: $105.00

Mark McCormick
CUSTOMER SIGNATURE

Cordova Electronics
612 Kent Avenue
Brooklyn, NY 11205

DATE: May 28, 20-- NO. 610

SOLD TO: Marianne Martino

CLERK	CASH	CHARGE	TERMS
			2/10, n/30

QTY.	DESCRIPTION	UNIT PRICE	AMOUNT
1	car stereo	$200.00	$200.00
		SUBTOTAL	$200.00
		SALES TAX	10.00
		TOTAL	$210.00

Thank You!

Cordova Electronics 897
612 Kent Avenue
Brooklyn, NY 11205
74-103/720

DATE May 25 20--

PAY TO THE ORDER OF Surfside Insurance Co. $ 1,600.00

One thousand six hundred and 00/100 DOLLARS

UB Union Bank

MEMO annual insurance Tina Cordova

⑆0720 0103⑆ 6171 5222 ⑈0897

Office Suppliers, Inc.
613 Cedar Grove, #75
Bronx, NY 10451

INVOICE NO. 9489
DATE: May 29, 20--
ORDER NO.:
SHIPPED BY:
TERMS:

TO Cordova Electronics
612 Kent Avenue
Brooklyn, NY 11205

QTY.	ITEM	UNIT PRICE	TOTAL
2 packs	Manila Folders	$ 20.00	$ 40.00
11 pads	Stationery	10.00	110.00
			$ 150.00

Cordova Electronics
612 Kent Avenue
Brooklyn, NY 11205

MEMORANDUM 26

TO: Accounting Clerk
FROM: Senior Accountant
DATE: May 26, 20--
SUBJECT: Correcting entry

Please make the entry to correct the error in debiting Purchases rather than Transportation In last month for $50.00.

Cordova Electronics 898
612 Kent Avenue
Brooklyn, NY 11205
74-103/720

DATE May 30 20--

PAY TO THE ORDER OF Green Realty $ 1,500.00

One thousand five hundred and 00/100 DOLLARS

UB Union Bank

MEMO rent Tina Cordova

⑆0720 0103⑆ 6171 5222 ⑈0898

Computer Systems, Inc.
351 Wood Street
New York, NY 10005

INVOICE NO. CS75
DATE: May 27, 20--
ORDER NO.:
SHIPPED BY:
TERMS: 2/10, n/30

TO Cordova Electronics
612 Kent Avenue
Brooklyn, NY 11205

QTY.	ITEM	UNIT PRICE	TOTAL
20	Various CDs	$ 50.00	$ 1,000.00
1	VCR	400.00	400.00
			$ 1,400.00

Dec. 31
Tape 22

1,200.00	CA
60.00	ST
900.00	BCS
45.00	ST

Name	Date	Class

Mini Practice Set 4 (continued)

$ 1,858.75 — No. 899
Date 5/31 20--
To Payroll Account
For Payroll—May 31

	Dollars	Cents
Balance brought forward	8,093	20
less 12/31 bank svc. fee	25	00
12/31 bankcard fee	100	00
Total		
Less this check	1,858	75
Balance carried forward	6,109	45

PAYROLL REGISTER

PAY PERIOD ENDING May 31 20--   DATE OF PAYMENT May 31, 20--

	EMPLOYEE NUMBER	NAME	MAR. STATUS	ALLOW.	TOTAL HOURS	RATE	EARNINGS REGULAR	EARNINGS OVERTIME	EARNINGS TOTAL	DEDUCTIONS SOC. SEC. TAX	DEDUCTIONS MED. TAX	DEDUCTIONS FED. INC. TAX	DEDUCTIONS STATE INC. TAX	DEDUCTIONS HOSP. INS.	DEDUCTIONS OTHER	DEDUCTIONS TOTAL	NET PAY	CK. NO.	
24																			24
25																			25
						TOTALS	2500 00			155 00	36 25	400 00	50 00			641 25	1858 75		

Other Deductions: Write the appropriate code letter to the left of the amount: B—U.S. Savings Bonds; C—Credit Union; UD—Union Dues; UW—United Way.

Cordova Electronics
612 Kent Avenue
Brooklyn, NY 11205

MEMORANDUM 27

TO: *Accounting Clerk*
FROM: *Payroll Dept.*
DATE: *May 31, 20--*
SUBJECT: *Payroll Tax*

Please record employer payroll taxes for May 31 payroll.
FICA rate = 6.2%
Medicare rate = 1.45%
Fed. unemployment tax rate = 0.8%
State unemployment tax rate = 5.4%

Name Date Class

Mini Practice Set 4 (continued)

SALES JOURNAL

PAGE 18

	DATE		SALES SLIP NO.	CUSTOMER'S ACCOUNT DEBITED	POST. REF.	SALES CREDIT	SALES TAX PAYABLE CREDIT	ACCOUNTS RECEIVABLE DEBIT	
1	20--								1
2	May	1	602	Sam Lorenzo	✓	180 00	9 00	189 00	2
3		3	603	Marianne Martino	✓	90 00	4 50	94 50	3
4		8	604	Tom Trout	✓	120 00	6 00	126 00	4
5		12	605	Mark McCormick	✓	200 00	10 00	210 00	5
6		13	606	Sue Ellen Scott	✓	300 00	15 00	315 00	6
7									7
8									8
9									9
10									10
11									11
12									12
13									13
14									14
15									15
16									16
17									17
18									18
19									19
20									20
21									21
22									22
23									23
24									24
25									25
26									26
27									27
28									28
29									29
30									30
31									31
32									32
33									33
34									34
35									35
36									36

Mini Practice Set 4 (continued)

CASH RECEIPTS JOURNAL

PAGE 15

	DATE		DOC. NO.	ACCOUNT NAME	POST. REF.	GENERAL CREDIT	SALES CREDIT	SALES TAX PAYABLE CREDIT	ACCOUNTS RECEIVABLE CREDIT	SALES DISCOUNTS DEBIT	CASH IN BANK DEBIT	
1	20--											1
2	May	3	R350	Sue Ellen Scott	✓				350 00	7 00	343 00	2
3		5	R351	Sam Lorenzo	✓				300 00	6 00	294 00	3
4		7	T20	Cash Sales	—		2100 00	105 00			2205 00	4
5		7	T20	Bankcard Sales	—		1860 00	93 00			1953 00	5
6		8	R352	Marianne Martino	✓				375 00		375 00	6
7		12	R353	Tom Trout	✓				225 00		225 00	7
8		14	R354	Sam Lorenzo	✓				189 00		189 00	8
9		15	R355	Mark McCormick	✓				250 00		250 00	9
10		15	T21	Cash Sales	—		1940 00	97 00			2037 00	10
11		15	T21	Bankcard Sales	—		1660 00	83 00			1743 00	11
12												12
13												13
14												14
15												15
16												16
17												17
18												18
19												19
20												20
21												21
22												22
23												23
24												24
25												25
26												26

Mini Practice Set 4 (continued)

PURCHASES JOURNAL

PAGE 12

	DATE		INVOICE NO.	CREDITOR'S ACCOUNT CREDITED	POST. REF.	ACCOUNTS PAYABLE CREDIT	PURCHASES DEBIT	GENERAL ACCOUNT DEBITED	GENERAL POST. REF.	GENERAL DEBIT	
1	20--										1
2	May	3	CS60	Computer Systems Inc.	✓	600 00	600 00				2
3		4	HT88	Hi-Tech Elec. Outlet	✓	350 00	350 00				3
4		6	9451	Office Suppliers Inc.	✓	770 00		Office Equipment	155	770 00	4
5		8	DW65	Desktop Wholesalers	✓	800 00		Office Equipment	155	800 00	5
6		10	601	Laser & Ink Jet Products	✓	1000 00	1000 00				6
7											7
8											8
9											9
10											10
11											11
12											12
13											13
14											14
15											15
16											16
17											17
18											18
19											19
20											20
21											21
22											22
23											23
24											24
25											25
26											26

Mini Practice Set 4 (continued)

CASH PAYMENTS JOURNAL

PAGE 14

	DATE		DOC. NO.	ACCOUNT NAME	POST. REF.	GENERAL DEBIT	GENERAL CREDIT	ACCOUNTS PAYABLE DEBIT	PURCHASES DISCOUNTS CREDIT	CASH IN BANK CREDIT	
1	20--										1
2	May	1	887	Utilities Expense	635	125 00				125 00	2
3		2	888	Desktop Wholesalers	✓			900 00		900 00	3
4		4	889	Laser & Ink Jet Products	✓			750 00	15 00	735 00	4
5		7	890	Office Suppliers Inc.	✓			1300 00		1300 00	5
6		10	891	Transportation In	505	175 00				175 00	6
7											7
8											8
9											9
10											10
11											11
12											12
13											13
14											14
15											15
16											16
17											17
18											18
19											19
20											20
21											21
22											22
23											23
24											24
25											25
26											26
27											27
28											28

Name Date Class

Mini Practice Set 4 (continued)

GENERAL JOURNAL PAGE 7

	DATE		DESCRIPTION	POST. REF.	DEBIT	CREDIT	
1	20--						1
2	May	5	Purchases	501	150000		2
3			Merchandise Inventory	110		150000	3
4			Memo 25				4
5							5
6							6
7							7
8							8
9							9
10							10
11							11
12							12
13							13
14							14
15							15
16							16
17							17
18							18
19							19
20							20
21							21
22							22
23							23
24							24
25							25
26							26
27							27
28							28
29							29
30							30
31							31
32							32
33							33
34							34
35							35
36							36
37							37
38							38

Name Date Class

Mini Practice Set 4 (continued)

ACCOUNTS RECEIVABLE SUBSIDIARY LEDGER

Name *Sam Lorenzo*

Address *362 Oceanview, Miami, FL 33101*

DATE		DESCRIPTION	POST. REF.	DEBIT	CREDIT	BALANCE
20--						
May	1	Balance	✓			300 00
	1		S18	189 00		489 00
	5		CR15		300 00	189 00
	14		CR15		189 00	—

Name *Mark McCormick*

Address *14 Garden Place, Clearwater, FL 34618*

DATE		DESCRIPTION	POST. REF.	DEBIT	CREDIT	BALANCE
20--						
May	1	Balance	✓			250 00
	12		S18	210 00		460 00
	15		CR15		250 00	210 00

Name *Marianne Martino*

Address *92 Stafford Court, Fort Lauderdale, FL 33310*

DATE		DESCRIPTION	POST. REF.	DEBIT	CREDIT	BALANCE
20--						
May	1	Balance	✓			375 00
	3		S18	94 50		469 50
	8		CR15		375 00	94 50

Name ____ Date ____ Class ____

Mini Practice Set 4 (continued)

Name *Sue Ellen Scott*

Address *302 Palm Drive, Jacksonville, FL 32203*

DATE		DESCRIPTION	POST. REF.	DEBIT	CREDIT	BALANCE
20--						
May	1	Balance	✓			350 00
	3		CR15		350 00	—
	13		S18	315 00		315 00

Name *Tom Trout*

Address *16 Del Mar, Boca Raton, FL 33431*

DATE		DESCRIPTION	POST. REF.	DEBIT	CREDIT	BALANCE
20--						
May	1	Balance	✓			225 00
	8		S18	126 00		351 00
	12		CR15		225 00	126 00

Mini Practice Set 4 (continued)

ACCOUNTS PAYABLE SUBSIDIARY LEDGER

Name *Computer Systems Inc.*

Address *Six Gulf Place, Hialeah, FL 33010*

DATE		DESCRIPTION	POST. REF.	DEBIT	CREDIT	BALANCE
20--						
May	1	Balance	✓			1200 00
	3		P12		600 00	1800 00

Name *Desktop Wholesalers*

Address *Three Surfside, Palm Springs, FL 33460*

DATE		DESCRIPTION	POST. REF.	DEBIT	CREDIT	BALANCE
20--						
May	1	Balance	✓			900 00
	2		CP14	900 00		—
	8		P12		800 00	800 00

Name *Hi-Tech Electronics Outlet*

Address *Quadrangle Complex, Orlando, FL 32802*

DATE		DESCRIPTION	POST. REF.	DEBIT	CREDIT	BALANCE
20--						
May	1	Balance	✓			1400 00
	4		P12		350 00	1750 00

Mini Practice Set 4 (continued)

Name *Laser & Ink Jet Products*

Address *32 Cypress Blvd., Tampa, FL 33602*

DATE		DESCRIPTION	POST. REF.	DEBIT	CREDIT	BALANCE
20--						
May	1	Balance	✓			750 00
	4		CP14	750 00		—
	10		P12		1 000 00	1 000 00

Name *Office Suppliers Inc.*

Address *56 Sunset Blvd., Panama City, FL 32401*

DATE		DESCRIPTION	POST. REF.	DEBIT	CREDIT	BALANCE
20--						
May	1	Balance	✓			1 300 00
	6		P12		770 00	2 070 00
	7		CP14	1 300 00		770 00

Name Date Class

Mini Practice Set 4 (continued)

GENERAL LEDGER

ACCOUNT *Cash in Bank* ACCOUNT NO. *101*

DATE		DESCRIPTION	POST. REF.	DEBIT	CREDIT	BALANCE DEBIT	BALANCE CREDIT
20--							
May	*1*	*Balance*	✓			*7500 00*	

ACCOUNT *Accounts Receivable* ACCOUNT NO. *105*

DATE		DESCRIPTION	POST. REF.	DEBIT	CREDIT	BALANCE DEBIT	BALANCE CREDIT
20--							
May	*1*	*Balance*	✓			*1500 00*	

ACCOUNT *Merchandise Inventory* ACCOUNT NO. *110*

DATE		DESCRIPTION	POST. REF.	DEBIT	CREDIT	BALANCE DEBIT	BALANCE CREDIT
20--							
May	*1*	*Balance*	✓			*57949 00*	
	5		*G7*		*1500 00*	*56449 00*	

ACCOUNT *Supplies* ACCOUNT NO. *115*

DATE		DESCRIPTION	POST. REF.	DEBIT	CREDIT	BALANCE DEBIT	BALANCE CREDIT
20--							
May	*1*	*Balance*	✓			*500 00*	

ACCOUNT *Prepaid Insurance* ACCOUNT NO. *120*

DATE		DESCRIPTION	POST. REF.	DEBIT	CREDIT	BALANCE DEBIT	BALANCE CREDIT
20--							
May	*1*	*Balance*	✓			*300 00*	

Name Date Class

Mini Practice Set 4 (continued)

ACCOUNT *Store Equipment* ACCOUNT NO. *150*

DATE		DESCRIPTION	POST. REF.	DEBIT	CREDIT	BALANCE DEBIT	BALANCE CREDIT
20--							
May	*1*	*Balance*	✓			*1300000*	

ACCOUNT *Office Equipment* ACCOUNT NO. *155*

DATE		DESCRIPTION	POST. REF.	DEBIT	CREDIT	BALANCE DEBIT	BALANCE CREDIT
20--							
May	*1*	*Balance*	✓			*320000*	
	6		*P12*	*77000*		*397000*	
	8		*P12*	*80000*		*477000*	

ACCOUNT *Accounts Payable* ACCOUNT NO. *201*

DATE		DESCRIPTION	POST. REF.	DEBIT	CREDIT	BALANCE DEBIT	BALANCE CREDIT
20--							
May	*1*	*Balance*	✓				*555000*

ACCOUNT *Sales Tax Payable* ACCOUNT NO. *205*

DATE		DESCRIPTION	POST. REF.	DEBIT	CREDIT	BALANCE DEBIT	BALANCE CREDIT
20--							
May	*1*	*Balance*	✓				*41200*

ACCOUNT *Employees' Federal Income Tax Payable* ACCOUNT NO. *210*

DATE		DESCRIPTION	POST. REF.	DEBIT	CREDIT	BALANCE DEBIT	BALANCE CREDIT
20--							
May	*1*	*Balance*	✓				*150000*

Name Date Class

Mini Practice Set 4 (continued)

ACCOUNT *Employees' State Income Tax Payable* ACCOUNT NO. *211*

DATE		DESCRIPTION	POST. REF.	DEBIT	CREDIT	BALANCE DEBIT	BALANCE CREDIT
20--							
May	*1*	*Balance*	✓				*215 00*

ACCOUNT *Social Security Tax Payable* ACCOUNT NO. *212*

DATE		DESCRIPTION	POST. REF.	DEBIT	CREDIT	BALANCE DEBIT	BALANCE CREDIT
20--							
May	*1*	*Balance*	✓				*975 00*

ACCOUNT *Medicare Tax Payable* ACCOUNT NO. *213*

DATE		DESCRIPTION	POST. REF.	DEBIT	CREDIT	BALANCE DEBIT	BALANCE CREDIT
20--							
May	*1*	*Balance*	✓				*180 00*

ACCOUNT *Federal Unemployment Tax Payable* ACCOUNT NO. *214*

DATE		DESCRIPTION	POST. REF.	DEBIT	CREDIT	BALANCE DEBIT	BALANCE CREDIT
20--							
May	*1*	*Balance*	✓				*95 00*

ACCOUNT *State Unemployment Tax Payable* ACCOUNT NO. *215*

DATE		DESCRIPTION	POST. REF.	DEBIT	CREDIT	BALANCE DEBIT	BALANCE CREDIT
20--							
May	*1*	*Balance*	✓				*130 00*

Mini Practice Set 4 (continued)

ACCOUNT *Capital Stock* ACCOUNT NO. *301*

DATE		DESCRIPTION	POST. REF.	DEBIT	CREDIT	BALANCE DEBIT	BALANCE CREDIT
20--							
May	1	Balance	✓				35000 00

ACCOUNT *Retained Earnings* ACCOUNT NO. *302*

DATE		DESCRIPTION	POST. REF.	DEBIT	CREDIT	BALANCE DEBIT	BALANCE CREDIT
20--							
May	1	Balance	✓				9260 00

ACCOUNT *Income Summary* ACCOUNT NO. *303*

DATE		DESCRIPTION	POST. REF.	DEBIT	CREDIT	BALANCE DEBIT	BALANCE CREDIT

ACCOUNT *Sales* ACCOUNT NO. *401*

DATE		DESCRIPTION	POST. REF.	DEBIT	CREDIT	BALANCE DEBIT	BALANCE CREDIT
20--							
May	1	Balance	✓				60000 00

ACCOUNT *Sales Discounts* ACCOUNT NO. *405*

DATE		DESCRIPTION	POST. REF.	DEBIT	CREDIT	BALANCE DEBIT	BALANCE CREDIT
20--							
May	1	Balance	✓			110 00	

Mini Practice Set 4 (continued)

ACCOUNT *Sales Returns and Allowances* ACCOUNT NO. *410*

DATE		DESCRIPTION	POST. REF.	DEBIT	CREDIT	BALANCE DEBIT	BALANCE CREDIT
20--							
May	1	Balance	✓			375 00	

ACCOUNT *Purchases* ACCOUNT NO. *501*

DATE		DESCRIPTION	POST. REF.	DEBIT	CREDIT	BALANCE DEBIT	BALANCE CREDIT
20--							
May	1	Balance	✓			12000 00	
	5		G7	1500 00		13500 00	

ACCOUNT *Transportation In* ACCOUNT NO. *505*

DATE		DESCRIPTION	POST. REF.	DEBIT	CREDIT	BALANCE DEBIT	BALANCE CREDIT
20--							
May	1	Balance	✓			600 00	
	10		CP14	175 00		775 00	

ACCOUNT *Purchases Discounts* ACCOUNT NO. *510*

DATE		DESCRIPTION	POST. REF.	DEBIT	CREDIT	BALANCE DEBIT	BALANCE CREDIT
20--							
May	1	Balance	✓				350 00

ACCOUNT *Purchases Returns and Allowances* ACCOUNT NO. *515*

DATE		DESCRIPTION	POST. REF.	DEBIT	CREDIT	BALANCE DEBIT	BALANCE CREDIT
20--							
May	1	Balance	✓				412 00

ACCOUNT *Advertising Expense* ACCOUNT NO. *605*

DATE		DESCRIPTION	POST. REF.	DEBIT	CREDIT	BALANCE DEBIT	BALANCE CREDIT
20--							
May	1	Balance	✓			510 00	

Mini Practice Set 4 (continued)

ACCOUNT *Bankcard Fees Expense* ACCOUNT NO. *610*

DATE		DESCRIPTION	POST. REF.	DEBIT	CREDIT	BALANCE DEBIT	BALANCE CREDIT
20--							
May	1	Balance	✓			60000	

ACCOUNT *Miscellaneous Expense* ACCOUNT NO. *615*

DATE		DESCRIPTION	POST. REF.	DEBIT	CREDIT	BALANCE DEBIT	BALANCE CREDIT
20--							
May	1	Balance	✓			7500	

ACCOUNT *Payroll Tax Expense* ACCOUNT NO. *620*

DATE		DESCRIPTION	POST. REF.	DEBIT	CREDIT	BALANCE DEBIT	BALANCE CREDIT
20--							
May	1	Balance	✓			138000	

ACCOUNT *Rent Expense* ACCOUNT NO. *625*

DATE		DESCRIPTION	POST. REF.	DEBIT	CREDIT	BALANCE DEBIT	BALANCE CREDIT
20--							
May	1	Balance	✓			600000	

ACCOUNT *Salaries Expense* ACCOUNT NO. *630*

DATE		DESCRIPTION	POST. REF.	DEBIT	CREDIT	BALANCE DEBIT	BALANCE CREDIT
20--							
May	1	Balance	✓			800000	

ACCOUNT *Utilities Expense* ACCOUNT NO. *635*

DATE		DESCRIPTION	POST. REF.	DEBIT	CREDIT	BALANCE DEBIT	BALANCE CREDIT
20--							
May	1	Balance	✓			48000	
	1		CP14	12500		60500	

Mini Practice Set 4 (continued)

Cordova Electronics

Cash Proof

May 31, 20--

Mini Practice Set 4 (continued)

Cordova Electronics
Schedule of Accounts Receivable
May 31, 20--

Cordova Electronics
Schedule of Accounts Payable
May 31, 20--

Name Date Class

Mini Practice Set 4 (concluded)

Analyze: **1.**

2.

3.

Name Date Class

Notes

Name Date Class

Cordova Electronics

Audit Test

Directions: *Use your completed solutions to answer the following questions. Write the answer in the space to the left of each question.*

______________ **1.** How many accounts receivable customers does the business have?

______________ **2.** How many transactions were recorded in the sales journal for this period?

______________ **3.** What total amount was posted from the Sales Tax Payable Credit column of the sales journal to the Sales Tax Payable account?

______________ **4.** What were the totals for debits and credits in the sales journal?

______________ **5.** What account was credited for May 18 transaction?

______________ **6.** What was the total of the Cash in Bank Debit column for the cash receipts journal?

______________ **7.** Which account was debited for the second May 21 transaction?

______________ **8.** What was the total of the Purchases Debit column in the purchases journal?

______________ **9.** How many transactions were recorded in the purchases journal?

______________ **10.** How many transactions in the cash payments journal affected the Purchases account?

______________ **11.** How many transactions were recorded in the general journal in the month of May?

______________ **12.** For the payroll entry recorded on May 31, what amount was debited to Payroll Tax Expense?

Name ______ Date ______ Class ______

______ **13.** What is the total of all accounts receivable subsidiary ledger accounts at month end?

______ **14.** What is the total of all accounts payable subsidiary ledger accounts at month end?

______ **15.** What is the balance of Cash in Bank at the end of the month?

______ **16.** What is the total of any payroll tax liabilities at May 31?

______ **17.** How many accounts are listed on the trial balance?

______ **18.** Which account has the largest balance on the trial balance?

______ **19.** Which customer owes Cordova Electronics the most at the end of the month?

______ **20.** What is the balance of the Sales account at month end?

Name Date Class

CHAPTER 20 Completing the Accounting Cycle for a Merchandising Corporation

Study Guide

Section Assessment

Section 1 *Read Section 1 on pages 591–594 and complete the following exercises on page 595.*

- ☐ Reinforce the Main Idea
- ☐ Math for Accounting
- ☐ Problem 20-1 *Identifying Accounts Affected by Closing Entries*

Section 2 *Read Section 2 on pages 596–601 and complete the following exercises on page 602.*

- ☐ Reinforce the Main Idea
- ☐ Math for Accounting
- ☐ Problem 20-2 *Analyzing a Source Document*
- ☐ Problem 20-3 *Organizing the Steps in the Accounting Cycle*

Chapter Assessment

Summary *Review the Chapter 22 Visual Summary on page 603 in your textbook.*

- ☐ Key Concepts

Review and Activities *Complete the following questions and exercises on page 604 in your textbook.*

- ☐ After You Read: Answering the Essential Question
- ☐ Vocabulary Check
- ☐ Concept Check

Standardized Test Practice *Complete the exercises on page 605 in your textbook.*

Computerized Accounting *Read the Computerized Accounting information on page 606 in your textbook.*

- ☐ Making the Transition from a Manual to a Computerized System

Problems *Complete the following End-of-Chapter Problems for Chapter 20 in your textbook.*

- ☐ Problem 20-4 *Journalizing Closing Entries*
- ☐ Problem 20-5 *Journalizing and Posting Closing Entries*
- ☐ Problem 20-6 *Identifying Accounts for Closing Entries*
- ☐ Problem 20-7 *Completing End-of-Period Activities*

Challenge Problem

- ☐ Problem 20-8 *Preparing Adjusting and Closing Entries*

Real-World Applications and Connections *Complete the following applications on pages 612–613 in your textbook.*

- ☐ Case Study
- ☐ 21st Century Skills
- ☐ Career Wise
- ☐ H.O.T. Audit

Working Papers *for Section Problems*

Problem 20-1 Identifying Accounts Affected by Closing Entries *(textbook p. 595)*

Account	Is the account affected by a closing entry?	During closing, is the account debited or credited?	During closing, is Income Summary debited or credited?
Accounts Receivable			
Bankcard Fees Expense			
Capital Stock			
Cash in Bank			
Equipment			
Federal Corporate Income Tax Expense			
Federal Corporate Income Tax Payable			
Income Summary			
Insurance Expense			
Merchandise Inventory			
Miscellaneous Expense			
Prepaid Insurance			
Purchases			
Purchases Discounts			
Purchases Returns and Allowances			
Retained Earnings			
Sales			
Sales Discounts			
Sales Returns and Allowances			
Sales Tax Payable			
Supplies			
Supplies Expense			
Transportation In			
Utilities Expense			

Name Date Class

Problem 20-2 Analyzing a Source Document *(textbook p. 602)*

Your Backpack Inc.
29000 White Road
Cold Springs, TX 77282-4513

MEMORANDUM 42

TO: *Robert Chan, Chief Accountant*
FROM: *James Perkins, President*
DATE: *July 12, 20--*
SUBJECT: *New Storage Facility Rent*

Would you please make a check out to Warehouse Inc. for $750. The check is for the new storage facility we are renting. Please mail the check to:

Mr. James Skiller, Controller
Warehouse Inc.
7576 County Line Highway
Crossplains, TX 77361-8411

CASH PAYMENTS JOURNAL PAGE ______

	DATE	DOC. NO.	ACCOUNT NAME	POST. REF.	GENERAL DEBIT	GENERAL CREDIT	ACCOUNTS PAYABLE DEBIT	PURCHASES DISCOUNTS CREDIT	CASH IN BANK CREDIT	
1										1
2										2
3										3
4										4

Name Date Class

Problem 20-3 Organizing the Steps in the Accounting Cycle *(textbook p. 602)*

1. ______
2. ______
3. ______
4. ______
5. ______
6. ______
7. ______
8. ______
9. ______
10. ______

Name Date Class

Working Papers *for End-of-Chapter Problems*

Problem 20-4 Journalizing Closing Entries *(textbook p. 607)*

GENERAL JOURNAL PAGE ____

	DATE		DESCRIPTION	POST. REF.	DEBIT	CREDIT	
1							1
2							2
3							3
4							4
5							5
6							6
7							7
8							8
9							9
10							10
11							11
12							12
13							13
14							14
15							15
16							16
17							17
18							18
19							19
20							20
21							21
22							22
23							23
24							24
25							25
26							26
27							27
28							28
29							29
30							30

Analyze:

Name Date Class

Problem 20-5 Journalizing and Posting Closing Entries *(textbook p. 608)*

(1)

GENERAL JOURNAL PAGE ____

	DATE		DESCRIPTION	POST. REF.	DEBIT	CREDIT	
1							1
2							2
3							3
4							4
5							5
6							6
7							7
8							8
9							9
10							10
11							11
12							12
13							13
14							14
15							15
16							16
17							17

(2)

GENERAL LEDGER (PARTIAL)

ACCOUNT *Retained Earnings* ACCOUNT NO. *305*

DATE		DESCRIPTION	POST. REF.	DEBIT	CREDIT	BALANCE DEBIT	BALANCE CREDIT
20--							
Dec.	*1*	*Balance*	✓				*2041000*

ACCOUNT *Income Summary* ACCOUNT NO. *310*

DATE		DESCRIPTION	POST. REF.	DEBIT	CREDIT	BALANCE DEBIT	BALANCE CREDIT
20--							
Dec.	*31*	*Adjusting Entry*	*G13*	*400000*		*400000*	

Name Date Class

Problem 20-5 (continued)

ACCOUNT *Sales* ACCOUNT NO. *401*

DATE		DESCRIPTION	POST. REF.	DEBIT	CREDIT	BALANCE DEBIT	BALANCE CREDIT
20--							
Dec.	1	Balance	✓				150000 00

ACCOUNT *Sales Returns and Allowances* ACCOUNT NO. *410*

DATE		DESCRIPTION	POST. REF.	DEBIT	CREDIT	BALANCE DEBIT	BALANCE CREDIT
20--							
Dec.	1	Balance	✓			5000 00	

ACCOUNT *Purchases* ACCOUNT NO. *501*

DATE		DESCRIPTION	POST. REF.	DEBIT	CREDIT	BALANCE DEBIT	BALANCE CREDIT
20--							
Dec.	1	Balance	✓			90000 00	

ACCOUNT *Transportation In* ACCOUNT NO. *505*

DATE		DESCRIPTION	POST. REF.	DEBIT	CREDIT	BALANCE DEBIT	BALANCE CREDIT
20--							
Dec.	1	Balance	✓			5000 00	

ACCOUNT *Purchases Discounts* ACCOUNT NO. *510*

DATE		DESCRIPTION	POST. REF.	DEBIT	CREDIT	BALANCE DEBIT	BALANCE CREDIT
20--							
Dec.	1	Balance	✓				1000 00

Problem 20-5 (concluded)

ACCOUNT *Purchases Returns and Allowances* ACCOUNT NO. *515*

DATE		DESCRIPTION	POST. REF.	DEBIT	CREDIT	BALANCE DEBIT	BALANCE CREDIT
20--							
Dec.	1	Balance	✓				1500 00

ACCOUNT *Federal Corporate Income Tax Expense* ACCOUNT NO. *620*

DATE		DESCRIPTION	POST. REF.	DEBIT	CREDIT	BALANCE DEBIT	BALANCE CREDIT
20--							
Dec.	1	Balance	✓			3900 00	
	31	Adjusting Entry	G13	800 00		4700 00	

ACCOUNT *Miscellaneous Expense* ACCOUNT NO. *645*

DATE		DESCRIPTION	POST. REF.	DEBIT	CREDIT	BALANCE DEBIT	BALANCE CREDIT
20--							
Dec.	1	Balance	✓			300 00	

ACCOUNT *Rent Expense* ACCOUNT NO. *650*

DATE		DESCRIPTION	POST. REF.	DEBIT	CREDIT	BALANCE DEBIT	BALANCE CREDIT
20--							
Dec.	1	Balance	✓			6000 00	

ACCOUNT *Supplies Expense* ACCOUNT NO. *660*

DATE		DESCRIPTION	POST. REF.	DEBIT	CREDIT	BALANCE DEBIT	BALANCE CREDIT
20--							
Dec.	31	Adjusting Entry	G13	1630 00		1630 00	

ACCOUNT *Utilities Expense* ACCOUNT NO. *670*

DATE		DESCRIPTION	POST. REF.	DEBIT	CREDIT	BALANCE DEBIT	BALANCE CREDIT
20--							
Dec.	1	Balance	✓			3000 00	

Analyze:

Name Date Class

Problem 20-6 Identifying Accounts for Closing Entries *(textbook p. 608)*

Accounts Debited	Accounts Credited

Analyze:

Name Date Class

Problem 20-7 Completing End-of-Period Activities *(textbook p. 609)*

(1), (2)

River's Edge
Work
For the Year Ended

	ACCT. NO.	ACCOUNT NAME	TRIAL BALANCE DEBIT	TRIAL BALANCE CREDIT	ADJUSTMENTS DEBIT	ADJUSTMENTS CREDIT
1	101	Cash in Bank	22,236.57			
2	115	Accounts Receivable	7,400.00			
3	130	Merchandise Inventory	25,000.00			
4	135	Supplies	4,100.00			
5	140	Prepaid Insurance	3,000.00			
6	145	Delivery Truck	67,900.00			
7	201	Accounts Payable		13,000.00		
8	210	Fed. Corporate Income Tax Pay.		—		
9	215	Sales Tax Payable		526.57		
10	301	Capital Stock		40,000.00		
11	305	Retained Earnings		25,400.00		
12	310	Income Summary	—	—		
13	401	Sales		175,000.00		
14	405	Sales Discounts	3,775.00			
15	410	Sales Returns and Allowances	2,500.00			
16	501	Purchases	75,300.00			
17	505	Transportation In	5,000.00			
18	510	Purchases Discounts		2,300.00		
19	515	Purchases Returns and Allow.		5,600.00		
20	605	Bankcard Fees Expense	3,515.00			
21	625	Fed. Corporate Income Tax Exp.	2,940.00			
22	635	Insurance Expense	—			
23	655	Miscellaneous Expense	5,960.00			
24	660	Rent Expense	9,000.00			
25	665	Salaries Expense	22,200.00			
26	670	Supplies Expense	—			
27	680	Utilities Expense	2,000.00			
28						
29						
30						
31						
32						

Name **Date** **Class**

Canoe & Kayak

Sheet

December 31, 20--

ADJUSTED TRIAL BALANCE		INCOME STATEMENT		BALANCE SHEET		
DEBIT	CREDIT	DEBIT	CREDIT	DEBIT	CREDIT	
						1
						2
						3
						4
						5
						6
						7
						8
						9
						10
						11
						12
						13
						14
						15
						16
						17
						18
						19
						20
						21
						22
						23
						24
						25
						26
						27
						28
						29
						30
						31
						32

Name Date Class

Problem 20-7 (continued)

(3)

Name Date Class

Problem 20-7 (continued)

(4)

(5)

Problem 20-7 (continued)

(6), (7)

GENERAL JOURNAL

PAGE ______

	DATE		DESCRIPTION	POST. REF.	DEBIT	CREDIT	
1							1
2							2
3							3
4							4
5							5
6							6
7							7
8							8
9							9
10							10
11							11
12							12
13							13
14							14
15							15
16							16
17							17
18							18
19							19
20							20
21							21
22							22
23							23
24							24
25							25
26							26
27							27
28							28
29							29
30							30
31							31
32							32
33							33
34							34
35							35
36							36

Name Date Class

Problem 20-7 (continued)

(7)

ACCOUNT *Cash in Bank* ACCOUNT NO. *101*

DATE		DESCRIPTION	POST. REF.	DEBIT	CREDIT	BALANCE DEBIT	BALANCE CREDIT
20--							
Dec.	1	Balance	✓			20,482.97	
	31		CR19	17,151.70		37,634.67	
	31		CP22		15,398.10	22,236.57	

ACCOUNT *Accounts Receivable* ACCOUNT NO. *115*

DATE		DESCRIPTION	POST. REF.	DEBIT	CREDIT	BALANCE DEBIT	BALANCE CREDIT
20--							
Dec.	1	Balance	✓			11,194.38	
	7		G12		175.00	11,019.38	
	31		S17	6,951.62		17,971.00	
	31		CR19		10,571.00	7,400.00	

ACCOUNT *Merchandise Inventory* ACCOUNT NO. *130*

DATE		DESCRIPTION	POST. REF.	DEBIT	CREDIT	BALANCE DEBIT	BALANCE CREDIT
20--							
Dec.	1	Balance	✓			25,000.00	

ACCOUNT *Supplies* ACCOUNT NO. *135*

DATE		DESCRIPTION	POST. REF.	DEBIT	CREDIT	BALANCE DEBIT	BALANCE CREDIT
20--							
Dec.	1	Balance	✓			3,966.50	
	10		P16	106.00		4,072.50	
	21		P16	27.50		4,100.00	

ACCOUNT *Prepaid Insurance* ACCOUNT NO. *140*

DATE		DESCRIPTION	POST. REF.	DEBIT	CREDIT	BALANCE DEBIT	BALANCE CREDIT
20--							
Dec.	1	Balance	✓			3,000.00	

Name Date Class

Problem 20-7 (continued)

ACCOUNT *Delivery Truck* ACCOUNT NO. *145*

DATE		DESCRIPTION	POST. REF.	DEBIT	CREDIT	BALANCE DEBIT	BALANCE CREDIT
20--							
Dec.	1	Balance	✓			67900 00	

ACCOUNT *Accounts Payable* ACCOUNT NO. *201*

DATE		DESCRIPTION	POST. REF.	DEBIT	CREDIT	BALANCE DEBIT	BALANCE CREDIT
20--							
Dec.	1	Balance	✓				13030 50
	19		G12	256 00			12774 50
	31		P16		9433 50		22208 00
	31		CP22	9208 00			13000 00

ACCOUNT *Federal Corporate Income Tax Payable* ACCOUNT NO. *210*

DATE		DESCRIPTION	POST. REF.	DEBIT	CREDIT	BALANCE DEBIT	BALANCE CREDIT

ACCOUNT *Sales Tax Payable* ACCOUNT NO. *215*

DATE		DESCRIPTION	POST. REF.	DEBIT	CREDIT	BALANCE DEBIT	BALANCE CREDIT
20--							
Dec.	1	Balance	✓				463 00
	14		CP22	463 00			—
	31		S17		267 37		267 37
	31		CR19		259 20		526 57

ACCOUNT *Capital Stock* ACCOUNT NO. *301*

DATE		DESCRIPTION	POST. REF.	DEBIT	CREDIT	BALANCE DEBIT	BALANCE CREDIT
20--							
Dec.	1	Balance	✓				40000 00

Problem 20-7 (continued)

ACCOUNT *Retained Earnings* ACCOUNT NO. *305*

DATE		DESCRIPTION	POST. REF.	DEBIT	CREDIT	BALANCE DEBIT	BALANCE CREDIT
20--							
Dec.	1	Balance	✓				25400 00

ACCOUNT *Income Summary* ACCOUNT NO. *310*

DATE		DESCRIPTION	POST. REF.	DEBIT	CREDIT	BALANCE DEBIT	BALANCE CREDIT

ACCOUNT *Sales* ACCOUNT NO. *401*

DATE		DESCRIPTION	POST. REF.	DEBIT	CREDIT	BALANCE DEBIT	BALANCE CREDIT
20--							
Dec.	1	Balance	✓				161835 75
	31		S17		6684 25		168520 00
	31		CR19		6480 00		175000 00

ACCOUNT *Sales Discounts* ACCOUNT NO. *405*

DATE		DESCRIPTION	POST. REF.	DEBIT	CREDIT	BALANCE DEBIT	BALANCE CREDIT
20--							
Dec.	1	Balance	✓			3616 50	
	31		CR19	158 50		3775 00	

ACCOUNT *Sales Returns and Allowances* ACCOUNT NO. *410*

DATE		DESCRIPTION	POST. REF.	DEBIT	CREDIT	BALANCE DEBIT	BALANCE CREDIT
20--							
Dec.	1	Balance	✓			2325 00	
	7		G12	175 00		2500 00	

Name Date Class

Problem 20-7 (continued)

ACCOUNT *Purchases* ACCOUNT NO. *501*

DATE		DESCRIPTION	POST. REF.	DEBIT	CREDIT	BALANCE DEBIT	BALANCE CREDIT
20--							
Dec.	1	Balance	✓			64385 00	
	11		CP22	1615 00		66000 00	
	31		P16	9300 00		75300 00	

ACCOUNT *Transportation In* ACCOUNT NO. *505*

DATE		DESCRIPTION	POST. REF.	DEBIT	CREDIT	BALANCE DEBIT	BALANCE CREDIT
20--							
Dec.	1	Balance	✓			4949 00	
	21		CP22	51 00		5000 00	

ACCOUNT *Purchases Discounts* ACCOUNT NO. *510*

DATE		DESCRIPTION	POST. REF.	DEBIT	CREDIT	BALANCE DEBIT	BALANCE CREDIT
20--							
Dec.	1	Balance	✓				2162 00
	31		CP22		138 00		2300 00

ACCOUNT *Purchases Returns and Allowances* ACCOUNT NO. *515*

DATE		DESCRIPTION	POST. REF.	DEBIT	CREDIT	BALANCE DEBIT	BALANCE CREDIT
20--							
Dec.	1	Balance	✓				5344 00
	19		G12		256 00		5600 00

ACCOUNT *Bankcard Fees Expense* ACCOUNT NO. *605*

DATE		DESCRIPTION	POST. REF.	DEBIT	CREDIT	BALANCE DEBIT	BALANCE CREDIT
20--							
Dec.	1	Balance	✓			3253 00	
	27		CP22	262 00		3515 00	

Problem 20-7 (continued)

ACCOUNT *Federal Corporate Income Tax Expense* ACCOUNT NO. *625*

DATE		DESCRIPTION	POST. REF.	DEBIT	CREDIT	BALANCE DEBIT	BALANCE CREDIT
20--							
Dec.	1	Balance	✓			2 205 00	
	15		CP22	735 00		2 940 00	

ACCOUNT *Insurance Expense* ACCOUNT NO. *635*

DATE		DESCRIPTION	POST. REF.	DEBIT	CREDIT	BALANCE DEBIT	BALANCE CREDIT

ACCOUNT *Miscellaneous Expense* ACCOUNT NO. *655*

DATE		DESCRIPTION	POST. REF.	DEBIT	CREDIT	BALANCE DEBIT	BALANCE CREDIT
20--							
Dec.	1	Balance	✓			5 520 00	
	6		CP22	425 00		5 945 00	
	27		CP22	15 00		5 960 00	

ACCOUNT *Rent Expense* ACCOUNT NO. *660*

DATE		DESCRIPTION	POST. REF.	DEBIT	CREDIT	BALANCE DEBIT	BALANCE CREDIT
20--							
Dec.	1	Balance	✓			8 250 00	
	1		CP22	750 00		9 000 00	

ACCOUNT *Salaries Expense* ACCOUNT NO. *665*

DATE		DESCRIPTION	POST. REF.	DEBIT	CREDIT	BALANCE DEBIT	BALANCE CREDIT
20--							
Dec.	1	Balance	✓			20 350 00	
	12		CP22	1 850 00		22 200 00	

Name Date Class

Problem 20-7 (concluded)

ACCOUNT *Supplies Expense* ACCOUNT NO. *670*

DATE		DESCRIPTION	POST. REF.	DEBIT	CREDIT	BALANCE DEBIT	BALANCE CREDIT

ACCOUNT *Utilities Expense* ACCOUNT NO. *680*

DATE		DESCRIPTION	POST. REF.	DEBIT	CREDIT	BALANCE DEBIT	BALANCE CREDIT
20--							
Dec.	*1*	*Balance*	✓			*1837 90*	
	9		*CP22*	*57 50*		*1895 40*	
	23		*CP22*	*104 60*		*2000 00*	

(8)

Analyze:

Name Date Class

Problem 20-8 Preparing Adjusting and Closing Entries *(textbook p. 610)*

(1)

GENERAL JOURNAL PAGE ______

	DATE		DESCRIPTION	POST. REF.	DEBIT	CREDIT	
1							1
2							2
3							3
4							4
5							5
6							6
7							7
8							8
9							9
10							10
11							11
12							12
13							13
14							14
15							15
16							16
17							17
18							18
19							19
20							20
21							21
22							22
23							23
24							24
25							25
26							26
27							27
28							28
29							29
30							30
31							31
32							32
33							33
34							34
35							35
36							36

Name Date Class

Problem 20-8 (concluded)

(2)

Analyze:

CHAPTER 21 Accounting for Publicly Held Corporations

Study Guide

Section Assessment

Section 1 *Read Section 1 on pages 617–621 and complete the following exercises on page 622.*
- ☐ Reinforce the Main Idea
- ☐ Math for Accounting
- ☐ Problem 21-1 *Examining Capital Stock Transactions*

Section 2 *Read Section 2 on pages 622–624 and complete the following exercises on page 625.*
- ☐ Reinforce the Main Idea
- ☐ Math for Accounting
- ☐ Problem 21-2 *Distributing Corporate Earnings*
- ☐ Problem 21-3 *Analyzing a Source Document*

Section 3 *Read Section 3 on pages 626–628 and complete the following exercises on page 629.*
- ☐ Reinforce the Main Idea
- ☐ Math for Accounting
- ☐ Problem 21-4 *Examining the Statement of Stockholders' Equity*

Chapter Assessment

Summary *Review the Chapter 21 Visual Summary on page 630 in your textbook.*
- ☐ Key Concepts

Review and Activities *Complete the following questions and exercises on page 631 in your textbook.*
- ☐ After You Read: Answering the Essential Question
- ☐ Vocabulary Check
- ☐ Concept Check

Standardized Test Practice *Complete the exercises on page 632 in your textbook.*

Computerized Accounting *Read the Computerized Accounting information on page 633 in your textbook.*
- ☐ Making the Transition from a Manual to a Computerized System

Problems *Complete the following End-of-Chapter Problems for Chapter 21 in your textbook.*
- ☐ Problem 21-5 *Distributing Corporate Earnings*
- ☐ Problem 21-6 *Journalizing the Issue of Stock*
- ☐ Problem 21-7 *Journalizing Common and Preferred Stock Dividend Transactions*
- ☐ Problem 21-8 *Preparing Corporate Financial Statements*

Challenge Problem
- ☐ Problem 21-9 *Recording Stockholders' Equity Transactions*

Real-World Applications and Connections *Complete the following applications on pages 638–639 in your textbook.*
- ☐ Career Wise
- ☐ Global Accounting
- ☐ A Matter of Ethics
- ☐ Analyzing Financial Reports
- ☐ H.O.T. Audit

Name Date Class

Working Papers *for Section Problems*

Problem 21-1 Examining Capital Stock Transactions *(textbook p. 621)*

1.

2.

3.

Problem 21-2 Distributing Corporate Earnings *(textbook p. 625)*

1.

2.

Name Date Class

Problem 21-3 Analyzing a Source Document *(textbook p. 625)*

GENERAL JOURNAL PAGE ______

	DATE		DESCRIPTION	POST. REF.	DEBIT	CREDIT	
1							1
2							2
3							3
4							4
5							5
6							6
7							7
8							8
9							9
10							10
11							11
12							12
13							13
14							14
15							15
16							16
17							17
18							18
19							19
20							20
21							21
22							22

Problem 21-4 Examining the Statement of Stockholders' Equity *(textbook p. 629)*

Transaction	Reported on Statement of Stockholders' Equity? (Yes/No)
1	
2	
3	
4	
5	
6	
7	
8	

Name Date Class

Working Papers *for End-of-Chapter Problems*

Problem 21-5 Distributing Corporate Earnings *(textbook p. 634)*

1. ______

2. ______

Analyze: ______

Problem 21-6 Journalizing the Issue of Stock *(textbook p. 634)*

GENERAL JOURNAL PAGE ______

	DATE		DESCRIPTION	POST. REF.	DEBIT	CREDIT	
1							1
2							2
3							3
4							4
5							5
6							6
7							7
8							8
9							9
10							10
11							11
12							12
13							13
14							14
15							15
16							16
17							17
18							18
19							19
20							20
21							21
22							22

Analyze: ______

Name Date Class

Problem 21-7 Journalizing Common and Preferred Stock Dividend Transactions *(textbook p. 635)*

(1)

GENERAL JOURNAL PAGE ______

	DATE		DESCRIPTION	POST. REF.	DEBIT	CREDIT	
1							1
2							2
3							3
4							4
5							5
6							6
7							7
8							8
9							9
10							10
11							11
12							12
13							13
14							14
15							15
16							16
17							17
18							18
19							19
20							20
21							21
22							22

Name ____________ Date ____________ Class ____________

Problem 21-7 (concluded)

(2)

GENERAL LEDGER (PARTIAL)

ACCOUNT *Cash in Bank* ACCOUNT NO. *101*

DATE		DESCRIPTION	POST. REF.	DEBIT	CREDIT	BALANCE DEBIT	BALANCE CREDIT
20--							
Dec.	*1*	*Balance*	✓			*98650 00*	

ACCOUNT *Dividends Payable—Preferred* ACCOUNT NO. *203*

DATE		DESCRIPTION	POST. REF.	DEBIT	CREDIT	BALANCE DEBIT	BALANCE CREDIT

ACCOUNT *Dividends Payable—Common* ACCOUNT NO. *204*

DATE		DESCRIPTION	POST. REF.	DEBIT	CREDIT	BALANCE DEBIT	BALANCE CREDIT

ACCOUNT *Dividends—Preferred* ACCOUNT NO. *307*

DATE		DESCRIPTION	POST. REF.	DEBIT	CREDIT	BALANCE DEBIT	BALANCE CREDIT

ACCOUNT *Dividends—Common* ACCOUNT NO. *308*

DATE		DESCRIPTION	POST. REF.	DEBIT	CREDIT	BALANCE DEBIT	BALANCE CREDIT

Analyze: ____________________

Name Date Class

Problem 21-8 Preparing Corporate Financial Statements *(textbook p. 635)*

(1)

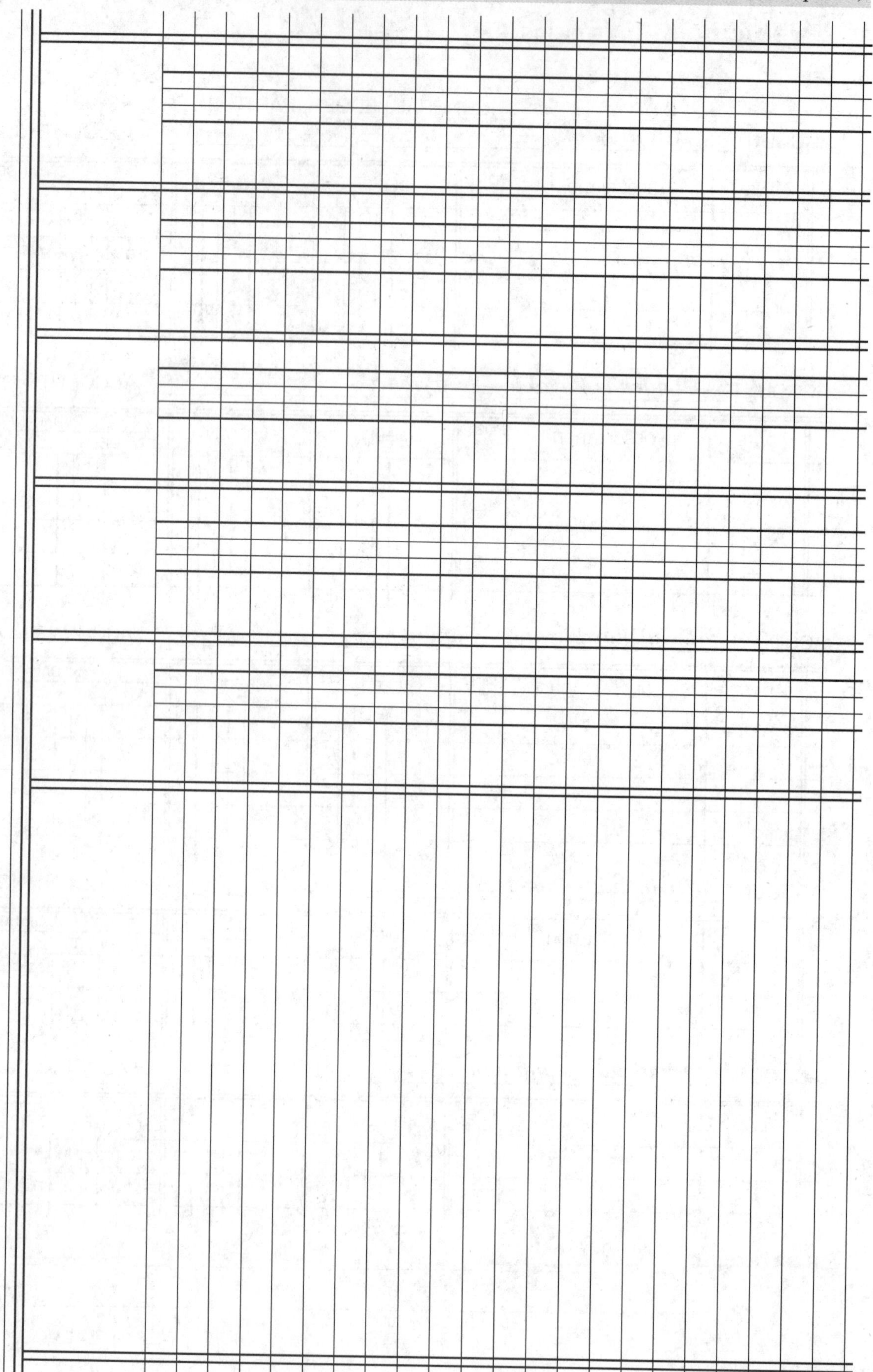

Name Date Class

Problem 21-8 (concluded)

(2)

Analyze:

Name Date Class

Problem 21-9 Recording Stockholder's Equity Transactions *(textbook p. 636)*

Instructions: *Use the following source documents to record the transactions for this problem.*

BUZZ NEWSSTAND
Union Terminal Building, #101
Tacoma, WA 98402

MEMORANDUM 635

TO: *Accounting Clerk*
FROM: *Corporate Accountant as per Board of Directors' Meeting*
DATE: *March 15, 20--*
SUBJECT: *Declared Dividends*

The board of directors approved a semiannual cash dividend of $62,250 for preferred and common stockholders. The dividend is payable to stockholders of record as of April 15 with payment on May 1.

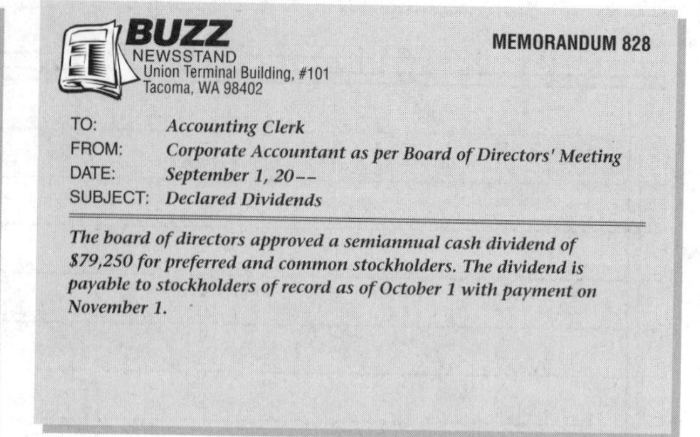
BUZZ NEWSSTAND
Union Terminal Building, #101
Tacoma, WA 98402

MEMORANDUM 828

TO: *Accounting Clerk*
FROM: *Corporate Accountant as per Board of Directors' Meeting*
DATE: *September 1, 20--*
SUBJECT: *Declared Dividends*

The board of directors approved a semiannual cash dividend of $79,250 for preferred and common stockholders. The dividend is payable to stockholders of record as of October 1 with payment on November 1.

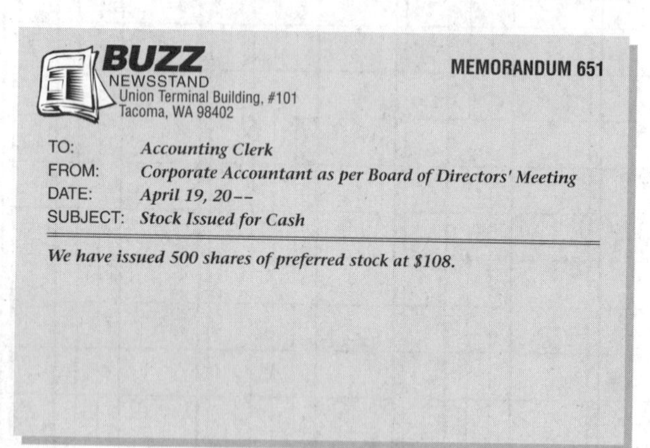
BUZZ NEWSSTAND
Union Terminal Building, #101
Tacoma, WA 98402

MEMORANDUM 651

TO: *Accounting Clerk*
FROM: *Corporate Accountant as per Board of Directors' Meeting*
DATE: *April 19, 20--*
SUBJECT: *Stock Issued for Cash*

We have issued 500 shares of preferred stock at $108.

$ *79,250.00* No. 2451
Date *November 1* 20--
To *Dividends Checking Account*
For *Dividends Payable*

	Dollars	Cents
Balance brought forward	*323,908*	*00*
Add deposits		
Total	*323,908*	*00*
Less this check	*79,250*	*00*
Balance carried forward	*244,658*	*00*

$ *62,250.00* No. 1256
Date *May 1* 20--
To *Dividends Checking Account*
For *Dividends Payable*

	Dollars	Cents
Balance brought forward	*357,225*	*00*
Add deposits		
Total	*357,225*	*00*
Less this check	*62,250*	*00*
Balance carried forward	*294,975*	*00*

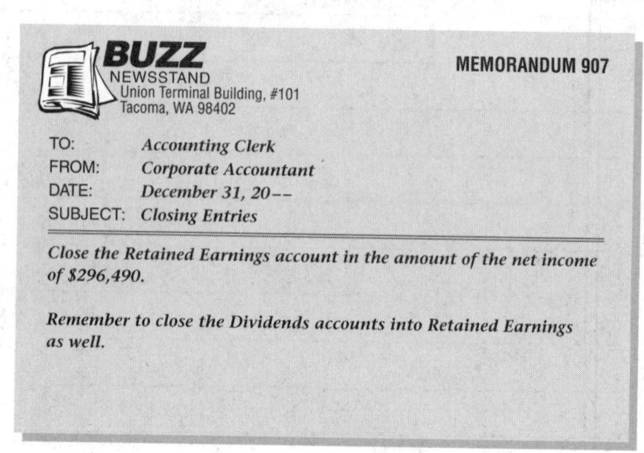
BUZZ NEWSSTAND
Union Terminal Building, #101
Tacoma, WA 98402

MEMORANDUM 907

TO: *Accounting Clerk*
FROM: *Corporate Accountant*
DATE: *December 31, 20--*
SUBJECT: *Closing Entries*

Close the Retained Earnings account in the amount of the net income of $296,490.

Remember to close the Dividends accounts into Retained Earnings as well.

Name Date Class

Problem 21-9 (continued)

(1)

GENERAL JOURNAL PAGE ______

	DATE		DESCRIPTION	POST. REF.	DEBIT	CREDIT	
1							1
2							2
3							3
4							4
5							5
6							6
7							7
8							8
9							9
10							10
11							11
12							12
13							13
14							14
15							15
16							16
17							17
18							18
19							19
20							20
21							21
22							22
23							23
24							24
25							25
26							26
27							27
28							28
29							29
30							30
31							31
32							32
33							33
34							34
35							35
36							36

Problem 21-9 (concluded)

(2)

Analyze:

Name Date Class

CHAPTER 22 Cash Funds

Study Guide

Section Assessment

Section 1 *Read Section 1 on pages 645–648 and complete the following exercises on page 649.*

- ☐ Reinforce the Main Idea
- ☐ Math for Accounting
- ☐ Problem 22-1 *Preparing a Cash Proof*
- ☐ Problem 22-2 *Recording a Cash Overage*

Section 2 *Read Section 2 on pages 650–657 and complete the following exercises on page 658.*

- ☐ Reinforce the Main Idea
- ☐ Math for Accounting
- ☐ Problem 22-3 *Analyzing a Source Document*

Chapter Assessment

Summary *Review the Chapter 22 Visual Summary on page 659 in your textbook.*

- ☐ Key Concepts

Review and Activities *Complete the following questions and exercises on page 660 in your textbook.*

- ☐ After You Read: Answering the Essential Question
- ☐ Vocabulary Check
- ☐ Concept Check

Standardized Test Practice *Complete the exercises on page 661 in your textbook.*

Computerized Accounting *Read the Computerized Accounting information on page 662 in your textbook.*

- ☐ Making the Transition from a Manual to a Computerized System

Problems *Complete the following End-of-Chapter Problems for Chapter 22 in your textbook.*

- ☐ Problem 22-4 *Establishing a Change Fund*
- ☐ Problem 22-5 *Establishing and Replenishing a Petty Cash Fund*
- ☐ Problem 22-6 *Establishing and Replenishing a Petty Cash Fund*
- ☐ Problem 22-7 *Using a Petty Cash Register*
- ☐ Problem 22-8 *Handling a Petty Cash Fund*

Challenge Problem

- ☐ Problem 22-9 *Locating Errors in a Petty Cash Register*

Real-World Applications and Connections *Complete the following applications on pages 668–669 in your textbook.*

- ☐ Case Study
- ☐ 21st Century Skills
- ☐ Career Wise
- ☐ Spotlight on Personal Finance
- ☐ H.O.T. Audit

Name Date Class

Working Papers *for Section Problems*

Problem 22-1 Preparing a Cash Proof *(textbook p. 649)*

(1)

CASH PROOF

Date ______________

Cash Register No. ________

Total cash received (from cash register tape)		$ ______
Cash in drawer	$ ______	
Less change fund	______	
Net cash received		$ ______
Cash short		______
Cash over		______

Salesclerk ______________________

Supervisor ______________________

(2)

GENERAL JOURNAL

PAGE ______

	DATE		DESCRIPTION	POST. REF.	DEBIT	CREDIT	
1							1
2							2
3							3
4							4
5							5
6							6
7							7
8							8
9							9
10							10
11							11
12							12

Name Date Class

Problem 22-2 Recording a Cash Overage *(textbook p. 649)*

(1)

CASH PROOF

Date ____________

Cash Register No. ________

Total cash received (from cash register tape)		$
Cash in drawer	$	
Less change fund		
Net cash received		$
Cash short		
Cash over		

Salesclerk ____________________

Supervisor ____________________

(2)

GENERAL JOURNAL PAGE ______

	DATE		DESCRIPTION	POST. REF.	DEBIT	CREDIT	
1							1
2							2
3							3
4							4
5							5
6							6
7							7
8							8
9							9
10							10
11							11
12							12

Name Date Class

Problem 22-3 Analyzing a Source Document *(textbook p. 658)*

$ ______ No. 973
Date ______ 20___
To ______
For ______

	Dollars	Cents
Balance brought forward	77,432	86
Add deposits		
Total		
Less this check		
Balance carried forward		

Riddle's Card Shop
1500 Main Street
Concord, MA 01742

973

53-215
113

DATE ______ 20___

PAY TO THE
ORDER OF ______ $______

______ DOLLARS

Patriot Bank
CONCORD, MASSACHUSETTS

MEMO ______ ______

⑆011302153⑆ 331 234 9⑈ 0973

Working Papers *for End-of-Chapter Problems*

Problem 22-4 Establishing a Change Fund *(textbook p. 663)*

(1), (3)

GENERAL JOURNAL PAGE ______

	DATE		DESCRIPTION	POST. REF.	DEBIT	CREDIT	
1							1
2							2
3							3
4							4
5							5
6							6
7							7
8							8
9							9
10							10

Analyze: ______

(2)

CASH PROOF

Date ______

Cash Register No. *1*

Total cash received (from cash register tape)		$ ______
Cash in drawer	$ ______	
Less change fund	______	
Net cash received		$ ______
Cash short		______
Cash over		______

Salesclerk ______

Supervisor ______

Name Date Class

Problem 22-5 Establishing and Replenishing a Petty Cash Fund *(textbook p. 663)*

(1)

GENERAL JOURNAL PAGE ______

	DATE		DESCRIPTION	POST. REF.	DEBIT	CREDIT	
1							1
2							2
3							3
4							4
5							5
6							6
7							7
8							8
9							9
10							10

(2)

GENERAL JOURNAL PAGE ______

	DATE		DESCRIPTION	POST. REF.	DEBIT	CREDIT	
1							1
2							2
3							3
4							4
5							5
6							6
7							7
8							8
9							9
10							10

Analyze: ______

Name Date Class

Problem 22-6 Establishing and Replenishing a Petty Cash Fund *(textbook p. 664)*

(1)

GENERAL JOURNAL PAGE ______

	DATE		DESCRIPTION	POST. REF.	DEBIT	CREDIT	
1							1
2							2
3							3
4							4
5							5
6							6
7							7
8							8
9							9
10							10

(5)

GENERAL JOURNAL PAGE ______

	DATE		DESCRIPTION	POST. REF.	DEBIT	CREDIT	
1							1
2							2
3							3
4							4
5							5
6							6
7							7
8							8
9							9
10							10

Problem 22-6 (concluded)

(2)

Voucher No.	Account Name	Amount
101	Supplies	$ ________
102	Advertising Expense	________
103	Miscellaneous Expense	________
104	Delivery Expense	________
105	Supplies	________
106	Miscellaneous Expense	________
107	Delivery Expense	________
108	Miscellaneous Expense	________
109	Supplies	________
110	Delivery Expense	________
111	Advertising Expense	________
112	Miscellaneous Expense	________
113	Advertising Expense	________
	TOTAL	$ ________

(3)

Supplies	$ ________
Advertising Expense	________
Delivery Expense	________
Miscellaneous Expense	________

(4)

PETTY CASH REQUISITION

Accounts for which payments were made:	Amount
________	$ ________
________	________
________	________
________	________
________	________
________	________

TOTAL CASH NEEDED TO REPLENISH FUND: $ ________

Requested by: ________ (PETTY CASHIER) Date ________

Approved by: ________ (ACCOUNTANT) Date ________

Check No. ________

Analyze: ________________

Problem 22-7 Using a Petty Cash Register *(textbook p. 665)*

Instructions: *Use the following source documents to record the transactions for this problem.*

PETTY CASH VOUCHER No. 0001

DATE *February 2* 20--

PAID TO *Silver City Star* $ *9.25*

FOR *Newspaper ad*

ACCOUNT *Advertising Expense*

APPROVED BY

PAYMENT RECEIVED BY *Dudley Hartel*

PETTY CASH VOUCHER No. 0002

DATE *February 5* 20--

PAID TO *Maxwell Office Supplies* $ *5.00*

FOR *Pens and pencils*

ACCOUNT *Supplies*

APPROVED BY

PAYMENT RECEIVED BY *Joshua Maxwell*

PETTY CASH VOUCHER No. 0003

DATE *February 9* 20--

PAID TO *Tumbleweed Florist* $ *12.50*

FOR *Flowers for employee's birthday*

ACCOUNT *Miscellaneous Expense*

APPROVED BY

PAYMENT RECEIVED BY *Louise Wicker*

PETTY CASH VOUCHER No. 0004

DATE *February 12* 20--

PAID TO *Maxwell Office Supplies* $ *3.95*

FOR *Cash register tape*

ACCOUNT *Supplies*

APPROVED BY

PAYMENT RECEIVED BY *Joshua Maxwell*

PETTY CASH VOUCHER No. 0005

DATE *February 19* 20--

PAID TO *National Express* $ *15.00*

FOR *Parts delivered*

ACCOUNT *Delivery Expense*

APPROVED BY

PAYMENT RECEIVED BY *Jessica Kirby*

PETTY CASH VOUCHER No. 0006

DATE *February 20* 20--

PAID TO *Postmaster* $ *3.90*

FOR *Postage stamps*

ACCOUNT *Miscellaneous Expense*

APPROVED BY

PAYMENT RECEIVED BY *Sam Haygood*

PETTY CASH VOUCHER No. 0007

DATE *February 22* 20--

PAID TO *Krystal Clean* $ *16.00*

FOR *Show window cleaned*

ACCOUNT *Miscellaneous Expense*

APPROVED BY

PAYMENT RECEIVED BY *Krystal Adams*

PETTY CASH VOUCHER No. 0008

DATE *February 24* 20--

PAID TO *Silver City Star* $ *11.00*

FOR *Newspaper ad*

ACCOUNT *Advertising Expense*

APPROVED BY

PAYMENT RECEIVED BY *Dudley Hartel*

Problem 22-7 (continued)

PETTY CASH VOUCHER No. 0009

DATE *February 25* 20--

PAID TO *Maxwell Office Supplies* $ *10.00*

FOR *Stationery*

ACCOUNT *Supplies*

APPROVED BY

PAYMENT RECEIVED BY *Joshua Maxwell*

PETTY CASH VOUCHER No. 0010

DATE *February 26* 20--

PAID TO *National Express* $ *8.25*

FOR *Packages delivered*

ACCOUNT *Delivery Expense*

APPROVED BY

PAYMENT RECEIVED BY *Jessica Kirby*

PETTY CASH VOUCHER No. 0011

DATE *February 27* 20--

PAID TO *Maxwell Office Supplies* $ *8.00*

FOR *Supplies*

ACCOUNT

APPROVED BY

PAYMENT RECEIVED BY

VOID

PETTY CASH VOUCHER No. 0012

DATE *February 27* 20--

PAID TO *Maxwell Office Supplies* $ *3.00*

FOR *Memo pads*

ACCOUNT *Supplies*

APPROVED BY

PAYMENT RECEIVED BY *Joshua Maxwell*

PETTY CASH VOUCHER No. 0013

DATE *February 28* 20--

PAID TO *Lara Allen* $ *4.00*

FOR *Tip for daily newspaper delivery*

ACCOUNT *Miscellaneous Expense*

APPROVED BY

PAYMENT RECEIVED BY *Lara Allen*

PETTY CASH VOUCHER No. 0014

DATE *February 28* 20--

PAID TO *Postmaster* $ *6.80*

FOR *Postage stamps*

ACCOUNT *Miscellaneous Expense*

APPROVED BY

PAYMENT RECEIVED BY *Sam Haygood*

PETTY CASH VOUCHER No. 0015

DATE *February 28* 20--

PAID TO *Silver City Star* $ *10.00*

FOR *Newspaper ad*

ACCOUNT *Advertising Expense*

APPROVED BY

PAYMENT RECEIVED BY *Dudley Hartel*

Name Date Class

Problem 22-7 (continued)

(1)

GENERAL JOURNAL PAGE ______

	DATE		DESCRIPTION	POST. REF.	DEBIT	CREDIT	
1							1
2							2
3							3
4							4
5							5
6							6
7							7
8							8
9							9
10							10

(7)

GENERAL JOURNAL PAGE ______

	DATE		DESCRIPTION	POST. REF.	DEBIT	CREDIT	
1							1
2							2
3							3
4							4
5							5
6							6
7							7
8							8
9							9
10							10

Name Date Class

Problem 22-7 (continued) (2), (3), (4), (5)

PETTY CASH REGISTER

PAGE ____

	DATE		VOU. NO.	DESCRIPTION	PAYMENTS	DISTRIBUTION OF PAYMENTS					
						SUPPLIES	DELIVERY EXPENSE	MISC. EXPENSE	GENERAL		
									ACCOUNT NAME	AMOUNT	
1											1
2											2
3											3
4											4
5											5
6											6
7											7
8											8
9											9
10											10
11											11
12											12
13											13
14											14
15											15
16											16
17											17
18											18
19											19
20											20
21											21
22											22
23											23
24											24
25											25

Problem 22-7 (concluded)

(6)

PETTY CASH REQUISITION

Accounts for which payments were made:	Amount
______________________	$________
______________________	________
______________________	________
______________________	________
______________________	________
______________________	________

TOTAL CASH NEEDED TO REPLENISH FUND: $________

Requested by: ______________ (PETTY CASHIER) Date ________

Approved by: ______________ (ACCOUNTANT) Date ________

Check No. ________

Analyze: ____

____

Name Date Class

Problem 22-8 Handling a Petty Cash Fund *(textbook p. 666)*

(1)

GENERAL JOURNAL PAGE ______

	DATE		DESCRIPTION	POST. REF.	DEBIT	CREDIT	
1							1
2							2
3							3
4							4
5							5
6							6
7							7

(7)

GENERAL JOURNAL PAGE ______

	DATE		DESCRIPTION	POST. REF.	DEBIT	CREDIT	
1							1
2							2
3							3
4							4
5							5
6							6
7							7
8							8
9							9
10							10

(9)

GENERAL JOURNAL PAGE ______

	DATE		DESCRIPTION	POST. REF.	DEBIT	CREDIT	
1							1
2							2
3							3
4							4
5							5
6							6
7							7

Name Date Class

Problem 22-8 (continued) (2), (3), (4), (5), (8)

PETTY CASH REGISTER

PAGE ______

	DATE	VOU. NO.	DESCRIPTION	PAYMENTS	DISTRIBUTION OF PAYMENTS					
					SUPPLIES	DELIVERY EXPENSE	MISC. EXPENSE	GENERAL		
								ACCOUNT NAME	AMOUNT	
1										1
2										2
3										3
4										4
5										5
6										6
7										7
8										8
9										9
10										10
11										11
12										12
13										13
14										14
15										15
16										16
17										17
18										18
19										19
20										20
21										21
22										22
23										23
24										24

Problem 22-8 (concluded)

(6)

PETTY CASH REQUISITION

Accounts for which payments were made: Amount

______________________ $________

______________________ ________

______________________ ________

______________________ ________

______________________ ________

______________________ ________

TOTAL CASH NEEDED TO REPLENISH FUND: $________

Requested by: ______________ (PETTY CASHIER) Date ________

Approved by: ______________ (ACCOUNTANT) Date ________

Check No. ________

Analyze: ______________________________

Name Date Class

Problem 22-9 Locating Errors in a Petty Cash Register *(textbook p. 667)*

Petty Cash Disbursements

Item	Date	Amt.
Delivery charge	Feb. 4	$ 7.60
Delivery charge	14	9.65
Delivery charge	27	8.75
Newspaper ad	Feb. 7	$10.00
Newspaper ad	10	8.50
Stamps	Feb. 2	$ 8.25
Stamps	11	9.00

Item	Date	Amt.
Order forms	Feb. 5	$ 9.45
Memo pads	6	12.14
Writing tablets	9	9.43
Wrapping paper	9	8.49
Pens/pencils	20	7.24
Coffee filters	25	3.14
Fax paper	28	9.30
Gasoline	28	11.42
Gasket	28	6.28
Telephone directory	28	4.30

Analyze: ____________________

Problem 22-9 (concluded) (1), (2), (3), (4)

PETTY CASH REGISTER

PAGE ______

	DATE		VOU. NO.	DESCRIPTION	PAYMENTS	SUPPLIES	DELIVERY EXPENSE	MISC. EXPENSE	GENERAL ACCOUNT NAME	GENERAL AMOUNT	
1	20--										1
2	Feb.	1	——	Est. fund $150 Ck. 948							2
3		2	101	Postage stamps	8 25			8 25			3
4		4	102	Delivery charge	6 70			6 70			4
5		5	103	Order forms	9 45			9 45			5
6		6	104	Memo pads	12 14	12 14					6
7		7	105	Newspaper ad	10 00				Advertising Expense	10 00	7
8		9	106	Writing tablets	9 43	9 34					8
9		9	107	Wrapping paper	8 49	8 49					9
10		10	108	Newspaper ad	8 52			8 50			10
11		11	109	Stamps	9 00				Postage	9 00	11
12		14	110	VOID	——						12
13		14	111	Delivery charge	9 65		9 65				13
14		20	112	Pens/pencils	7 24	7 24					14
15		25	113	Coffee filters	3 14			3 14			15
16		27	114	Delivery charge	8 75		6 75				16
17		28	115	Fax paper	9 30	9 30					17
18		28	116	Gasoline	11 42				Gasoline Expense	11 42	18
19		28	117	Gasket	6 28				Maintenance Expense	6 28	19
20		28	118	Telephone directory	4 30			4 30			20
21		28		Totals	138 90	46 51	16 46	38 34		36 70	21
22											22
23				Reconciled Balance	7 06						23
24				Cash Over	1 04						24
25				Replenishment Check	141 90						25
26				Total	150 00						26
27											27
28											28

Name Date Class

CHAPTER 23 Plant Assets and Depreciation

Study Guide

Section Assessment

Section 1 *Read Section 1 on pages 673–675 and complete the following exercises on page 676.*

- ☐ Reinforce the Main Idea
- ☐ Math for Accounting
- ☐ Problem 23-1 *Classifying Asset Accounts*

Section 2 *Read Section 2 on pages 677–678 and complete the following exercises on page 679.*

- ☐ Reinforce the Main Idea
- ☐ Math for Accounting
- ☐ Problem 23-2 *Calculating Depreciation Expense*
- ☐ Problem 23-3 *Completing a Plant Asset Record*

Section 3 *Read Section 3 on pages 680–686 and complete the following exercises on page 687.*

- ☐ Reinforce the Main Idea
- ☐ Math for Accounting
- ☐ Problem 23-4 *Analyzing a Source Document*
- ☐ Problem 23-5 *Preparing a Depreciation Schedule and Journalizing the Depreciation Adjusting Entry*

Chapter Assessment

Summary *Review the Chapter 23 Visual Summary on page 688 in your textbook.*

- ☐ Key Concepts

Review and Activities *Complete the following questions and exercises on page 689 in your textbook.*

- ☐ After You Read: Answering the Essential Question
- ☐ Vocabulary Check
- ☐ Concept Check

Standardized Test Practice *Complete the exercises on page 690 in your textbook.*

Computerized Accounting *Read the Computerized Accounting information on page 691 in your textbook.*

- ☐ Making the Transition from a Manual to a Computerized System

Problems *Complete the following End-of-Chapter Problems for Chapter 23 in your textbook.*

- ☐ Problem 23-6 *Opening a Plant Asset Record*
- ☐ Problem 23-7 *Recording Adjusting Entries for Depreciation*
- ☐ Problem 23-8 *Reporting Depreciation Expense on the Work Sheet and Financial Statements*
- ☐ Problem 23-9 *Calculating and Recording Depreciation Expense*
- ☐ Problem 23-10 *Calculating and Recording Adjustments*

Challenge Problem ☐ Problem 23-11 *Examining Depreciation Adjustments*

Real-World Applications and Connections *Complete the following applications on pages 696–697 in your textbook.*

- ☐ Career Wise
- ☐ Global Accounting
- ☐ Analyzing Financial Reports
- ☐ H.O.T Audit

Name Date Class

Working Papers *for Section Problems*

Problem 23-1 Classifying Asset Accounts *(textbook p. 676)*

Asset	Current Asset	Plant Asset
Accounts Receivable	✓	
Building		
Cash in Bank		
Change Fund		
Delivery Equipment		
Land		
Merchandise Inventory		
Office Equipment		
Office Furniture		
Petty Cash Fund		
Prepaid Insurance		
Store Equipment		
Supplies		

Problem 23-2 Calculating Depreciation Expense *(textbook p. 679)*

	Asset	(1) Amount to be Depreciated	Depreciation Rate	(2) Annual Depreciation	Months Owned	(3) First Year Depreciation
1	Cash register	$		$		$
2	Computer	$		$		$
3	Conference table	$		$		$
4	Delivery truck	$		$		$
5	Desk	$		$		$

Name Date Class

Problem 23-3 Completing a Plant Asset Record *(textbook p. 679)*

PLANT ASSET RECORD

ITEM ______ GENERAL LEDGER ACCOUNT ______

SERIAL NUMBER ______ MANUFACTURER ______

PURCHASED FROM ______ EST. DISPOSAL VALUE ______

ESTIMATED LIFE ______ LOCATION ______

DEPRECIATION METHOD ______ DEPRECIATION PER YEAR ______

DATE	EXPLANATION	ASSET			ACCUMULATED DEPRECIATION			BOOK VALUE
		DEBIT	CREDIT	BALANCE	DEBIT	CREDIT	BALANCE	

Problem 23-4 Analyzing a Source Document *(textbook p. 687)*

(1)

GENERAL JOURNAL PAGE ______

	DATE	DESCRIPTION	POST. REF.	DEBIT	CREDIT	
1						1
2						2
3						3

(2)

GENERAL JOURNAL PAGE ______

	DATE	DESCRIPTION	POST. REF.	DEBIT	CREDIT	
1						1
2						2
3						3

(3)

GENERAL JOURNAL PAGE ______

	DATE	DESCRIPTION	POST. REF.	DEBIT	CREDIT	
1						1
2						2
3						3

Name Date Class

Problem 23-5 Preparing a Depreciation Schedule and Journalizing the Depreciation Adjusting Entry *(textbook p. 687)*

(1)

Date	Cost	Annual Depreciation	Accumulated Depreciation	Book Value
January 7	*$ 2,360*	———	———	*$ 2,360*
First year				
Second year				
Third year				
Fourth year				
Fifth year				

(2), (3)

GENERAL JOURNAL PAGE *40*

	DATE		DESCRIPTION	POST. REF.	DEBIT	CREDIT	
1							1
2							2
3							3
4							4
5							5
6							6
7							7
8							8
9							9
10							10
11							11
12							12

(4)

Name Date Class

Working Papers *for End-of-Chapter Problems*

Problem 23-6 Opening a Plant Asset Record *(textbook p. 692)*

PLANT ASSET RECORD

ITEM ______ GENERAL LEDGER ACCOUNT ______

SERIAL NUMBER ______ MANUFACTURER ______

PURCHASED FROM ______ EST. DISPOSAL VALUE ______

ESTIMATED LIFE ______ LOCATION ______

DEPRECIATION METHOD ______ DEPRECIATION PER YEAR ______

DATE	EXPLANATION	ASSET			ACCUMULATED DEPRECIATION			BOOK VALUE
		DEBIT	CREDIT	BALANCE	DEBIT	CREDIT	BALANCE	

Analyze: ______

Problem 23-7 Recording Adjusting Entries for Depreciation *(textbook p. 692)*

GENERAL JOURNAL PAGE ______

	DATE	DESCRIPTION	POST. REF.	DEBIT	CREDIT	
1						1
2						2
3						3
4						4
5						5
6						6
7						7

Analyze: ______

Problem 23-8 Reporting Depreciation Expense on the Work Sheet and Financial Statements *(textbook p. 693)*

(1), (2)

Shutterbug
Work
For the Year Ended

	ACCT. NO.	ACCOUNT NAME	TRIAL BALANCE DEBIT	TRIAL BALANCE CREDIT	ADJUSTMENTS DEBIT	ADJUSTMENTS CREDIT
1	101	Cash in Bank	9,300.00			
2	105	Change Fund	500.00			
3	110	Petty Cash Fund	200.00			
4	115	Accounts Receivable	1,200.00			
5	125	Merchandise Inventory	50,000.00			(a) 3,690.00
6	130	Supplies	4,000.00			(c) 2,960.00
7	135	Prepaid Insurance	2,400.00			(b) 1,200.00
8	140	Office Equipment	26,000.00			
9	142	Accum. Depr.—Office Equip.		7,500.00		
10	145	Store Equipment	19,200.00			
11	147	Accum. Depr.—Store Equip.		3,600.00		
12	201	Accounts Payable		1,510.00		
13	207	Fed. Corporate Income Tax Pay.	—	—		(d) 600.00
14	215	Sales Tax Payable		1,320.00		
15	301	Capital Stock		51,365.00		
16	305	Retained Earnings		24,000.00		
17	310	Income Summary	—	—	(a) 3,690.00	
18	401	Sales		66,940.00		
19	410	Sales Returns and Allowances	875.00			
20	501	Purchases	21,000.00			
21	505	Transportation In	310.00			
22	510	Purchases Discounts		215.00		
23	515	Purchases Returns and Allow.		1,600.00		
24	601	Advertising Expense	3,000.00			
25	610	Cash Short & Over	50.00			
26	615	Depr. Exp.—Office Equip.	—			
27	617	Depr. Exp.—Store Equip.	—			
28	620	Fed. Corporate Income Tax Exp.	5,000.00		(d) 600.00	
29		Carry Forward	143,035.00	158,050.00		
30						
31						
32						
33						

Name Date Class

Cameras

Sheet

December 31, 20--

ADJUSTED TRIAL BALANCE		INCOME STATEMENT		BALANCE SHEET		
DEBIT	CREDIT	DEBIT	CREDIT	DEBIT	CREDIT	
						1
						2
						3
						4
						5
						6
						7
						8
						9
						10
						11
						12
						13
						14
						15
						16
						17
						18
						19
						20
						21
						22
						23
						24
						25
						26
						27
						28
						29
						30
						31
						32
						33

Name Date Class

Problem 23-8 (continued)

Shutterbug
Work Sheet
For the Year Ended

	ACCT. NO.	ACCOUNT NAME	TRIAL BALANCE DEBIT	TRIAL BALANCE CREDIT	ADJUSTMENTS DEBIT	ADJUSTMENTS CREDIT
1		*Brought Forward*	143,035.00	158,050.00		
2						
3	630	*Insurance Expense*	—		(b) 1,200.00	
4	640	*Maintenance Expense*	1,400.00			
5	645	*Miscellaneous Expense*	425.00			
6	650	*Rent Expense*	6,000.00			
7	655	*Salaries Expense*	6,040.00			
8	660	*Supplies Expense*	—		(c) 2,960.00	
9	670	*Utilities Expense*	1,150.00			
10			158,050.00	158,050.00		
11		*Net Income*				
12						
13						
14						
15						
16						
17						
18						
19						
20						
21						
22						
23						
24						
25						
26						
27						
28						
29						
30						
31						
32						

Name Date Class

Cameras

(continued)

December 31, 20--

ADJUSTED TRIAL BALANCE		INCOME STATEMENT		BALANCE SHEET		
DEBIT	CREDIT	DEBIT	CREDIT	DEBIT	CREDIT	
						1
						2
						3
						4
						5
						6
						7
						8
						9
						10
						11
						12
						13
						14
						15
						16
						17
						18
						19
						20
						21
						22
						23
						24
						25
						26
						27
						28
						29
						30
						31
						32

Name Date Class

Problem 23-8 (continued)

(3)

Name Date Class

Problem 23-8 (concluded)

Analyze:

Problem 23-9 Calculating and Recording Depreciation Expense *(textbook p. 693)*

(1)

Date	Cost	Annual Depreciation	Accumulated Depreciation	Book Value
Purchased Aug. 1	$410,000	———	———	$410,000
First year				
Second year				

(2)

Depreciation Expense—
Manufacturing Equipment
Account 623

Accumulated Depreciation—
Manufacturing Equipment
Account 152

(3)

GENERAL JOURNAL PAGE ______

	DATE		DESCRIPTION	POST. REF.	DEBIT	CREDIT	
1							1
2							2
3							3
4							4
5							5
6							6
7							7

Name Date Class

Problem 23-9 (concluded)

(4)

GENERAL LEDGER

ACCOUNT ______ ACCOUNT NO. ______

DATE		DESCRIPTION	POST. REF.	DEBIT	CREDIT	BALANCE	
						DEBIT	CREDIT

ACCOUNT ______ ACCOUNT NO. ______

DATE		DESCRIPTION	POST. REF.	DEBIT	CREDIT	BALANCE	
						DEBIT	CREDIT

Analyze: ______

Name Date Class

Problem 23-10 Calculating and Recording Adjustments *(textbook p. 694)*

(1), (2)

River's Edge

Work

For the Year Ended

	ACCT. NO.	ACCOUNT NAME	TRIAL BALANCE DEBIT	TRIAL BALANCE CREDIT	ADJUSTMENTS DEBIT	ADJUSTMENTS CREDIT
1	101	Cash in Bank	6690 00			
2	105	Change Fund	200 00			
3	115	Accounts Receivable	12400 00			
4	130	Merchandise Inventory	16300 00			
5	135	Supplies	4850 00			
6	140	Prepaid Insurance	6000 00			
7	145	Delivery Truck	32000 00			
8	147	Accum. Depr.—Delivery Truck		16000 00		
9	150	Store Equipment	13000 00			
10	152	Accum. Depr.—Store Equip.		6000 00		
11	155	Building	160000 00			
12	157	Accum. Depr.—Building		60000 00		
13	160	Land	55000 00			
14	201	Accounts Payable		2300 00		
15	204	Fed. Corporate Income Tax Pay.	—	—		
16	215	Sales Tax Payable		1620 00		
17	301	Capital Stock		140000 00		
18	305	Retained Earnings		20520 00		
19	310	Income Summary	—	—		
20	401	Sales		180000 00		
21	501	Purchases	96000 00			
22	505	Transportation In	5000 00			
23	601	Advertising Expense	3500 00			
24	615	Depr. Exp.—Store Equip.	—			
25	620	Depr. Exp.—Delivery Truck	—			
26	622	Depr. Exp.—Building	—			
27	625	Fed. Corporate Income Tax Exp.	2400 00			
28		Carry Forward	413340 00	426440 00		
29						
30						
31						
32						
33						

Name Date Class

Canoe & Kayak

Sheet

December 31, 20--

ADJUSTED TRIAL BALANCE		INCOME STATEMENT		BALANCE SHEET		
DEBIT	CREDIT	DEBIT	CREDIT	DEBIT	CREDIT	
						1
						2
						3
						4
						5
						6
						7
						8
						9
						10
						11
						12
						13
						14
						15
						16
						17
						18
						19
						20
						21
						22
						23
						24
						25
						26
						27
						28
						29
						30
						31
						32
						33

Problem 23-10 (continued)

River's Edge
Work Sheet
For the Year Ended

	ACCT. NO.	ACCOUNT NAME	TRIAL BALANCE DEBIT	TRIAL BALANCE CREDIT	ADJUSTMENTS DEBIT	ADJUSTMENTS CREDIT
1		*Brought Forward*	413,340.00	426,440.00		
2						
3	630	*Gas Expense*	1,400.00			
4	635	*Insurance Expense*	—			
5	655	*Miscellaneous Expense*	5,400.00			
6	670	*Supplies Expense*	—			
7	680	*Utilities Expense*	6,300.00			
8			426,440.00	426,440.00		
9		*Net Income*				
10						
11						
12						
13						
14						
15						
16						
17						
18						
19						
20						
21						
22						
23						
24						
25						
26						
27						
28						
29						
30						
31						
32						

Name Date Class

Canoe & Kayak

(continued)

December 31, 20--

ADJUSTED TRIAL BALANCE		INCOME STATEMENT		BALANCE SHEET		
DEBIT	CREDIT	DEBIT	CREDIT	DEBIT	CREDIT	
						1
						2
						3
						4
						5
						6
						7
						8
						9
						10
						11
						12
						13
						14
						15
						16
						17
						18
						19
						20
						21
						22
						23
						24
						25
						26
						27
						28
						29
						30
						31
						32

Problem 23-10 (continued)

(3), (4)

GENERAL JOURNAL PAGE ______

	DATE		DESCRIPTION	POST. REF.	DEBIT	CREDIT	
1							1
2							2
3							3
4							4
5							5
6							6
7							7
8							8
9							9
10							10
11							11
12							12
13							13
14							14
15							15
16							16
17							17
18							18
19							19
20							20
21							21
22							22
23							23
24							24
25							25
26							26
27							27
28							28
29							29
30							30
31							31
32							32
33							33
34							34
35							35
36							36

Name Date Class

Problem 23-10 (continued)

GENERAL LEDGER (PARTIAL)

ACCOUNT *Merchandise Inventory* ACCOUNT NO. *130*

DATE		DESCRIPTION	POST. REF.	DEBIT	CREDIT	BALANCE DEBIT	BALANCE CREDIT
20--							
Dec.	*31*	*Balance*	✓			*16300 00*	

ACCOUNT *Supplies* ACCOUNT NO. *135*

DATE		DESCRIPTION	POST. REF.	DEBIT	CREDIT	BALANCE DEBIT	BALANCE CREDIT
20--							
Dec.	*31*	*Balance*	✓			*4850 00*	

ACCOUNT *Prepaid Insurance* ACCOUNT NO. *140*

DATE		DESCRIPTION	POST. REF.	DEBIT	CREDIT	BALANCE DEBIT	BALANCE CREDIT
20--							
Dec.	*31*	*Balance*	✓			*6000 00*	

ACCOUNT *Accumulated Depreciation—Delivery Truck* ACCOUNT NO. *147*

DATE		DESCRIPTION	POST. REF.	DEBIT	CREDIT	BALANCE DEBIT	BALANCE CREDIT
20--							
Dec.	*31*	*Balance*	✓				*16000 00*

Name Date Class

Problem 23-10 (continued)

ACCOUNT *Accumulated Depreciation—Store Equipment* ACCOUNT NO. *152*

DATE		DESCRIPTION	POST. REF.	DEBIT	CREDIT	BALANCE DEBIT	BALANCE CREDIT
20--							
Dec.	*31*	*Balance*	✓				*600000*

ACCOUNT *Accumulated Depreciation—Building* ACCOUNT NO. *157*

DATE		DESCRIPTION	POST. REF.	DEBIT	CREDIT	BALANCE DEBIT	BALANCE CREDIT
20--							
Dec.	*31*	*Balance*	✓				*6000000*

ACCOUNT *Federal Corporate Income Tax Payable* ACCOUNT NO. *204*

DATE		DESCRIPTION	POST. REF.	DEBIT	CREDIT	BALANCE DEBIT	BALANCE CREDIT

ACCOUNT *Retained Earnings* ACCOUNT NO. *305*

DATE		DESCRIPTION	POST. REF.	DEBIT	CREDIT	BALANCE DEBIT	BALANCE CREDIT
20--							
Dec.	*31*	*Balance*	✓				*2052000*

Problem 23-10 (continued)

ACCOUNT *Income Summary* ACCOUNT NO. *310*

DATE		DESCRIPTION	POST. REF.	DEBIT	CREDIT	BALANCE DEBIT	BALANCE CREDIT

ACCOUNT *Sales* ACCOUNT NO. *401*

DATE		DESCRIPTION	POST. REF.	DEBIT	CREDIT	BALANCE DEBIT	BALANCE CREDIT
20--							
Dec.	*31*	*Balance*	✓				*180000 00*

ACCOUNT *Purchases* ACCOUNT NO. *501*

DATE		DESCRIPTION	POST. REF.	DEBIT	CREDIT	BALANCE DEBIT	BALANCE CREDIT
20--							
Dec.	*31*	*Balance*	✓			*96000 00*	

ACCOUNT *Transportation In* ACCOUNT NO. *505*

DATE		DESCRIPTION	POST. REF.	DEBIT	CREDIT	BALANCE DEBIT	BALANCE CREDIT
20--							
Dec.	*31*	*Balance*	✓			*5000 00*	

Problem 23-10 (continued)

ACCOUNT *Advertising Expense* ACCOUNT NO. *601*

DATE		DESCRIPTION	POST. REF.	DEBIT	CREDIT	BALANCE DEBIT	BALANCE CREDIT
20--							
Dec.	*31*	*Balance*	✓			*3500 00*	

ACCOUNT *Depreciation Expense—Store Equipment* ACCOUNT NO. *615*

DATE		DESCRIPTION	POST. REF.	DEBIT	CREDIT	BALANCE DEBIT	BALANCE CREDIT

ACCOUNT *Depreciation Expense—Delivery Truck* ACCOUNT NO. *620*

DATE		DESCRIPTION	POST. REF.	DEBIT	CREDIT	BALANCE DEBIT	BALANCE CREDIT

ACCOUNT *Depreciation Expense—Building* ACCOUNT NO. *622*

DATE		DESCRIPTION	POST. REF.	DEBIT	CREDIT	BALANCE DEBIT	BALANCE CREDIT

Problem 23-10 (continued)

ACCOUNT *Federal Corporate Income Tax Expense* ACCOUNT NO. *625*

DATE		DESCRIPTION	POST. REF.	DEBIT	CREDIT	BALANCE DEBIT	BALANCE CREDIT
20--							
Dec.	*31*	*Balance*	✓			*240000*	

ACCOUNT *Gas Expense* ACCOUNT NO. *630*

DATE		DESCRIPTION	POST. REF.	DEBIT	CREDIT	BALANCE DEBIT	BALANCE CREDIT
20--							
Dec.	*31*	*Balance*	✓			*140000*	

ACCOUNT *Insurance Expense* ACCOUNT NO. *635*

DATE		DESCRIPTION	POST. REF.	DEBIT	CREDIT	BALANCE DEBIT	BALANCE CREDIT

ACCOUNT *Miscellaneous Expense* ACCOUNT NO. *655*

DATE		DESCRIPTION	POST. REF.	DEBIT	CREDIT	BALANCE DEBIT	BALANCE CREDIT
20--							
Dec.	*31*	*Balance*	✓			*540000*	

Name Date Class

Problem 23-10 (concluded)

ACCOUNT *Supplies Expense* ACCOUNT NO. *670*

DATE		DESCRIPTION	POST. REF.	DEBIT	CREDIT	BALANCE DEBIT	BALANCE CREDIT

ACCOUNT *Utilities Expense* ACCOUNT NO. *680*

DATE		DESCRIPTION	POST. REF.	DEBIT	CREDIT	BALANCE DEBIT	BALANCE CREDIT
20--							
Dec.	*31*	*Balance*	✓			*630000*	

Analyze:

Problem 23-11 Examining Depreciation Adjustments *(textbook p. 694)*

1.

2.

Analyze:

Name Date Class

Study Guide

Section Assessment

Section 1 *Read Section 1 on pages 701–704 and complete the following exercises on page 705.*

- ☐ Reinforce the Main Idea
- ☐ Math for Accounting
- ☐ Problem 24-1 *Using the Direct Write-Off Method*

Section 2 *Read Section 2 on pages 706–713 and complete the following exercises on page 714.*

- ☐ Reinforce the Main Idea
- ☐ Math for Accounting
- ☐ Problem 24-2 *Writing Off Accounts Using the Allowance Method*

Section 3 *Read Section 3 on pages 715–717 and complete the following exercises on page 718.*

- ☐ Reinforce the Main Idea
- ☐ Math for Accounting
- ☐ Problem 24-3 *Estimating Uncollectible Accounts Expense Using the Percentage of Net Sales Method*

Chapter Assessment

Summary *Review the Chapter 24 Visual Summary on page 719 in your textbook.*

- ☐ Key Concepts

Review and Activities *Complete the following questions and exercises on page 720 in your textbook.*

- ☐ After You Read: Answering the Essential Question
- ☐ Vocabulary Check
- ☐ Concept Check

Standardized Test Practice *Complete the exercises on page 721 in your textbook.*

Computerized Accounting *Read the Computerized Accounting information on page 722 in your textbook.*

- ☐ Making the Transition from a Manual to a Computerized System

Problems *Complete the following End-of-Chapter Problems for Chapter 24 in your textbook.*

- ☐ Problem 24-4 *Using the Direct Write-Off Method*
- ☐ Problem 24-5 *Calculating and Recording Estimated Uncollectible Accounts Expense*
- ☐ Problem 24-6 *Writing off Accounts Under the Allowance Method*
- ☐ Problem 24-7 *Estimating Uncollectible Accounts Expense*
- ☐ Problem 24-8 *Reporting Uncollectible Amounts on the Financial Statements*

Challenge Problem

- ☐ Problem 24-9 *Using the Allowance Method for Write-Offs*

Real-World Applications and Connections *Complete the following applications on pages 726–727 in your textbook.*

- ☐ Case Study
- ☐ 21st Century Skills
- ☐ Career Wise
- ☐ Spotlight on Personal Finance
- ☐ H.O.T. Audit

Name Date Class

Working Papers *for Section Problems*

Problem 24-1 Using the Direct Write-Off Method *(textbook p. 705)*

(1)

GENERAL JOURNAL PAGE ______

	DATE		DESCRIPTION	POST. REF.	DEBIT	CREDIT	
1							1
2							2
3							3
4							4
5							5
6							6
7							7
8							8
9							9
10							10
11							11
12							12
13							13
14							14
15							15
16							16
17							17
18							18
19							19
20							20
21							21
22							22
23							23
24							24
25							25
26							26
27							27
28							28
29							29
30							30

Problem 24-1 (continued)

(2)

GENERAL LEDGER

ACCOUNT *Cash in Bank* ACCOUNT NO. *101*

DATE		DESCRIPTION	POST. REF.	DEBIT	CREDIT	BALANCE DEBIT	BALANCE CREDIT
20--							
Apr.	1	Balance	✓			9,428.00	

ACCOUNT *Accounts Receivable* ACCOUNT NO. *115*

DATE		DESCRIPTION	POST. REF.	DEBIT	CREDIT	BALANCE DEBIT	BALANCE CREDIT
20—							
Apr.	1	Balance	✓			7,290.00	

ACCOUNT *Sales Tax Payable* ACCOUNT NO. *215*

DATE		DESCRIPTION	POST. REF.	DEBIT	CREDIT	BALANCE DEBIT	BALANCE CREDIT
20--							
Apr.	1	Balance	✓				248.00

ACCOUNT *Sales* ACCOUNT NO. *401*

DATE		DESCRIPTION	POST. REF.	DEBIT	CREDIT	BALANCE DEBIT	BALANCE CREDIT
20--							
Apr.	1	Balance	✓				24,160.00

ACCOUNT *Uncollectible Accounts Expense* ACCOUNT NO. *680*

DATE		DESCRIPTION	POST. REF.	DEBIT	CREDIT	BALANCE DEBIT	BALANCE CREDIT
20--							
Apr.	1	Balance	✓			928.00	

Name Date Class

Problem 24-1 (concluded)

(2)

ACCOUNTS RECEIVABLE SUBSIDIARY LEDGER

Name *Sonya Dickson*

Address

DATE		DESCRIPTION	POST. REF.	DEBIT	CREDIT	BALANCE

Name Date Class

Problem 24-2 Writing Off Accounts Using the Allowance Method
(textbook p. 714)

(1)

GENERAL JOURNAL PAGE ______

	DATE		DESCRIPTION	POST. REF.	DEBIT	CREDIT	
1							1
2							2
3							3
4							4
5							5
6							6
7							7
8							8
9							9
10							10
11							11
12							12
13							13
14							14
15							15
16							16
17							17
18							18
19							19
20							20
21							21
22							22
23							23
24							24
25							25
26							26
27							27
28							28
29							29
30							30

Problem 24-2 (continued)

(2)

ACCOUNTS RECEIVABLE SUBSIDIARY LEDGER

Name *Jack Bowers*

Address

DATE		DESCRIPTION	POST. REF.	DEBIT	CREDIT	BALANCE
20--						
May	1	Balance	✓			1 050 00

GENERAL LEDGER (PARTIAL)

ACCOUNT *Cash in Bank* ACCOUNT NO. *101*

DATE		DESCRIPTION	POST. REF.	DEBIT	CREDIT	BALANCE DEBIT	BALANCE CREDIT
20--							
Nov.	1	Balance	✓			9 420 00	

ACCOUNT *Accounts Receivable* ACCOUNT NO. *115*

DATE		DESCRIPTION	POST. REF.	DEBIT	CREDIT	BALANCE DEBIT	BALANCE CREDIT
20--							
May	1	Balance	✓			20 400 00	

Name Date Class

Problem 24-2 (concluded)

ACCOUNT *Allowance for Uncollectible Accounts* ACCOUNT NO. *117*

DATE		DESCRIPTION	POST. REF.	DEBIT	CREDIT	BALANCE DEBIT	BALANCE CREDIT
20--							
May	*1*	*Balance*	✓				*1200 00*

ACCOUNT *Uncollectible Accounts Expense* ACCOUNT NO. *675*

DATE		DESCRIPTION	POST. REF.	DEBIT	CREDIT	BALANCE DEBIT	BALANCE CREDIT

(3)

Name Date Class

Problem 24-3 Estimating Uncollectible Accounts Expense Using the Percentage of Net Sales Method *(textbook p. 718)*

(1)

Company	Net Sales	Percentage of Net Sales	Uncollectible Accounts Expense
Andrews Co.		2%	
The Book Nook		1%	
Cable, Inc.		1½%	
Davis, Inc.		2%	
Ever-Sharp Co.		1¼%	

(2)

GENERAL JOURNAL PAGE *21*

	DATE		DESCRIPTION	POST. REF.	DEBIT	CREDIT	
1							1
2							2
3							3
4							4
5							5
6							6
7							7
8							8
9							9
10							10
11							11
12							12

Working Papers *for End-of-Chapter Problems*

Problem 24-4 Using the Direct Write-Off Method *(textbook p. 723)*

(1)

GENERAL JOURNAL PAGE ______

	DATE		DESCRIPTION	POST. REF.	DEBIT	CREDIT	
1							1
2							2
3							3
4							4
5							5
6							6
7							7
8							8
9							9
10							10
11							11
12							12
13							13
14							14
15							15
16							16
17							17
18							18
19							19
20							20
21							21
22							22
23							23
24							24
25							25
26							26
27							27
28							28
29							29
30							30
31							31
32							32
33							33
34							34

Problem 24-4 (continued)

(2)

ACCOUNTS RECEIVABLE SUBSIDIARY LEDGER

Name *Martha Adams*

Address

DATE		DESCRIPTION	POST. REF.	DEBIT	CREDIT	BALANCE
20--						
June	*1*	*Balance*	✓			*100 80*

Name *Alex Hamilton*

Address

DATE		DESCRIPTION	POST. REF.	DEBIT	CREDIT	BALANCE
20--						
June	*1*	*Balance*	✓			*288 75*

Name *Helen Jun*

Address

DATE		DESCRIPTION	POST. REF.	DEBIT	CREDIT	BALANCE
20--						
June	*1*	*Balance*	✓			*243 60*

Name *Nate Moulder*

Address

DATE		DESCRIPTION	POST. REF.	DEBIT	CREDIT	BALANCE
20--						
June	*1*	*Balance*	✓			*57 75*

Name Date Class

Problem 24-4 (concluded)

GENERAL LEDGER

ACCOUNT *Cash in Bank* ACCOUNT NO. *101*

DATE		DESCRIPTION	POST. REF.	DEBIT	CREDIT	BALANCE DEBIT	BALANCE CREDIT
20--							
June	*1*	*Balance*	✓			*10650 16*	

ACCOUNT *Accounts Receivable* ACCOUNT NO. *115*

DATE		DESCRIPTION	POST. REF.	DEBIT	CREDIT	BALANCE DEBIT	BALANCE CREDIT
20--							
June	*1*	*Balance*	✓			*8016 50*	

ACCOUNT *Uncollectible Accounts Expense* ACCOUNT NO. *670*

DATE		DESCRIPTION	POST. REF.	DEBIT	CREDIT	BALANCE DEBIT	BALANCE CREDIT

Analyze:

Name Date Class

Problem 24-5 Calculating and Recording Estimated Uncollectible Accounts Expense *(textbook p. 723)*

(1) ______________________________

(2)

GENERAL JOURNAL PAGE ____

	DATE		DESCRIPTION	POST. REF.	DEBIT	CREDIT	
1							1
2							2
3							3
4							4
5							5
6							6

(3)

GENERAL LEDGER (PARTIAL)

ACCOUNT *Allowance for Uncollectible Accounts* ACCOUNT NO. *117*

DATE		DESCRIPTION	POST. REF.	DEBIT	CREDIT	BALANCE DEBIT	BALANCE CREDIT
20--							
June	*1*	*Balance*	✓				*400000*

ACCOUNT *Uncollectible Accounts Expense* ACCOUNT NO. *670*

DATE		DESCRIPTION	POST. REF.	DEBIT	CREDIT	BALANCE DEBIT	BALANCE CREDIT

Analyze: ______________________________

Problem 24-6 Writing Off Accounts Under the Allowance Method

(textbook p. 724)

Instructions: *Use the following source documents to record the transactions for this problem.*

Shutterbug Cameras
1111 Gulf Breeze Drive
Gulf Shores, AL 36542

MEMORANDUM 329

TO: *Accounting Clerk*
FROM: *Whitney Henderson, Senior Accountant*
DATE: *June 2, 20--*
SUBJECT: *Uncollectible Account*

Please write off the $593.25 account of Kalla Booth as uncollectible.

Shutterbug Cameras
1111 Gulf Breeze Drive
Gulf Shores, AL 36542

MEMORANDUM 474

TO: *Accounting Clerk*
FROM: *Whitney Henderson, Senior Accountant*
DATE: *June 12, 20--*
SUBJECT: *Uncollectible Account*

Please write off the account of FastForward Productions ($945.00) as uncollectible.

Shutterbug Cameras
1111 Gulf Breeze Drive
Gulf Shores, AL 36542

MEMORANDUM 343

TO: *Accounting Clerk*
FROM: *Whitney Henderson, Senior Accountant*
DATE: *June 9, 20--*
SUBJECT: *Uncollectible Account*

Please write off the account of Click Studios ($840.00) as uncollectible.

Shutterbug Cameras
1111 Gulf Breeze Drive
Gulf Shores, AL 36542

MEMORANDUM 478

TO: *Accounting Clerk*
FROM: *Whitney Henderson, Senior Accountant*
DATE: *June 30, 20--*
SUBJECT: *Closing Entries*

The adjusting entry for estimated uncollectible accounts for the period is to be recorded. The uncollectible account expense estimate is based on 2% of net sales of $150,000.00.

Shutterbug Cameras
1111 Gulf Breeze Drive
Gulf Shores, AL 36542

RECEIPT
No. 210

June 10 20 --

RECEIVED FROM *Jimmy Thompson* $ *131.25*

One hundred thirty-one and 25/100 DOLLARS

FOR *Payment on past due account*

RECEIVED BY *Whitney Henderson*

Shutterbug Cameras
1111 Gulf Breeze Drive
Gulf Shores, AL 36542

MEMORANDUM 479

TO: *Accounting Clerk*
FROM: *Whitney Henderson, Senior Accountant*
DATE: *June 30, 20--*
SUBJECT: *Closing Entries*

Please record the closing entry for Uncollectible Accounts Expense.

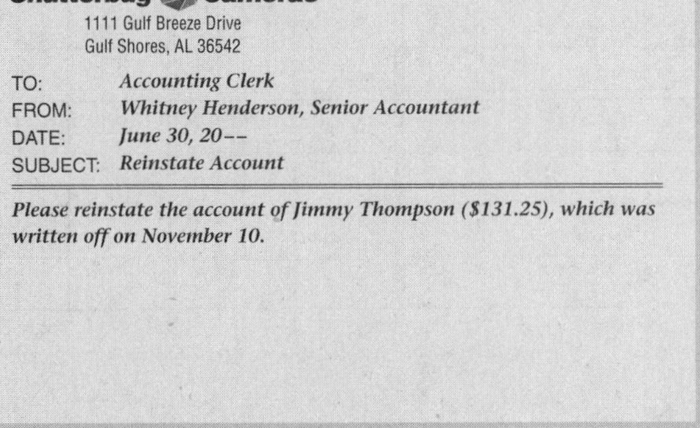

Shutterbug Cameras
1111 Gulf Breeze Drive
Gulf Shores, AL 36542

MEMORANDUM 349

TO: *Accounting Clerk*
FROM: *Whitney Henderson, Senior Accountant*
DATE: *June 30, 20--*
SUBJECT: *Reinstate Account*

Please reinstate the account of Jimmy Thompson ($131.25), which was written off on November 10.

Name Date Class

Problem 24-6 (continued)

(1)

GENERAL JOURNAL

PAGE ______

	DATE		DESCRIPTION	POST. REF.	DEBIT	CREDIT	
1							1
2							2
3							3
4							4
5							5
6							6
7							7
8							8
9							9
10							10
11							11
12							12
13							13
14							14
15							15
16							16
17							17
18							18
19							19
20							20
21							21
22							22
23							23
24							24
25							25
26							26
27							27
28							28
29							29
30							30
31							31
32							32
33							33
34							34

Name Date Class

Problem 24-6 (continued)

(2)

GENERAL LEDGER

ACCOUNT *Cash in Bank* ACCOUNT NO. *101*

DATE		DESCRIPTION	POST. REF.	DEBIT	CREDIT	BALANCE DEBIT	BALANCE CREDIT
20--							
June	*1*	*Balance*	✓			*9 306 54*	

ACCOUNT *Accounts Receivable* ACCOUNT NO. *115*

DATE		DESCRIPTION	POST. REF.	DEBIT	CREDIT	BALANCE DEBIT	BALANCE CREDIT
20--							
June	*1*	*Balance*	✓			*23 102 00*	

ACCOUNT *Allowance for Uncollectible Accounts* ACCOUNT NO. *117*

DATE		DESCRIPTION	POST. REF.	DEBIT	CREDIT	BALANCE DEBIT	BALANCE CREDIT
20--							
June	*1*	*Balance*	✓				*3 164 00*

ACCOUNT *Income Summary* ACCOUNT NO. *310*

DATE		DESCRIPTION	POST. REF.	DEBIT	CREDIT	BALANCE DEBIT	BALANCE CREDIT

ACCOUNT *Uncollectible Accounts Expense* ACCOUNT NO. *665*

DATE		DESCRIPTION	POST. REF.	DEBIT	CREDIT	BALANCE DEBIT	BALANCE CREDIT

Problem 24-6 (continued)

(2)

ACCOUNTS RECEIVABLE SUBSIDIARY LEDGER

Name *Kalla Booth*

Address *1416 Halprin Avenue, Mobile, AL 36604*

DATE		DESCRIPTION	POST. REF.	DEBIT	CREDIT	BALANCE
20--						
June	1	Balance	✓			593 25

Name *Click Studios*

Address *1300 Nice Avenue, Mobile, AL 36610*

DATE		DESCRIPTION	POST. REF.	DEBIT	CREDIT	BALANCE
20--						
June	1	Balance	✓			840 00

Name *FastForward Productions*

Address *3937 Channel Drive, Mobile, AL 36617*

DATE		DESCRIPTION	POST. REF.	DEBIT	CREDIT	BALANCE
20--						
June	1	Balance	✓			945 00

Name *Jimmy Thompson*

Address *1616 Parkway Drive, Mobile, AL 36609*

DATE		DESCRIPTION	POST. REF.	DEBIT	CREDIT	BALANCE
20--						
June	1	Balance	✓			—

Name Date Class

Problem 24-6 (concluded)

(3)

Analyze:

Name Date Class

Problem 24-7 Estimating Uncollectible Accounts Expense *(textbook p. 724)*

(1)

Customer Name	Total Amount Owed	Not Yet Due	Days Past Due				
			1-30 Days	31-60 Days	61-90 Days	91-180 Days	Over 180
N. Bellis	$ 722	$ 722					
G. Buresh	1,362		$ 761		$601		
Rachel D'Souza	209	209					
S. Garfield	449		132	$317			
Greg Kellogg	271					$ 271	
Rishi Nadal	1,066	640		426			
Megan O'Hara	48					48	
ProTeam Sponsors Inc.	1,998	1,998					
Heidi Spencer	790	428	362				
Ed Young	296						$296
Totals							

(2)

Age Group	Amount	Estimated Percentage Uncollectible	Estimated Uncollectible Amount
Not yet due		2%	
1–30 days past due		4%	
31–60 days past due		20%	
61–90 days past due		30%	
91–180 days past due		45%	
Over 180 days past due		60%	
Totals			

Name Date Class

Problem 24-7 (concluded)

(3)

GENERAL JOURNAL PAGE

	DATE		DESCRIPTION	POST. REF.	DEBIT	CREDIT	
1							1
2							2
3							3
4							4
5							5
6							6

(4)

GENERAL LEDGER (PARTIAL)

ACCOUNT *Accounts Receivable* ACCOUNT NO. *115*

DATE		DESCRIPTION	POST. REF.	DEBIT	CREDIT	BALANCE DEBIT	BALANCE CREDIT
20--							
June	*30*	*Balance*	*3*			*7 211 00*	

ACCOUNT *Allowance for Uncollectible Accounts* ACCOUNT NO. *117*

DATE		DESCRIPTION	POST. REF.	DEBIT	CREDIT	BALANCE DEBIT	BALANCE CREDIT
20--							
June	*30*	*Balance*	*3*				*142 00*

ACCOUNT *Uncollectible Accounts Expense* ACCOUNT NO. *670*

DATE		DESCRIPTION	POST. REF.	DEBIT	CREDIT	BALANCE DEBIT	BALANCE CREDIT

Analyze:

Name Date Class

Problem 24-8 Reporting Uncollectible Amounts on the Financial Statements *(textbook p. 725)*

(1), (2)

River's Edge
Work
For the Year Ended

	ACCT. NO.	ACCOUNT NAME	TRIAL BALANCE DEBIT	TRIAL BALANCE CREDIT	ADJUSTMENTS DEBIT	ADJUSTMENTS CREDIT
1	101	Cash in Bank	21,633.50			
2	115	Accounts Receivable	10,168.45			
3	117	Allow. for Uncollectible Accounts		400.00		
4	130	Merchandise Inventory	39,391.75			(b) 3,630.25
5	135	Supplies	2,875.00			(c) 1,900.00
6	140	Prepaid Insurance	3,100.00			(d) 2,000.00
7	150	Store Equipment	30,000.00			
8	152	Accum. Depr.—Store Equip.		3,610.00		(e) 500.00
9	201	Accounts Payable		3,960.00		
10	210	Fed. Corporate Income Tax Pay.	—	—		(f) 1,806.00
11	215	Sales Tax Payable		613.10		
12	301	Capital Stock		40,000.00		
13	305	Retained Earnings		9,764.15		
14	310	Income Summary	—	—	(b) 3,630.25	
15	401	Sales		152,875.20		
16	410	Sales Returns and Allowances	3,585.00			
17	501	Purchases	81,860.00			
18	505	Transportation In	3,956.00			
19	510	Purchases Discounts		740.00		
20	515	Purchases Returns and Allow.		1,221.00		
21	605	Bankcard Fees Expense	452.75			
22	615	Depr. Exp.—Store Equip.	—		(e) 500.00	
23	625	Fed. Corporate Income Tax Exp.	3,750.00		(f) 1,806.00	
24	635	Insurance Expense	—		(d) 2,000.00	
25	655	Miscellaneous Expense	730.00			
26	660	Rent Expense	9,600.00			
27	670	Supplies Expense	—		(c) 1,900.00	
28	675	Uncollectible Accounts Expense	—			
29	680	Utilities Expense	2,081.00			
30			213,183.45	213,183.45		
31						
32						
33						

Name Date Class

Canoe & Kayak

Sheet

June 30, 20––

ADJUSTED TRIAL BALANCE		INCOME STATEMENT		BALANCE SHEET		
DEBIT	CREDIT	DEBIT	CREDIT	DEBIT	CREDIT	
						1
						2
						3
						4
						5
						6
						7
						8
						9
						10
						11
						12
						13
						14
						15
						16
						17
						18
						19
						20
						21
						22
						23
						24
						25
						26
						27
						28
						29
						30
						31
						32
						33

Name Date Class

Problem 24-8 (continued)

(3)

Problem 24-8 (continued)

(3)

(3)

Problem 24-8 (continued)

(4), (5)

GENERAL JOURNAL PAGE ______

	DATE		DESCRIPTION	POST. REF.	DEBIT	CREDIT	
1							1
2							2
3							3
4							4
5							5
6							6
7							7
8							8
9							9
10							10
11							11
12							12
13							13
14							14
15							15
16							16
17							17
18							18
19							19
20							20
21							21
22							22
23							23
24							24
25							25
26							26
27							27
28							28
29							29
30							30
31							31
32							32
33							33
34							34
35							35
36							36

Name Date Class

Problem 24-8 (continued)

(5)

GENERAL LEDGER

ACCOUNT *Cash in Bank* ACCOUNT NO. *101*

DATE		DESCRIPTION	POST. REF.	DEBIT	CREDIT	BALANCE DEBIT	BALANCE CREDIT
20--							
June	*30*	*Balance*	✓			*21,633.50*	

ACCOUNT *Accounts Receivable* ACCOUNT NO. *115*

DATE		DESCRIPTION	POST. REF.	DEBIT	CREDIT	BALANCE DEBIT	BALANCE CREDIT
20--							
June	*30*	*Balance*	✓			*10,168.45*	

ACCOUNT *Allowance for Uncollectible Accounts* ACCOUNT NO. *117*

DATE		DESCRIPTION	POST. REF.	DEBIT	CREDIT	BALANCE DEBIT	BALANCE CREDIT
20--							
June	*30*	*Balance*	✓				*400.00*

ACCOUNT *Merchandise Inventory* ACCOUNT NO. *130*

DATE		DESCRIPTION	POST. REF.	DEBIT	CREDIT	BALANCE DEBIT	BALANCE CREDIT
20--							
June	*30*	*Balance*	✓			*39,391.75*	

ACCOUNT *Supplies* ACCOUNT NO. *135*

DATE		DESCRIPTION	POST. REF.	DEBIT	CREDIT	BALANCE DEBIT	BALANCE CREDIT
20--							
June	*30*	*Balance*	✓			*2,875.00*	

ACCOUNT *Prepaid Insurance* ACCOUNT NO. *140*

DATE		DESCRIPTION	POST. REF.	DEBIT	CREDIT	BALANCE DEBIT	BALANCE CREDIT
20--							
June	*30*	*Balance*	✓			*3,100.00*	

Problem 24-8 (continued)

ACCOUNT *Store Equipment* ACCOUNT NO. *150*

DATE		DESCRIPTION	POST. REF.	DEBIT	CREDIT	BALANCE DEBIT	BALANCE CREDIT
20--							
June	30	Balance	✓			30000 00	

ACCOUNT *Accumulated Depreciation—Store Equipment* ACCOUNT NO. *152*

DATE		DESCRIPTION	POST. REF.	DEBIT	CREDIT	BALANCE DEBIT	BALANCE CREDIT
20--							
June	30	Balance	✓				3610 00

ACCOUNT *Accounts Payable* ACCOUNT NO. *201*

DATE		DESCRIPTION	POST. REF.	DEBIT	CREDIT	BALANCE DEBIT	BALANCE CREDIT
20--							
June	30	Balance	✓				3960 00

ACCOUNT *Federal Corporate Income Tax Payable* ACCOUNT NO. *204*

DATE		DESCRIPTION	POST. REF.	DEBIT	CREDIT	BALANCE DEBIT	BALANCE CREDIT

ACCOUNT *Sales Tax Payable* ACCOUNT NO. *215*

DATE		DESCRIPTION	POST. REF.	DEBIT	CREDIT	BALANCE DEBIT	BALANCE CREDIT
20--							
June	30	Balance	✓				613 10

ACCOUNT *Capital Stock* ACCOUNT NO. *301*

DATE		DESCRIPTION	POST. REF.	DEBIT	CREDIT	BALANCE DEBIT	BALANCE CREDIT
20--							
June	30	Balance	✓				40000 00

Problem 24-8 (continued)

ACCOUNT *Retained Earnings* ACCOUNT NO. *305*

DATE		DESCRIPTION	POST. REF.	DEBIT	CREDIT	BALANCE DEBIT	BALANCE CREDIT
20--							
June	*30*	*Balance*	✓				*9 764 15*

ACCOUNT *Income Summary* ACCOUNT NO. *310*

DATE		DESCRIPTION	POST. REF.	DEBIT	CREDIT	BALANCE DEBIT	BALANCE CREDIT

ACCOUNT *Sales* ACCOUNT NO. *401*

DATE		DESCRIPTION	POST. REF.	DEBIT	CREDIT	BALANCE DEBIT	BALANCE CREDIT
20--							
June	*30*	*Balance*	✓				*152 875 20*

ACCOUNT *Sales Returns and Allowances* ACCOUNT NO. *410*

DATE		DESCRIPTION	POST. REF.	DEBIT	CREDIT	BALANCE DEBIT	BALANCE CREDIT
20--							
June	*30*	*Balance*	✓			*3 585 00*	

ACCOUNT *Purchases* ACCOUNT NO. *501*

DATE		DESCRIPTION	POST. REF.	DEBIT	CREDIT	BALANCE DEBIT	BALANCE CREDIT
20--							
June	*30*	*Balance*	✓			*81 860 00*	

ACCOUNT *Transportation In* ACCOUNT NO. *505*

DATE		DESCRIPTION	POST. REF.	DEBIT	CREDIT	BALANCE DEBIT	BALANCE CREDIT
20--							
June	*30*	*Balance*	✓			*3 956 00*	

Name Date Class

Problem 24-8 (continued)

ACCOUNT *Purchases Discounts* ACCOUNT NO. *510*

DATE		DESCRIPTION	POST. REF.	DEBIT	CREDIT	BALANCE DEBIT	BALANCE CREDIT
20--							
June	*30*	*Balance*	✓				*740 00*

ACCOUNT *Purchases Returns and Allowances* ACCOUNT NO. *515*

DATE		DESCRIPTION	POST. REF.	DEBIT	CREDIT	BALANCE DEBIT	BALANCE CREDIT
20--							
June	*30*	*Balance*	✓				*1 221 00*

ACCOUNT *Bankcard Fees Expense* ACCOUNT NO. *605*

DATE		DESCRIPTION	POST. REF.	DEBIT	CREDIT	BALANCE DEBIT	BALANCE CREDIT
20--							
June	*30*	*Balance*	✓			*452 75*	

ACCOUNT *Depreciation Expense—Store Equipment* ACCOUNT NO. *620*

DATE		DESCRIPTION	POST. REF.	DEBIT	CREDIT	BALANCE DEBIT	BALANCE CREDIT

ACCOUNT *Federal Corporate Income Tax Expense* ACCOUNT NO. *625*

DATE		DESCRIPTION	POST. REF.	DEBIT	CREDIT	BALANCE DEBIT	BALANCE CREDIT
20--							
June	*30*	*Balance*	✓			*3 750 00*	

ACCOUNT *Insurance Expense* ACCOUNT NO. *635*

DATE		DESCRIPTION	POST. REF.	DEBIT	CREDIT	BALANCE DEBIT	BALANCE CREDIT

Name Date Class

Problem 24-8 (concluded)

ACCOUNT *Miscellaneous Expense* ACCOUNT NO. 655

DATE		DESCRIPTION	POST. REF.	DEBIT	CREDIT	BALANCE DEBIT	BALANCE CREDIT
20--							
June	30	Balance	✓			730 00	

ACCOUNT *Rent Expense* ACCOUNT NO. 660

DATE		DESCRIPTION	POST. REF.	DEBIT	CREDIT	BALANCE DEBIT	BALANCE CREDIT
20--							
June	30	Balance	✓			9,600 00	

ACCOUNT *Supplies Expense* ACCOUNT NO. 670

DATE		DESCRIPTION	POST. REF.	DEBIT	CREDIT	BALANCE DEBIT	BALANCE CREDIT

ACCOUNT *Uncollectible Accounts Expense* ACCOUNT NO. 675

DATE		DESCRIPTION	POST. REF.	DEBIT	CREDIT	BALANCE DEBIT	BALANCE CREDIT

ACCOUNT *Utilities Expense* ACCOUNT NO. 680

DATE		DESCRIPTION	POST. REF.	DEBIT	CREDIT	BALANCE DEBIT	BALANCE CREDIT
20--							
June	30	Balance	✓			2,081 00	

Analyze:

Problem 24-9 Using the Allowance Method for Write-Offs *(textbook p. 725)*

GENERAL JOURNAL

PAGE ______

	DATE		DESCRIPTION	POST. REF.	DEBIT	CREDIT	
1							1
2							2
3							3
4							4
5							5
6							6
7							7
8							8
9							9
10							10
11							11
12							12
13							13
14							14
15							15
16							16
17							17
18							18
19							19

ACCOUNTS RECEIVABLE SUBSIDIARY LEDGER

Name *Lee Adkins*

Address

DATE		DESCRIPTION	POST. REF.	DEBIT	CREDIT	BALANCE
20--						
Jan.	*1*	*Balance*	✓			*194 50*

Analyze:

Name Date Class

CHAPTER 25 Inventories

Study Guide

Section Assessment

Section 1 *Read Section 1 on pages 731–732 and complete the following exercises on page 733.*

- ☐ Reinforce the Main Idea
- ☐ Math for Accounting
- ☐ Problem 25-1 *Preparing Inventory Reports*

Section 2 *Read Section 2 on pages 734–737 and complete the following exercises on page 738.*

- ☐ Reinforce the Main Idea
- ☐ Math for Accounting
- ☐ Problem 25-2 *Determining Inventory Costs*

Section 3 *Read Section 3 on pages 739–740 and complete the following exercises on page 741.*

- ☐ Reinforce the Main Idea
- ☐ Math for Accounting
- ☐ Problem 25-3 *Analyzing a Source Document*

Chapter Assessment

Summary *Review the Chapter 25 Visual Summary on page 742 in your textbook.*

- ☐ Key Concepts

Review and Activities *Complete the following questions and exercises on page 743 in your textbook.*

- ☐ After You Read: Answering the Essential Question
- ☐ Vocabulary Check
- ☐ Concept Check

Standardized Test Practice *Complete the exercises on page 744 in your textbook.*

Computerized Accounting *Read the Computerized Accounting information on page 745 in your textbook.*

- ☐ Determining the Cost of Inventories in a Perpetual Inventory System

Problems *Complete the following End-of-Chapter Problems for Chapter 25 in your textbook.*

- ☐ Problem 25-4 *Calculating the Cost of Ending Inventory*
- ☐ Problem 25-5 *Completing an Inventory Sheet*
- ☐ Problem 25-6 *Calculating Gross Profit on Sales*
- ☐ Problem 25-7 *Reporting Ending Inventory on the Income Statement*

Challenge Problem ☐ Problem 25-8 *Calculating Cost of Merchandise Sold and Gross Profit on Sales*

Real-World Applications and Connections *Complete the following applications on pages 750–751 in your textbook.*

- ☐ Career Wise
- ☐ Global Accounting
- ☐ Analyzing Financial Reports
- ☐ H.O.T. Audit

Name Date Class

Working Papers *for Section Problems*

Problem 25-1 Preparing Inventory Reports (textbook p. 733)

INVENTORY SHEET

Date ______ Clerk ______ Page ______

STOCK NO.	ITEM	UNIT	QUANTITY	UNIT COST	TOTAL VALUE
1790	*Greeting Cards*	*Doz.*	*32*	*$6.00*	
2217	*Plush Toys*	*Each*	*20*	*2.50*	
1900	*Balloons*	*Doz.*	*12*	*0.50*	
1201	*Wrapping Paper*	*Each*	*30*	*1.12*	
1205	*Ribbon*	*Spool*	*25*	*0.75*	
3495	*Novelty Buttons*	*Doz.*	*12*	*2.50*	
2722	*Music Boxes*	*Doz.*	*6*	*60.00*	
4200	*Party Supplies*	*Doz.*	*10*	*6.50*	
1907	*Gift Boxes*	*Doz.*	*5*	*2.75*	
1742	*Vases*	*Doz.*	*2*	*12.50*	
				TOTAL	

Problem 25-2 Determining Inventory Costs (textbook p. 738)

(a) Specific Identification Method ______

(b) First-In, First-Out Method ______

(c) Last-In, First-Out Method ______

(d) Weighted Average Cost Method ______

Problem 25-3 Analyzing a Source Document (textbook p. 741)

1. ______

2. ______

Name Date Class

Working Papers *for End-of-Chapter Problems*

Problem 25-4 Calculating the Cost of Ending Inventory *(textbook p. 746)*

a. Specific Identification Method ______________

b. FIFO ______________

c. LIFO ______________

d. Weighted Average Method ______________

Analyze: ______________

Problem 25-5 Completing an Inventory Sheet *(textbook p. 746)*

INVENTORY RECORD

ITEM NO.	ITEM	ENDING INVENTORY	COST PER UNIT	CURRENT MARKET VALUE	PRICE TO BE USED	TOTAL COST
0247	*Blank CDs*	*24*	*2.67*	*2.88*	*2.67*	*64.08*
0391	*Blank CDs*	*36*	*2.80*	*2.74*		
0388	*Cable #4*	*21*	*2.91*	*3.05*		
0379	*CD Cleaner*	*6*	*6.36*	*8.33*		
0380	*CD Cleaner*	*19*	*7.49*	*7.51*		
0274	*Audio Plug*	*23*	*6.90*	*6.95*		
0276	*Dust Cover*	*12*	*8.13*	*7.95*		
0277	*Headset*	*14*	*9.25*	*9.57*		
0181	*Cable #9*	*18*	*2.06*	*2.52*		
0193	*Cable #5*	*9*	*2.29*	*2.74*		
0419	*Headset*	*8*	*8.42*	*8.73*		
0420	*Headset*	*14*	*8.98*	*9.19*		
					TOTAL COST	

Analyze: ______________

Name Date Class

Problem 25-6 Calculating Gross Profit on Sales *(textbook p. 747)*

	Specific Identification Method	First-In, First-Out Method	Last-In, First-Out Method	Weighted Average Cost Method
Net Sales	$	$	$	$
Cost of Merchandise Sold	$	$	$	$
Gross Profit on Sales	$	$	$	$

Analyze:

Problem 25-7 Reporting Ending Inventory on the Income Statement *(textbook p. 747)*

	FIFO Method	FIFO Method	Weighted Average Cost Method
Ending Inventory	$	$	$
Cost of Merchandise Sold			

FIFO Method

Name Date Class

Problem 25-7 (concluded)

LIFO Method

Weighted Average Cost Method

Analyze:

Name Date Class

Problem 25-8 Calculating Cost of Merchandise Sold and Gross Profit on Sales *(textbook p. 748)*

Instructions: *Use the following source documents to record the transactions for this problem.*

Delta Press
440 Dodger Drive
Brooklyn, NY 10112

INVOICE NO. DP1033
DATE: *May 2, 20--*
ORDER NO.:
SHIPPED BY: *Rizzo's Trucking*
TERMS: *net 30*

TO *Buzz Newsstand*
Union Terminal Bldg., #101
Tacoma, WA 98402

QTY.	ITEM	UNIT PRICE	TOTAL
10	#4931 Cameras	$8.45	$84.50

Delta Press
440 Dodger Drive
Brooklyn, NY 10112

INVOICE NO. DP1052
DATE: *May 14, 20--*
ORDER NO.:
SHIPPED BY: *Rizzo's Trucking*
TERMS: *net 30*

TO *Buzz Newsstand*
Union Terminal Bldg., #101
Tacoma, WA 98402

QTY.	ITEM	UNIT PRICE	TOTAL
5	#9265 Cameras	$8.25	$41.25

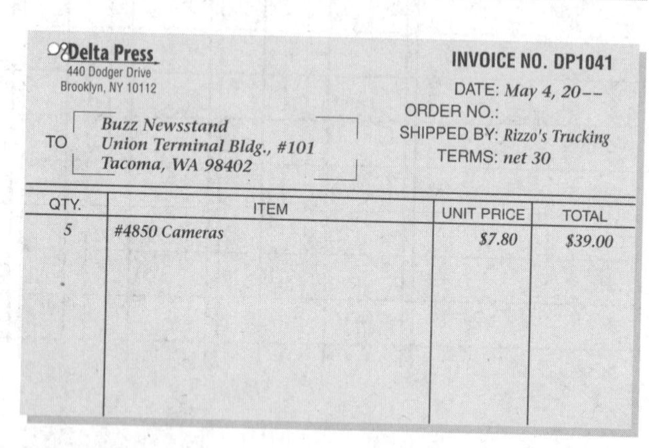

Delta Press
440 Dodger Drive
Brooklyn, NY 10112

INVOICE NO. DP1041
DATE: *May 4, 20--*
ORDER NO.:
SHIPPED BY: *Rizzo's Trucking*
TERMS: *net 30*

TO *Buzz Newsstand*
Union Terminal Bldg., #101
Tacoma, WA 98402

QTY.	ITEM	UNIT PRICE	TOTAL
5	#4850 Cameras	$7.80	$39.00

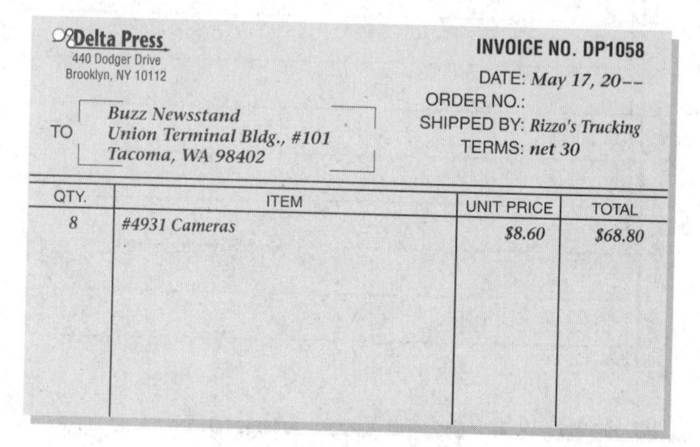

Delta Press
440 Dodger Drive
Brooklyn, NY 10112

INVOICE NO. DP1058
DATE: *May 17, 20--*
ORDER NO.:
SHIPPED BY: *Rizzo's Trucking*
TERMS: *net 30*

TO *Buzz Newsstand*
Union Terminal Bldg., #101
Tacoma, WA 98402

QTY.	ITEM	UNIT PRICE	TOTAL
8	#4931 Cameras	$8.60	$68.80

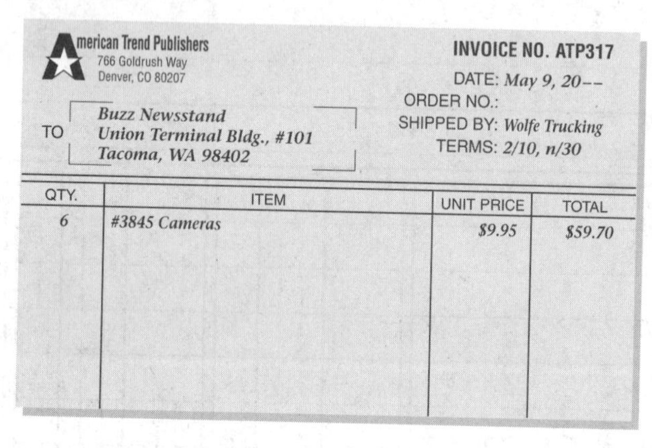

American Trend Publishers
766 Goldrush Way
Denver, CO 80207

INVOICE NO. ATP317
DATE: *May 9, 20--*
ORDER NO.:
SHIPPED BY: *Wolfe Trucking*
TERMS: *2/10, n/30*

TO *Buzz Newsstand*
Union Terminal Bldg., #101
Tacoma, WA 98402

QTY.	ITEM	UNIT PRICE	TOTAL
6	#3845 Cameras	$9.95	$59.70

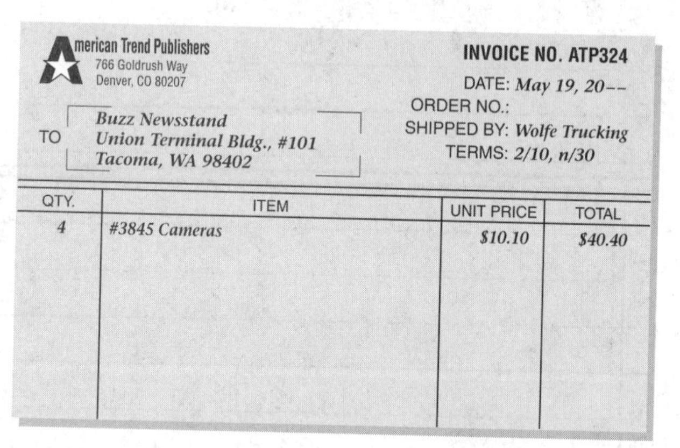

American Trend Publishers
766 Goldrush Way
Denver, CO 80207

INVOICE NO. ATP324
DATE: *May 19, 20--*
ORDER NO.:
SHIPPED BY: *Wolfe Trucking*
TERMS: *2/10, n/30*

TO *Buzz Newsstand*
Union Terminal Bldg., #101
Tacoma, WA 98402

QTY.	ITEM	UNIT PRICE	TOTAL
4	#3845 Cameras	$10.10	$40.40

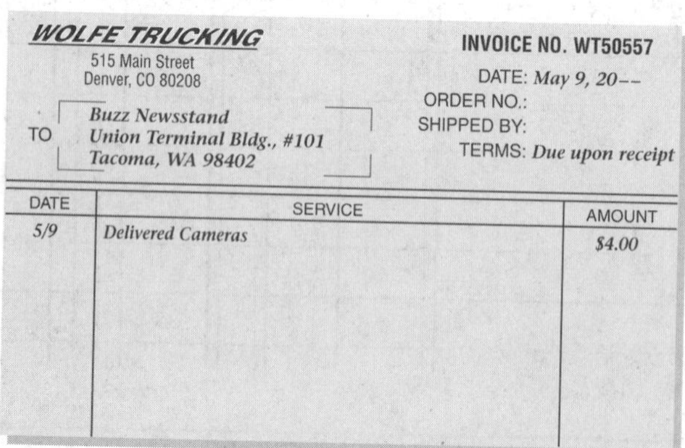

WOLFE TRUCKING
515 Main Street
Denver, CO 80208

INVOICE NO. WT50557
DATE: *May 9, 20--*
ORDER NO.:
SHIPPED BY:
TERMS: *Due upon receipt*

TO *Buzz Newsstand*
Union Terminal Bldg., #101
Tacoma, WA 98402

DATE	SERVICE	AMOUNT
5/9	Delivered Cameras	$4.00

WOLFE TRUCKING
515 Main Street
Denver, CO 80208

INVOICE NO. WT50603
DATE: *May 19, 20--*
ORDER NO.:
SHIPPED BY:
TERMS: *Due upon receipt*

TO *Buzz Newsstand*
Union Terminal Bldg., #101
Tacoma, WA 98402

DATE	SERVICE	AMOUNT
5/19	Delivered Cameras	$5.00

Problem 25-8 (continued)

Delta Press
440 Dodger Drive
Brooklyn, NY 10112

INVOICE NO. DP1067
DATE: *May 27, 20--*
ORDER NO.:
SHIPPED BY: *Rizzo's Trucking*
TERMS: *net 30*

TO *Buzz Newsstand*
Union Terminal Bldg., #101
Tacoma, WA 98402

QTY.	ITEM	UNIT PRICE	TOTAL
8	#9265 Cameras	$8.30	$66.40

Delta Press
440 Dodger Drive
Brooklyn, NY 10112

INVOICE NO. DP1071
DATE: *May 29, 20--*
ORDER NO.:
SHIPPED BY: *Rizzo's Trucking*
TERMS: *net 30*

TO *Buzz Newsstand*
Union Terminal Bldg., #101
Tacoma, WA 98402

QTY.	ITEM	UNIT PRICE	TOTAL
4	#4931 Cameras	$8.85	$35.40

Name _______________ Date _______ Class _______

Problem 25-8 (concluded)

(1)

#3845 ______________ #4931 ______________

#9265 ______________ #4850 ______________

(2)

	Item			
	3845	4931	9265	4850
Sales for Month				
Value of Beginning Inventory				
Purchases for May				
Transportation Costs				
Net Purchases for May				
Goods Available for Sale				
Value of Ending Inventory				
Cost of Merchandise Sold				
Gross Profit on Sales				

Analyze: ______________________________

Name Date Class

CHAPTER 26 Notes Payable and Receivable

Study Guide

Section Assessment

Section 1 *Read Section 1 on pages 755–758 and complete the following exercises on page 759.*

- ☐ Reinforce the Main Idea
- ☐ Math for Accounting
- ☐ Problem 26-1 *Calculating Interest and Finding Maturity Values*
- ☐ Problem 26-2 *Calculating Interest*

Section 2 *Read Section 2 on pages 760–766 and complete the following exercises on page 767.*

- ☐ Reinforce the Main Idea
- ☐ Math for Accounting
- ☐ Problem 26-3 *Recording the Issuance of an Interest-Bearing Note Payable*
- ☐ Problem 26-4 *Recording the Issuance of a Non-Interest-Bearing Note Payable*

Section 3 *Read Section 3 on pages 768–769 and complete the following exercises on page 770.*

- ☐ Reinforce the Main Idea
- ☐ Math for Accounting
- ☐ Problem 26-5 *Analyzing a Source Document*

Chapter Assessment

Summary *Review the Chapter 26 Visual Summary on page 771 in your textbook.*

- ☐ Key Concepts

Review and Activities *Complete the following questions and exercises on page 772 in your textbook.*

- ☐ After You Read: Answering the Essential Question
- ☐ Vocabulary Check
- ☐ Concept Check

Standardized Test Practice *Complete the exercises on page 773 in your textbook.*

Computerized Accounting *Read the Computerized Accounting information on page 774 in your textbook.*

- ☐ Making the Transition from a Manual to a Computerized System

Problems *Complete the following End-of-Chapter Problems for Chapter 26 in your textbook.*

- ☐ Problem 26-6 *Recording Transactions for Interest-Bearing Notes Payable*
- ☐ Problem 26-7 *Recording Transactions for Non-Interest-Bearing Notes Payable*
- ☐ Problem 26-8 *Recording Notes Payable and Notes Receivable*
- ☐ Problem 26-9 *Recording Notes Payable and Notes Receivable*

Challenge Problem

- ☐ Problem 26-10 *Renewing a Note Receivable*

Real-World Applications and Connections *Complete the following applications on pages 778–779 in your textbook.*

- ☐ Case Study
- ☐ 21st Century Skills
- ☐ Career Wise
- ☐ Spotlight on Personal Finance
- ☐ H.O.T. Audit

Name Date Class

Working Papers *for Section Problems*

Problem 26-1 Calculating Interest and Finding Maturity Values *(textbook p. 759)*

	Principal	Interest Rate	Term (in days)	Interest	Maturity Value
1	$ 4,000.00	11.50%	60	$	$
2	10,000.00	11.75%	90		
3	6,500.00	12.75%	60		
4	900.00	12.25%	120		

Problem 26-2 Calculating Interest *(textbook p. 759)*

	Principal	Interest Rate	Term	Interest
1	$ 600.00	15.00%	90 days	$
2	3,500.00	12.00%	60 days	
3	9,600.00	9.00%	4 months	
4	2,500.00	10.00%	180 days	

Problem 26-3 Recording the Issuance of an Interest-Bearing Note Payable *(textbook p. 767)*

1. ______________________________
2. ______________________________
3. ______________________________
4. ______________________________

Problem 26-4 Recording the Issuance of a Non-Interest-Bearing Note Payable *(textbook p. 767)*

1. ____________________

____

2. ____________________

____

Problem 26-5 Analyzing a Source Document *(textbook p. 770)*

GENERAL JOURNAL PAGE ______

	DATE		DESCRIPTION	POST. REF.	DEBIT	CREDIT	
1							1
2							2
3							3
4							4
5							5
6							6
7							7
8							8
9							9
10							10

Name Date Class

Working Papers *for End-of-Chapter Problems*

Problem 26-6 Recording Transactions for Interest-Bearing Notes Payable

(textbook p. 775)

PAGE ____

CASH RECEIPTS JOURNAL

	DATE	DOC. NO.	ACCOUNT NAME	POST. REF.	GENERAL		SALES CREDIT	SALES TAX PAYABLE CREDIT	ACCOUNTS RECEIVABLE CREDIT	CASH IN BANK DEBIT	
					DEBIT	CREDIT					
1											1
2											2
3											3
4											4
5											5
6											6
7											7
8											8
9											9
10											10

PAGE ____

CASH PAYMENTS JOURNAL

	DATE	DOC. NO.	ACCOUNT NAME	POST. REF.	GENERAL		ACCOUNTS PAYABLE DEBIT	PURCHASES DISCOUNTS CREDIT	CASH IN BANK CREDIT	
					DEBIT	CREDIT				
1										1
2										2
3										3
4										4
5										5
6										6
7										7
8										8
9										9
10										10

Analyze: ____________________

Name Date Class

Problem 26-7 Recording Transactions for Non-Interest-Bearing Notes Payable

(textbook p. 775)

CASH RECEIPTS JOURNAL

PAGE ____

	DATE	DOC. NO.	ACCOUNT NAME	POST. REF.	GENERAL DEBIT	GENERAL CREDIT	SALES CREDIT	SALES TAX PAYABLE CREDIT	ACCOUNTS RECEIVABLE CREDIT	CASH IN BANK DEBIT	
1											1
2											2
3											3
4											4
5											5
6											6
7											7
8											8
9											9
10											10

CASH PAYMENTS JOURNAL

PAGE ____

	DATE	DOC. NO.	ACCOUNT NAME	POST. REF.	GENERAL DEBIT	GENERAL CREDIT	ACCOUNTS PAYABLE DEBIT	PURCHASES DISCOUNTS CREDIT	CASH IN BANK CREDIT	
1										1
2										2
3										3
4										4
5										5
6										6
7										7
8										8
9										9
10										10

Analyze: ____________________

Name ______________________ Date ______________ Class ______________

Problem 26-8 Recording Notes Payable and Notes Receivable *(textbook p. 776)*

CASH RECEIPTS JOURNAL

PAGE ______

	DATE	DOC. NO.	ACCOUNT NAME	POST. REF.	GENERAL DEBIT	GENERAL CREDIT	SALES CREDIT	SALES TAX PAYABLE CREDIT	ACCOUNTS RECEIVABLE CREDIT	CASH IN BANK DEBIT	
1											1
2											2
3											3
4											4
5											5
6											6
7											7
8											8
9											9
10											10

CASH PAYMENTS JOURNAL

PAGE ______

	DATE	DOC. NO.	ACCOUNT NAME	POST. REF.	GENERAL DEBIT	GENERAL CREDIT	ACCOUNTS PAYABLE DEBIT	PURCHASES DISCOUNTS CREDIT	CASH IN BANK CREDIT	
1										1
2										2
3										3
4										4
5										5
6										6
7										7
8										8
9										9
10										10

Name Date Class

Problem 26-8 (concluded)

GENERAL JOURNAL PAGE ______

	DATE		DESCRIPTION	POST. REF.	DEBIT	CREDIT	
1							1
2							2
3							3
4							4
5							5
6							6
7							7
8							8
9							9
10							10
11							11
12							12
13							13
14							14
15							15
16							16
17							17
18							18
19							19
20							20
21							21
22							22
23							23
24							24
25							25
26							26

Analyze: ______

Name Date Class

Problem 26-9 Recording Notes Payable and Notes Receivable *(textbook p. 776)*

CASH RECEIPTS JOURNAL

PAGE ____

	DATE	DOC. NO.	ACCOUNT NAME	POST. REF.	GENERAL DEBIT	GENERAL CREDIT	SALES CREDIT	SALES TAX PAYABLE CREDIT	ACCOUNTS RECEIVABLE CREDIT	CASH IN BANK DEBIT	
1											1
2											2
3											3
4											4
5											5
6											6
7											7
8											8
9											9
10											10

CASH PAYMENTS JOURNAL

PAGE ____

	DATE	DOC. NO.	ACCOUNT NAME	POST. REF.	GENERAL DEBIT	GENERAL CREDIT	ACCOUNTS PAYABLE DEBIT	PURCHASES DISCOUNTS CREDIT	CASH IN BANK CREDIT	
1										1
2										2
3										3
4										4
5										5
6										6
7										7
8										8
9										9
10										10

Name Date Class

Problem 26-9 (concluded)

GENERAL JOURNAL PAGE ______

	DATE		DESCRIPTION	POST. REF.	DEBIT	CREDIT	
1							1
2							2
3							3
4							4
5							5
6							6
7							7
8							8
9							9
10							10
11							11
12							12
13							13
14							14
15							15
16							16
17							17
18							18
19							19
20							20
21							21
22							22
23							23
24							24
25							25
26							26

Analyze: ______

Name Date Class

Problem 26-10 Renewing a Note Receivable *(textbook p. 774)*

Instructions: *Use the following source documents to record the transactions for this business.*

BUZZ NEWSSTAND
Union Terminal Building, #101
Tacoma, WA 98402

DATE: *March 14, 20--* NO. *388*

SOLD TO: *Saba Nadal*
1306 Hampstead Ct.
Seattle, WA 98134

CLERK	CASH	CHARGE	TERMS
B.A.		✓	*n/30*

QTY.	DESCRIPTION	UNIT PRICE	AMOUNT	
30	*Travel planning software*	*$40.00*	*$1,200*	*00*
6 cs	*Magazines*	*100/cs*	*600*	*00*
		SUBTOTAL	*$1,800*	*00*
		SALES TAX	*108*	*00*
		TOTAL	*$1,908*	*00*

Thank You!

NOTE NO. 416

$ *1,908.00* Date *April 13* 20 *--*

Sixty days after date I promise to pay to

Buzz Newsstand the sum of

One thousand nine hundred eight dollars with interest at the

rate of *9%* per year.

Due date *June 12* 20 *--*

Saba Nadal

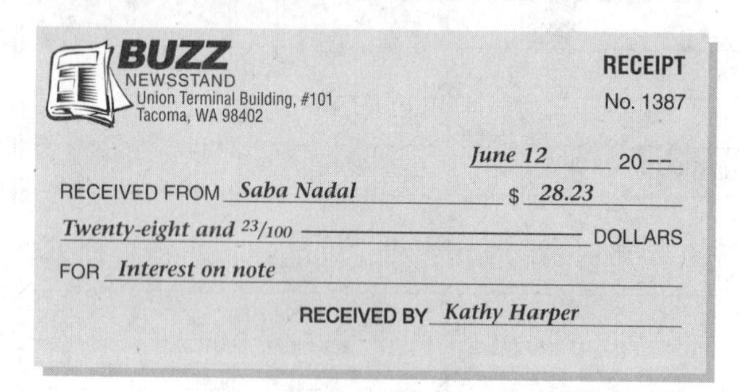

BUZZ NEWSSTAND
Union Terminal Building, #101
Tacoma, WA 98402

RECEIPT
No. 1387

June 12 20 *--*

RECEIVED FROM *Saba Nadal* $ *28.23*

Twenty-eight and 23/100 DOLLARS

FOR *Interest on note*

RECEIVED BY *Kathy Harper*

NOTE NO. 417

$ *1,908.00* Date *June 12* 20 *--*

Ninety days after date I promise to pay to

Buzz Newsstand the sum of

One thousand nine hundred eight dollars with interest at the

rate of *10%* per year.

Due date *September 10* 20 *--*

Saba Nadal

BUZZ NEWSSTAND
Union Terminal Building, #101
Tacoma, WA 98402

RECEIPT
No. 1555

September 10 20 *--*

RECEIVED FROM *Saba Nadal* $ *1,955.05*

One thousand nine hundred fifty-five and 05/100 DOLLARS

FOR *Payment for note issued June 12, 20 - -*

RECEIVED BY *Kathy Harper*

Problem 26-10 (concluded)

GENERAL JOURNAL PAGE ______

	DATE		DESCRIPTION	POST. REF.	DEBIT	CREDIT	
1							1
2							2
3							3
4							4
5							5
6							6
7							7
8							8
9							9
10							10
11							11
12							12
13							13
14							14
15							15
16							16
17							17
18							18
19							19
20							20
21							21
22							22
23							23
24							24
25							25
26							26

Analyze: ______________________________

Name Date Class

Notes

Name Date Class

MINI PRACTICE SET 5

Go Fly a Kite Inc.

CHART OF ACCOUNTS

ASSETS
101 Cash in Bank
105 Accounts Receivable
110 Merchandise Inventory
115 Supplies
120 Prepaid Insurance
125 Office Equipment
130 Store Equipment

LIABILITIES
201 Accounts Payable
205 Federal Corp. Income Tax Payable
210 Sales Tax Payable

STOCKHOLDERS' EQUITY
301 Capital Stock
305 Retained Earnings
310 Income Summary

REVENUE
401 Sales
405 Sales Discounts
410 Sales Returns and Allowances

COST OF MERCHANDISE
501 Purchases
505 Transportation In
510 Purchases Discounts
515 Purchases Returns and Allowances

EXPENSES
605 Advertising Expense
610 Bankcard Fees Expense
615 Insurance Expense
620 Miscellaneous Expense
625 Rent Expense
630 Salaries Expense
635 Supplies Expense
640 Utilities Expense
650 Federal Corp. Income Tax Expense

Accounts Receivable Subsidiary Ledger
BES Best Toy
LAR Lars' Specialties
SER Serendipity Shop
SMA Small Town Toys
TOY The Toy Store

Accounts Payable Subsidiary Ledger
BRA Brad Kites Ltd.
CRE Creative Kites Inc.
EAS Easy Glide Co.
RED Reddi-Bright Manufacturing
STA Stars Kites Outlet
TAY Taylor Office Supplies

Name Date Class

Mini Practice Set 5 *(textbook p. 778)*

Instructions: *Use the following source documents to record the transactions for this practice set.*

Reddi-Bright MANUFACTURING
127 Hill Street, #5000
Druid Hills, GA 30333

INVOICE NO. 410
DATE: *Dec. 16, 20--*
ORDER NO.:
SHIPPED BY:
TERMS:

TO *Go Fly a Kite Inc.*
112 Ashby Drive
Atlanta, GA 30308

QTY.	ITEM	UNIT PRICE	TOTAL
	General merchandise		*$1,475.00*

Taylor Office Supplies
212 Morningside Drive
Atlanta, GA 30305

INVOICE NO. 830
DATE: *December 17, 20--*
ORDER NO.:
SHIPPED BY:
TERMS:

TO *Go Fly a Kite Inc.*
112 Ashby Drive
Atlanta, GA 30308

QTY.	ITEM	UNIT PRICE	TOTAL
2	*Calendar/Planner*	*$40.00*	*$80.00*

Go Fly a Kite Inc.
112 Ashby Drive
Atlanta, GA 30308

610
4-571/6212

DATE *December 16* 20--

PAY TO THE ORDER OF *United States Treasury* $ *1,050.00*

One thousand fifty and 00/100 DOLLARS

Sanwa Bank

MEMO *Qtrly. fed. inc. tax* *Michael Ramspart*

⑆621245711⑆ 2323 1112⑈ 0610

Go Fly a Kite Inc.
112 Ashby Drive
Atlanta, GA 30308

RECEIPT
No. 358

December 17 20--

RECEIVED FROM *Best Toys* $ *1,965.60*

One thousand nine hundred sixty-five and 60/100 DOLLARS

FOR *Sales slip #479 for $2,003.40, less $37.80 discount*

RECEIVED BY *Michael Ramspart*

Go Fly a Kite Inc.
112 Ashby Drive
Atlanta, GA 30308

611
4-571/6212

DATE *December 16* 20--

PAY TO THE ORDER OF *Brad Kites, Ltd.* $ *2,548.00*

Two thousand five hundred forty-eight and 00/100 DOLLARS

Sanwa Bank

MEMO *#112 $2600 less disc.* *Michael Ramspart*

⑆621245711⑆ 2323 1112⑈ 0611

Go Fly a Kite Inc.
112 Ashby Drive
Atlanta, GA 30308

DATE: *December 19, 20--* NO. *484*

SOLD TO *Best Toys*

CLERK	CASH	CHARGE	TERMS

QTY.	DESCRIPTION	UNIT PRICE	AMOUNT	
26	*Kites*	*$100.00*	*$2,600*	*00*
		SUBTOTAL	*$2,600*	*00*
		SALES TAX	*156*	*00*
		TOTAL	*$2,756*	*00*

Thank You!

Go Fly a Kite Inc.
112 Ashby Drive
Atlanta, GA 30308

612
4-571/6212

DATE *December 17* 20--

PAY TO THE ORDER OF *Sanwa Bank* $ *4,750.00*

Four thousand seven hundred fifty and 00/100 DOLLARS

Sanwa Bank

MEMO *Monthly payroll* *Michael Ramspart*

⑆621245711⑆ 2323 1112⑈ 0612

Mini Practice Set 5 (continued)

Go Fly a Kite Inc.
112 Ashby Drive
Atlanta, GA 30308

RECEIPT
No. 359

December 19 20--

RECEIVED FROM *Lars' Specialties* $ *1,716.00*

One thousand seven hundred sixteen and 00/100 DOLLARS

FOR *Payment of sales slip #480 for $1,749, less $33 discount*

RECEIVED BY *Michael Ramspart*

Brad Kites, Ltd.
633 Louise Street
Atlanta, GA 30303

INVOICE NO. 215
DATE: *Dec. 20, 20--*
ORDER NO.:
SHIPPED BY:
TERMS:

TO *Go Fly a Kite Inc.*
112 Ashby Drive
Atlanta, GA 30308

QTY.	ITEM	UNIT PRICE	TOTAL
50	Kites	$31.20	$1,560.00

Go Fly a Kite Inc.
112 Ashby Drive
Atlanta, GA 30308

DATE: *December 23, 20--* NO. *485*

SOLD TO *Lars' Specialties*

CLERK	CASH	CHARGE	TERMS

QTY.	DESCRIPTION	UNIT PRICE	AMOUNT
100	Kites	$15.80	$1,580 00
		SUBTOTAL	$1,580 00
		SALES TAX	94 80
		TOTAL	$1,674 80

Thank You!

Go Fly a Kite Inc.
112 Ashby Drive
Atlanta, GA 30308

613
4-571/6212

DATE *December 20* 20--

PAY TO THE ORDER OF *Creative Kites, Inc.* $ *375.00*

Three hundred seventy-five and 00/100 DOLLARS

Sanwa Bank

MEMO *on account* *Michael Ramspart*

⑆621245710⑆ 2323 1112⑈ 0613

Go Fly a Kite Inc.
112 Ashby Drive
Atlanta, GA 30308

RECEIPT
No. 360

December 23 20--

RECEIVED FROM *Serendipity Shop* $ *300.00*

Three hundred and 00/100 DOLLARS

FOR *Payment on account*

RECEIVED BY *Michael Ramspart*

Go Fly a Kite Inc.
112 Ashby Drive
Atlanta, GA 30308

CREDIT MEMORANDUM NO. *44*

DATE: *December 21, 20--*
NAME: *Best Toys*
ADDRESS:

ORIGINAL SALES DATE	ORIGINAL SALES SLIP	APPROVAL	MDSE RET
Dec. 19, 20--	484	M.R.	X

QTY.	DESCRIPTION	AMOUNT
1	Kite	$ 100 00
REASON FOR RETURN: damaged	SUB TOTAL	$ 100 00
THE TOTAL SHOWN AT THE RIGHT WILL BE CREDITED TO YOUR ACCOUNT.	SALES TAX	6 00
	TOTAL	$ 106 00

Katie Sims
CUSTOMER SIGNATURE

Go Fly a Kite Inc.
112 Ashby Drive
Atlanta, GA 30308

614
4-571/6212

DATE *December 23* 20--

PAY TO THE ORDER OF *Easy Glide Co.* $ *1,852.20*

One thousand eight hundred fifty-two and 20/100 DOLLARS

Sanwa Bank

MEMO *#326 $1890 less disc.* *Michael Ramspart*

⑆621245710⑆ 2323 1112⑈ 0614

Go Fly a Kite Inc.
112 Ashby Drive
Atlanta, GA 30308

RECEIPT
No. 361

December 26 20--

RECEIVED FROM *The Toy Store* $ *1,102.40*

One thousand one hundred two and 40/100 DOLLARS

FOR *Sales slip #483 for $1,123.60, less $21.20 discount*

RECEIVED BY *Michael Ramspart*

Name Date Class

Mini Practice Set 5 (continued)

DEBIT MEMORANDUM No. 28

Go Fly a Kite Inc.
112 Ashby Drive
Atlanta, GA 30308

Date: *December 26, 20--*
Invoice No.: *215*

To: *Brad Kites, Ltd.*
633 Louise Street
Atlanta, GA 30303

This day we have debited your account as follows:

Quantity	Item	Unit Price	Total
1	*misc. merchandise*	*$150.00*	*$150.00*

Go Fly a Kite Inc.
112 Ashby Drive
Atlanta, GA 30308

616
4-571/6212

DATE *December 29* 20--

PAY TO THE ORDER OF *Stars Kites Outlet* $ *1,625.00*

One thousand six hundred twenty-five and 00/100 DOLLARS

Sanwa Bank

MEMO *on account* *Michael Ramspart*

⑆621245714⑆ 2323 1112⑈ 0616

EASY GLIDE CO.
124 Merric Blvd., #2A
Atlanta, GA 30301

INVOICE NO. 335
DATE: *Dec. 26, 20--*
ORDER NO.:
SHIPPED BY:
TERMS:

TO *Go Fly a Kite Inc.*
112 Ashby Drive
Atlanta, GA 30308

QTY.	ITEM	UNIT PRICE	TOTAL
	Specialty kites		*$1,630.00*

Go Fly a Kite Inc.
112 Ashby Drive
Atlanta, GA 30308

DATE: *December 29, 20--* NO. *486*

SOLD TO *The Toy Store*

CLERK	CASH	CHARGE	TERMS

QTY.	DESCRIPTION	UNIT PRICE	AMOUNT	
50	*Kites Variety Pack*	*$39.80*	*$1,990*	*00*
		SUBTOTAL	*$1,990*	*00*
		SALES TAX	*119*	*40*
		TOTAL	*$2,109*	*40*

Thank You!

Go Fly a Kite Inc.
112 Ashby Drive
Atlanta, GA 30308

615
4-571/6212

DATE *December 28* 20--

PAY TO THE ORDER OF *Daily Examiner* $ *120.00*

One hundred twenty and 00/100 DOLLARS

Sanwa Bank

MEMO *monthly advertising* *Michael Ramspart*

⑆621245714⑆ 2323 1112⑈ 0615

Go Fly a Kite Inc.
112 Ashby Drive
Atlanta, GA 30308

617
4-571/6212

DATE *December 30* 20--

PAY TO THE ORDER OF *Reddi-Bright Manufacturing* $ *700.00*

Seven hundred and 00/100 DOLLARS

Sanwa Bank

MEMO *on account* *Michael Ramspart*

⑆621245714⑆ 2323 1112⑈ 0617

Go Fly a Kite Inc.
112 Ashby Drive
Atlanta, GA 30308

RECEIPT
No. 362

December 28 20 --

RECEIVED FROM *Small Town Toys* $ *450.00*

Four hundred fifty and 00/100 DOLLARS

FOR *Payment on account*

RECEIVED BY *Michael Ramspart*

Go Fly a Kite Inc.
112 Ashby Drive
Atlanta, GA 30308

DATE: *December 30, 20--* NO. *487*

SOLD TO *Serendipity Shop*

CLERK	CASH	CHARGE	TERMS

QTY.	DESCRIPTION	UNIT PRICE	AMOUNT	
28	*Kites*	*$20.00*	*$560*	*00*
		SUBTOTAL	*$560*	*00*
		SALES TAX	*33*	*60*
		TOTAL	*$593*	*60*

Thank You!

Name Date Class

Mini Practice Set 5 (continued)

$	No. 618	
Date *December 31* 20--		
To		
For		
	Dollars	Cents
Balance brought forward		
Less Bank Svc. Chg.	*10*	*00*
Less Bankcard fee	*150*	*00*
Total		
Less this check		
Balance carried forward		

Go Fly a Kite Inc.
112 Ashby Drive
Atlanta, GA 30308

618
4-571
6212

DATE *December 31* 20--

PAY TO THE ORDER OF *Remote Trucking Co.* $ *51.60*

Fifty-one and 60/100 DOLLARS

Sanwa Bank

MEMO *transport. charges* *Michael Ramspart*

62124571 2323 1112 0618

$	No. 619	
Date *December 31* 20--		
To		
For		
	Dollars	Cents
Balance brought forward		
Add deposits *12/31/-- (T41)*	*4,234*	*81*
12/31/-- (T41)	*1,840*	*45*
Total		
Less this check		
Balance carried forward		

Dec 31
Tape 41

3,995.10	CA
239.71	TX
4,234.81	TTL
1,736.27	CA
104.18	TX
1,840.45	TTL

Name Date Class

Notes

Name Date Class

Mini Practice Set 5 (continued)

(1), (4)

SALES JOURNAL

PAGE 22

	DATE		SALES SLIP NO.	CUSTOMER'S ACCOUNT DEBITED	POST. REF.	SALES CREDIT	SALES TAX PAYABLE CREDIT	ACCOUNTS RECEIVABLE DEBIT	
1	20--								1
2	Dec.	7	479	Best Toys	✓	1890 00	113 40	2003 40	2
3		9	480	Lars' Specialties	✓	1650 00	99 00	1749 00	3
4		9	481	Serendipity Shop	✓	1219 00	73 14	1292 14	4
5		12	482	Small Town Toys	✓	875 00	52 50	927 50	5
6		15	483	The Toy Store	✓	1060 00	63 60	1123 60	6
7									7
8									8
9									9
10									10
11									11
12									12
13									13
14									14
15									15
16									16
17									17
18									18
19									19
20									20
21									21
22									22
23									23
24									24
25									25
26									26
27									27
28									28
29									29
30									30
31									31
32									32
33									33

CASH RECEIPTS JOURNAL

PAGE 23

	DATE		DOC. NO.	ACCOUNT NAME	POST. REF.	GENERAL CREDIT	SALES CREDIT	SALES TAX PAYABLE CREDIT	ACCOUNTS RECEIVABLE CREDIT	SALES DISCOUNTS DEBIT	CASH IN BANK DEBIT	
1	20--											1
2	Dec.	2	R351	Best Toys	✓				3195 90	60 30	3135 60	2
3		3	R352	Store Equipment	130	200 00					200 00	3
4		6	R353	Lars' Specialties	✓				1897 40	35 80	1861 60	4
5		8	R354	Serendipity Shop	✓				763 60	14 40	749 20	5
6		10	R355	Small Town Toys	✓				1284 80		1284 80	6
7		12	R356	The Toy Store	✓				1240 20	23 40	1216 80	7
8		13	R357	Supplies	115	30 00					30 00	8
9		15	T40	Cash Sales	—		3650 70	219 04			3869 74	9
10		15	T40	Bankcard Sales	—		1812 40	108 74			1921 14	10
11												11
12												12
13												13
14												14
15												15
16												16
17												17
18												18
19												19
20												20
21												21
22												22
23												23
24												24
25												25
26												26

Mini Practice Set 5 (continued)

PURCHASES JOURNAL

PAGE 21

	DATE		INVOICE NO.	CREDITOR'S ACCOUNT CREDITED	POST. REF.	ACCOUNTS PAYABLE CREDIT	PURCHASES DEBIT	GENERAL ACCOUNT DEBITED	GENERAL POST. REF.	GENERAL DEBIT	
1	20--										1
2	Dec.	3	CL213	Creative Kites Inc.	✓	1500 00	1500 00				2
3		4	803	Taylor Office Supplies	✓	125 00		Office Equipment	125	125 00	3
4		7	112	Brad Kites Ltd.	✓	2600 00	2600 00				4
5		11	514	Stars Kites Outlet	✓	3250 00	3250 00				5
6		14	326	Easy Glide Co.	✓	1890 00	1890 00				6
7											7
8											8
9											9
10											10
11											11
12											12
13											13
14											14
15											15
16											16
17											17
18											18
19											19
20											20
21											21
22											22
23											23
24											24
25											25

Mini Practice Set 5 (continued)

CASH PAYMENTS JOURNAL

PAGE 24

	DATE		DOC. NO.	ACCOUNT NAME	POST. REF.	GENERAL DEBIT	ACCOUNTS PAYABLE DEBIT	PURCHASES DISCOUNTS CREDIT	CASH IN BANK CREDIT	
1	20--									1
2	Dec.	2	601	Rent Expense	625	700 00			700 00	2
3		5	602	Brad Kites Ltd.	✓		1375 00	27 50	1347 50	3
4		6	603	Stars Kites Outlet	✓		1470 00	29 40	1440 60	4
5		7	604	Transportation In	505	37 20			37 20	5
6		9	605	Creative Kites Inc.	✓		1090 00	21 80	1068 20	6
7		11	606	Easy Glide Co.	✓		1235 00	24 70	1210 30	7
8		14	607	Reddi-Bright Mfg.	✓		2280 00		2280 00	8
9		15	608	Utilities Expense	640	165 00			165 00	9
10		15	609	Taylor Office Supplies	✓		125 00		125 00	10
11										11
12										12
13										13
14										14
15										15
16										16
17										17
18										18
19										19
20										20
21										21
22										22
23										23
24										24
25										25
26										26
27										27
28										28

Mini Practice Set 5 (continued)

(1), (13), (14)

GENERAL JOURNAL PAGE 12

	DATE		DESCRIPTION	POST. REF.	DEBIT	CREDIT	
1	20--						1
2	Dec.	3	Purchases	501	1500 00		2
3			Merchandise Inventory	110		1500 00	3
4			Memo 30				4
5		5	Sales Returns and Allowances	410	120 00		5
6			Sales Tax Payable	210	7 20		6
7			Accts. Rec./Small Town Toys	105/✓		127 20	7
8			Credit Memo 43				8
9		12	Accts. Pay./Reddi-Bright Mfg.	201/✓	80 00		9
10			Purchases Returns and Allowances	515		80 00	10
11			Debit Memo 27				11
12							12
13							13
14							14
15							15
16							16
17							17
18							18
19							19
20							20
21							21
22							22
23							23
24							24
25							25
26							26
27							27
28							28
29							29
30							30
31							31
32							32
33							33
34							34
35							35
36							36

Name Date Class

Mini Practice Set 5 (continued)

(1)

GENERAL JOURNAL

PAGE ______

	DATE		DESCRIPTION	POST. REF.	DEBIT	CREDIT	
1							1
2							2
3							3
4							4
5							5
6							6
7							7
8							8
9							9
10							10
11							11
12							12
13							13
14							14
15							15
16							16
17							17
18							18
19							19
20							20

(2)

ACCOUNTS RECEIVABLE SUBSIDIARY LEDGER

Name *Best Toys*

Address *13400 Midway Road, Dallas, TX 75244*

DATE		DESCRIPTION	POST. REF.	DEBIT	CREDIT	BALANCE
20--						
Dec.	*1*	*Balance*	✓			*3195 90*
	2		*CR23*		*3195 90*	———
	7		*S22*	*2003 40*		*2003 40*

Name Date Class

Mini Practice Set 5 (continued)

ACCOUNTS RECEIVABLE SUBSIDIARY LEDGER

Name *Lars' Specialties*

Address *601 O'Hara Road, Arlington, TX 76010*

DATE		DESCRIPTION	POST. REF.	DEBIT	CREDIT	BALANCE
20--						
Dec.	1	Balance	✓			1,897.40
	6		CR23		1,897.40	—
	9		S22	1,749.00		1,749.00

Name *Serendipity Shop*

Address *835 Coronado Drive, Corpus Christi, TX 78403*

DATE		DESCRIPTION	POST. REF.	DEBIT	CREDIT	BALANCE
20--						
Dec.	1	Balance	✓			763.60
	8		CR23		763.60	—
	9		S22	1,292.14		1,292.14

Name *Small Town Toys*

Address *103 Cedar Park, Dallas, TX 75244*

DATE		DESCRIPTION	POST. REF.	DEBIT	CREDIT	BALANCE
20--						
Dec.	1	Balance	✓			1,412.00
	5		G12		127.20	1,284.80
	10		CR23		1,284.80	—
	12		S22	927.50		927.50

Name Date Class

Mini Practice Set 5 (continued)

ACCOUNTS RECEIVABLE SUBSIDIARY LEDGER

Name *The Toy Store*

Address *70 South Washington Street, Fort Worth, TX 76101*

DATE		DESCRIPTION	POST. REF.	DEBIT	CREDIT	BALANCE
20--						
Dec.	1	Balance	✓			1,240.20
	12		CR23		1,240.20	—
	15		S22	1,123.60		1,123.60

ACCOUNTS PAYABLE SUBSIDIARY LEDGER

Name *Brad Kites Ltd.*

Address *633 Louise Street NW, Atlanta, GA 30303*

DATE		DESCRIPTION	POST. REF.	DEBIT	CREDIT	BALANCE
20--						
Dec.	1	Balance	✓			1,375.00
	5		CP24	1,375.00		—
	7		P21		2,600.00	2,600.00

Name *Creative Kites Inc.*

Address *1900 Talman Avenue North, Chicago, IL 60647*

DATE		DESCRIPTION	POST. REF.	DEBIT	CREDIT	BALANCE
20--						
Dec.	1	Balance	✓			1,090.00
	3		P21		1,500.00	2,590.00
	9		CP24	1,090.00		1,500.00

Mini Practice Set 5 (continued)

ACCOUNTS PAYABLE SUBSIDIARY LEDGER

Name *Easy Glide Co.*

Address *124 Merric Blvd. #2A, Atlanta, GA 30301*

DATE		DESCRIPTION	POST. REF.	DEBIT	CREDIT	BALANCE
20--						
Dec.	1	Balance	✓			1235 00
	11		CP24	1235 00		—
	14		P21		1890 00	1890 00

Name *Reddi-Bright Manufacturing*

Address *127 Hill Street #5000, Druid Hills, GA 30333*

DATE		DESCRIPTION	POST. REF.	DEBIT	CREDIT	BALANCE
20--						
Dec.	1	Balance	✓			2360 00
	12		G12	80 00		2280 00
	14		CP24	2280 00		—

Name *Stars Kites Outlet*

Address *150 Vista Avenue, St. Louis, MO 63110*

DATE		DESCRIPTION	POST. REF.	DEBIT	CREDIT	BALANCE
20--						
Dec.	1	Balance	✓			1470 00
	6		CP24	1470 00		—
	11		P21		3250 00	3250 00

Mini Practice Set 5 (continued)

ACCOUNTS PAYABLE SUBSIDIARY LEDGER

Name *Taylor Office Supplies*

Address *212 Morningside Drive, Atlanta, GA 30305*

DATE		DESCRIPTION	POST. REF.	DEBIT	CREDIT	BALANCE
20--						
Dec.	4		P21		125 00	125 00
	15		CP24	125 00		—

(3)

GENERAL LEDGER

ACCOUNT *Cash in Bank* ACCOUNT NO. *101*

DATE		DESCRIPTION	POST. REF.	DEBIT	CREDIT	BALANCE DEBIT	BALANCE CREDIT
20--							
Dec.	1	Balance	✓			18 480 29	

ACCOUNT *Accounts Receivable* ACCOUNT NO. *105*

DATE		DESCRIPTION	POST. REF.	DEBIT	CREDIT	BALANCE DEBIT	BALANCE CREDIT
20--							
Dec.	1	Balance	✓			8 509 10	
	5		G12		127 20	8 381 90	

ACCOUNT *Merchandise Inventory* ACCOUNT NO. *110*

DATE		DESCRIPTION	POST. REF.	DEBIT	CREDIT	BALANCE DEBIT	BALANCE CREDIT
20--							
Dec.	1	Balance	✓			31 766 98	
	3		G12		1 500 00	30 266 98	

Name Date Class

Mini Practice Set 5 (continued)

ACCOUNT *Supplies* ACCOUNT NO. *115*

DATE		DESCRIPTION	POST. REF.	DEBIT	CREDIT	BALANCE DEBIT	BALANCE CREDIT
20--							
Dec.	1	Balance	✓			1 251 46	
	13		CR23		30 00	1 221 46	

ACCOUNT *Prepaid Insurance* ACCOUNT NO. *120*

DATE		DESCRIPTION	POST. REF.	DEBIT	CREDIT	BALANCE DEBIT	BALANCE CREDIT
20--							
Dec.	1	Balance	✓			2 460 00	

ACCOUNT *Office Equipment* ACCOUNT NO. *125*

DATE		DESCRIPTION	POST. REF.	DEBIT	CREDIT	BALANCE DEBIT	BALANCE CREDIT
20--							
Dec.	1	Balance	✓			6 600 00	
	4		P21	125 00		6 725 00	

ACCOUNT *Store Equipment* ACCOUNT NO. *130*

DATE		DESCRIPTION	POST. REF.	DEBIT	CREDIT	BALANCE DEBIT	BALANCE CREDIT
20--							
Dec.	1	Balance	✓			10 800 00	
	3		CR23		200 00	10 600 00	

ACCOUNT *Accounts Payable* ACCOUNT NO. *201*

DATE		DESCRIPTION	POST. REF.	DEBIT	CREDIT	BALANCE DEBIT	BALANCE CREDIT
20--							
Dec.	1	Balance	✓				7 530 00
	12		G12	80 00			7 450 00

Name Date Class

Mini Practice Set 5 (continued)

ACCOUNT *Federal Corporate Income Tax Payable* ACCOUNT NO. *205*

DATE		DESCRIPTION	POST. REF.	DEBIT	CREDIT	BALANCE DEBIT	BALANCE CREDIT

ACCOUNT *Sales Tax Payable* ACCOUNT NO. *210*

DATE		DESCRIPTION	POST. REF.	DEBIT	CREDIT	BALANCE DEBIT	BALANCE CREDIT
20--							
Dec.	*1*	*Balance*	✓				*895 80*
	5		*G12*	*7 20*			*888 60*

ACCOUNT *Capital Stock* ACCOUNT NO. *301*

DATE		DESCRIPTION	POST. REF.	DEBIT	CREDIT	BALANCE DEBIT	BALANCE CREDIT
20--							
Dec.	*1*	*Balance*	✓				*25,000 00*

ACCOUNT *Retained Earnings* ACCOUNT NO. *305*

DATE		DESCRIPTION	POST. REF.	DEBIT	CREDIT	BALANCE DEBIT	BALANCE CREDIT
20--							
Dec.	*1*	*Balance*	✓				*13,000 00*

ACCOUNT *Income Summary* ACCOUNT NO. *310*

DATE		DESCRIPTION	POST. REF.	DEBIT	CREDIT	BALANCE DEBIT	BALANCE CREDIT

Name Date Class

Mini Practice Set 5 (continued)

ACCOUNT *Sales* ACCOUNT NO. *401*

DATE		DESCRIPTION	POST. REF.	DEBIT	CREDIT	BALANCE DEBIT	BALANCE CREDIT
20--							
Dec.	*1*	*Balance*	✓				*108 1 5 1 39*

ACCOUNT *Sales Discounts* ACCOUNT NO. *405*

DATE		DESCRIPTION	POST. REF.	DEBIT	CREDIT	BALANCE DEBIT	BALANCE CREDIT
20--							
Dec.	*1*	*Balance*	✓			*2 1 0 00*	

ACCOUNT *Sales Returns and Allowances* ACCOUNT NO. *410*

DATE		DESCRIPTION	POST. REF.	DEBIT	CREDIT	BALANCE DEBIT	BALANCE CREDIT
20--							
Dec.	*1*	*Balance*	✓			*1 7 5 40*	
	5		*G12*	*1 2 0 00*		*2 9 5 40*	

ACCOUNT *Purchases* ACCOUNT NO. *501*

DATE		DESCRIPTION	POST. REF.	DEBIT	CREDIT	BALANCE DEBIT	BALANCE CREDIT
20--							
Dec.	*1*	*Balance*	✓			*23 7 6 1 13*	
	3		*G12*	*1 5 0 0 00*		*25 2 6 1 13*	

Name Date Class

Mini Practice Set 5 (continued)

ACCOUNT *Transportation In* ACCOUNT NO. *505*

DATE		DESCRIPTION	POST. REF.	DEBIT	CREDIT	BALANCE DEBIT	BALANCE CREDIT
20--							
Dec.	1	Balance	✓			1,275.80	
	7		CP24	37.20		1,313.00	

ACCOUNT *Purchases Discounts* ACCOUNT NO. *510*

DATE		DESCRIPTION	POST. REF.	DEBIT	CREDIT	BALANCE DEBIT	BALANCE CREDIT
20--							
Dec.	1	Balance	✓				415.75

ACCOUNT *Purchases Returns and Allowances* ACCOUNT NO. *515*

DATE		DESCRIPTION	POST. REF.	DEBIT	CREDIT	BALANCE DEBIT	BALANCE CREDIT
20--							
Dec.	1	Balance	✓				390.85
	12		G12		80.00		470.85

ACCOUNT *Advertising Expense* ACCOUNT NO. *605*

DATE		DESCRIPTION	POST. REF.	DEBIT	CREDIT	BALANCE DEBIT	BALANCE CREDIT
20--							
Dec.	1	Balance	✓			430.00	

ACCOUNT *Bankcard Fees Expense* ACCOUNT NO. *610*

DATE		DESCRIPTION	POST. REF.	DEBIT	CREDIT	BALANCE DEBIT	BALANCE CREDIT
20--							
Dec.	1	Balance	✓			1,420.57	

Mini Practice Set 5 (continued)

ACCOUNT *Insurance Expense* ACCOUNT NO. *615*

DATE		DESCRIPTION	POST. REF.	DEBIT	CREDIT	BALANCE DEBIT	BALANCE CREDIT

ACCOUNT *Miscellaneous Expense* ACCOUNT NO. *620*

DATE		DESCRIPTION	POST. REF.	DEBIT	CREDIT	BALANCE DEBIT	BALANCE CREDIT
20--							
Dec.	*1*	*Balance*	✓			*247 52*	

ACCOUNT *Rent Expense* ACCOUNT NO. *625*

DATE		DESCRIPTION	POST. REF.	DEBIT	CREDIT	BALANCE DEBIT	BALANCE CREDIT
20--							
Dec.	*1*	*Balance*	✓			*7 700 00*	
	2		*CP24*	*700 00*		*8 400 00*	

ACCOUNT *Salaries Expense* ACCOUNT NO. *630*

DATE		DESCRIPTION	POST. REF.	DEBIT	CREDIT	BALANCE DEBIT	BALANCE CREDIT
20--							
Dec.	*1*	*Balance*	✓			*34 871 18*	

ACCOUNT *Supplies Expense* ACCOUNT NO. *635*

DATE		DESCRIPTION	POST. REF.	DEBIT	CREDIT	BALANCE DEBIT	BALANCE CREDIT

Name Date Class

Mini Practice Set 5 (continued)

ACCOUNT *Utilities Expense* ACCOUNT NO. *640*

DATE		DESCRIPTION	POST. REF.	DEBIT	CREDIT	BALANCE DEBIT	BALANCE CREDIT
20--							
Dec.	*1*	*Balance*	✓			*2274 36*	
	15		*CP24*	*165 00*		*2439 36*	

ACCOUNT *Federal Corporate Income Tax Expense* ACCOUNT NO. *650*

DATE		DESCRIPTION	POST. REF.	DEBIT	CREDIT	BALANCE DEBIT	BALANCE CREDIT
20--							
Dec.	*1*	*Balance*	✓			*3150 00*	

(6)

Name Date Class

Mini Practice Set 5 (continued)

(7)

(7)

Name Date Class

Mini Practice Set 5 (continued)

(8), (9)

	ACCT. NO.	ACCOUNT NAME	TRIAL BALANCE DEBIT	TRIAL BALANCE CREDIT	ADJUSTMENTS DEBIT	ADJUSTMENTS CREDIT
1						
2						
3						
4						
5						
6						
7						
8						
9						
10						
11						
12						
13						
14						
15						
16						
17						
18						
19						
20						
21						
22						
23						
24						
25						
26						
27						
28						
29						
30						
31						
32						
33						

Name Date Class

ADJUSTED TRIAL BALANCE		INCOME STATEMENT		BALANCE SHEET		
DEBIT	CREDIT	DEBIT	CREDIT	DEBIT	CREDIT	
						1
						2
						3
						4
						5
						6
						7
						8
						9
						10
						11
						12
						13
						14
						15
						16
						17
						18
						19
						20
						21
						22
						23
						24
						25
						26
						27
						28
						29
						30
						31
						32
						33

Name Date Class

Mini Practice Set 5 (continued)

(11)

(12)

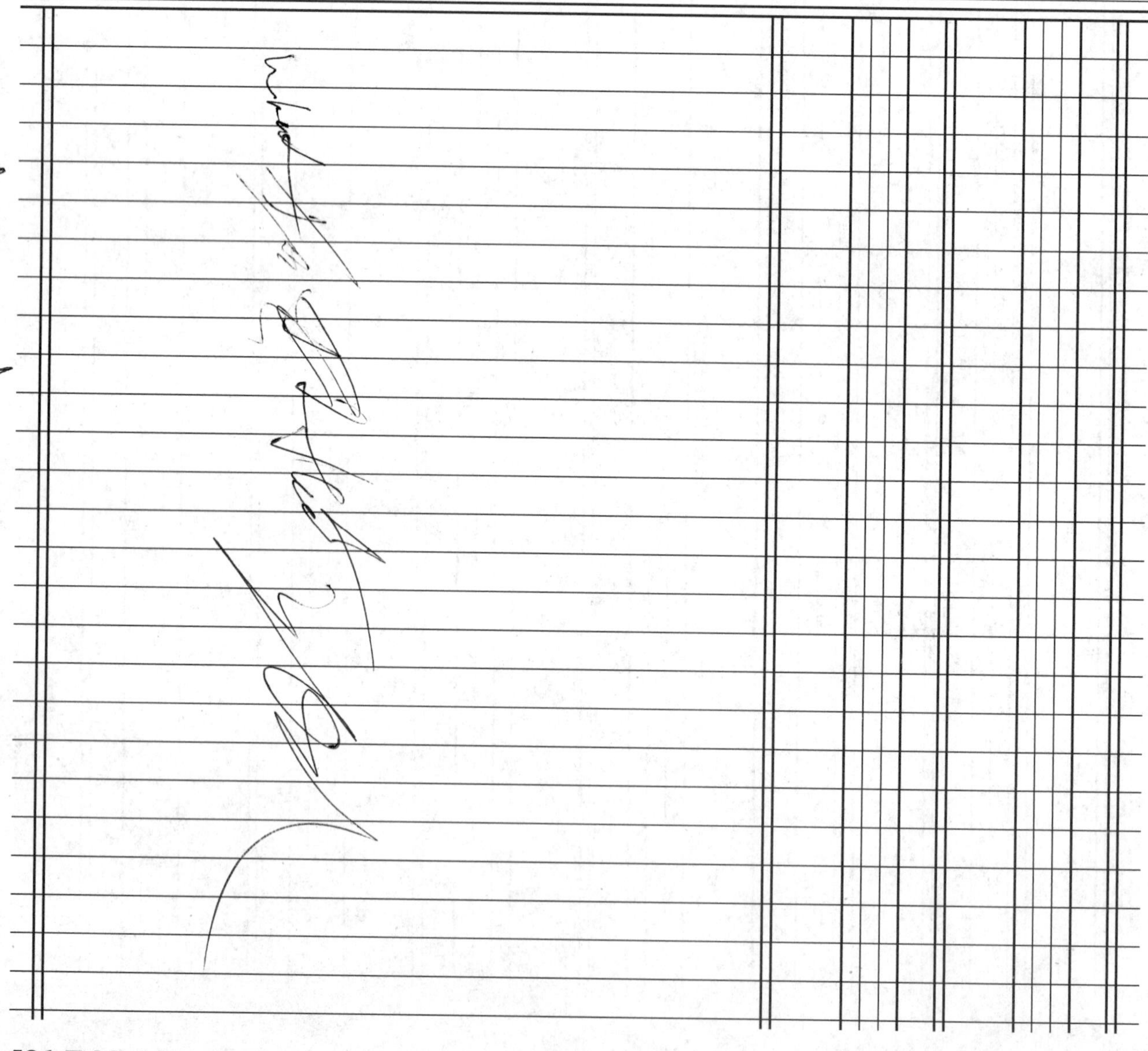

Name Date Class

Mini Practice Set 5 (continued)

(10)

Name Date Class

Mini Practice Set 5 (continued)

(15)

Analyze:

1.

2.

3.

Name Date Class

MINI PRACTICE SET 5

Go Fly a Kite Inc.

Audit Test

Directions: *Use your completed solutions to answer the following questions. Write the answer in the space to the left of each question.*

Answer

______________________ **1.** What is the total of debits and credits in the Sales journal at the end of December?

______________________ **2.** What is the total of debits and credits in the Cash Receipts journal at the end of December?

______________________ **3.** What is the total of debits and credits in the Purchases journal at the end of December?

______________________ **4.** What is the total of debits and credits in the Cash Payments journal at the end of December?

______________________ **5.** For the first transaction on December 26, which account was credited?

______________________ **6.** What amount was credited to the Merchandise Inventory account as an adjustment to inventory?

______________________ **7.** What amount was debited to the Income Summary account to close the expense accounts for the month?

______________________ **8.** What is the ending balance of the Best Toys accounts receivable subsidiary ledger account?

______________________ **9.** What is the ending balance for the Accounts Receivable general ledger account? Does the balance agree with the total of the subsidiary ledger accounts?

______________________ **10.** What is the ending balance for the Reddi-Bright Manufacturing accounts payable subsidiary ledger account?

_______________ **11.** What is the ending balance for the Accounts Payable general ledger account? Does the balance agree with the total of the subsidiary ledger accounts?

_______________ **12.** How many transactions during the month of December affected the Cash in Bank account?

_______________ **13.** Has the amount owed to Stars Kites Outlet been paid off by the end of December?

_______________ **14.** How many checks were issued by the business in December?

_______________ **15.** What was the total amount credited to Sales for the month?

_______________ **16.** What was the date of the trial balance?

_______________ **17.** How many accounts were affected by adjusting entries?

_______________ **18.** What was the total of operating expenses for the period?

_______________ **19.** What is the ending balance for Retained Earnings for the period?

_______________ **20.** What is the amount of total assets for the business at December 31?

_______________ **21.** How many accounts are listed on the trial balance?

_______________ **22.** How many accounts on the trial balance have debit balances?

_______________ **23.** Which account on the trial balance has the largest balance?

_______________ **24.** What is the amount of total liabilities for the business at December 31?

_______________ **25.** How many accounts are listed on the post-closing trial balance?

CHAPTER 27 Introduction to Partnerships

Study Guide

Section Assessment

Section 1 *Read Section 1 on pages 789–791 and complete the following exercises on page 792.*
- ☐ Reinforce the Main Idea
- ☐ Math for Accounting
- ☐ Problem 27-1 *Recording Partners' Investments*

Section 2 *Read Section 2 on pages 793–797 and complete the following exercises on page 798.*
- ☐ Reinforce the Main Idea
- ☐ Math for Accounting
- ☐ Problem 27-2 *Determining Partners' Fractional Shares*
- ☐ Problem 27-3 *Analyzing a Source Document*

Chapter Assessment

Summary *Review the Chapter 27 Visual Summary on page 799 in your textbook.*
- ☐ Key Concepts

Review and Activities *Complete the following questions and exercises on page 800 in your textbook.*
- ☐ After You Read: Answering the Essential Question
- ☐ Vocabulary Check
- ☐ Concept Check

Standardized Test Practice *Complete the exercises on page 801 in your textbook.*

Computerized Accounting *Read the Computerized Accounting information on page 802 in your textbook.*
- ☐ Making the Transition from a Manual to a Computerized System

Problems *Complete the following End-of-Chapter Problems for Chapter 27 in your textbook.*
- ☐ Problem 27-4 *Dividing Partnership Earnings*
- ☐ Problem 27-5 *Calculating the Percentage of a Partner's Capital Investment*
- ☐ Problem 27-6 *Recording Investments of Partners*
- ☐ Problem 27-7 *Sharing Losses Based on Capital Balances*
- ☐ Problem 27-8 *Partners' Withdrawals*
- ☐ Problem 27-9 *Preparing Closing Entries for a Partnership*

Challenge Problem
- ☐ Problem 27-10 *Evaluating Methods of Dividing Partnership Earnings*

Real-World Applications and Connections *Complete the following applications on pages 806–807 in your textbook.*
- ☐ Career Wise
- ☐ Global Accounting
- ☐ A Matter of Ethics
- ☐ Analyzing Financial Reports
- ☐ H.O.T. Audit

Name Date Class

Working Papers *for Section Problems*

Problem 27-1 Recording Partners' Investments *(textbook p. 792)*

GENERAL JOURNAL PAGE ______

	DATE		DESCRIPTION	POST. REF.	DEBIT	CREDIT	
1							1
2							2
3							3
4							4
5							5
6							6
7							7
8							8
9							9
10							10
11							11
12							12
13							13
14							14
15							15
16							16
17							17

Problem 27-2 Determining Partners' Fractional Shares *(textbook p. 798)*

Ratio	Fractions
1. 3:1	
2. 5:3:1	
3. 3:2:2:1	
4. 2:1:1	
5. 2:1	

Problem 27-3 Analyzing a Source Document *(textbook p. 798)*

GENERAL JOURNAL PAGE *42*

	DATE		DESCRIPTION	POST. REF.	DEBIT	CREDIT	
1							1
2							2
3							3
4							4
5							5

Name Date Class

Working Papers *for End-of-Chapter Problems*

Problem 27-4 Dividing Partnership Earnings *(textbook p. 803)*

Net Income	Share of Net Income		
	Partner 1	Partner 2	Partner 3
1. $45,000			
2. $89,700			
3. $22,000			
4. $32,000			
5. $92,700			

Analyze: ______

Problem 27-5 Calculating the Percentage of a Partner's Capital Investment *(textbook p. 803)*

1. ______

2. ______

3. ______

4. ______

Analyze: ______

Name Date Class

Problem 27-6 Recording Investments of Partners *(textbook p. 803)*

GENERAL JOURNAL PAGE ______

	DATE		DESCRIPTION	POST. REF.	DEBIT	CREDIT	
1							1
2							2
3							3
4							4
5							5
6							6
7							7
8							8
9							9
10							10
11							11
12							12

Analyze: ______

Problem 27-7 Sharing Losses Based on Capital Balances *(textbook p. 804)*

GENERAL JOURNAL PAGE 14

	DATE		DESCRIPTION	POST. REF.	DEBIT	CREDIT	
1							1
2							2
3							3
4							4
5							5
6							6
7							7
8							8
9							9
10							10
11							11
12							12

Analyze: ______

Name Date Class

Problem 27-8 Partners' Withdrawals *(textbook p. 804)*

GENERAL JOURNAL PAGE 42

	DATE		DESCRIPTION	POST. REF.	DEBIT	CREDIT	
1							1
2							2
3							3
4							4
5							5
6							6
7							7
8							8
9							9
10							10
11							11
12							12

Analyze:

Problem 27-9 Preparing Closing Entries for a Partnership *(textbook p. 805)*

GENERAL JOURNAL PAGE

	DATE		DESCRIPTION	POST. REF.	DEBIT	CREDIT	
1							1
2							2
3							3
4							4
5							5
6							6
7							7
8							8
9							9
10							10
11							11
12							12

Name Date Class

Problem 27-9 (concluded)

GENERAL LEDGER (PARTIAL)

ACCOUNT *Barbara Scott, Capital* ACCOUNT NO. *301*

DATE		DESCRIPTION	POST. REF.	DEBIT	CREDIT	BALANCE DEBIT	BALANCE CREDIT
20--							
Dec.	*31*	*Balance*	✓				*67312 00*

ACCOUNT *Barbara Scott, Withdrawals* ACCOUNT NO. *305*

DATE		DESCRIPTION	POST. REF.	DEBIT	CREDIT	BALANCE DEBIT	BALANCE CREDIT
20--							
Dec.	*31*	*Balance*	✓			*6600 00*	

ACCOUNT *Martin Towers, Capital* ACCOUNT NO. *303*

DATE		DESCRIPTION	POST. REF.	DEBIT	CREDIT	BALANCE DEBIT	BALANCE CREDIT
20--							
Dec.	*31*	*Balance*	✓				*49601 00*

ACCOUNT *Martin Towers, Withdrawals* ACCOUNT NO. *307*

DATE		DESCRIPTION	POST. REF.	DEBIT	CREDIT	BALANCE DEBIT	BALANCE CREDIT
20--							
Dec.	*1*	*Balance*	✓			*5400 00*	

ACCOUNT *Income Summary* ACCOUNT NO. *310*

DATE		DESCRIPTION	POST. REF.	DEBIT	CREDIT	BALANCE DEBIT	BALANCE CREDIT

Analyze:

Name Date Class

Problem 27-10 Evaluating Methods of Dividing Partnership Earnings *(textbook p. 805)*

1. Garrity: ______

   O'Riley: ______

   White: ______

2. Garrity: ______

   O'Riley: ______

   White: ______

3. Garrity: ______

   O'Riley: ______

   White: ______

Analyze: ______

Name Date Class

Notes

Name Date Class

CHAPTER 28 Financial Statements and Liquidation of a Partnership

Study Guide

Section Assessment

Section 1 *Read Section 1 on pages 811–812 and complete the following exercises on page 813.*

- ☐ Reinforce the Main Idea
- ☐ Math for Accounting
- ☐ Problem 28-1 *Preparing the Income Statement and Balance Sheet for a Partnership*
- ☐ Problem 28-2 *Analyzing a Source Document*

Section 2 *Read Section 2 on pages 814–817 and complete the following exercises on page 818.*

- ☐ Reinforce the Main Idea
- ☐ Math for Accounting
- ☐ Problem 28-3 *Recording a Loss and a Gain on the Sale of Noncash Assets by a Partnership*

Chapter Assessment

Summary *Review the Chapter 28 Visual Summary on page 819 in your textbook.*

- ☐ Key Concepts

Review and Activities *Complete the following questions and exercises on page 820 in your textbook.*

- ☐ After You Read: Answering the Essential Question
- ☐ Vocabulary Check
- ☐ Concept Check

Standardized Test Practice *Complete the exercises on page 821 in your textbook.*

Computerized Accounting *Read the Computerized Accounting information on page 822 in your textbook.*

- ☐ Making the Transition from a Manual to a Computerized System

Problems *Complete the following End-of-Chapter Problems for Chapter 28 in your textbook.*

- ☐ Problem 28-4 *Preparing an Income Statement and Balance Sheet for a Partnership*
- ☐ Problem 28-5 *Liquidating the Partnership with Losses on the Sale of Noncash Assets*
- ☐ Problem 28-6 *Recording a Gain or a Loss on the Sale of Noncash Assets by a Partnership*
- ☐ Problem 28-7 *Preparing a Statement of Changes in Partners' Equity*
- ☐ Problem 28-8 *Liquidating the Partnership*

Challenge Problem

- ☐ Problem 28-9 *Completing End-of-Period Activities for a Partnership*

Real-World Applications and Connections *Complete the following applications on pages 826–827 in your textbook.*

- ☐ Case Study
- ☐ 21st Century Skills
- ☐ Career Wise
- ☐ Analyzing Financial Reports
- ☐ H.O.T. Audit

Working Papers *for Section Problems*

Problem 28-1 Preparing the Income Statement and Balance Sheet for a Partnership *(textbook p. 813)*

Name Date Class

Problem 28-2 Analyzing a Source Document *(textbook p. 813)*

Gain = $26,400
Shares of gain:

Larry Bass = ______________________

John Buie = ______________________

Teri Anderson = ______________________

Robert Norman = ______________________

Paula Dunham = ______________________

John Ruppe = ______________________

Name Date Class

Problem 28-3 Recording a Loss and Gain on the Sale of Noncash Assets by a Partnership *(textbook p. 818)*

GENERAL JOURNAL

PAGE ______

	DATE		DESCRIPTION	POST. REF.	DEBIT	CREDIT	
1							1
2							2
3							3
4							4
5							5
6							6
7							7
8							8
9							9
10							10
11							11
12							12
13							13
14							14
15							15
16							16
17							17
18							18
19							19
20							20

Working Papers *for End-of-Chapter Problems*

Problem 28-4 Preparing an Income Statement and Balance Sheet for a Partnership *(textbook p. 823)*

Webster and Ruiz
Income Statement (partial)
For Period Ending December 31, 20--

Webster and Ruiz
Balance Sheet (partial)
December 31, 20--

Analyze:

Name Date Class

Problem 28-5 Liquidating the Partnership With Losses on the Sale of Noncash Assets *(textbook p. 823)*

GENERAL JOURNAL

PAGE ______

	DATE		DESCRIPTION	POST. REF.	DEBIT	CREDIT	
1							1
2							2
3							3
4							4
5							5
6							6
7							7
8							8
9							9
10							10
11							11
12							12
13							13
14							14
15							15
16							16
17							17
18							18
19							19
20							20
21							21
22							22
23							23
24							24
25							25
26							26
27							27
28							28
29							29
30							30

Analyze:

Name Date Class

Problem 28-6 Recording a Gain or Loss on the Sale of Noncash Assets by a Partnership *(textbook p. 824)*

GENERAL JOURNAL PAGE ______

	DATE	DESCRIPTION	POST. REF.	DEBIT	CREDIT	
1						1
2						2
3						3
4						4
5						5
6						6
7						7
8						8
9						9
10						10
11						11
12						12
13						13
14						14
15						15
16						16
17						17
18						18
19						19
20						20
21						21
22						22
23						23
24						24
25						25
26						26
27						27
28						28
29						29
30						30

Analyze:

Name Date Class

Problem 28-7 Preparing a Statement of Changes in Partners' Equity *(textbook p. 824)*

Analyze:

Name Date Class

Problem 28-8 Liquidating the Partnership *(textbook p. 825)*

GENERAL JOURNAL PAGE ______

	DATE		DESCRIPTION	POST. REF.	DEBIT	CREDIT	
1							1
2							2
3							3
4							4
5							5
6							6
7							7
8							8
9							9
10							10
11							11
12							12
13							13
14							14
15							15
16							16
17							17
18							18
19							19
20							20
21							21
22							22
23							23
24							24
25							25
26							26
27							27
28							28
29							29
30							30

Analyze:

Name Date Class

Problem 28-9 Completing End-of-Period Activities for a Partnership *(textbook p. 825)*

R&C

Work

For the Year Ended

	ACCT. NO.	ACCOUNT NAME	TRIAL BALANCE DEBIT	TRIAL BALANCE CREDIT	ADJUSTMENTS DEBIT	ADJUSTMENTS CREDIT
1	101	Cash in Bank	17928 00			
2	105	Accounts Receivable	4310 00			
3	110	Office Supplies	495 00			(a) 335 00
4	115	Roofing Supplies	15610 00			(b) 11470 00
5	120	Prepaid Insurance	2400 00			(c) 1200 00
6	150	Office Equipment	2650 00			
7	155	Accum. Depr.—Office Equip.		1016 00		(d) 185 00
8	160	Truck	19890 00			
9	165	Accum. Depr.—Truck		3100 00		(e) 3900 00
10	170	Building	30000 00			
11	175	Accum. Depr.—Building		3600 00		(f) 1200 00
12	180	Land	10000 00			
13	201	Accounts Payable		7945 00		
14	301	R. Smooth, Capital		42238 00		
15	305	R. Smooth, Withdrawals	8700 00			
16	310	C. Overhill, Capital		17538 00		
17	315	C. Overhill, Withdrawals	8100 00			
18	320	Income Summary	—	—		
19	401	Consulting Fees		15900 00		
20	405	Roofing Fees		62750 00		
21	501	Advertising Expense	2400 00			
22	505	Depr. Exp.—Office Equip.	—		(d) 185 00	
23	510	Depr. Expense—Truck	—		(e) 3900 00	
24	515	Depr. Expense—Building	—		(f) 1200 00	
25	520	Insurance Expense	—		(c) 1200 00	
26	525	Office Supplies Expense	—		(a) 335 00	
27	530	Roofing Supplies Expense	—		(b) 11470 00	
28	535	Salaries Expense	28109 00			
29	540	Truck Expense	1400 00			
30	545	Utilities Expense	2095 00			
31			154087 00	154087 00	18290 00	18290 00
32		Net Income				
33						

Name Date Class

Problem 28-9 (continued)

Roofing
Sheet
December 31, 20--

ADJUSTED TRIAL BALANCE		INCOME STATEMENT		BALANCE SHEET		
DEBIT	CREDIT	DEBIT	CREDIT	DEBIT	CREDIT	
17928 00				17928 00		1
4310 00				4310 00		2
160 00				160 00		3
4140 00				4140 00		4
1200 00				1200 00		5
2650 00				2650 00		6
	1201 00				1201 00	7
19890 00				19890 00		8
	7000 00				7000 00	9
30000 00				30000 00		10
	4800 00				4800 00	11
10000 00				10000 00		12
	7945 00				7945 00	13
	42238 00				42238 00	14
8700 00				8700 00		15
	17538 00				17538 00	16
8100 00				8100 00		17
						18
	15900 00		15900 00			19
	62750 00		62750 00			20
2400 00		2400 00				21
185 00		185 00				22
3900 00		3900 00				23
1200 00		1200 00				24
1200 00		1200 00				25
335 00		335 00				26
11470 00		11470 00				27
28109 00		28109 00				28
1400 00		1400 00				29
2095 00		2095 00				30
159372 00	159372 00	52294 00	78650 00	107078 00	80722 00	31
		26356 00			26356 00	32
		78650 00	78650 00	107078 00	107078 00	33

Name Date Class

Problem 28-9 (continued)

Name Date Class

Problem 28-9 (continued)

Name ____________ Date ____________ Class ____________

Problem 28-9 (concluded)

GENERAL JOURNAL

PAGE ____

	DATE	DESCRIPTION	POST. REF.	DEBIT	CREDIT	
1						1
2						2
3						3
4						4
5						5
6						6
7						7
8						8
9						9
10						10
11						11
12						12
13						13
14						14
15						15
16						16
17						17
18						18
19						19
20						20
21						21
22						22
23						23
24						24
25						25
26						26
27						27
28						28
29						29
30						30
31						31
32						32
33						33
34						34
35						35
36						36
37						37

Analyze: ____________

Name Date Class

MINI PRACTICE SET 6

Paint Works

CHART OF ACCOUNTS

ASSETS

101 Cash in Bank
105 Accounts Receivable—Mountain View City School District
120 Computer Equipment
130 Office Supplies
135 Office Equipment
140 Painting Supplies
145 Painting Equipment

LIABILITIES

205 Accounts Payable—Custom Color
210 Accounts Payable—J & J Hardware and Lumber
215 Accounts Payable—Paint Palace

PARTNERS' EQUITY

301 Laura Andersen, Capital
302 Laura Andersen, Withdrawals
303 David Ingram, Capital
304 David Ingram, Withdrawals
305 Sean Woo, Capital
306 Sean Woo, Withdrawals
310 Income Summary

REVENUE

401 Painting Fees
405 Consultation Fees

EXPENSES

505 Advertising Expense
510 Miscellaneous Expense
515 Rent Expense
520 Utilities Expense

Name Date Class

Mini Practice Set 6 *(textbook p. 826)*

Instructions: *Use the following source documents to record the transactions for this practice set.*

Paint Works
755 Brewton Street
Forest Hills, AL 36105

MEMORANDUM 1

TO: *Accounting Clerk*
FROM: *Senior Accountant*
DATE: *February 1, 20--*
SUBJECT: *Partner Investment*

Record partners' investments with following amounts:

	Andersen	Ingram	Woo
Cash	$1,500.00	$1,000.00	$1,200.00
Computer Equip.	–	2,800.00	–
Office Equip.	100.00	–	–
Painting Supplies	150.00	–	225.00
Painting Equip.	1,375.00	–	1,675.00
Total	$3,125.00	$3,800.00	$3,100.00

Paint Works
755 Brewton Street
Forest Hills, AL 36105

1101
71-821/3321

DATE *February 1* 20--

PAY TO THE ORDER OF *Taft Leasing Co.* $ *1,500.00*

One thousand five hundred and 00/100 DOLLARS

Barclays Bank

MEMO *Rent* *Laura Andersen*

⑆332171821⑆ 4516 2133⑈ 1101

Paint Works
755 Brewton Street
Forest Hills, AL 36105

1102
71-821/3321

DATE *February 1* 20--

PAY TO THE ORDER OF *Call an Expert* $ *25.00*

Twenty-five and 00/100 DOLLARS

Barclays Bank

MEMO *Newspaper ad* *Laura Andersen*

⑆332171821⑆ 4516 2133⑈ 1102

Paint Works
755 Brewton Street
Forest Hills, AL 36105

1103
71-821/3321

DATE *February 2* 20--

PAY TO THE ORDER OF *Western Utilities* $ *100.00*

One hundred and 00/100 DOLLARS

Barclays Bank

MEMO *Utilities* *Laura Andersen*

⑆332171821⑆ 4516 2133⑈ 1104

Paint Works
755 Brewton Street
Forest Hills, AL 36105

1104
71-821/3321

DATE *February 1* 20--

PAY TO THE ORDER OF *GTE* $ *175.00*

One hundred seventy-five and 00/100 DOLLARS

Barclays Bank

MEMO *Telephone svc* *Laura Andersen*

⑆332171821⑆ 4516 2133⑈ 1105

Paint Works
755 Brewton Street
Forest Hills, AL 36105

RECEIPT
No. 01

February 2 20--

RECEIVED FROM *McGuires* $ *250.00*

Two hundred fifty and 00/100 DOLLARS

FOR *$250 deposit for McGuires contract*

RECEIVED BY *Laura Andersen*

Custom Color
3167 Turner Place, #1A
Wildwood, AL 36120

INVOICE NO. 742
DATE: *Feb. 2, 20--*
ORDER NO.:
SHIPPED BY:
TERMS:

TO *Paint Works*
755 Brewton Street
Forest Hills, AL 36105

QTY.	ITEM	UNIT PRICE	TOTAL
5	Paint & Border Stencils	$40.00	$200.00

Paint Works
755 Brewton Street
Forest Hills, AL 36105

1105
71-821/3321

DATE *February 2* 20--

PAY TO THE ORDER OF *City of Mountain View* $ *55.00*

Fifty-five and 00/100 DOLLARS

Barclays Bank

MEMO *Business license* *Laura Andersen*

⑆332171821⑆ 4516 2133⑈ 1103

Name Date Class

Mini Practice Set 6 (continued)

Paint Works
755 Brewton Street
Forest Hills, AL 36105

1106
71-821
3321

DATE *February 4* 20--

PAY TO THE ORDER OF *Office Max* $ *115.00*

One hundred fifteen and 00/100 DOLLARS

Barclays Bank

MEMO *Office supplies* *Laura Andersen*

⑆332171821⑆ 4516 2133⑈ 1106

Paint Palace
612 James Avenue
Montgomery, AL 36105

INVOICE NO. 1162
DATE: *Feb. 8, 20--*
ORDER NO.:
SHIPPED BY:
TERMS:

TO *Paint Works*
755 Brewton Street
Forest Hills, AL 36105

QTY.	ITEM	UNIT PRICE	TOTAL
2	Painting equipment	$187.50	$375.00

Paint Works
755 Brewton Street
Forest Hills, AL 36105

RECEIPT
No. 02

February 5 20--

RECEIVED FROM *McGuires* $ *450.00*

Four hundred fifty and 00/100 DOLLARS

FOR *Balance on McGuires contract*

RECEIVED BY *Laura Andersen*

Paint Works
755 Brewton Street
Forest Hills, AL 36105

RECEIPT
No. 03

February 10 20--

RECEIVED FROM *Prospective Client* $ *60.00*

Sixty and 00/100 DOLLARS

FOR *Color and painting consultation*

RECEIVED BY *Laura Andersen*

Paint Works
755 Brewton Street
Forest Hills, AL 36105

1107
71-821
3321

DATE *February 6* 20--

PAY TO THE ORDER OF *Mountain View Chamber of Commerce* $ *45.00*

Forty-five and 00/100 DOLLARS

Barclays Bank

MEMO *Membership* *Laura Andersen*

⑆332171821⑆ 4516 2133⑈ 1107

Paint Works
755 Brewton Street
Forest Hills, AL 36105

INVOICE NO. 101
DATE: *Feb. 12, 20--*
ORDER NO.:
TERMS:

TO *Mountain View*
City School District

DATE	SERVICE	AMOUNT
	Cafeteria Painting at elementary school	$835.00

Paint Works
755 Brewton Street
Forest Hills, AL 36105

1108
71-821
3321

DATE *February 14* 20--

PAY TO THE ORDER OF *Custom Color* $ *200.00*

Two hundred and 00/100 DOLLARS

Barclays Bank

MEMO *On account* *Laura Andersen*

⑆332171821⑆ 4516 2133⑈ 1108

Mini Practice Set 6 (continued)

Paint Works
755 Brewton Street
Forest Hills, AL 36105

1109
71-821
3321

DATE *February 15* 20--

PAY TO THE ORDER OF *Laura Andersen* $ *650.00*

Six hundred fifty and 00/100 DOLLARS

Barclays Bank

MEMO *Personal withdrawal* *Laura Andersen*

⑆3321718214⑆ 4516 2133⑈ 1109

Paint Works
755 Brewton Street
Forest Hills, AL 36105

1110
71-821
3321

DATE *February 15* 20--

PAY TO THE ORDER OF *David Ingram* $ *650.00*

Six hundred fifty and 00/100 DOLLARS

Barclays Bank

MEMO *Personal withdrawal* *Laura Andersen*

⑆3321718214⑆ 4516 2133⑈ 1110

Paint Works
755 Brewton Street
Forest Hills, AL 36105

1111
71-821
3321

DATE *February 15* 20--

PAY TO THE ORDER OF *Sean Woo* $ *650.00*

Six hundred fifty and 00/100 DOLLARS

Barclays Bank

MEMO *Personal withdrawal* *Laura Andersen*

⑆3321718214⑆ 4516 2133⑈ 1111

Paint Works
755 Brewton Street
Forest Hills, AL 36105

RECEIPT
No. 04

February 15 20 --

RECEIVED FROM *Wicker & Hartel Law Office* $ *1,000.00*

One thousand and 00/100 DOLLARS

FOR *Deposit on contract*

RECEIVED BY *Laura Andersen*

Paint Works
755 Brewton Street
Forest Hills, AL 36105

1112
71-821
3321

DATE *February 16* 20--

PAY TO THE ORDER OF *Odds & Ends (Painting Supplies)* $ *135.00*

One hundred thirty-five and 00/100 DOLLARS

Barclays Bank

MEMO *Painting supplies* *Laura Andersen*

⑆3321718214⑆ 4516 2133⑈ 1112

Custom Color
3167 Turner Place, #1A
Wildwood, AL 36120

INVOICE NO. 750
DATE: *Feb. 16, 20--*
ORDER NO.:
SHIPPED BY:
TERMS:

TO *Paint Works*
755 Brewton Street
Forest Hills, AL 36105

QTY.	ITEM	UNIT PRICE	TOTAL
5	Paint gallons	$79.00	$395.00

Paint Works
755 Brewton Street
Forest Hills, AL 36105

1113
71-821
3321

DATE *February 17* 20--

PAY TO THE ORDER OF *Mountain View Realtors* $ *77.00*

Seventy-seven and 00/100 DOLLARS

Barclays Bank

MEMO *Advertisement* *Laura Andersen*

⑆3321718214⑆ 4516 2133⑈ 1113

Paint Works
755 Brewton Street
Forest Hills, AL 36105

RECEIPT
No. 05

February 18 20 --

RECEIVED FROM *Prospective Client* $ *125.00*

One hundred twenty-five and 00/100 DOLLARS

FOR *Painting consultation*

RECEIVED BY *Laura Andersen*

Name Date Class

Mini Practice Set 6 (continued)

Paint Works
755 Brewton Street
Forest Hills, AL 36105

1114
71-821/3321

DATE *February 19* 20--

PAY TO THE ORDER OF *A-1 Repair Services* $ *85.00*

Eighty-five and 00/100 DOLLARS

Barclays Bank

MEMO *Computer repair* *Laura Andersen*

⑆3321718210⑆ 4516 2133⑈ 1114

Paint Works
755 Brewton Street
Forest Hills, AL 36105

1115
71-821/3321

DATE *February 21* 20--

PAY TO THE ORDER OF *Paint Palace* $ *375.00*

Three hundred seventy-five and 00/100 DOLLARS

Barclays Bank

MEMO *On account* *Laura Andersen*

⑆3321718210⑆ 4516 2133⑈ 1115

Paint Works
755 Brewton Street
Forest Hills, AL 36105

RECEIPT
No. 06

February 22 20 --

RECEIVED FROM *Wicker & Hartel Law Office* $ *2,000.00*

Two thousand and 00/100 DOLLARS

FOR *Final payment*

RECEIVED BY *Laura Andersen*

J&J Hardware & Lumber
315 Rooster Lane
Wildwood, AL 36121

INVOICE NO. 207
DATE: *Feb. 24, 20--*
ORDER NO.:
SHIPPED BY:
TERMS:

TO *Paint Works*
755 Brewton Street
Forest Hills, AL 36105

QTY.	ITEM	UNIT PRICE	TOTAL
10	Paint brushes	$9.00	$90.00

Paint Works
755 Brewton Street
Forest Hills, AL 36105

RECEIPT
No. 07

February 25 20 --

RECEIVED FROM *Maintenance Service* $ *575.00*

Five hundred seventy-five and 00/100 DOLLARS

FOR *Minor repairs to garage*

RECEIVED BY *Laura Andersen*

Paint Works
755 Brewton Street
Forest Hills, AL 36105

1116
71-821/3321

DATE *February 28* 20--

PAY TO THE ORDER OF *Laura Andersen* $ *650.00*

Six hundred fifty and 00/100 DOLLARS

Barclays Bank

MEMO *Personal withdrawal* *David Ingram*

⑆3321718210⑆ 4516 2133⑈ 1116

Paint Works
755 Brewton Street
Forest Hills, AL 36105

1117
71-821/3321

DATE *February 28* 20--

PAY TO THE ORDER OF *David Ingram* $ *650.00*

Six hundred fifty and 00/100 DOLLARS

Barclays Bank

MEMO *Personal withdrawal* *Laura Andersen*

⑆3321718210⑆ 4516 2133⑈ 1117

Paint Works
755 Brewton Street
Forest Hills, AL 36105

1118
71-821/3321

DATE *February 28* 20--

PAY TO THE ORDER OF *Sean Woo* $ *650.00*

Six hundred fifty and 00/100 DOLLARS

Barclays Bank

MEMO *Personal withdrawal* *David Ingram*

⑆3321718210⑆ 4516 2133⑈ 1118

Name Date Class

Notes

Name Date Class

Mini Practice Set 6 (continued)

(1), (4), (9)

GENERAL LEDGER

ACCOUNT ______________________ ACCOUNT NO. ________

DATE		DESCRIPTION	POST. REF.	DEBIT	CREDIT	BALANCE DEBIT	BALANCE CREDIT

ACCOUNT ______________________ ACCOUNT NO. ________

DATE		DESCRIPTION	POST. REF.	DEBIT	CREDIT	BALANCE DEBIT	BALANCE CREDIT

Name Date Class

Mini Practice Set 6 (continued)

GENERAL LEDGER

ACCOUNT ______ ACCOUNT NO. ______

DATE		DESCRIPTION	POST. REF.	DEBIT	CREDIT	BALANCE	
						DEBIT	CREDIT

ACCOUNT ______ ACCOUNT NO. ______

DATE		DESCRIPTION	POST. REF.	DEBIT	CREDIT	BALANCE	
						DEBIT	CREDIT

ACCOUNT ______ ACCOUNT NO. ______

DATE		DESCRIPTION	POST. REF.	DEBIT	CREDIT	BALANCE	
						DEBIT	CREDIT

ACCOUNT ______ ACCOUNT NO. ______

DATE		DESCRIPTION	POST. REF.	DEBIT	CREDIT	BALANCE	
						DEBIT	CREDIT

ACCOUNT ______ ACCOUNT NO. ______

DATE		DESCRIPTION	POST. REF.	DEBIT	CREDIT	BALANCE	
						DEBIT	CREDIT

Name ____________________ Date ____________ Class ____________

Mini Practice Set 6 (continued)

GENERAL LEDGER

ACCOUNT ________________________ ACCOUNT NO. ________

DATE		DESCRIPTION	POST. REF.	DEBIT	CREDIT	BALANCE	
						DEBIT	CREDIT

ACCOUNT ________________________ ACCOUNT NO. ________

DATE		DESCRIPTION	POST. REF.	DEBIT	CREDIT	BALANCE	
						DEBIT	CREDIT

ACCOUNT ________________________ ACCOUNT NO. ________

DATE		DESCRIPTION	POST. REF.	DEBIT	CREDIT	BALANCE	
						DEBIT	CREDIT

ACCOUNT ________________________ ACCOUNT NO. ________

DATE		DESCRIPTION	POST. REF.	DEBIT	CREDIT	BALANCE	
						DEBIT	CREDIT

ACCOUNT ________________________ ACCOUNT NO. ________

DATE		DESCRIPTION	POST. REF.	DEBIT	CREDIT	BALANCE	
						DEBIT	CREDIT

Mini Practice Set 6 (continued)

GENERAL LEDGER

ACCOUNT ______ ACCOUNT NO. ______

DATE		DESCRIPTION	POST. REF.	DEBIT	CREDIT	BALANCE DEBIT	BALANCE CREDIT

ACCOUNT ______ ACCOUNT NO. ______

DATE		DESCRIPTION	POST. REF.	DEBIT	CREDIT	BALANCE DEBIT	BALANCE CREDIT

ACCOUNT ______ ACCOUNT NO. ______

DATE		DESCRIPTION	POST. REF.	DEBIT	CREDIT	BALANCE DEBIT	BALANCE CREDIT

ACCOUNT ______ ACCOUNT NO. ______

DATE		DESCRIPTION	POST. REF.	DEBIT	CREDIT	BALANCE DEBIT	BALANCE CREDIT

Mini Practice Set 6 (continued)

GENERAL LEDGER

ACCOUNT ______ ACCOUNT NO. ______

DATE		DESCRIPTION	POST. REF.	DEBIT	CREDIT	BALANCE	
						DEBIT	CREDIT

ACCOUNT ______ ACCOUNT NO. ______

DATE		DESCRIPTION	POST. REF.	DEBIT	CREDIT	BALANCE	
						DEBIT	CREDIT

ACCOUNT ______ ACCOUNT NO. ______

DATE		DESCRIPTION	POST. REF.	DEBIT	CREDIT	BALANCE	
						DEBIT	CREDIT

Name Date Class

Mini Practice Set 6 (continued)

GENERAL LEDGER

ACCOUNT ______ ACCOUNT NO. ______

DATE		DESCRIPTION	POST. REF.	DEBIT	CREDIT	BALANCE	
						DEBIT	CREDIT

ACCOUNT ______ ACCOUNT NO. ______

DATE		DESCRIPTION	POST. REF.	DEBIT	CREDIT	BALANCE	
						DEBIT	CREDIT

ACCOUNT ______ ACCOUNT NO. ______

DATE		DESCRIPTION	POST. REF.	DEBIT	CREDIT	BALANCE	
						DEBIT	CREDIT

ACCOUNT ______ ACCOUNT NO. ______

DATE		DESCRIPTION	POST. REF.	DEBIT	CREDIT	BALANCE	
						DEBIT	CREDIT

Mini Practice Set 6 (continued)

(2), (3), (9)

GENERAL JOURNAL PAGE ____

	DATE		DESCRIPTION	POST. REF.	DEBIT	CREDIT	
1							1
2							2
3							3
4							4
5							5
6							6
7							7
8							8
9							9
10							10
11							11
12							12
13							13
14							14
15							15
16							16
17							17
18							18
19							19
20							20
21							21
22							22
23							23
24							24
25							25
26							26
27							27
28							28
29							29
30							30
31							31
32							32
33							33
34							34
35							35
36							36
37							37

Name Date Class

Mini Practice Set 6 (continued)

GENERAL JOURNAL

PAGE ______

	DATE		DESCRIPTION	POST. REF.	DEBIT	CREDIT	
1							1
2							2
3							3
4							4
5							5
6							6
7							7
8							8
9							9
10							10
11							11
12							12
13							13
14							14
15							15
16							16
17							17
18							18
19							19
20							20
21							21
22							22
23							23
24							24
25							25
26							26
27							27
28							28
29							29
30							30
31							31
32							32
33							33
34							34
35							35
36							36
37							37
38							38

Name Date Class

Mini Practice Set 6 (continued)

GENERAL JOURNAL

PAGE ______

	DATE		DESCRIPTION	POST. REF.	DEBIT	CREDIT	
1							1
2							2
3							3
4							4
5							5
6							6
7							7
8							8
9							9
10							10
11							11
12							12
13							13
14							14
15							15
16							16
17							17
18							18
19							19
20							20
21							21
22							22
23							23
24							24
25							25
26							26
27							27
28							28
29							29
30							30
31							31
32							32
33							33
34							34
35							35
36							36
37							37
38							38

Name Date Class

Mini Practice Set 6 (continued)

GENERAL JOURNAL

PAGE ______

	DATE		DESCRIPTION	POST. REF.	DEBIT	CREDIT	
1							1
2							2
3							3
4							4
5							5
6							6
7							7
8							8
9							9
10							10
11							11
12							12
13							13
14							14
15							15
16							16
17							17
18							18
19							19
20							20
21							21
22							22
23							23
24							24
25							25
26							26
27							27
28							28
29							29
30							30
31							31
32							32
33							33
34							34
35							35
36							36
37							37
38							38

Name Date Class

Mini Practice Set 6 (continued) (5)

	ACCT. NO.	ACCOUNT NAME	TRIAL BALANCE DEBIT	TRIAL BALANCE CREDIT	INCOME STATEMENT DEBIT	INCOME STATEMENT CREDIT	BALANCE SHEET DEBIT	BALANCE SHEET CREDIT	
1									1
2									2
3									3
4									4
5									5
6									6
7									7
8									8
9									9
10									10
11									11
12									12
13									13
14									14
15									15
16									16
17									17
18									18
19									19
20									20
21									21
22									22
23									23
24									24
25									25
26									26

Name Date Class

Mini Practice Set 6 (continued)

(6)

(7)

Name Date Class

Mini Practice Set 6 (continued)

(8)

Name Date Class

Mini Practice Set 6 (concluded)

(10)

Analyze:

Name Date Class

MINI PRACTICE SET 6

Paint Works

Audit Test

Directions: *Use your completed solutions to answer the following questions. Write the answer in the space to the left of each question.*

Answer

_______________ **1.** How many checks were issued by Fine Finishes in the month of February?

_______________ **2.** What is the total ending balance for the Accounts Payable accounts at February 28?

_______________ **3.** What is the ending balance of the Accounts Receivable account at February 28?

_______________ **4.** What total amount was credited to the Painting Fees revenue account for the month?

_______________ **5.** What were the total expenses for the month?

_______________ **6.** What amount was debited to the Income Summary account to close the expense accounts for the period?

_______________ **7.** How many accounts were listed on the trial balance dated February 28?

_______________ **8.** What was the net income for the period?

_______________ **9.** When net income was divided between the partners, how much was allocated to Laura Andersen?

_______________ **10.** What total withdrawals were made by all three partners for the period?

_______________ **11.** What was the ending balance for the David Ingram, Capital account?

_______________ **12.** What was the amount of total assets for the business at February 28?

_______________ **13.** What was the amount of total liabilities for the business at February 28?

_______________ **14.** How many accounts were listed on the post-closing trial balance?

_______________ **15.** At month end, what debts remain unpaid by Paint Works?

_______________ **16.** What was the total amount of debits to the Cash in Bank account for the period?

Name Date Class

CHAPTER 29 Ethics in Accounting

Study Guide

Section Assessment

Section 1 *Read Section 1 on pages 835–837 and complete the following exercises on page 838.*

- ☐ Reinforce the Main Idea
- ☐ Math for Accounting
- ☐ Problem 29-1 *Reporting Ethics Violations*
- ☐ Problem 29-2 *Exploring the Difference Between Ethics and Law*

Section 2 *Read Section 2 on pages 839–841 and complete the following exercises on page 842.*

- ☐ Reinforce the Main Idea
- ☐ Math for Accounting
- ☐ Problem 29-3 *Promoting Principles of Conduct*

Chapter Assessment

Summary *Review the Chapter 29 Visual Summary on page 843 in your textbook.*

- ☐ Key Concepts

Review and Activities *Complete the following questions and exercises on page 844 in your textbook.*

- ☐ After You Read: Answering the Essential Question
- ☐ Vocabulary Check
- ☐ Concept Check

Problems *Complete the following End-of-Chapter Problems for Chapter 29 in your textbook.*

- ☐ Problem 29-4 *Researching Ethics in the News*
- ☐ Problem 29-5 *Creating a Business Ethics Program*
- ☐ Problem 29-6 *Making Ethical Decisions*
- ☐ Problem 29-7 *Making Ethical Decisions*
- ☐ Problem 29-8 *Examining the Impact of Unethical Decisions*
- ☐ Problem 29-9 *Finding Out What Ethical Principles Mean to Your Classmates*
- ☐ Problem 29-10 *Finding Out What Ethical Principles Mean to Adults*
- ☐ Problem 29-11 *Applying a Code of Ethics to Personal Behavior*

Challenge Problem

- ☐ Problem 29-12 *Analyzing the Preamble to the Principles Section of the AICPA Code of Professional Conduct*

Real-World Applications and Connections *Complete the following applications on pages 847–848 in your textbook.*

- ☐ Career Wise
- ☐ Global Accounting
- ☐ A Matter of Ethics
- ☐ Analyzing Financial Reports
- ☐ H.O.T. Audit

Name Date Class

Working Papers *for Section Problems*

Problem 29-1 Reporting Ethics Violations *(textbook p. 838)*

Problem 29-2 Exploring the Difference Between Ethics and Law *(textbook p. 838)*

Problem 29-3 Promoting Principles of Conduct *(textbook p. 842)*

Name Date Class

Working Papers *for End-of-Chapter Problems*

Problem 29-4 Researching Ethics in the News *(textbook p. 845)*

Problem 29-5 Creating a Business Ethics Program *(textbook p. 845)*

Problem 29-6 Making Ethical Decisions *(textbook p. 845)*

Problem 29-7 Making Ethical Decisions *(textbook p. 845)*

Name Date Class

Working Papers for End-of-Chapter Problems

Problem 29-8 Examining the Impact of Unethical Decisions

(textbook p. 846)

Problem 29-9 Finding Out What Ethical Principles Mean to Your Classmates

(textbook p. 846)

Problem 29-10 Finding Out What Ethical Principles Mean to Adults

(textbook p. 846)

Problem 29-11 Applying a Code of Ethics to Personal Behavior

(textbook p. 846)

Name Date Class

Problem 29-12 Analyzing the Preamble to the Principles Section of the AICPA Code of Professional Conduct *(textbook p. 846)*

Name Date Class

The Accrual Basis of Accounting

Problem A-1 Identifying Accruals and Deferrals *(textbook p. A–10)*

Item	Prepaid Expense	Unearned Revenue	Accrued Expense	Accrued Revenue
1				
2				
3				
4				
5				
6				
7				
8				
9				
10				
11				

Name Date Class

Problem A-2 Recording Adjusting Entries *(textbook p. A–10)*

GENERAL JOURNAL PAGE ______

	DATE		DESCRIPTION	POST. REF.	DEBIT	CREDIT	
1							1
2							2
3							3
4							4
5							5
6							6
7							7
8							8
9							9
10							10
11							11
12							12
13							13
14							14
15							15
16							16
17							17
18							18
19							19
20							20

Name Date Class

Problem A-3 Recording Transactions for Notes Payable *(textbook p. A–11)*

GENERAL JOURNAL

PAGE ______

	DATE		DESCRIPTION	POST. REF.	DEBIT	CREDIT	
1							1
2							2
3							3
4							4
5							5
6							6
7							7
8							8
9							9
10							10
11							11
12							12
13							13
14							14
15							15
16							16
17							17
18							18
19							19
20							20

Name Date Class

Problem A-4 Recording Accrued Expenses *(textbook p. A–11)*

GENERAL JOURNAL PAGE ______

	DATE		DESCRIPTION	POST. REF.	DEBIT	CREDIT	
1							1
2							2
3							3
4							4
5							5
6							6
7							7
8							8
9							9
10							10
11							11
12							12
13							13
14							14
15							15
16							16
17							17
18							18
19							19
20							20

Name Date Class

Notes

Name Date Class

APPENDIX B Federal Personal Income Tax

20-- Tax Table

See the instructions for line 43 that begin on page 33 to see if you must use the Tax Table below to figure your tax.

Example. Mr. and Mrs. Brown are filing a joint return. Their taxable income on Form 1040, line 42, is $25,300. First, they find the $25,300–25,350 taxable income line. Next, they find the column for married filing jointly and read down the column. The amount shown where the taxable income line and filing status column meet is $3,084. This is the tax amount they should enter on Form 1040, line 43.

Sample Table

At least	But less than	Single	Married filing jointly *	Married filing separately	Head of a household
			Your tax is—		
25,200	25,250	3,426	3,069	3,426	3,274
25,250	25,300	3,434	3,076	3,434	3,281
25,300	25,350	3,441	(3,084)	3,441	3,289
25,350	25,400	3,449	3,091	3,449	3,296

If line 42 (taxable income) is—		And you are—			
At least	But less than	Single	Married filing jointly *	Married filing separately	Head of a household
		Your tax is—			
0	5	0	0	0	0
5	15	1	1	1	1
15	25	2	2	2	2
25	50	4	4	4	4
50	75	6	6	6	6
75	100	9	9	9	9
100	125	11	11	11	11
125	150	14	14	14	14
150	175	16	16	16	16
175	200	19	19	19	19
200	225	21	21	21	21
225	250	24	24	24	24
250	275	26	26	26	26
275	300	29	29	29	29
300	325	31	31	31	31
325	350	34	34	34	34
350	375	36	36	36	36
375	400	39	39	39	39
400	425	41	41	41	41
425	450	44	44	44	44
450	475	46	46	46	46
475	500	49	49	49	49
500	525	51	51	51	51
525	550	54	54	54	54
550	575	56	56	56	56
575	600	59	59	59	59
600	625	61	61	61	61
625	650	64	64	64	64
650	675	66	66	66	66
675	700	69	69	69	69
700	725	71	71	71	71
725	750	74	74	74	74
750	775	76	76	76	76
775	800	79	79	79	79
800	825	81	81	81	81
825	850	84	84	84	84
850	875	86	86	86	86
875	900	89	89	89	89
900	925	91	91	91	91
925	950	94	94	94	94
950	975	96	96	96	96
975	1,000	99	99	99	99
1,000					
1,000	1,025	101	101	101	101
1,025	1,050	104	104	104	104
1,050	1,075	106	106	106	106
1,075	1,100	109	109	109	109
1,100	1,125	111	111	111	111
1,125	1,150	114	114	114	114
1,150	1,175	116	116	116	116
1,175	1,200	119	119	119	119
1,200	1,225	121	121	121	121
1,225	1,250	124	124	124	124
1,250	1,275	126	126	126	126
1,275	1,300	129	129	129	129

If line 42 (taxable income) is—		And you are—			
At least	But less than	Single	Married filing jointly *	Married filing separately	Head of a household
		Your tax is—			
1,300	1,325	131	131	131	131
1,325	1,350	134	134	134	134
1,350	1,375	136	136	136	136
1,375	1,400	139	139	139	139
1,400	1,425	141	141	141	141
1,425	1,450	144	144	144	144
1,450	1,475	146	146	146	146
1,475	1,500	149	149	149	149
1,500	1,525	151	151	151	151
1,525	1,550	154	154	154	154
1,550	1,575	156	156	156	156
1,575	1,600	159	159	159	159
1,600	1,625	161	161	161	161
1,625	1,650	164	164	164	164
1,650	1,675	166	166	166	166
1,675	1,700	169	169	169	169
1,700	1,725	171	171	171	171
1,725	1,750	174	174	174	174
1,750	1,775	176	176	176	176
1,775	1,800	179	179	179	179
1,800	1,825	181	181	181	181
1,825	1,850	184	184	184	184
1,850	1,875	186	186	186	186
1,875	1,900	189	189	189	189
1,900	1,925	191	191	191	191
1,925	1,950	194	194	194	194
1,950	1,975	196	196	196	196
1,975	2,000	199	199	199	199
2,000					
2,000	2,025	201	201	201	201
2,025	2,050	204	204	204	204
2,050	2,075	206	206	206	206
2,075	2,100	209	209	209	209
2,100	2,125	211	211	211	211
2,125	2,150	214	214	214	214
2,150	2,175	216	216	216	216
2,175	2,200	219	219	219	219
2,200	2,225	221	221	221	221
2,225	2,250	224	224	224	224
2,250	2,275	226	226	226	226
2,275	2,300	229	229	229	229
2,300	2,325	231	231	231	231
2,325	2,350	234	234	234	234
2,350	2,375	236	236	236	236
2,375	2,400	239	239	239	239
2,400	2,425	241	241	241	241
2,425	2,450	244	244	244	244
2,450	2,475	246	246	246	246
2,475	2,500	249	249	249	249
2,500	2,525	251	251	251	251
2,525	2,550	254	254	254	254
2,550	2,575	256	256	256	256
2,575	2,600	259	259	259	259
2,600	2,625	261	261	261	261
2,625	2,650	264	264	264	264
2,650	2,675	266	266	266	266
2,675	2,700	269	269	269	269

If line 42 (taxable income) is—		And you are—			
At least	But less than	Single	Married filing jointly *	Married filing separately	Head of a household
		Your tax is—			
2,700	2,725	271	271	271	271
2,725	2,750	274	274	274	274
2,750	2,775	276	276	276	276
2,775	2,800	279	279	279	279
2,800	2,825	281	281	281	281
2,825	2,850	284	284	284	284
2,850	2,875	286	286	286	286
2,875	2,900	289	289	289	289
2,900	2,925	291	291	291	291
2,925	2,950	294	294	294	294
2,950	2,975	296	296	296	296
2,975	3,000	299	299	299	299
3,000					
3,000	3,050	303	303	303	303
3,050	3,100	308	308	308	308
3,100	3,150	313	313	313	313
3,150	3,200	318	318	318	318
3,200	3,250	323	323	323	323
3,250	3,300	328	328	328	328
3,300	3,350	333	333	333	333
3,350	3,400	338	338	338	338
3,400	3,450	343	343	343	343
3,450	3,500	348	348	348	348
3,500	3,550	353	353	353	353
3,550	3,600	358	358	358	358
3,600	3,650	363	363	363	363
3,650	3,700	368	368	368	368
3,700	3,750	373	373	373	373
3,750	3,800	378	378	378	378
3,800	3,850	383	383	383	383
3,850	3,900	388	388	388	388
3,900	3,950	393	393	393	393
3,950	4,000	398	398	398	398
4,000					
4,000	4,050	403	403	403	403
4,050	4,100	408	408	408	408
4,100	4,150	413	413	413	413
4,150	4,200	418	418	418	418
4,200	4,250	423	423	423	423
4,250	4,300	428	428	428	428
4,300	4,350	433	433	433	433
4,350	4,400	438	438	438	438
4,400	4,450	443	443	443	443
4,450	4,500	448	448	448	448
4,500	4,550	453	453	453	453
4,550	4,600	458	458	458	458
4,600	4,650	463	463	463	463
4,650	4,700	468	468	468	468
4,700	4,750	473	473	473	473
4,750	4,800	478	478	478	478
4,800	4,850	483	483	483	483
4,850	4,900	488	488	488	488
4,900	4,950	493	493	493	493
4,950	5,000	498	498	498	498

(Continued on page 61)

* This column must also be used by a qualifying widow(er).

Name Date Class

Problem B-1 Preparing Form 1040EZ *(textbook p. A–17)*

Form **1040EZ** — Department of the Treasury—Internal Revenue Service
Income Tax Return for Single and Joint Filers With No Dependents (99) **20--**
OMB No. 1545-0675

Label (See page 11.) **Use the IRS label.** Otherwise, please print or type.
LABEL HERE

Your first name and initial | Last name | Your social security number
If a joint return, spouse's first name and initial | Last name | Spouse's social security number
Home address (number and street). If you have a P.O. box, see page 11. | Apt. no.
City, town or post office, state, and ZIP code. If you have a foreign address, see page 11.

▲ Important! ▲ You **must** enter your SSN(s) above.

Presidential Election Campaign (page 11)
Note. Checking "Yes" will not change your tax or reduce your refund.
Do you, or your spouse if a joint return, want $3 to go to this fund? ▶ You ☐ Yes ☐ No Spouse ☐ Yes ☐ No

Income
Attach Form(s) W-2 here. Enclose, but do not attach, any payment.

1	Wages, salaries, and tips. This should be shown in box 1 of your Form(s) W-2. Attach your Form(s) W-2.	1
2	Taxable interest. If the total is over $1,500, you cannot use Form 1040EZ.	2
3	Unemployment compensation and Alaska Permanent Fund dividends (see page 13).	3
4	Add lines 1, 2, and 3. This is your **adjusted gross income.**	4
5	Can your parents (or someone else) claim you on their return? **Yes.** ☐ Enter amount from worksheet on back. **No.** ☐ If **single,** enter $7,950. If **married filing jointly,** enter $15,900. See back for explanation.	5
6	Subtract line 5 from line 4. If line 5 is larger than line 4, enter -0-. This is your **taxable income.** ▶	6

Note. You **must** check Yes or No.

Payments and tax

7	Federal income tax withheld from box 2 of your Form(s) W-2.	7
8a	**Earned income credit (EIC).**	8a
b	Nontaxable combat pay election. 8b	
9	Add lines 7 and 8a. These are your **total payments.** ▶	9
10	**Tax.** Use the amount on **line 6 above** to find your tax in the tax table on pages 24–32 of the booklet. Then, enter the tax from the table on this line.	10

Refund
Have it directly deposited! See page 18 and fill in 11b, 11c, and 11d.

11a	If line 9 is larger than line 10, subtract line 10 from line 9. This is your **refund.** ▶	11a
▶ b	Routing number ▶ c Type: ☐ Checking ☐ Savings	
▶ d	Account number	

Amount you owe

12	If line 10 is larger than line 9, subtract line 9 from line 10. This is the **amount you owe.** For details on how to pay, see page 19. ▶	12

Third party designee
Do you want to allow another person to discuss this return with the IRS (see page 19)? ☐ **Yes.** Complete the following. ☐ **No**
Designee's name ▶ Phone no. ▶ ( ) Personal identification number (PIN) ▶

Sign here
Joint return? See page 11. Keep a copy for your records.
Under penalties of perjury, I declare that I have examined this return, and to the best of my knowledge and belief, it is true, correct, and accurately lists all amounts and sources of income I received during the tax year. Declaration of preparer (other than the taxpayer) is based on all information of which the preparer has any knowledge.
Your signature | Date | Your occupation | Daytime phone number ( )
Spouse's signature. If a joint return, **both** must sign. | Date | Spouse's occupation

Paid preparer's use only
Preparer's signature | Date | Check if self-employed ☐ | Preparer's SSN or PTIN
Firm's name (or yours if self-employed), address, and ZIP code | EIN | Phone no. ( )

For Disclosure, Privacy Act, and Paperwork Reduction Act Notice, see page 23. Cat. No. 11329W Form **1040EZ** (20--)

Name Date Class

Problem B-1 (concluded)

Form 1040EZ (20 _) Page 2

Use this form if

- Your filing status is single or married filing jointly. If you are not sure about your filing status, see page 11.
- You (and your spouse if married filing jointly) were under age 65 and not blind at the end of 20 --. If you were born on January 1, 1940, you are considered to be age 65 at the end of 20--.
- You do not claim any dependents. For information on dependents, use TeleTax topic 354 (see page 6).
- Your taxable income (line 6) is less than $100,000.
- You do not claim any adjustments to income. For information on adjustments to income, use TeleTax topics 451-458 (see page 6).
- The only tax credit you can claim is the earned income credit. For information on credits, use TeleTax topics 601-608 and 610 (see page 6).
- You had only wages, salaries, tips, taxable scholarship or fellowship grants, unemployment compensation, or Alaska Permanent Fund dividends, and your taxable interest was not over $1,500. But if you earned tips, including allocated tips, that are not included in box 5 and box 7 of your Form W-2, you may not be able to use Form 1040EZ (see page 12). If you are planning to use Form 1040EZ for a child who received Alaska Permanent Fund dividends, see page 13.
- You did not receive any advance earned income credit payments.

If you cannot use this form, use TeleTax topic 352 (see page 6).

Filling in your return

For tips on how to avoid common mistakes, see page 20.

If you received a scholarship or fellowship grant or tax-exempt interest income, such as on municipal bonds, see the booklet before filling in the form. Also, see the booklet if you received a Form 1099-INT showing federal income tax withheld or if federal income tax was withheld from your unemployment compensation or Alaska Permanent Fund dividends.

Remember, you must report all wages, salaries, and tips even if you do not get a Form W-2 from your employer. You must also report all your taxable interest, including interest from banks, savings and loans, credit unions, etc., even if you do not get a Form 1099-INT.

Worksheet for dependents who checked "Yes" on line 5

(keep a copy for your records)

Use this worksheet to figure the amount to enter on line 5 if someone can claim you (or your spouse if married filing jointly) as a dependent, even if that person chooses not to do so. To find out if someone can claim you as a dependent, use TeleTax topic 354 (see page 6).

A. Amount, if any, from line 1 on front ________
\+ 250.00 Enter total ▶ **A.** ________

B. Minimum standard deduction . . . . **B.** 800.00

C. Enter the **larger** of line A or line B here . . . . **C.** ________

D. Maximum standard deduction. If **single,** enter $4,850; if **married filing jointly,** enter $9,700 . . . . **D.** ________

E. Enter the **smaller** of line C or line D here. This is your standard deduction . . . . **E.** ________

F. Exemption amount.
- If single, enter -0-.
- If married filing jointly and—
  - —both you and your spouse can be claimed as dependents, enter -0-.
  - —only one of you can be claimed as a dependent, enter $3,100.

F. ________

G. Add lines E and F. Enter the total here and on line 5 on the front . . **G.** ________

If you checked "No" on line 5 because no one can claim you (or your spouse if married filing jointly) as a dependent, enter on line 5 the amount shown below that applies to you.

- Single, enter $7,950. This is the total of your standard deduction ($4,850) and your exemption ($3,100).
- Married filing jointly, enter $15,900. This is the total of your standard deduction ($9,700), your exemption ($3,100), and your spouse's exemption ($3,100).

Mailing return

Mail your return by **April 15, 20--.** Use the envelope that came with your booklet. If you do not have that envelope or if you moved during the year, see the back cover for the address to use.

Form **1040EZ** (20--)

Name Date Class

Problem B-2 Preparing Form 1040EZ *(textbook p. A–17)*

Form **1040EZ**

Department of the Treasury—Internal Revenue Service

Income Tax Return for Single and Joint Filers With No Dependents (99) **20--**

OMB No. 1545-0675

Label
(See page 11.)
Use the IRS label.
Otherwise, please print or type.

LABEL HERE

Your first name and initial | Last name | **Your social security number**

If a joint return, spouse's first name and initial | Last name | **Spouse's social security number**

Home address (number and street). If you have a P.O. box, see page 11. | Apt. no.

City, town or post office, state, and ZIP code. If you have a foreign address, see page 11.

▲ Important! ▲
You **must** enter your SSN(s) above.

Presidential Election Campaign (page 11)

Note. Checking "Yes" will not change your tax or reduce your refund.
Do you, or your spouse if a joint return, want $3 to go to this fund? . . . . . . ▶

You ☐ Yes ☐ No **Spouse** ☐ Yes ☐ No

Income

Attach Form(s) W-2 here.
Enclose, but do not attach, any payment.

1 Wages, salaries, and tips. This should be shown in box 1 of your Form(s) W-2. Attach your Form(s) W-2. — 1

2 Taxable interest. If the total is over $1,500, you cannot use Form 1040EZ. — 2

3 Unemployment compensation and Alaska Permanent Fund dividends (see page 13). — 3

4 Add lines 1, 2, and 3. This is your **adjusted gross income.** — 4

Note. You **must** check Yes or No.

5 Can your parents (or someone else) claim you on their return?
Yes. ☐ Enter amount from worksheet on back.
No. ☐ If **single,** enter $7,950.
If **married filing jointly,** enter $15,900.
See back for explanation. — 5

6 Subtract line 5 from line 4. If line 5 is larger than line 4, enter -0-.
This is your **taxable income.** ▶ — 6

Payments and tax

7 Federal income tax withheld from box 2 of your Form(s) W-2. — 7

8a **Earned income credit (EIC).** — 8a

b Nontaxable combat pay election. — 8b

9 Add lines 7 and 8a. These are your **total payments.** ▶ — 9

10 **Tax.** Use the amount on **line 6 above** to find your tax in the tax table on pages 24–32 of the booklet. Then, enter the tax from the table on this line. — 10

Refund

Have it directly deposited! See page 18 and fill in 11b, 11c, and 11d.

11a If line 9 is larger than line 10, subtract line 10 from line 9. This is your **refund.** ▶ — 11a

▶ b Routing number ☐☐☐☐☐☐☐☐☐ ▶ c Type: ☐ Checking ☐ Savings

▶ d Account number ☐☐☐☐☐☐☐☐☐☐☐☐☐☐☐☐☐

Amount you owe

12 If line 10 is larger than line 9, subtract line 9 from line 10. This is the **amount you owe.** For details on how to pay, see page 19. ▶ — 12

Third party designee

Do you want to allow another person to discuss this return with the IRS (see page 19)? ☐ **Yes.** Complete the following. ☐ **No**

Designee's name ▶ | Phone no. ▶ ( ) | Personal identification number (PIN) ▶ ☐☐☐☐☐

Sign here

Joint return? See page 11.
Keep a copy for your records.

Under penalties of perjury, I declare that I have examined this return, and to the best of my knowledge and belief, it is true, correct, and accurately lists all amounts and sources of income I received during the tax year. Declaration of preparer (other than the taxpayer) is based on all information of which the preparer has any knowledge.

Your signature | Date | Your occupation | Daytime phone number ( )

Spouse's signature. If a joint return, **both** must sign. | Date | Spouse's occupation

Paid preparer's use only

Preparer's signature | Date | Check if self-employed ☐ | Preparer's SSN or PTIN

Firm's name (or yours if self-employed), address, and ZIP code | EIN | Phone no. ( )

For Disclosure, Privacy Act, and Paperwork Reduction Act Notice, see page 23. Cat. No. 11329W Form **1040EZ** (20--)

Problem B-2 (concluded)

Form 1040EZ (20) Page 2

Use this form if

- Your filing status is single or married filing jointly. If you are not sure about your filing status, see page 11.
- You (and your spouse if married filing jointly) were under age 65 and not blind at the end of 20--. If you were born on January 1, 1940, you are considered to be age 65 at the end of 20--.
- You do not claim any dependents. For information on dependents, use TeleTax topic 354 (see page 6).
- Your taxable income (line 6) is less than $100,000.
- You do not claim any adjustments to income. For information on adjustments to income, use TeleTax topics 451-458 (see page 6).
- The only tax credit you can claim is the earned income credit. For information on credits, use TeleTax topics 601-608 and 610 (see page 6).
- You had only wages, salaries, tips, taxable scholarship or fellowship grants, unemployment compensation, or Alaska Permanent Fund dividends, and your taxable interest was not over $1,500. But if you earned tips, including allocated tips, that are not included in box 5 and box 7 of your Form W-2, you may not be able to use Form 1040EZ (see page 12). If you are planning to use Form 1040EZ for a child who received Alaska Permanent Fund dividends, see page 13.
- You did not receive any advance earned income credit payments.

If you cannot use this form, use TeleTax topic 352 (see page 6).

Filling in your return

For tips on how to avoid common mistakes, see page 20.

If you received a scholarship or fellowship grant or tax-exempt interest income, such as on municipal bonds, see the booklet before filling in the form. Also, see the booklet if you received a Form 1099-INT showing federal income tax withheld or if federal income tax was withheld from your unemployment compensation or Alaska Permanent Fund dividends.

Remember, you must report all wages, salaries, and tips even if you do not get a Form W-2 from your employer. You must also report all your taxable interest, including interest from banks, savings and loans, credit unions, etc., even if you do not get a Form 1099-INT.

Worksheet for dependents who checked "Yes" on line 5

(keep a copy for your records)

Use this worksheet to figure the amount to enter on line 5 if someone can claim you (or your spouse if married filing jointly) as a dependent, even if that person chooses not to do so. To find out if someone can claim you as a dependent, use TeleTax topic 354 (see page 6).

A. Amount, if any, from line 1 on front ________
+ 250.00 Enter total ▶ **A.** ________

B. Minimum standard deduction . . . . **B.** 800.00

C. Enter the **larger** of line A or line B here . . . . **C.** ________

D. Maximum standard deduction. If **single,** enter $4,850; if **married filing jointly,** enter $9,700 . . . . **D.** ________

E. Enter the **smaller** of line C or line D here. This is your standard deduction . . . . **E.** ________

F. Exemption amount.
- If single, enter -0-.
- If married filing jointly and—
  - —both you and your spouse can be claimed as dependents, enter -0-.
  - —only one of you can be claimed as a dependent, enter $3,100.

F. ________

G. Add lines E and F. Enter the total here and on line 5 on the front . . **G.** ________

If you checked "No" on line 5 because no one can claim you (or your spouse if married filing jointly) as a dependent, enter on line 5 the amount shown below that applies to you.

- Single, enter $7,950. This is the total of your standard deduction ($4,850) and your exemption ($3,100).
- Married filing jointly, enter $15,900. This is the total of your standard deduction ($9,700), your exemption ($3,100), and your spouse's exemption ($3,100).

Mailing return

Mail your return by **April 15, 20--.** Use the envelope that came with your booklet. If you do not have that envelope or if you moved during the year, see the back cover for the address to use.

Form **1040EZ** (20--)

Name Date Class

Using the Numeric Keypad

Using the 4, 5, and 6 Keys

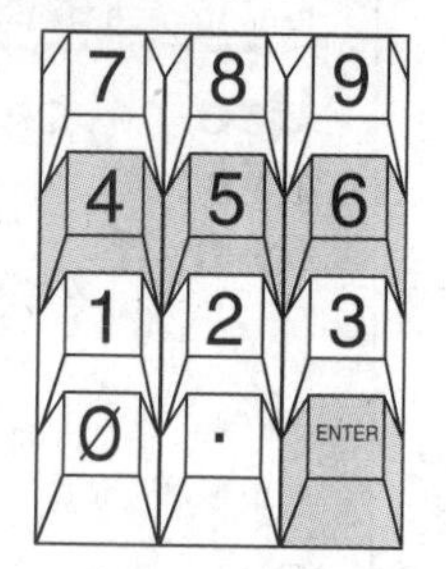

Exercises 1–6 are from your textbook on page A–19. Exercises 7–24 are provided to give you additional practice.

Practice at a comfortable pace until you feel confident about each key's location.

1.	2.	3.	4.	5.	6.
444	555	666	456	554	664
555	666	454	654	445	445
666	444	545	465	564	566
456	654	446	556	664	645
564	546	646	656	565	465
646	465	546	465	655	654
3,331	3,330	3,303	3,252	3,447	3,439

7.	8.	9.	10.	11.	12.
456	564	646	555	666	444
654	546	465	666	454	545
446	646	546	456	654	465
556	656	465	554	445	564
664	565	655	664	466	566
645	465	654	444	555	666
3,421	3,442	3,431	3,339	3,240	3,250

13.	14.	15.	16.	17.	18.
654	666	464	666	456	555
546	546	656	654	454	545
456	546	656	654	454	545
465	646	546	555	446	454
444	654	654	556	445	456
555	564	546	554	444	654
3,120	3,622	3,522	3,639	2,699	3,209

19.	20.	21.	22.	23.	24.
5,655	4,556	456	55	445	6,656
45	645	4,564	4	56	4,655
6	54	655	54	6,664	566
456	46	4,545	5,554	465	465
664	564	5,664	564	5,644	64
56	5	65	445	56	544
6,882	5,870	15,949	6,676	13,330	12,950

Name Date Class

Using the 1, 7, and 0 Keys

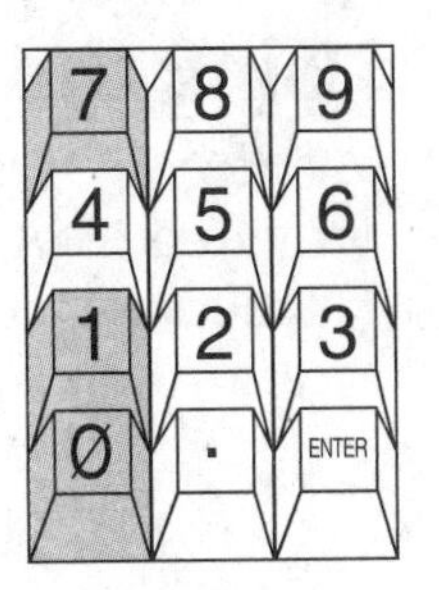

Exercises 1–6 are from your textbook on page A–20. Exercises 7–24 are provided to give you additional practice.

Practice at a comfortable pace until you feel confident about each key's location.

1.	**2.**	**3.**	**4.**	**5.**	**6.**
444	014	140	107	011	141
471	107	701	074	170	117
174	740	701	104	710	417
741	101	704	007	004	047
710	114	471	411	471	104
407	441	117	047	174	114
2,947	1,517	2,834	750	1,540	940

7.	**8.**	**9.**	**10.**	**11.**	**12.**
741	710	407	014	147	740
101	114	441	140	701	701
704	471	117	107	074	104
007	411	017	011	170	710
004	471	174	141	117	417
047	104	114	444	471	174
1,604	2,281	1,270	857	1,680	2,846

13.	**14.**	**15.**	**16.**	**17.**	**18.**
170	140	104	111	777	410
701	147	107	147	111	140
107	014	401	174	444	014
741	041	701	741	714	741
147	074	101	710	741	471
410	047	010	410	704	147
2,276	463	1,424	2,293	3,491	1,923

19.	**20.**	**21.**	**22.**	**23.**	**24.**
1,044	456	145	17	101	1,404
540	4,540	6,147	7,100	47	40
7,055	74	567	1,105	1,075	140
607	415	10	574	157	1,714
4,441	510	106	177	7,775	1,570
17	1,750	1,045	50	147	1,104
13,704	7,745	8,020	9,023	9,302	5,972

Name Date Class

Using the 3 and 9 Keys

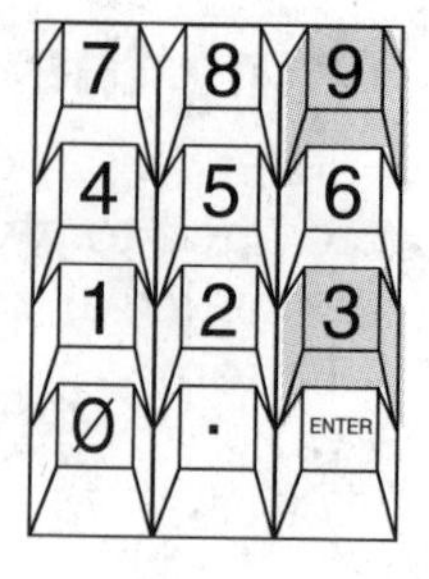

Exercises 1–6 are from your textbook on page A–20. Exercises 7–12 are provided to give you additional practice.

Practice at a comfortable pace until you feel confident about each key's location.

1.	2.	3.	4.	5.	6.
666	669	339	966	939	699
999	663	363	393	363	936
333	936	336	966	393	939
963	396	936	633	639	336
639	936	636	393	369	696
399	363	996	993	369	939
3,999	3,963	3,606	4,344	3,072	4,545

7.	8.	9.	10.	11.	12.
963	639	399	669	663	936
396	936	363	339	363	336
936	636	993	966	393	966
633	393	993	939	363	393
639	369	369	699	936	939
336	696	939	666	999	333
3,903	3,669	4,056	4,278	3,717	3,903

Using the 2 and 8 Keys

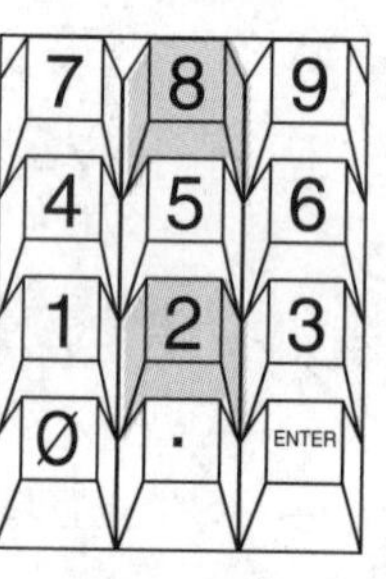

Exercises 1–6 are from your textbook on page A–20. Exercises 7–12 are provided to give you additional practice.

Practice at a comfortable pace until you feel confident about each key's location.

1.	2.	3.	4.	5.	6.
555	228	885	285	582	828
888	852	285	258	558	825
222	522	825	525	582	852
582	252	588	858	825	258
822	528	258	582	525	885
522	855	852	825	582	282
3,591	3,237	3,693	3,333	3,654	3,930

7.	8.	9.	10.	11.	12.
582	822	522	228	852	522
252	528	855	885	285	825
588	258	258	285	825	525
858	582	825	582	558	582
825	525	582	828	528	852
852	885	282	555	888	222
3,957	3,600	3,324	3,363	3,936	3,528

Name Date Class

Using the Decimal Key

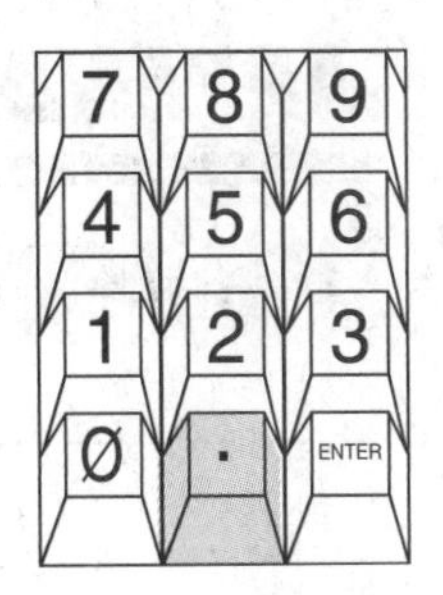

Exercises 1–18 are from your textbook on page A–21. Exercises 19–24 are provided to give you additional practice.

Practice at a comfortable pace until you feel confident about each key's location.

1.	**2.**	**3.**	**4.**	**5.**	**6.**
.777	.978	.998	8.78	7.88	8.79
.888	.987	.879	8.89	7.87	7.98
.999	.878	.787	8.87	8.97	9.89
.789	.987	.878	7.88	9.77	9.87
.897	.789	.797	9.87	7.97	7.89
.978	.797	.899	7.98	8.79	9.78
5.328	5.416	5.238	52.27	51.25	54.20

7.	**8.**	**9.**	**10.**	**11.**	**12.**
468.	48.2	.8	284.0	41.87	154.88
.489	2,537.	5,827.	100.	4,057.4	888.
214.2	852.	.024	8.45	89.45	.0082
7.12	3.978	18.73	56.0	2.25	200.08
6,394.4	257.0	85.00	23.00	20.0	632.48
.58	.2684	1.045	.89	36.248	64.1
7,084.789	3,698.4464	5,932.599	472.34	4,247.218	1,939.5482

13.	**14.**	**15.**	**16.**	**17.**	**18.**
267.50	425.21	1.25	467.54	65.27	9.78
4.19	414.50	0.18	95.14	102.38	5.94
87.64	1,684.84	585.56	6,926.95	8,216.58	652.25
654.84	49.95	7.50	35.00	1,852.84	3,782.70
1,750.67	720.65	11.60	7.13	4.60	39.25
141.82	77.61	23.55	154.95	79.15	36.87
2,906.66	3,372.76	629.64	7,686.71	10,320.82	4,526.79

19.	**20.**	**21.**	**22.**	**23.**	**24.**
61.93	446.00	20.67	78.30	519.02	8.68
1,296.13	4,466.73	216.37	14.39	3,113.56	62.36
200.00	61.45	445.39	14.60	102.55	43.12
157.43	258.16	5,650.00	352.49	39.95	611.18
14.97	900.62	1,426.15	617.32	1,874.05	21.67
869.42	25.15	109.15	803.70	3,130.78	1,972.32
2,599.88	6,158.11	7,867.73	1,880.80	8,779.91	2,719.33

Name Date Class

APPENDIX D Advanced Accounting Concepts

Problem D-1 (p. A–26)

Problem D-2 (p. A–26)

Name Date Class

APPENDIX E Additional Reinforcement Problems

Reinforcement Problem 3A Determining the Effects of Business Transactions on the Accounting Equation

	Assets					=	Liabilities	+	Owner's Equity
Transaction	Cash in Bank	Accounts Receivable	Office Furniture	Computer Equipment	Office Equipment	=	Accounts Payable	+	Pamela Wong, Capital
1									
Balance						=		+	
2									
Balance						=		+	
3									
Balance						=		+	
4									
Balance						=		+	
5									
Balance						=		+	
6									
Balance						=		+	
7									
Balance						=		+	
8									
Balance						=		+	
9									
Balance						=		+	
10									
Balance						=		+	
11									
Balance						=		+	

Reinforcement Problem 3A (concluded)

Analyze: **a.** ______________________

b. ______________________

c. ______________________

d. ______________________

Name Date Class

Reinforcement Problem 4A Analyzing Transactions Affecting Assets, Liabilities, and Owner's Equity

(1), (2), (3)

(4) Sum of debit balances: ______

(5) Sum of credit balances: ______

Analyze: ______

Name Date Class

Reinforcement Problem 5A — Analyzing Transactions Affecting Revenue, Expenses, and Withdrawal

Chart of Accounts (partial)

Cash in Bank	Accounts Payable—Computer Warehouse Inc.	Design Revenue
Accounts Receivable—Adams, Bell, and Cox Inc.	Pamela Wong, Capital	Maintenance Expense
Office Equipment	Pamela Wong, Withdrawals	Rent Expense
Computer Equipment		Utilities Expense

Name Date Class

Reinforcement Problem 5A (concluded)

(4)

Account Name	*Debit Balances*	*Credit Balances*

Analyze:

Name Date Class

Reinforcement Problem 6A Recording General Journal Transactions

GENERAL JOURNAL PAGE ______

	DATE		DESCRIPTION	POST. REF.	DEBIT	CREDIT	
1							1
2							2
3							3
4							4
5							5
6							6
7							7
8							8
9							9
10							10
11							11
12							12
13							13
14							14
15							15
16							16
17							17
18							18
19							19
20							20
21							21
22							22
23							23
24							24
25							25
26							26
27							27
28							28
29							29
30							30
31							31
32							32
33							33
34							34
35							35

Analyze: ______

Name Date Class

Reinforcement Problem 7A Journalizing and Posting Transactions

(1), (3)

GENERAL LEDGER

ACCOUNT ______ ACCOUNT NO. ______

DATE		DESCRIPTION	POST. REF.	DEBIT	CREDIT	BALANCE	
						DEBIT	CREDIT

ACCOUNT ______ ACCOUNT NO. ______

DATE		DESCRIPTION	POST. REF.	DEBIT	CREDIT	BALANCE	
						DEBIT	CREDIT

ACCOUNT ______ ACCOUNT NO. ______

DATE		DESCRIPTION	POST. REF.	DEBIT	CREDIT	BALANCE	
						DEBIT	CREDIT

ACCOUNT ______ ACCOUNT NO. ______

DATE		DESCRIPTION	POST. REF.	DEBIT	CREDIT	BALANCE	
						DEBIT	CREDIT

ACCOUNT ______ ACCOUNT NO. ______

DATE		DESCRIPTION	POST. REF.	DEBIT	CREDIT	BALANCE	
						DEBIT	CREDIT

Name Date Class

Reinforcement Problem 7A (continued)

ACCOUNT ACCOUNT NO.

DATE	DESCRIPTION	POST. REF.	DEBIT	CREDIT	BALANCE DEBIT	BALANCE CREDIT

ACCOUNT ACCOUNT NO.

DATE	DESCRIPTION	POST. REF.	DEBIT	CREDIT	BALANCE DEBIT	BALANCE CREDIT

ACCOUNT ACCOUNT NO.

DATE	DESCRIPTION	POST. REF.	DEBIT	CREDIT	BALANCE DEBIT	BALANCE CREDIT

ACCOUNT ACCOUNT NO.

DATE	DESCRIPTION	POST. REF.	DEBIT	CREDIT	BALANCE DEBIT	BALANCE CREDIT

ACCOUNT ACCOUNT NO.

DATE	DESCRIPTION	POST. REF.	DEBIT	CREDIT	BALANCE DEBIT	BALANCE CREDIT

ACCOUNT ACCOUNT NO.

DATE	DESCRIPTION	POST. REF.	DEBIT	CREDIT	BALANCE DEBIT	BALANCE CREDIT

Reinforcement Problem 7A (continued)

(2)

GENERAL JOURNAL PAGE ______

	DATE	DESCRIPTION	POST. REF.	DEBIT	CREDIT	
1						1
2						2
3						3
4						4
5						5
6						6
7						7
8						8
9						9
10						10
11						11
12						12
13						13
14						14
15						15
16						16
17						17
18						18
19						19
20						20
21						21
22						22
23						23
24						24
25						25
26						26
27						27
28						28
29						29
30						30
31						31
32						32
33						33
34						34
35						35

Name Date Class

Reinforcement Problem 7A (concluded)

(4)

Analyze:

Name Date Class

Reinforcement Problem 8A Preparing a Six-Column Work Sheet

	ACCT. NO.	ACCOUNT NAME	TRIAL BALANCE		INCOME STATEMENT		BALANCE SHEET		
			DEBIT	CREDIT	DEBIT	CREDIT	DEBIT	CREDIT	
1									1
2									2
3									3
4									4
5									5
6									6
7									7
8									8
9									9
10									10
11									11
12									12
13									13
14									14
15									15
16									16
17									17
18									18
19									19
20									20
21									21
22									22
23									23
24									24
25									25
26									26

Name Date Class

Reinforcement Problem 8A (concluded)

Analyze:

Reinforcement Problem 9A Interpreting Financial Information

Analyze:

Name Date Class

Reinforcement Problem 10A Preparing Closing Entries

Thunder Graphics Desktop Publishing

Work Sheet

For the Year Ended December 31, 20--

	ACCT. NO.	ACCOUNT NAME	TRIAL BALANCE DEBIT	TRIAL BALANCE CREDIT	INCOME STATEMENT DEBIT	INCOME STATEMENT CREDIT	BALANCE SHEET DEBIT	BALANCE SHEET CREDIT	
1	101	Cash in Liberty State Bank	3400 00				3400 00		1
2	105	Accts. Rec.—Adams, Bell, and Cox	1400 00				1400 00		2
3	110	Accts. Rec.—Roger McFall	400 00				400 00		3
4	113	Accts. Rec.—Designers Boutique	1200 00				1200 00		4
5	115	Accts. Rec.—Pat Cooper	600 00				600 00		5
6	120	Office Equipment	3000 00				3000 00		6
7	125	Office Furniture	9300 00				9300 00		7
8	130	Computer Equipment	21000 00				21000 00		8
9	201	Accts. Pay.—Solutions Software		2100 00				2100 00	9
10	205	Accts. Pay.—Pro Computer Co.		1200 00				1200 00	10
11	207	Accts. Pay.—Computer Warehouse		17000 00				17000 00	11
12	301	Pamela Wong, Capital		14300 00				14300 00	12
13	305	Pamela Wong, Withdrawals	8000 00				8000 00		13
14	310	Income Summary	—	—	—	—			14
15	401	Design Revenue		24000 00		24000 00			15
16	405	Print Production Revenue		15000 00		15000 00			16
17	501	Rent Expense	12000 00		12000 00				17
18	515	Maintenance Expense	3200 00		3200 00				18
19	520	Advertising Expense	2000 00		2000 00				19
20	525	Utilities Expense	4800 00		4800 00				20
21	540	Office Supplies Expense	1800 00		1800 00				21
22	545	Miscellaneous Expense	1500 00		1500 00				22
23			73600 00	73600 00	25300 00	39000 00	48300 00	34600 00	23
24		Net Income			13700 00			13700 00	24
25					39000 00	39000 00	48300 00	48300 00	25
26									26

Name Date Class

Reinforcement Problem 10A (concluded)

GENERAL JOURNAL

PAGE ______

	DATE		DESCRIPTION	POST. REF.	DEBIT	CREDIT	
1							1
2							2
3							3
4							4
5							5
6							6
7							7
8							8
9							9
10							10
11							11
12							12
13							13
14							14
15							15
16							16
17							17
18							18
19							19
20							20
21							21
22							22
23							23
24							24
25							25
26							26
27							27
28							28
29							29
30							30

Analyze:

Name Date Class

Reinforcement Problem 11A Recording Deposits in the Checkbook

(1)

Date ____________ 20 ____

Checks and other items are received for deposit subject to the terms and conditions of this bank's collection agreement.

First Pacific Bank

⑆0650 01334⑆ 27 10749⑈

BE SURE EACH ITEM IS ENDORSED

	DOLLARS	CENTS
CASH		
CHECKS (List Singly)		
1		
2		
3		
4		
5		
6		
7		
8		
TOTAL		

(2), (3)

$ ____________ **No. 1068**
Date ____________ 20 ____
To ____________
For ____________

	Dollars	Cents
Balance brought forward		
Add deposits		
Total		
Less this check		
Balance carried forward		

THUNDER GRAPHICS
desktop publishing

1068

51-160/111

DATE ____________ 20 ____

PAY TO THE ORDER OF ____________ $ ____________

____________ DOLLARS

First Pacific Bank

MEMO ____________ ____________

⑆0111 01602⑆ 749 2454⑈ 1068

(4)

$ ____________ **No. 1069**
Date ____________ 20 ____
To ____________
For ____________

	Dollars	Cents
Balance brought forward		
Add deposits		
Total		
Less this check		
Balance carried forward		

Name Date Class

Reinforcement Problem 11A (concluded)

(5)

GENERAL JOURNAL PAGE 21

	DATE		DESCRIPTION	POST. REF.	DEBIT	CREDIT	
1							1
2							2
3							3
4							4
5							5
6							6
7							7
8							8
9							9
10							10

(6)

a.

b.

c.

d.

e.

Analyze:

Name Date Class

Reinforcement Problem 12A Preparing a Payroll Register

PAYROLL REGISTER

PAY PERIOD ENDING ____________ 20 ____ DATE OF PAYMENT ____________

	EMPLOYEE NUMBER	NAME	MAR. STATUS	ALLOW.	TOTAL HOURS	RATE	EARNINGS			DEDUCTIONS							NET PAY	CK. NO.	
							REGULAR	OVERTIME	TOTAL	SOC. SEC. TAX	MED. TAX	FED. INC. TAX	STATE INC. TAX	HOSP. INS.	OTHER	TOTAL			
1																			1
2																			2
3																			3
4																			4
25																			25
		TOTALS																	

Other Deductions: Write the appropriate code letter to the left of the amount: B—U.S. Savings Bonds; C—Credit Union; UD—Union Dues; UW—United Way.

Analyze: ________________________________

____

Reinforcement Problem 13A Recording Payroll Transactions

PAYROLL REGISTER

PAY PERIOD ENDING *December 17* 20 *--* DATE OF PAYMENT *December 17, 20--*

	EMPLOYEE NUMBER	NAME	MAR. STATUS	ALLOW.	TOTAL HOURS	RATE	EARNINGS REGULAR	EARNINGS OVERTIME	EARNINGS TOTAL	DEDUCTIONS SOC. SEC. TAX	DEDUCTIONS MED. TAX	DEDUCTIONS FED. INC. TAX	DEDUCTIONS STATE INC. TAX	DEDUCTIONS HOSP. INS.	DEDUCTIONS OTHER	DEDUCTIONS TOTAL	NET PAY	CK. NO.	
1	*173*	*Don Hoffman*	*M*	*1*	*22*	*6.95*	*152 90*		*152 90*	*9 48*	*2 22*	*24 00*	*2 29*	*7 85*		*45 84*	*107 06*		1
2	*168*	*Manual Gongas*	*S*	*0*	*36*	*7.10*	*255 60*		*255 60*	*15 85*	*3 71*	*39 00*	*3 83*	*4 75*	*UD 3 25*	*70 39*	*185 21*		2
3	*167*	*Riley Sullivan*	*M*	*2*	*40*	*7.40*	*296 00*		*296 00*	*18 35*	*4 29*	*43 00*	*4 44*	*7 85*	*UD 3 25*	*81 18*	*214 82*		3
4	*175*	*Marcy Jackson*	*S*	*1*	*38*	*6.95*	*264 10*		*264 10*	*16 37*	*3 83*	*39 00*	*3 96*	*4 75*	*UD 3 25*	*71 16*	*192 94*		4
25																			25
		TOTALS					*968 60*		*968 60*	*60 05*	*14 05*	*145 00*	*14 52*	*25 20*	*9 75*	*268 57*	*700 03*		

Other Deductions: Write the appropriate code letter to the left of the amount: B—U.S. Savings Bonds; C—Credit Union; UD—Union Dues; UW—United Way.

Name Date Class

Reinforcement Problem 13A (concluded)

GENERAL JOURNAL

PAGE ______

	DATE		DESCRIPTION	POST. REF.	DEBIT	CREDIT	
1							1
2							2
3							3
4							4
5							5
6							6
7							7
8							8
9							9
10							10
11							11
12							12
13							13
14							14
15							15
16							16
17							17
18							18
19							19
20							20
21							21
22							22
23							23
24							24
25							25
26							26
27							27
28							28
29							29
30							30

Analyze:

Name Date Class

Reinforcement Problem 14A Recording and Posting Sales and Cash Receipt Transactions

(1), (4)

GENERAL LEDGER

ACCOUNT ACCOUNT NO.

DATE		DESCRIPTION	POST. REF.	DEBIT	CREDIT	BALANCE	
						DEBIT	CREDIT

ACCOUNT ACCOUNT NO.

DATE		DESCRIPTION	POST. REF.	DEBIT	CREDIT	BALANCE	
						DEBIT	CREDIT

ACCOUNT ACCOUNT NO.

DATE		DESCRIPTION	POST. REF.	DEBIT	CREDIT	BALANCE	
						DEBIT	CREDIT

Name ____________ Date ____________ Class ____________

Reinforcement Problem 14A (continued)

ACCOUNT ____________ ACCOUNT NO. ____________

DATE		DESCRIPTION	POST. REF.	DEBIT	CREDIT	BALANCE DEBIT	BALANCE CREDIT

ACCOUNT ____________ ACCOUNT NO. ____________

DATE		DESCRIPTION	POST. REF.	DEBIT	CREDIT	BALANCE DEBIT	BALANCE CREDIT

ACCOUNT ____________ ACCOUNT NO. ____________

DATE		DESCRIPTION	POST. REF.	DEBIT	CREDIT	BALANCE DEBIT	BALANCE CREDIT

Name Date Class

Reinforcement Problem 14A (continued)

(2)

ACCOUNTS RECEIVABLE SUBSIDIARY LEDGER

Name ______

Address ______

DATE		DESCRIPTION	POST. REF.	DEBIT	CREDIT	BALANCE

Name ______

Address ______

DATE		DESCRIPTION	POST. REF.	DEBIT	CREDIT	BALANCE

Name ______

Address ______

DATE		DESCRIPTION	POST. REF.	DEBIT	CREDIT	BALANCE

Name ______

Address ______

DATE		DESCRIPTION	POST. REF.	DEBIT	CREDIT	BALANCE

Analyze: ______

Name Date Class

Reinforcement Problem 14A (concluded)

(3)

GENERAL JOURNAL PAGE ______

	DATE	DESCRIPTION	POST. REF.	DEBIT	CREDIT	
1						1
2						2
3						3
4						4
5						5
6						6
7						7
8						8
9						9
10						10
11						11
12						12
13						13
14						14
15						15
16						16
17						17
18						18
19						19
20						20
21						21
22						22
23						23
24						24
25						25
26						26
27						27
28						28
29						29
30						30
31						31
32						32
33						33
34						34
35						35

Name Date Class

Reinforcement Problem 15A Recording Purchases and Cash Payment Transactions

General Ledger (partial)		Accounts Payable Subsidiary Ledger (partial)
Cash in Bank	Purchases	Carter Office Supply
Accounts Receivable	Purchases Discounts	Dancing Wind Clothing Manufacturers
Prepaid Insurance	Transportation In	Wilmington Shirt Factory
Supplies	Purchases Returns and Allowances	
Accounts Payable		
Sales Tax Payable		

GENERAL JOURNAL PAGE ______

	DATE		DESCRIPTION	POST. REF.	DEBIT	CREDIT	
1							1
2							2
3							3
4							4
5							5
6							6
7							7
8							8
9							9
10							10
11							11
12							12
13							13
14							14
15							15
16							16
17							17
18							18
19							19
20							20
21							21
22							22
23							23
24							24
25							25
26							26
27							27
28							28

Name Date Class

Reinforcement Problem 15A (concluded)

GENERAL JOURNAL

PAGE ______

	DATE		DESCRIPTION	POST. REF.	DEBIT	CREDIT	
1							1
2							2
3							3
4							4
5							5
6							6
7							7
8							8
9							9
10							10
11							11
12							12
13							13
14							14
15							15

Analyze:

Name Date Class

Reinforcement Problem 16A Recording and Posting Sales, Cash Receipts, and General Journal Transactions

(1)

GENERAL LEDGER

ACCOUNT ______ ACCOUNT NO. ______

DATE		DESCRIPTION	POST. REF.	DEBIT	CREDIT	BALANCE DEBIT	BALANCE CREDIT

ACCOUNT ______ ACCOUNT NO. ______

DATE		DESCRIPTION	POST. REF.	DEBIT	CREDIT	BALANCE DEBIT	BALANCE CREDIT

ACCOUNT ______ ACCOUNT NO. ______

DATE		DESCRIPTION	POST. REF.	DEBIT	CREDIT	BALANCE DEBIT	BALANCE CREDIT

ACCOUNT ______ ACCOUNT NO. ______

DATE		DESCRIPTION	POST. REF.	DEBIT	CREDIT	BALANCE DEBIT	BALANCE CREDIT

Name Date Class

Reinforcement Problem 16A (continued)

ACCOUNT ACCOUNT NO.

DATE		DESCRIPTION	POST. REF.	DEBIT	CREDIT	BALANCE	
						DEBIT	CREDIT

ACCOUNT ACCOUNT NO.

DATE		DESCRIPTION	POST. REF.	DEBIT	CREDIT	BALANCE	
						DEBIT	CREDIT

ACCOUNT ACCOUNT NO.

DATE		DESCRIPTION	POST. REF.	DEBIT	CREDIT	BALANCE	
						DEBIT	CREDIT

(9)

Name Date Class

Reinforcement Problem 16A (continued)

(2)

ACCOUNTS RECEIVABLE SUBSIDIARY LEDGER

Name

Address

DATE		DESCRIPTION	POST. REF.	DEBIT	CREDIT	BALANCE

Name

Address

DATE		DESCRIPTION	POST. REF.	DEBIT	CREDIT	BALANCE

Name

Address

DATE		DESCRIPTION	POST. REF.	DEBIT	CREDIT	BALANCE

Name

Address

DATE		DESCRIPTION	POST. REF.	DEBIT	CREDIT	BALANCE

Name Date Class

Reinforcement Problem 16A (continued)

Name

Address

DATE		DESCRIPTION	POST. REF.	DEBIT	CREDIT	BALANCE

Name

Address

DATE		DESCRIPTION	POST. REF.	DEBIT	CREDIT	BALANCE

Name

Address

DATE		DESCRIPTION	POST. REF.	DEBIT	CREDIT	BALANCE

Name Date Class

Reinforcement Problem 16A (continued)

SALES JOURNAL

PAGE ____

	DATE		SALES SLIP NO.	CUSTOMER'S ACCOUNT DEBITED	POST. REF.	SALES CREDIT	SALES TAX PAYABLE CREDIT	ACCOUNTS RECEIVABLE DEBIT	
1									1
2									2
3									3
4									4
5									5
6									6
7									7
8									8
9									9
10									10
11									11
12									12
13									13
14									14
15									15
16									16
17									17
18									18
19									19
20									20
21									21
22									22
23									23
24									24
25									25
26									26
27									27
28									28
29									29
30									30
31									31
32									32
33									33
34									34

Reinforcement Problem 16A (continued)

CASH RECEIPTS JOURNAL

PAGE ____

	DATE	DOC. NO.	ACCOUNT NAME	POST. REF.	GENERAL CREDIT	SALES CREDIT	SALES TAX PAYABLE CREDIT	ACCOUNTS RECEIVABLE CREDIT	SALES DISCOUNTS DEBIT	CASH IN BANK DEBIT	
1											1
2											2
3											3
4											4
5											5
6											6
7											7
8											8
9											9
10											10
11											11
12											12
13											13
14											14
15											15
16											16
17											17
18											18
19											19
20											20
21											21
22											22
23											23
24											24
25											25

Name Date Class

Reinforcement Problem 16A (concluded)

GENERAL JOURNAL PAGE ____

	DATE		DESCRIPTION	POST. REF.	DEBIT	CREDIT	
1							1
2							2
3							3
4							4
5							5
6							6
7							7
8							8
9							9
10							10
11							11
12							12
13							13
14							14
15							15
16							16
17							17
18							18
19							19
20							20
21							21
22							22
23							23
24							24
25							25
26							26
27							27
28							28
29							29
30							30
31							31
32							32
33							33

Analyze:

Name Date Class

Reinforcement Problem 17A Recording Special Journal and General Journal Transactions

SALES JOURNAL

PAGE ______

	DATE	SALES SLIP NO.	CUSTOMER'S ACCOUNT DEBITED	POST. REF.	SALES CREDIT	SALES TAX PAYABLE CREDIT	ACCOUNTS RECEIVABLE DEBIT	
1								1
2								2
3								3
4								4
5								5
6								6
7								7
8								8
9								9
10								10
11								11
12								12
13								13
14								14
15								15
16								16
17								17
18								18
19								19
20								20
21								21
22								22
23								23
24								24
25								25
26								26
27								27
28								28
29								29
30								30
31								31
32								32
33								33
34								34

Name Date Class

Reinforcement Problem 17A (continued)

CASH RECEIPTS JOURNAL

PAGE ____

	DATE	DOC. NO.	ACCOUNT NAME	POST. REF.	GENERAL CREDIT	SALES CREDIT	SALES TAX PAYABLE CREDIT	ACCOUNTS RECEIVABLE CREDIT	SALES DISCOUNTS DEBIT	CASH IN BANK DEBIT	
1											1
2											2
3											3
4											4
5											5
6											6
7											7
8											8
9											9
10											10
11											11
12											12
13											13
14											14
15											15
16											16
17											17
18											18
19											19
20											20
21											21
22											22
23											23
24											24
25											25

Name Date Class

Reinforcement Problem 17A (continued)

PURCHASES JOURNAL

PAGE ______

	DATE		INVOICE NO.	CREDITOR'S ACCOUNT CREDITED	POST. REF.	ACCOUNTS PAYABLE CREDIT	PURCHASES DEBIT	GENERAL ACCOUNT DEBITED	GENERAL POST. REF.	GENERAL DEBIT	
1											1
2											2
3											3
4											4
5											5
6											6
7											7
8											8
9											9
10											10
11											11
12											12
13											13
14											14
15											15
16											16
17											17
18											18
19											19
20											20
21											21
22											22
23											23
24											24
25											25
26											26

Name ____________ Date ____________ Class ____________

Reinforcement Problem 17A (continued)

CASH PAYMENTS JOURNAL

PAGE ______

	DATE		DOC. NO.	ACCOUNT NAME	POST. REF.	GENERAL DEBIT	GENERAL CREDIT	ACCOUNTS PAYABLE DEBIT	PURCHASES DISCOUNTS CREDIT	CASH IN BANK CREDIT	
1	20--										1
2	July	1	534	Sullivan Screen Printers				325 00		325 00	2
3											3
4											4
5											5
6											6
7											7
8											8
9											9
10											10
11											11
12											12
13											13
14											14
15											15
16											16
17											17
18											18
19											19
20											20
21											21
22											22
23											23
24											24
25											25
26											26

Name Date Class

Reinforcement Problem 17A (continued)

GENERAL JOURNAL PAGE ______

	DATE		DESCRIPTION	POST. REF.	DEBIT	CREDIT	
1							1
2							2
3							3
4							4
5							5
6							6
7							7
8							8
9							9
10							10
11							11
12							12
13							13
14							14
15							15
16							16
17							17
18							18
19							19
20							20
21							21
22							22
23							23
24							24
25							25
26							26
27							27
28							28
29							29
30							30
31							31
32							32
33							33
34							34
35							35

Name Date Class

Reinforcement Problem 17A (concluded)

Analyze:

Name Date Class

Notes

Name Date Class

Reinforcement Problem 18A — Calculating Adjustments and Preparing the Ten-Column Work Sheet

T-Shirt

Work

For the Year Ended

	ACCT. NO.	ACCOUNT NAME	TRIAL BALANCE DEBIT	TRIAL BALANCE CREDIT	ADJUSTMENTS DEBIT	ADJUSTMENTS CREDIT
1	101	Cash in Bank	14729 00			
2	115	Accounts Receivable	5702 00			
3	130	Merchandise Inventory	51215 00			
4	135	Supplies	3197 00			
5	140	Prepaid Insurance	1800 00			
6	145	Office Equipment	7837 00			
7	150	Store Equipment	18504 00			
8	155	Delivery Equipment	11754 00			
9	201	Accounts Payable		13039 00		
10	204	Fed. Corporate Income Tax Pay.				
11	210	Employees' Fed. Inc. Tax Pay.		636 00		
12	211	Employees' State Inc. Tax Pay.		117 00		
13	212	Social Security Tax Payable		479 00		
14	213	Medicare Tax Payable		113 00		
15	215	Sales Tax Payable		3931 00		
16	216	Fed. Unemployment Tax Pay.		79 00		
17	217	State Unemployment Tax Pay.		315 00		
18	301	Capital Stock		50000 00		
19	305	Retained Earnings		25425 00		
20	310	Income Summary				
21	401	Sales		133123 00		
22	405	Sales Discounts	258 00			
23	410	Sales Returns and Allow.	1342 00			
24	501	Purchases	72510 00			
25	505	Transportation In	1141 00			
26	510	Purchases Discounts		1292 00		
27	515	Purchases Returns and Allow.		571 00		
28	601	Advertising Expense	4205 00			
29		Carried Forward	194194 00	229120 00		
30						
31						
32						

Name Date Class

Trends

Sheet

December 31, 20--

ADJUSTED TRIAL BALANCE		INCOME STATEMENT		BALANCE SHEET		
DEBIT	CREDIT	DEBIT	CREDIT	DEBIT	CREDIT	
						1
						2
						3
						4
						5
						6
						7
						8
						9
						10
						11
						12
						13
						14
						15
						16
						17
						18
						19
						20
						21
						22
						23
						24
						25
						26
						27
						28
						29
						30
						31
						32

Name Date Class

Reinforcement Problem 18A (concluded)

T-Shirt

Work Sheet

For the Year Ended

	ACCT. NO.	ACCOUNT NAME	TRIAL BALANCE DEBIT	TRIAL BALANCE CREDIT	ADJUSTMENTS DEBIT	ADJUSTMENTS CREDIT
1		*Brought Forward*	194,194.00	229,120.00		
2						
3	605	*Bankcard Fees Expense*	619.00			
4	630	*Fed. Corporate Income Tax Exp.*	2,480.00			
5	640	*Insurance Expense*				
6	655	*Maintenance Expense*	1,322.00			
7	660	*Miscellaneous Expense*	3,772.00			
8	663	*Payroll Tax Expense*	1,251.00			
9	665	*Rent Expense*	10,900.00			
10	670	*Salaries Expense*	11,989.00			
11	675	*Supplies Expense*				
12	685	*Utilities Expense*	2,593.00			
13			229,120.00	229,120.00		
14						
15						
16						
17						
18						
19						
20						
21						
22						
23						
24						
25						
26						
27						
28						
29						
30						
31						
32						

Name **Date** **Class**

Trends

(continued)

December 31, 20--

ADJUSTED TRIAL BALANCE		INCOME STATEMENT		BALANCE SHEET		
DEBIT	CREDIT	DEBIT	CREDIT	DEBIT	CREDIT	
						1
						2
						3
						4
						5
						6
						7
						8
						9
						10
						11
						12
						13
						14
						15
						16
						17
						18
						19
						20
						21
						22
						23
						24
						25
						26
						27
						28
						29
						30
						31
						32

Analyze:

Name Date Class

Reinforcement Problem 19A Preparing Financial Statements

T-Shirt

Work

For the Year Ended

	ACCT. NO.	ACCOUNT NAME	TRIAL BALANCE DEBIT	TRIAL BALANCE CREDIT	ADJUSTMENTS DEBIT	ADJUSTMENTS CREDIT
1	101	Cash in Bank	19731 00			
2	115	Accounts Receivable	6462 00			
3	130	Merchandise Inventory	25192 00		(a) 1228 00	
4	135	Supplies	4669 00			(b) 2938 00
5	140	Prepaid Insurance	2400 00			(c) 625 00
6	145	Office Equipment	14895 00			
7	150	Store Equipment	25223 00			
8	155	Delivery Truck	12750 00			
9	201	Accounts Payable		15824 00		
10	210	Fed. Corporate Income Tax Pay.				(d) 142 00
11	211	Employees' Fed. Inc. Tax Pay.		534 00		
12	212	Employees' State Inc. Tax Pay.		151 00		
13	213	Social Security Tax Payable		451 00		
14	214	Medicare Tax Payable		180 00		
15	215	Sales Tax Payable		2413 00		
16	216	Fed. Unemployment Tax Pay.		54 00		
17	217	State Unemployment Tax Pay.		282 00		
18	301	Capital Stock		50000 00		
19	305	Retained Earnings		10811 00		
20	310	Income Summary				(a) 1228 00
21	401	Sales		131551 00		
22	405	Sales Discounts	196 00			
23	410	Sales Returns and Allow.	1668 00			
24	501	Purchases	65819 00			
25	505	Transportation In	1321 00			
26	510	Purchases Discounts		789 00		
27	515	Purchases Returns and Allow.		967 00		
28	601	Advertising Expense	2117 00			
29		Carried Forward	182443 00	214007 00	1228 00	4933 00
30						
31						
32						

Trends

Sheet

December 31, 20--

	ADJUSTED TRIAL BALANCE		INCOME STATEMENT		BALANCE SHEET	
	DEBIT	CREDIT	DEBIT	CREDIT	DEBIT	CREDIT
1	19731 00				19731 00	
2	6462 00				6462 00	
3	26420 00				26420 00	
4	1731 00				1731 00	
5	1775 00				1775 00	
6	14895 00				14895 00	
7	25223 00				25223 00	
8	12750 00				12750 00	
9		15824 00				15824 00
10		142 00				142 00
11		534 00				534 00
12		151 00				151 00
13		451 00				451 00
14		180 00				180 00
15		2413 00				2413 00
16		54 00				54 00
17		282 00				282 00
18		50000 00				50000 00
19		10811 00				10811 00
20		1228 00		1228 00		
21		131551 00		131551 00		
22	196 00		196 00			
23	1668 00		1668 00			
24	65819 00		65819 00			
25	1321 00		1321 00			
26		789 00		789 00		
27		967 00		967 00		
28	2117 00		2117 00			
29	180108 00	215377 00	71121 00	134535 00	108987 00	80842 00
30						
31						
32						

Reinforcement Problem 19A (continued)

T-Shirt

Work Sheet

For the Year Ended

	ACCT. NO.	ACCOUNT NAME	TRIAL BALANCE DEBIT	TRIAL BALANCE CREDIT	ADJUSTMENTS DEBIT	ADJUSTMENTS CREDIT
1		*Brought Forward*	182443 00	214007 00	1228 00	4933 00
2						
3	605	*Bankcard Fees Expense*	328 00			
4	630	*Fed. Corporate Income Tax Exp.*	3510 00		(d) 142 00	
5	640	*Insurance Expense*			(c) 625 00	
6	655	*Maintenance Expense*	1350 00			
7	660	*Miscellaneous Expense*	931 00			
8	663	*Payroll Tax Expense*	834 00			
9	665	*Rent Expense*	12700 00			
10	670	*Salaries Expense*	7234 00			
11	675	*Supplies Expense*			(b) 2938 00	
12	685	*Utilities Expense*	4677 00			
13			214007 00	214007 00	4933 00	4933 00
14		*Net Income*				
15						
16						
17						
18						
19						
20						
21						
22						
23						
24						
25						
26						
27						
28						
29						
30						
31						
32						

Name Date Class

Trends

(continued)

December 31, 20--

	ADJUSTED TRIAL BALANCE		INCOME STATEMENT		BALANCE SHEET	
	DEBIT	CREDIT	DEBIT	CREDIT	DEBIT	CREDIT
1	180108 00	215377 00	71121 00	134535 00	108987 00	80842 00
2						
3	328 00		328 00			
4	3652 00		3652 00			
5	625 00		625 00			
6	1350 00		1350 00			
7	931 00		931 00			
8	834 00		834 00			
9	12700 00		12700 00			
10	7234 00		7234 00			
11	2938 00		2938 00			
12	4677 00		4677 00			
13	215377 00	215377 00	106390 00	134535 00	108987 00	80842 00
14			28145 00			28145 00
15			134535 00	134535 00	108987 00	108987 00
16						
17						
18						
19						
20						
21						
22						
23						
24						
25						
26						
27						
28						
29						
30						
31						
32						

Name Date Class

Reinforcement Problem 19A (continued)

(2)

(3)

Name Date Class

Reinforcement Problem 19A (continued)

(1)

Name ______ Date ______ Class ______

Reinforcement Problem 19A (concluded)

Analyze: ______

Reinforcement Problem 20A Journalizing Closing Entries

Account Names and Balances as of December 31, 20--:

Sales	*$94,412.00*
Purchases Discounts	*750.00*
Purchases Returns and Allowances	*455.00*
Sales Discounts	*867.00*
Sales Returns and Allowances	*1,735.00*
Purchases	*35,000.00*
Transportation In	*1,700.00*
Advertising Expense	*900.00*
Bankcard Fees Expense	*647.00*
Federal Income Tax Expense	*5,343.00*
Insurance Expense	*1,200.00*
Miscellaneous Expense	*369.00*
Rent Expense	*18,000.00*
Supplies Expense	*2,612.00*
Utilities Expense	*4,200.00*

Name Date Class

Reinforcement Problem 20A (concluded)

GENERAL JOURNAL PAGE ______

	DATE		DESCRIPTION	POST. REF.	DEBIT	CREDIT	
1							1
2							2
3							3
4							4
5							5
6							6
7							7
8							8
9							9
10							10
11							11
12							12
13							13
14							14
15							15
16							16
17							17
18							18
19							19
20							20
21							21
22							22
23							23
24							24
25							25
26							26
27							27
28							28
29							29
30							30
31							31
32							32
33							33

Analyze: ______

Name Date Class

Reinforcement Problem 21A Recording Stockholders' Equity Transactions

GENERAL JOURNAL PAGE ______

	DATE		DESCRIPTION	POST. REF.	DEBIT	CREDIT	
1							1
2							2
3							3
4							4
5							5
6							6
7							7
8							8
9							9
10							10
11							11
12							12
13							13
14							14
15							15
16							16
17							17
18							18
19							19
20							20
21							21
22							22
23							23
24							24
25							25
26							26
27							27
28							28
29							29
30							30
31							31
32							32
33							33
34							34
35							35
36							36
37							37

Name _______________ Date _______________ Class _______________

Reinforcement Problem 21A (concluded)

GENERAL JOURNAL

PAGE ______

	DATE		DESCRIPTION	POST. REF.	DEBIT	CREDIT	
1							1
2							2
3							3
4							4
5							5
6							6
7							7
8							8
9							9
10							10
11							11
12							12
13							13
14							14
15							15

Analyze: _______________

Name Date Class

Reinforcement Problem 22A Maintaining a Petty Cash Register

PETTY CASH REGISTER

PAGE ____

	DATE	VOU. NO.	DESCRIPTION	PAYMENTS	DISTRIBUTION OF PAYMENTS					
					OFFICE SUPPLIES	DELIVERY EXPENSE	MISC. EXPENSE	GENERAL		
								ACCOUNT NAME	AMOUNT	
1										1
2										2
3										3
4										4
5										5
6										6
7										7
8										8
9										9
10										10
11										11
12										12
13										13
14										14
15										15
16										16
17										17
18										18
19										19
20										20
21										21
22										22
23										23
24										24

Analyze: ____

Name Date Class

Reinforcement Problem 23A Calculating and Recording Depreciation Expense

(1)

Date	Cost	Annual Depreciation	Accumulated Depreciation	Book Value

(2)

GENERAL JOURNAL PAGE ______

	DATE		DESCRIPTION	POST. REF.	DEBIT	CREDIT	
1							1
2							2
3							3
4							4
5							5
6							6
7							7
8							8
9							9
10							10

Reinforcement Problem 23A (concluded)

ACCOUNT *Accumulated Depreciation—Delivery Truck* ACCOUNT NO. *155*

DATE		DESCRIPTION	POST. REF.	DEBIT	CREDIT	BALANCE DEBIT	BALANCE CREDIT

(3) a.

b.

c.

d.

Analyze:

Name Date Class

Reinforcement Problem 24A — Calculating and Recording Uncollectible Accounts Expense

(1)

Estimate of uncollectible accounts: ______________________

(2)

GENERAL JOURNAL PAGE ______

	DATE		DESCRIPTION	POST. REF.	DEBIT	CREDIT	
1							1
2							2
3							3
4							4
5							5
6							6

(3)

GENERAL LEDGER (PARTIAL)

ACCOUNT ______________________ ACCOUNT NO. *110*

DATE		DESCRIPTION	POST. REF.	DEBIT	CREDIT	BALANCE	
						DEBIT	CREDIT

ACCOUNT ______________________ ACCOUNT NO. *605*

DATE		DESCRIPTION	POST. REF.	DEBIT	CREDIT	BALANCE	
						DEBIT	CREDIT

(4)

Book value of accounts receivable: ______________________

Analyze: ______________________

Name Date Class

Reinforcement Problem 25A Accounting for Inventories

Cost of Ending Inventory:

Specific Identification

FIFO

LIFO

Weighted Average Cost

Analyze:

Name Date Class

Reinforcement Problem 26A Calculating Current and Future Interest

	Maturity Date	Interest	
		Current Year	Following Year
1.			
2.			
3.			
4.			
5.			
6.			
7.			
8.			
9.			
10.			

Analyze:

Name Date Class

Reinforcement Problem 26B Recording Non-Interest-Bearing Notes Payable

GENERAL JOURNAL PAGE ______

	DATE		DESCRIPTION	POST. REF.	DEBIT	CREDIT	
1							1
2							2
3							3
4							4
5							5
6							6
7							7
8							8
9							9
10							10
11							11
12							12
13							13
14							14
15							15
16							16
17							17
18							18
19							19
20							20
21							21
22							22
23							23
24							24
25							25
26							26

Analyze:

Name Date Class

Reinforcement Problem 27A Recording Partners' Investments

GENERAL JOURNAL PAGE ______

	DATE		DESCRIPTION	POST. REF.	DEBIT	CREDIT	
1							1
2							2
3							3
4							4
5							5
6							6
7							7
8							8
9							9
10							10
11							11
12							12
13							13
14							14
15							15
16							16
17							17
18							18
19							19
20							20
21							21
22							22
23							23
24							24
25							25
26							26

Analyze:

Name Date Class

Reinforcement Problem 28A Liquidation of a Partnership

GENERAL JOURNAL

PAGE ______

	DATE		DESCRIPTION	POST. REF.	DEBIT	CREDIT	
1							1
2							2
3							3
4							4
5							5
6							6
7							7
8							8
9							9
10							10
11							11
12							12
13							13
14							14
15							15
16							16
17							17
18							18
19							19
20							20
21							21
22							22
23							23
24							24
25							25
26							26
27							27
28							28
29							29
30							30
31							31
32							32

Analyze: